Nonprofits and Government

Nonprofits and Government

Collaboration and Conflict

Edited by
Elizabeth T. Boris and C. Eugene Steuerle

COPUBLISHED WITH
THE URBAN INSTITUTE PRESS

ROWMAN & LITTLEFIELD
Lanham • Boulder • New York • London

Copublished with the Urban Institute Press
Editorial Advisory Board
Bridget Lowell, vice president for strategic communications and outreach
Margery Austin Turner, senior vice president for program planning and management
John Rogers, executive vice president, treasurer, and chief financial officer
Scott Forrey, editorial consultant

Published by Rowman & Littlefield
A wholly owned subsidiary of The Rowman & Littlefield Publishing Group, Inc.
4501 Forbes Boulevard, Suite 200, Lanham, Maryland 20706
www.rowman.com

Unit A, Whitacre Mews, 26-34 Stannary Street, London SE11 4AB

Copyright © 2017 by Rowman & Littlefield

All rights reserved. No part of this book may be reproduced in any form or by any electronic or mechanical means, including information storage and retrieval systems, without written permission from the publisher, except by a reviewer who may quote passages in a review.

British Library Cataloguing in Publication Information Available

Library of Congress Cataloging-in-Publication Data Available
ISBN: 978-1-4422-7177-7 (cloth : alk. paper)
ISBN: 978-1-4422-7178-4 (pbk. : alk. paper)
ISBN: 978-1-4422-7179-1 (electronic)

∞™ The paper used in this publication meets the minimum requirements of American National Standard for Information Sciences—Permanence of Paper for Printed Library Materials, ANSI/NISO Z39.48-1992.

Printed in the United States of America

Contents

Foreword   vii

Acknowledgments   ix

Introduction: Roles and Responsibilities of Nonprofit
Organizations in a Democracy   1
Elizabeth T. Boris, Brice McKeever, and Béatrice Leydier

1   Supplementary, Complementary, or Adversarial?:
Nonprofit-Government Relations   37
Dennis R. Young and John Casey

2   Meeting Social Needs through Charitable
and Government Resources   71
*C. Eugene Steuerle, Alan J. Abramson, Ellen Steele,
and Virginia Hodgkinson*

3   Cross-Sector Nonprofit-Government Financing   103
Steven Rathgeb Smith

4   Tax Treatment of Nonprofit Organizations:
A Two-Edged Sword?   133
Evelyn Brody and Joseph J. Cordes

5   State Regulatory and Legal Framework   163
Cindy M. Lott and Marion Fremont-Smith

6   Nonprofits and Advocacy   191
Roger Colinvaux

7	No Taxation, No Representation: How Government Is Organized—or Not—to Address Nonprofit Issues *Alan J. Abramson*	217
8	Philanthropy: Shaping and Being Shaped by Public Policy *Lewis Faulk and Jasmine McGinnis Johnson*	237
9	New Ways of Creating Social Value: Hybrids and Impact Investing *Joseph Cordes, Nathan Dietz, C. Eugene Steuerle, and Erica Broadus*	263
10	Performance Measurement and Management: The Tangled Web of Nonprofit-Government Relationships *Saunji D. Fyffe, Teresa Derrick-Mills, and Mary K. Winkler*	291
11	International Trends in Government-Nonprofit Relations: Constancy, Change, and Contradictions *Susan D. Phillips and Mark Blumberg*	313

Index	343
About the Contributors	359

Foreword

In the decade since the last edition of *Nonprofits and Government: Collaboration and Conflict*, the pace of change in the nonprofit sector has accelerated and the interconnections between the nonprofit, government, and business sectors have deepened. New organizational forms like the B Corp, the emergence of a new group of major donors with a social enterprise bent, and new multi-sector financing opportunities, such as social impact bonds, are all rapidly reshaping the nonprofit sector.

Nonprofits account for over 5 percent of gross domestic product, employ approximately 10 percent of the labor force, and, excluding churches, have some five trillion dollars in assets. Much of their activity, in healthcare, education, and beyond, is financed by government and through fees for services. In an era of fiscal constraint, policymakers need more than ever high quality research about how effectively nonprofits deliver public services; and taxpayers need to understand the costs and benefits received from the range of tax incentives that federal, state and local governments provide to nonprofits.

Evidence-informed insight is critical for the nonprofits as well. Their charitable contributions are modest when compared to the public support and public benefits (like tax expenditures) that they receive.

As the title of this volume indicates, nonprofits and government collaborate and conflict; they both complement and substitute for each other; at times they criticize each other while at other times they learn from one another. Meanwhile, businesses employ and partner with nonprofits to pursue social and political objectives. Recently, entrepreneurs have been seeking to develop hybrid organizational forms that both make a profit and innovate for social causes, under a combination of legal constraints on what businesses and charities can do. Government and other funders promote market models and performance metrics, seeking greater effectiveness and impact, and, in the language of markets, higher return on their social investments.

Despite how much we invest in nonprofits and their import to achieving public objectives, regulation and oversight of nonprofits has always been quite limited. At the state level, attorneys general and charity offices often employ at most a handful of employees to protect those making contributions. Congress has cut back IRS resources devoted to tax law enforcement, even as it weighs new requirements and nonprofit transparency on, for example, use of endowments and other assets.

Some of the leading researchers on charity and nonprofits provide the scholarship in this volume. Here they describe the data, laws, and social developments that help explain the historical evolution of the nonprofit sector and examine recent trends in nonprofit-government relationships in the United States and in other countries.

As the sector evolves, research about it must be renewed as well, with new questions posed and new insights found. Previous editions of this volume have become must-reads for those studying the nonprofit sector, whether as individuals or in courses now offered in universities around the country. I expect this volume will as well.

—*Sarah Rosen Wartell*

Acknowledgments

In this third edition of *Nonprofits and Government: Collaboration and Conflict*, we again tapped exceptional scholars from a variety of backgrounds and institutions to provide a comprehensive portrait of the relationships of nonprofit organizations and philanthropy to governments at all levels in the United States and across the globe. While research on this sector has blossomed in recent years, our outreach to colleagues revealed demand for updated analyses of these important relationships in a text suitable for academic courses that draw mixed groups of students and nonprofit leaders.

In response, we invited authors to update core chapters from earlier editions: for example, tax policies, government spending, advocacy, and federal and state regulatory issues. We also asked authors to delve into new topics not covered in earlier editions, such as philanthropy, hybrid organizations and impact investing, representation of nonprofit issues in government, performance measurement and management, and analysis of regulatory regimes across countries.

We are extremely grateful for the quality of the products that these authors produced. It has also been a joy to work with individuals who have both a passion for their work and an appreciation for the realities of producing a volume.

A volume like this depends upon many people, but one person needs to keep all the wheels turning. In this case, Ellen Steele, Urban Institute, did a terrific job of overall coordination, along with co-authoring one of the chapters. We are also grateful to Erica Broadus, George Washington University, who started us down the path toward this volume while she was an emerging scholar at the Urban Institute and to Béatrice Leydier, Georgetown University, who provided background research.

Scott Forrey was instrumental in setting up the publication process and helped us navigate the technicalities with Rowman & Littlefield, who were accommodating and helpful throughout this process.

We also wish to acknowledge support from our institutions: Urban Institute's Center on Nonprofits and Philanthropy, directed by Shena Ashley; the Urban-Brookings Tax Policy Center, directed by Leonard Burman; and Georgetown's McCourt School of Public Policy, Edward Montgomery, dean. These fine institutions are sources of intellectual as well as material nourishment.

This book was funded in part by the Bill & Melinda Gates Foundation and the Charles Stewart Mott Foundation. We are grateful to them and to all our funders, who make it possible for the Urban Institute to advance its mission.

The views expressed are those of the authors and should not be attributed to the Urban Institute, its trustees, or its funders. Funders do not determine research findings or the insights and recommendations of Urban experts. Further information on the Urban Institute's funding principles is available at www.urban.org/support.

Introduction

Roles and Responsibilities of Nonprofit Organizations in a Democracy

Elizabeth T. Boris, Brice McKeever, and Béatrice Leydier

NONPROFIT ORGANIZATIONS OF CIVIL SOCIETY

Nonprofit organizations are a vital force of civil society, distinct from both government and business, although they display elements of both. Their basic role as enablers of civic engagement and promoters of the common good is the cornerstone of our pluralistic democracy. Nonprofits and government interact in many fascinating ways, yet we must understand the variety of roles played by nonprofit organizations before we can thoroughly explore these relationships. Because their spheres of activity intersect in so many ways, the nature, scope, and impacts of nonprofit organizations are sensitive to changes in public policy and vice versa. Simplistic assumptions about what nonprofit organizations do, their finances, and how they affect society may lead to public policies that are ineffective or have unintended negative consequences both for the organizations and for society. Partly to avoid these perils, this volume analyzes the relationships of nonprofits and government in myriad detail. At the same time, there has been significant growth in the nonprofit sector of civil society over the past decade, with major changes in types of institutions, financing mechanisms, and interactions with government, politics, and business, which we will document in this volume.

In this introduction, we define nonprofit organizations, identify common types and activities, provide data on their scope and finances, and discuss their roles in society as background for the chapters that follow. "Nonprofit" is the generic term used in this chapter and in this volume to describe organizations that make up the "nonprofit" sector, in contrast to the government and business sectors. The nonprofit sector includes philanthropic foundations, religious congregations, universities, hospitals, environmental groups, art museums, youth recreation associations, civil rights groups, community development organizations, labor unions, political parties, social clubs, and many more. These organizations are even more diverse than the terms typically associated with them: charities, nongovernmental organizations, civil society, philanthropic sector, tax exempt organizations, voluntary associations, civic sector organizations, third sector organizations, independent sector organizations, nonprofit organizations, and social sector organizations.

Nonprofits exhibit a wide diversity of missions, activities, reach, and impacts, but what they have in common is that they all are voluntary and self-governing, may not distribute profits, and serve public purposes or the common goals of their members. Nonprofits promote and defend values and competing visions of the public good, and many harness altruism and public and private resources to serve those who need assistance. All of these activities require the freedom to associate, deliberate, and act in the public sphere—freedoms guaranteed by the United States Constitution and Bill of Rights. Inevitably, however, competing values and interests often produce conflict. Also inevitably, where public resources are directly or indirectly involved, government regulation and oversight follow.

Like government, nonprofits generally promote the common good or public benefit, but in contrast to government, they are not bound by majority preferences. They embody democratic pluralism, promoting individual or particularistic conceptions of the public good that may conflict with others' notions of the public good. Through both collaboration and conflict, however, nonprofits shape and are shaped by government policies and funding.

Like businesses, nonprofits must obtain revenues to cover the costs of services they provide, as well as capital to scale up or branch out. Revenues can be from individual, corporate or foundation donors, volunteer labor (including labor at below market wages), fees for services or products, government grants and contracts, earnings on endowments or other assets, and special events. Capital can come from individuals, foundations, and government bonds and increasingly from social and impact investors that may include a mix of nonprofit, government, and business resources. Unlike businesses, nonprofits may not have owners or shareholders to whom they distribute profits; any surplus revenues must be used for the organization's mission.

Nonprofit organizations play prominent social, economic, and political roles in society as service providers, but many are also employers and advocates. Their numbers and economic impact have grown significantly as they increasingly earn fees and contract with government to deliver a variety of services, particularly health care and social services (see chapter 3 by Smith). These relationships are usually collaborative, or, in economic terms, complementary or supplementary to government (see chapter 1 by Young and Casey), although the scale of nonprofit resources are dwarfed by those of government (see chapter 2 by Steurele et al.). In their civic role, they are often advocates; they provide a voice for their constituents, and may lobby for or against government policies that affect their constituencies or interests, often invoking conflict and adversarial relationships with government, businesses, and other nonprofits (see chapter 6 by Colinvaux).

Less visible but vital nonprofit roles are captured under the rubric of "civil society": fostering community engagement and civic participation, and promoting and preserving civic, cultural, and religious values. Scholars are exploring the central role that formal and informal nonprofit organizations play in creating the glue that holds communities together and the avenues they provide for civic participation and a robust civil society (O'Connell 1999; Putnam 2000; Sievers 2010; Skocpol and Fiorina 1999; Verba, Schlozman, and Brady 1995; Zuckerman 2014). These roles are usually financed through giving and volunteering rather than by fees and contracts, and they can involve either collaboration or conflict with government, although these types of activities typically fall outside of direct government purview.

The interaction between government and nonprofit organizations in civil society is complex and dynamic, ebbing and flowing with shifts in social and economic policy, political administrations, and social norms. Because nonprofits are heterogeneous, they reflect sharp differences as well as common aspirations. Their impacts can be positive or negative and antagonistic or conciliatory, depending on their activities as well as the perspective of the analyst. Of course, speaking about nonprofits in the aggregate invites overgeneralization—obscuring huge variation and diversity of nonprofit roles, contributions, and interactions with government, subjects to which we will turn.

REGULATION OF NONPROFIT ORGANIZATIONS

Nonprofit organizations in the United States are defined and regulated primarily under the federal tax code. They are exempt from federal income taxes by virtue of being organized for public purposes. Regulation of nonprofits is fragmented; there is no central US government agency that focuses solely on oversight of nonprofit organizations. At the national level, the Internal Revenue Service (IRS) is the primary regulator of nonprofit organizations and is charged with determining their legitimacy as tax exempt entities and overseeing that their activities are tax exempt and that charitable deductions are used for charitable purposes (see chapter 4 by Brody and Cordes for a discussion of federal tax treatment of nonprofits). State governments oversee and regulate nonprofits that operate in their jurisdictions, though usually more from a consumer protection standpoint (see chapter 5 by Lott and Fremont-Smith). The Federal Election Commission regulates nonprofits engaged in federal elections. Regulatory frameworks in other countries are varied but also generally involve tax incentives and greater or lesser limitation of political activity. They have in common with the United States the lack of an overarching philosophy or approach to nonprofit-government relationships (see chapter 11 by Phillips and Blumberg for a comparative analysis of nonprofit regulatory policies in other countries).

All US nonprofit organizations with annual gross receipts of $5,000 or more, except religious groups, are required to register with the IRS. Organizations with revenues (gross receipts) of more than $50,000 are required to complete and file an annual information form, IRS Form 990; all private foundations must file IRS Form 990-PF. These forms are public documents that provide the basis for federal and state oversight of nonprofits and the only financial data on nonprofit organizations required to be publicly available.[1]

Those nonprofit organizations that serve broad public purposes and are organized for educational, religious, scientific, literary, poverty relief, and other activities for the public benefit are eligible to apply for charitable status under section 501(c)(3) of the tax code. Charitable status permits organizations to receive tax-deductible contributions, an important incentive to encourage donations. Religious congregations, however, do not have to apply for charitable status; they are, by definition, charities. Charitable nonprofits serving broad public purposes account for the majority of tax exempt organizations and are the focus of most chapters in this volume. Membership organizations such as labor unions, recreation clubs, credit unions, and political parties are also tax exempt, but receive less attention here.

Even within the charitable portion of the nonprofit sector, the organizations are extremely diverse. They vary greatly in mission, origin, structure, size, sources of revenues, and financial means and are accountable to multiple constituencies—board and staff, members, donors, clients, volunteers, funders, and the public.[2] Public confidence and trust are crucial to their success, yet the public has limited understanding of the scope and operations of nonprofits. Lack of transparency, particularly about the use of donated money, and scandals of any type negatively affect the whole sector, often leading to public outcry, congressional inquiries, and new regulatory proposals.[3]

TYPES OF ORGANIZATIONS

Nonprofits' diversity confounds attempts to explain them through some overarching theory (see chapter 1, by Young and Casey, for discussions of theories of the government-nonprofit relationship). Researchers have made progress in categorizing and measuring the scope of formal organizations (McKeever 2015), but less has been accomplished in measuring the informal groups, coalitions, and religious organizations (Smith et al. 2010), although in-depth research on nonprofits in Indiana provides a window into groups not captured in IRS filings (Grønbjerg, Liu, and Pollak 2010).

The National Taxonomy of Exempt Entities (NTEE), developed by the National Center for Charitable Statistics,[4] classifies all nonprofit organizations into over 400 categories, demonstrating their diversity (Stevenson 1997). The basic divisions are as follows:

- Arts, culture, and humanities (e.g., art museums, theater companies, historical societies)
- Education, (e.g., private schools and universities, parent-teacher groups)
- Environment and animals (e.g., Humane Societies, the Chesapeake Bay Foundation)
- Health, hospitals (e.g., nonprofit hospitals and clinics, the American Lung Association)
- Human services (e.g., Girl Scouts, YMCA, food banks, homeless shelters)
- International, foreign affairs (e.g., CARE, the Asia Society, International Committee of the Red Cross)
- Public and societal benefit (private and public foundations, e.g., Rockefeller Foundation, the Cleveland Foundation, the Urban Institute, civil rights groups, United Ways)
- Religion related (e.g., interfaith coalitions, religious societies, congregations)

NTEE classifications permit researchers to track the growth of different types of nonprofits as in table I.1 which covers operating public charities.

Table I.1 Growth in Nonprofit Organizations by Type of Service, 2003–2013

Type	2003	2008	2013	2003–2013 # Change	2003–2013 % Change
Arts and culture	29,203	36,145	38,083	8,880	30.4
Education	38,872	48,644	48,287	9,415	24.2
Environment and animals	10,313	14,103	16,838	6,525	63.3
Health	31,263	35,436	37,440	6,177	19.8
Human service	91,546	110,743	120,241	28,695	31.3
International	4,749	6,202	7,877	3,128	65.9
Public and societal benefit	19,937	25,074	27,512	7,575	38.0
Religion related	15,114	20,608	23,758	8,644	57.2
Not classified	25	280	579	554	2216.0
Total	**241,022**	**297,235**	**320,615**	**79,593**	**33.0**

Note: Only operating public charities are included (see table I.2 for definition).
Source: The Urban Institute, NCCS Core Files, Public Charities, 2003, 2008, 2013.

NONPROFIT ACTIVITIES

The variety of nonprofit organizations is matched by a great diversity of activities. Among others, they produce and display art, culture, and music; generate knowledge through research and education; protect consumers, the environment, and animals; promote health; prevent and treat diseases; provide basic social services—housing, food and clothing; promote international understanding; provide international aid and relief; create community social and economic infrastructure; advocate for and against public policies; provide services and funding to other nonprofit groups; transmit religious values and traditions; provide solidarity, recreation, and services to members and others; and educate and register voters.

This laundry list gives some sense of the difficulty of defining and describing the nonprofit sector. It also makes it clear that voluntary organizations do many things that are also done by governments and businesses. There are no sharp boundaries among the sectors; in fact, there is increasing blurring of the boundaries, particularly with regard to commercial activities (see chapter 9 by Cordes et al.). There are, however, some activities (such as religious worship, membership activities, and monitoring of government) that are almost exclusively accomplished in the nonprofit sector and other activities (such as museums, botanical gardens, and zoos) that are more likely to be undertaken by nonprofits than by either government or business. Some activities are more evenly divided between government and nonprofits (such as providing social services), while others (such as primary education) are largely a government activity. Business and government also sometimes collaborate or cooperate with nonprofits in providing, for example, low-income housing and disaster relief.

Nonprofits have a long history of pioneering programs that were subsequently taken over by the other sectors. Primary education, kindergartens, and disease control were popularized by nonprofits and taken over by government when demand outpaced the ability of nonprofit providers to supply services. Recreation programs pioneered by nonprofits were picked up by businesses and developed into profit-making enterprises. Nonprofits are often lauded for being flexible and innovative, a source of discoveries for improving society with breakthroughs that transcend sectors.

Collaboration with government, however, is often difficult for both partners. Experiences with disaster relief in large-scale tragedies, such as the attacks of September 11, 2001, Hurricane Katrina in 2010, Hurricane Sandy in 2012, and the earthquake in Haiti in 2010, reveal the strengths and weaknesses of nonprofits in their collaboration with government. Nonprofits are quick to respond and galvanize volunteers and donations, but their capacity varies in different regions of this country and around the world. They are flexible problem solvers, but often weak on coordination and long-term logistics and follow-through (Morley and De Vita 2007). But, importantly, given their relative size, they cannot compensate for weak government leadership or inadequate government resources for large-scale disasters.

Some nonprofits have the characteristics of business corporations or of government programs, and a small proportion of organizations change from one type of organization to another (Goddeeris and Weisbrod 2006). Governments set up nonprofit corporations to carry out some public programs; for example, the Corporation for Public Broadcasting and the National Trust for Historic Preservation. Nonprofits may create profit-making subsidiaries to subsidize their charitable activities. Even though it has a charitable owner, such a subsidiary's income would generally be taxable unless it independently qualified as an exempt organization. They also engage in social enterprises that directly use market activities as part of their missions (Cordes and Steuerle 2009; Dees 1998; Kerlin 2005; Young, Salamon, Grinsfelder 2012). DC Central Kitchen, for example, picks up and distributes surplus food to hungry people and trains unemployed workers in culinary skills, preparing food that is sold to stores and schools (Moore 2014). (See chapter 9 by Cordes et al. for a discussion of hybrid forms that combine nonprofit social missions with for-profit business activities.)

The interaction of nonprofits with the business sector affects their relationships with government. A few nonprofits give up their tax exempt status when their missions can be accomplished more effectively as business corporations, or when economic incentives, government policies, or the need for capital make it profitable for them to become businesses. The conversion of nonprofit hospitals to for-profit businesses is one example. Conversions raise questions about whether it is in the public interest for businesses to take over hospitals and certain other types of services, but as long as the assets are reserved for charitable purposes, usually in a foundation, the current barriers to conversion seem to be minimal. Some members of Congress, however, are particularly interested in the rationale for permitting nonprofit hospitals to compete with for-profit hospitals when donations are a minor portion of their revenues and charity care is a small part of their services, or no more than profit-making hospitals. As a result, since 2008, nonprofit hospitals are required to document their community benefits on Forms 990. Efforts by scholars to discern whether there are differences in services and outcomes depending on whether hospitals operate as nonprofits or for-profits provide some evidence that the nonprofit form, on average, adds value (Gray and Schlesinger 2012).

The sometimes overlapping and complementary nature of the three sectors may at times seem inefficient, but it provides flexibility and adaptability. Public-serving activities are not restricted to government but can be undertaken through multiple avenues. Diverse populations with different tastes and requirements can create entities to meet their perceived needs. Government can contract with nonprofits to provide social and health services without expanding the government workforce. Social entrepreneurs can implement their visions through nonprofit organizations, and the alternatives they develop sometimes find their way into the public or business sectors. This complementarity can be leveraged when actors work together.

SCOPE OF NONPROFIT ORGANIZATIONS IN THE UNITED STATES

The nonprofit sector in the United States is dynamic and has grown significantly in recent decades. Although characterized by great diversity of organizations and activities, resources are concentrated in a small number of organizations, while activities are fragmented and vary in scale and by geographic area. In total, nonprofits (excluding religious congregations) have assets of approximately $5.2 trillion and expenses of $2.1 trillion. In economic terms, the nonprofit sector represents 5.4 percent of national gross domestic product and employs about 9–10 percent of the labor force (excluding volunteers) (Bureau of Labor Statistics 2014). (See chapter 2 by Steuerle et al. for a comparison of the resources of the nonprofit sector and government and a breakdown of nonprofit revenues by source.)

There were approximately 1.58 million tax exempt nonprofit organizations (including congregations) in 2013, up from about 1.44 million in 1998. This represents an increase of 9.7 percent (see table I.2).

Among the 1.44 million nonprofits required to register with the IRS because they had more than $5,000 in gross receipts in 2013, were just over one million "charitable" 501(c)(3) organizations that were eligible to receive tax-deductible contributions (see figure I.1). This group includes operating public charities (such as hospitals, universities, and soup kitchens) as well as supporting organizations (such as private and community foundations) that provide resources to other nonprofits and mutual membership and benefit organizations (such as nonprofit credit unions, labor unions, and fraternal organizations). Congregations are charitable organizations that are not required to register with the IRS, although many do.[5] The total number of charitable organizations registered with the IRS increased by 9.1 percent between 2003 and 2013 (from about 964,000 organizations to about 1,052,000 organizations) and rose from almost 60 percent to about two-thirds of all registered nonprofits (see table I.2).[6]

Among the 320,615 charitable operating nonprofits that report financial information to the IRS, environmental, international, and religion-related organizations increased most rapidly, while the number of health

Table I.2 Number of Nonprofit Entities in the United States, 1998–2013 (Numbers in Thousands)

	1998		2003		2008		2013		1998–2013
	Number	Percent	Number	Percent	Number	Percent	Number	Percent	% Change
Total private nonprofit organizations	**1,443**	**100.0**	**1,641**	**100.0**	**1,851**	**100.0**	**1,583**	**100.0**	**9.7**
Tax exempt orgs. registered with the IRS	1,273	88.3	1,502	91.5	1,711	92.4	1,442	91.1	13.3
Total 501(c)(3) charitable orgs.	734	50.9	964	58.8	1,187	64.1	1,052	66.5	43.4
Total public charities	675	46.8	883	53.8	1,091	59.0	957	60.4	41.7
Reporting with financial data	228	15.8	289	17.6	357	19.3	382	24.2	67.9
Out-of-scope orgs.	0.3	0.0	1.0	0.1	2.1	0.1	1.1	0.1	242.7
Reporting public charities	227.4	15.8	288.3	17.6	354.6	19.2	381.3	24.1	67.7
Operating	190.2	13.2	241.0	14.7	297.2	16.1	320.6	20.3	68.5
Supporting	36.7	2.5	46.8	2.9	56.7	3.1	59.9	3.8	63.1
Mutual benefit	0.4	0.0	0.5	0.0	0.6	0.0	0.8	0.0	74.1
Nonreporting	447	31.0	594	36.2	735	39.7	574	36.3	28.3
Private foundations	59	4.1	82	5.0	95	5.2	96	6.1	63.4
501(c)(4) social welfare orgs.	140	9.7	138	8.4	135	7.3	91	5.8	−34.7
Other registered tax exempt orgs.	400	27.7	400	24.3	388	21.0	299	18.9	−25.3
Religious congregations not registered with the IRS	169	11.7	139	8.5	140	7.6	141	8.9	−16.7

Sources: The Urban Institute, NCCS Core Files, Public Charities and Private Foundations, 1998, 2003, 2008, 2013; Internal Revenue Service Data Book, Publication 55B, 1998, 2003, 2008, 2013.

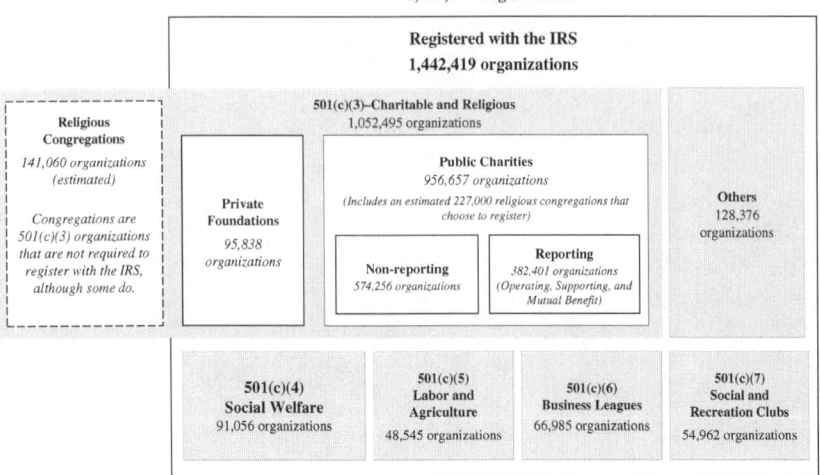

Figure I.1 Total Nonprofit Organizations (2013). *Sources*: The Urban Institute, NCCS Core File, Public Charities and Private Foundations, 2013; Internal Revenue Service Data Book, 2013, Table 25.

organizations grew much more slowly between 2003 and 2013 (see table I.1). In terms of numbers, however, human services added the most organizations (28,695), increasing by 31.3 percent from 2003 to 2013.

Small charities, many recently created, grew more quickly than charities overall. Defined as organizations with between $5,000 and $50,000 in revenues, they represented about 55 percent of 501(c)(3) charities in 2013 (574,000 organizations).[7] The information on these small charities is limited because they do not have to file the yearly IRS Form 990 that tax exempt organizations with $50,000 or more in gross receipts must submit.

There are probably million more small formal and informal associations (with less than $5,000 in revenues) that are not required to register or report to the IRS. Recent research is attempting to document the prevalence of these small and often volunteer-led organizations, as well as the many nonprofits that should be registering with the IRS, but are not (Gronbjerg, Liu, and Pollak 2010).

In addition to the "charitable" organizations, there were approximately 91,056 public-serving social welfare organizations that were tax exempt under IRC section 501(c)(4) in 2013. Most of these organizations may not receive tax-deductible gifts; some elect to do substantial lobbying and advocate for specific issues (Koulish 2016).[8] Along with public charities and congregations, they are considered a key component of the independent sector, as defined in various editions of the *Nonprofit Almanac* (Roeger et al. 2012).[9]

Table I.3 Tax exempt Organizations Registered with the IRS, 2013

Section	Description	Number
501(c)(1)	Corporations organized under act of Congress	615
501(c)(2)	Title-holding corporations	4,730
501(c)(3)	**Charitable and religious**	**1,052,495**
501(c)(4)	Social welfare organizations	91,056
501(c)(5)	Labor and agriculture organizations	48,545
501(c)(6)	Business leagues	66,985
501(c)(7)	Social and recreation clubs	54,962
501(c)(8)	Fraternal beneficiary societies	48,578
501(c)(9)	Voluntary employees' beneficiary associations	6,884
501(c)(10)	Domestic fraternal beneficiary societies	16,049
501(c)(12)	Benevolent life insurance associations	5,486
501(c)(13)	Cemetery companies	9,482
501(c)(14)	State-chartered credit unions	2,711
501(c)(15)	Mutual insurance companies	905
501(c)(17)	Supplemental unemployment benefit trusts	112
501(c)(19)	War veterans' organizations	31,674
501(c)(25)	Holding companies for pensions and other entities	813
	Other 501(c) subsections	115
501(d)	Religious and apostolic organizations	222
Total		**1,442,419**

Source: Internal Revenue Service Data Book, 2013, Table 25.

Other types of tax exempt organizations primarily serve their members, for example business leagues, social and recreational clubs, war veterans' organizations, nonprofit cemetery companies, labor unions, benevolent life insurance associations, and credit unions (see table I.3). Donations to these organizations are not tax deductible, although earnings on their assets are often tax exempt. Their numbers have not grown since 1993, and they are a declining proportion of the nonprofit sector. While all of these groups potentially contribute to the social fabric of the country, we know most about the "charitable" 501(c)(3) organizations and the "social welfare" 501(c)(4) organizations that make up the majority of formal nonprofit organizations. In this volume, we focus mainly on them because of their public-serving nature.

Regional Variation

Numbers, types, finances, and growth of charitable nonprofit organizations vary by state and region. Obviously, the numbers of nonprofits tend to increase with population. California, New York, and Texas have the largest numbers of charitable nonprofits. Similarly, the growth rates for nonprofits tend to be higher for states that have rapidly growing populations. Density of nonprofits across the states, however, varies widely and tells a different story. Sparsely populated states have the highest density of nonprofits. Vermont, for example, had a density of about 25 organizations per 10,000 people in 2013 and Montana 18, compared to just over 7 for Texas; almost 13 for New York, and almost 10 for California. There are 10 nonprofits per 10,000 people nationally (see figure I.2).

The West has proportionally more environmental groups than the other regions; the Northeast has proportionately more arts, culture, and humanities organizations, as well as human service organizations. The Northeast, with less than one-fifth of the population (17.7 percent), is home to almost a quarter (22.8 percent) of nonprofit organizations that account for 27.5 percent of the expenditures of the sector. In contrast, 32.2 percent of nonprofit organizations are located in the South (with only 26.7 percent of expenses), despite 37.4 percent of the American population residing there (see table I.4).

Some areas have higher rates of giving and volunteering and stronger civic and nonprofit infrastructure than others. Though the average charitable deduction per itemized income tax return was $1,339 in 2013, state averages ranged from $605 in West Virginia to $2,722 in Utah (National Center for

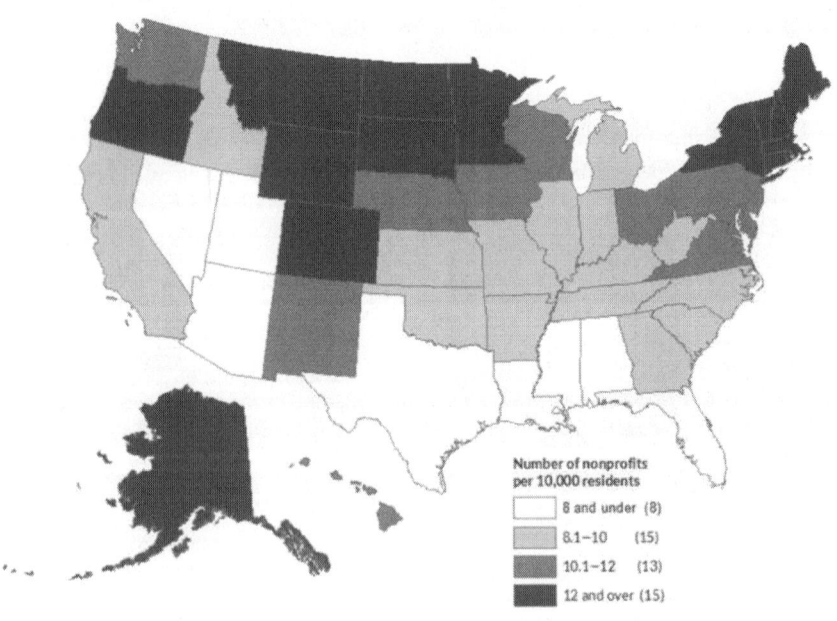

Figure I.2 Number of Nonprofit Organizations per 10,000 Residents, 2013. *Source*: The Urban Institute, NCCS Core File, Public Charities, 2013; U.S. Census Bureau, Population Division, table 1. Annual Estimates of the Resident Population for the United States, Regions, States, and Puerto Rico: April 1, 2010 to July 1, 2015. *Note*: Only operating public charities are included (see table I.2 for definition).

Table I.4 Total Number and Expenses of Nonprofit Organizations by Region, 2013

Region	Organizations	Percent	2013 Population (tens of thousands)	Non-profits per 10,000 residents	Expenses ($ millions)	Percent
Northeast	73,189	22.8	5,602	13.1	398,234	27.5
Midwest	69,218	21.6	6,757	10.2	334,804	23.1
South	103,098	32.2	11,849	8.7	386,701	26.7
West	75,110	23.4	7,435	10.1	329,137	22.7
Total	**320,615**	**100.0**	**31,643**	**10.1**	**1,448,876**	**100.0**

Note: Only operating public charities are included (see table I.2 for definition).
Source: The Urban Institute, NCCS Core File, Public Charities, 2013.

Charitable Statistics 2016). In-depth local studies are uncovering variations in giving amounts by demographics and motivations (Deitrick et al. 2014; Ong et al. 2014). Volunteering rates also vary from state to state (Rotolo and Wilson 2012). Wealthier areas have larger numbers of nonprofit organizations that provide amenities such as recreation, private schools, and art activities (Wolpert 1993). Cultural, political, economic, and historical factors all affect the types of organizations, their levels of contributions, and their financial strength in each region.

Associations at the local, state, and national levels provide a voice for nonprofits in the policy process, seeking to affect tax policy and funding decisions on the one hand and trying to enhance nonprofit capacity, conduct research, educate nonprofit managers, and encourage collaboration on the other (Abramson and McCarthy 2012). This infrastructure, dating generally from the early 1980s, has had significant, if rarely documented, impacts on the nonprofit sector, although as Alan J. Abramson discusses in chapter 7, these organizations are hampered in their policy work because there is no place within government where policy issues affecting nonprofits are of primary concern.

The portrait of the nonprofit sector that emerges is one of disparate groups, spread thinly and unevenly across the states, with a great range of missions and activities. Although their increasing economic strength raises their visibility as a whole, most are community based, modestly funded, and not well known outside of their neighborhoods. Despite their contributions and the increase in numbers of nonprofits and their visibility in recent decades, their resources pale in contrast to government and business.

Finances of Nonprofit Organizations

Nonprofits vary tremendously in resources and capacity. Almost all nonprofits, however, benefit financially from their tax exempt status, and charities additionally benefit from the incentives that charitable income tax deductions provide for the approximately 2 percent of personal income that individuals give to charities.[10] (See discussion of the value of tax incentives in chapter 4.) Most nonprofits are extremely small entities with meager resources that operate locally with modest budgets and volunteer labor. Some organizations, however, are large and professional, with hundreds of employees and many millions of dollars in expenditures; nonprofit resources are concentrated in these large organizations, mostly in hospitals, universities, and multipurpose service organizations.

Nonprofit revenue sources include fees for service, government and foundation grants, individual and corporate donations, income from special events, member dues, investments, revenues from commercial ventures, and miscellaneous other sources. Direct government grants are less important than fee-for-service income, which is the dominant source of revenue for the sector in aggregate terms. Government provides significant amounts of fee income, both directly and indirectly, although there is significant variation by type of organization. Fees involve payments for services provided (including, e.g., individual payments for tuition), government contracts through Medicare and Medicaid, and government or private vouchers for job training or childcare. According to Steven Rathgeb Smith (chapter 3), Medicaid is a driving force in the growth of government funding of nonprofits.

The resources of charities are highly concentrated in the largest organizations. Only 4 percent (13,536 organizations) of all operating charities (organizations such as health, education, and arts, which are required to register and report to the IRS) have $10 million or more in expenses. These large organizations are professionally staffed and account for 87.1 percent of the $1,448 billion in expenditures and 85.4 percent of the $2,510 billion in assets of operating charities.

In contrast, 44 percent of operating public charities (141,123) have expenses of less than $100,000 and represented only 0.4 percent of the total expenses for operating charities in 2013 (see figure I.3). These smaller organizations are largely volunteer run, with minimal, if any, paid staff. Because aggregate financial statistics are driven by large organizations and by the tremendous resources deployed in the health sector, they fail to reveal a great deal about the majority of organizations in the nonprofit sector.

Health and educational institutions dominate the finances of the nonprofit sector. About three-fifths of the total revenue and expenses of public charities are in health-related organizations. Hospitals make up about 1.1 percent of organizations, but 43.2 percent of expenditures and 36.5 percent of assets. Private higher education accounts for about 0.7 percent of organizations, but for 12 percent of expenses and 24.6 percent of assets. Human service organizations, in contrast, account for 37.5 percent of operating charities

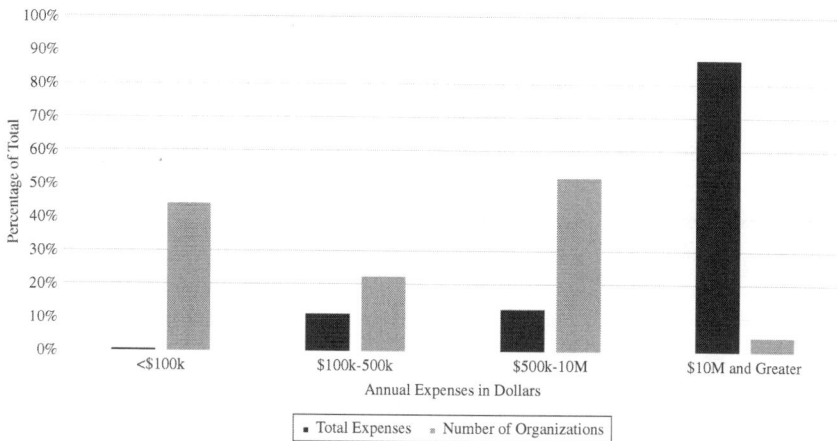

Figure I.3 Nonprofit Organizations by Total Annual Expenses, 2013.

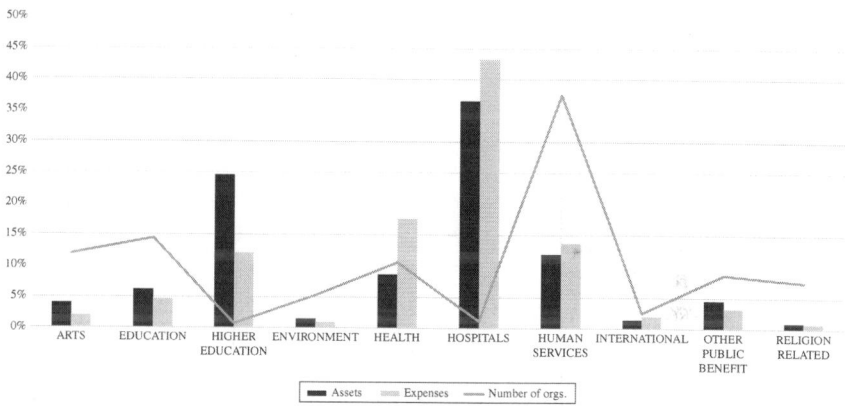

Figure I.4 Nonprofit Organizations by Type of Activity, 2013. *Note*: Only operating public charities are included (see table I.2 for definition). *Source*: The Urban Institute, NCCS Core File, Public Charities, 2013.

but less than 14 percent of expenses and just under 12 percent of assets (see figure I.4). They tend to be smaller, and their financial status is often quite weak.

Private and public foundations hold significant nonprofit assets in endowments that generate revenues used to make grants to nonprofit organizations. Private grantmaking foundations are 501(c)(3) organizations created by an individual or a family or by a corporation to fund other, mostly nonprofit, entities over time. Public foundations, including community foundations and similar funds, are endowed public charities that raise money from individuals to benefit a city, other geographic area, or specific set of causes. Together these organizations hold approximately one-fifth of the assets of the charitable sector (excluding religious congregations).[11] Donor-advised funds established by national providers, such as Fidelity Charitable, Vanguard Charitable, and others, are a rapidly growing vehicle for philanthropic giving. (See chapter 8 by Faulk and McGinnis Johnson for a description of foundations and their activities as well as of new forms of philanthropy.)

While hospitals and higher education have long relied on fees, commercial fee-for-service income is increasingly important for other types of charities. Recent analyses show that it had grown to approximately 58 percent (Kerlin and Pollak 2011). Increasing reliance on fee-for-service income from government and other sources inevitably affects the character and operations of many nonprofits (see chapter 3 by Smith). With the increase in contracting between government and nonprofits, competition for clients and for government contracts—among nonprofits and between nonprofits and businesses—has increased and has led to more businesslike marketing strategies and management practices.

Opportunities for commercial ventures and social enterprises have increased as social entrepreneurs start new organizations: nonprofits, for-profits, and hybrids (see chapter 9 by Cordes et al.). Concerned with lack of capital for scaling programs as well as sustainability of financial resources, some foundations are also using private sector models to finance nonprofits, shifting from almost exclusive reliance on grantmaking to making loans and using assets to make impact investments. These market-like investments require greater concern for efficiency, the financial bottom line, performance measurement, and outcome evaluation (see chapter 10 by Fyffe et al.).

There is a growing appreciation of the need for foundations to provide operating support grants to nonprofits (Brest 2003; Grantmakers for Effective Organizations 2007), joining the ranks of Venture Philanthropy Partners, the Edna McConnell Clark Foundation, and the Sobrato Family Foundation, among many others, in making significant capacity-building grants. Charity-monitoring organizations, however, are slow to change their nonprofit rating systems that rely significantly on low overhead and fundraising costs (efficiency) rather than on results attained (effectiveness) and sustainability (long-term effectiveness), thereby discouraging organizations from investing in strengthening their own internal operations, a necessary ingredient for effectiveness.

ROLES OF NONPROFIT ORGANIZATIONS

Why do nonprofits exist? Scholars answer this question in different ways, depending on their disciplines and orientations. Economic theories include the notions of "market failure," "government failure," and "nonprofit failure" as ways of explaining the public services delivered by nonprofits and the partnership of the government with the nonprofit sector in financing a variety of public services.

Market failure is based on the concept that there are desired services or collective "goods" that do not have sufficient potential for profit to attract business providers. Market failure is also precipitated by insufficient information on the quality of services, which may lead consumers to turn to nonprofit providers that are perceived as trustworthy because they do not have a profit motive. Similarly, government failure implies that there are public services that government will not provide for reasons that may include the cost or the limited constituency that desires the service (Hansman 1987; Weisbrod 1988). "Nonprofit failure" explains the nonprofit-government partnership as a consequence of the public demanding services best met by nonprofit provision but requiring government financing. In this theory, nonprofits are the preferred providers of services, and government action becomes necessary because nonprofits are unable to meet perceived needs (Salamon 1995) and raise the necessary revenues (see chapter 2 by Steuerle et al.). Young and Casey review economic theories of the relationship of nonprofits and government in chapter 1. Lester Salamon uses slightly different terms for a similar framework (Salamon 2012).

In contrast to economists, political scientists tend to stress the role of the nonprofit sector in terms of providing avenues of civic participation and representation of interests in the pluralistic political system of a heterogeneous society. Diverse values and interests are aggregated through associations and represented to the political system through political advocacy and lobbying of the government by many nonprofit groups (Berry 1984; Berry and Arons 2003; Boris and Krehely 2002; Boris and Maronick 2012; Clemens 2006; Sievers 2010; Verba, Schlozman, and Brady 1995; Warren 2002). Roger Lohmann builds on the idea of the commons as the civic arena in his book on the nonprofit sector (Lohmann 1992, 2003; Sievers 2010). While there is no agreement on the effectiveness of their representation of disadvantaged interests, there is an acknowledgment that, however imperfect, nonprofit advocacy provides some counterbalance to the interest advocacy of business institutions (Jenkins 2006).

The government-nonprofit relationship in the political sphere is delineated in part by the constitutionally guaranteed rights of free speech and association and in part by the limits on using dollars subsidized by the charitable tax deduction for advocacy, lobbying, and, particularly, political activity (Colinvaux 2014; Fremont-Smith 2004; Reid 2003). Conflict occurs when government and nonprofits disagree on the boundaries of permissible efforts to influence government policies and engage in political activities.[12] (See chapter 6 by Roger Colinvaux for a discussion of regulations affecting nonprofit advocacy and the implications of campaign finance reform for the political use of charities and other types of nonprofits.)

Interdisciplinary approaches to studying nonprofits provide valuable alternative perspectives. Communitarians view voluntary associations in organic terms, as the precursors of government and the market and, thus, among the most basic of social relationships that connect people and create communities. These relationships became more complex over time and evolved into the state and the market (Etzioni 1993). Robert Putnam and others use the concepts of social capital and civil society in a basically communitarian framework (Putnam 1993; Walzer 1995).

Scholars also look to the civic history of the United States—the suffrage, antislavery, and child welfare movements, for example—and to the religious roots of charity, altruism, and social justice to explain the giving and volunteering that characterize involvement in nonprofit organizations and rights-oriented social movements (Hess 2003; McCarthy 2003; O'Connell 1997; Payton 1988; Skocpol 1995; Wuthnow 1991).

Each of these approaches reveals a different aspect of nonprofits' roles and, thus, their relationship with government. A civil society approach examines the role of nonprofits in generating the social capital that links people to their communities and to others. A political analysis highlights efforts to influence the political process and create social change. An economic perspective looks at resources, at the creation of income, jobs, and knowledge, at service provision, and at economic development, often in collaboration with government. A value perspective helps explain the role of nonprofits in alleviating poverty and promoting and maintaining religious, ideological, cultural, and artistic values and beliefs, activities that sometimes lead to conflict with government. The chapters in this volume reflect the richness of these approaches.

Social Capital

Nonprofit organizations, regardless of origin, create networks and relationships that connect people to each other and to institutions quite apart from the organization's primary purposes. Research by Robert Putnam and others suggests that relationships such as those fostered by choral societies, bowling leagues, and other community associations build the trust and cooperation that is essential for the effective functioning of society, politics, and economy (Brown and Ferris 2007; Perks and Haan 2011; Putnam 1993).

Despite growing professionalism in the nonprofit arena, most nonprofits still facilitate relationships and connect people to each other and to the constituencies they serve. Members and volunteers are critical to the success of many nonprofits. Volunteers serve in governance capacities on boards of directors, in staff management and service positions, as fund-raisers, and in many other ways. Volunteers bring expertise from business, government, and the community to bear on local, national, and international problems. Volunteers enhance civic engagement and spread expertise: people of various backgrounds learn about the needs of their communities and others and act together to solve them. Volunteering also harnesses the enthusiasm of young and old and adds meaning to their lives. People who are involved in youth groups, churches, and other voluntary activities when young are more likely to give, volunteer, and be engaged in civic life in adulthood (Brown and Ferris 2007; Hodgkinson and Weitzman 1996; Perks and Haan 2011). Those who are involved in their communities are also more likely to be healthy and happy (Post 2011; Seligman 1991).

Civic Roles

Civic activities carried out by nonprofits include getting out the vote for elections, informing people about voting dates, times, and venues, conducting nonpartisan forums for discussing issues, and providing civic education classes for young people and new citizens. Indirectly, nonprofits are training grounds where people learn and use skills critical for civic participation. Members learn how to organize, lead, negotiate differences, adopt, and implement goals within organizations. These skills are transferable to civic activism and may also be employed in direct and indirect activities designed to influence attitudes, behavior, public policies, legislation, and elections.

Public education is a critical tool of civic life. Many nonprofits inform and influence domestic social and economic policies as well as international affairs through nonpartisan research, writing, evaluation, and demonstration projects. Expertise may be provided to inform and influence executive agencies or the legislative branch. Think tanks and universities conduct research and evaluations and make that information available to policymakers through publications, news media, forums, and individual conversations (Boris 1999; Boris and Maronick 2012). The role of the nonprofit policy expert is changing, however, as some think tanks have become advocates with ideological agendas, calling into question their expertise, credibility, and ability to conduct disinterested research (Rich 2004, 2005).

Grantmaking foundations and other nonprofits try to influence public policy by demonstrating the efficacy of alternative approaches to economic development, population issues, or hunger (Anheier and Hammack 2010; Fleishman 2007; Kania, Kramer, and Russell 2014). They may conduct experimental programs, evaluate the results, and communicate them to public authorities. Foundations may also promote policy agendas indirectly, for example the foundations that financed conservative think tanks that provided much of the intellectual capital for the Reagan and Bush administrations (Covington 1997; Mayer 2016; Rich 2004) and the liberal foundations that helped to finance the marriage equality movement, which resulted in the Supreme Court decision in the *Obergefell v. Hodges* case that legalized same-sex marriages in June 2015.

Advocacy, Lobbying, and Political Roles

Nonprofit advocacy groups try to educate the public and encourage individuals to contact their representatives directly or to sign petitions for or against certain positions; they may also try to influence public policy through demonstrations, sit-ins, parades, and boycotts. Jeffrey Berry maintains that public interest citizen groups have been very effective at setting and influencing the congressional agenda (Berry 1999). The National Committee for Responsive Philanthropy found that investments in advocacy leveraged significant state policy changes in Minnesota, resulting in measurable benefits of over $2 billion for residents (Gulati-Partee and Ranghelli 2009).

Certain nonprofits are involved more directly in politics, and some develop multiple organizational structures to permit them to do so in a variety of ways. They might have a 501(c)(3) charity, entitled to receive tax-deductible contributions, which permits them to provide services, and advocate and conduct limited lobbying for or against legislation. Such charities may be affiliated with a 501(c)(4) social welfare organization which can conduct unlimited lobbying for (or against) policies that affect their constituencies without revealing its donors. They may also be related to a 527 organization that is permitted to engage in issue advocacy during electoral campaigns. Some even have related political action committees (PACs) so they can be involved in partisan political campaigns, endorsing and supporting political candidate for office. These structures are a direct result of the different ways government regulates the various types of political activities, trying not to hinder free speech on the one hand while avoiding government subsidy of political activities on the other (Colinvaux 2014; Pekkanen et al. 2014; Reid and Kerlin 2003; Reid 2006). Roger Colinvaux, in chapter 6, discusses nonprofit advocacy and the principles and regulations that guide and constrain such activities.

Some of the most profound social changes of this century have been promoted through a combination of research, public education, advocacy, legislation, and litigation fostered by nonprofit organizations. These nonprofits usually work in coalitions, sometimes in collaboration with government and business interests, and sometimes in conflict with them and with other nonprofits (Boris and Maronick 2012). Civil rights groups, working with religious and other organizations, attacked racial segregation in this country through direct action, lobbying, advocacy, litigation, and public education. Environmental groups used research, public education, advocacy, and litigation in their pioneering efforts to reduce air and water pollution and protect the environment and wildlife. Currently, they are using public education to disseminate research and promote policies to curb global warming. Antismoking groups joined insurance companies, foundations, and government agencies to foster research and use the results to educate the public about the negative impacts of tobacco smoking on health. David Cole, in *Engines of Liberty: The Power of Citizen Activists to Make Constitutional Law* (2016), profiles three issues: marriage equality, right to bear arms, and human rights in the war on terror, in which advocacy organizations over time managed to change constitutional law.

Not all advocacy is designed to introduce change. Groups all along the political spectrum may aim to conserve or protect values that they espouse or may try to prevent the erosion of values they cherish or advantages they enjoy. The National Rifle Association, for example, promotes gun ownership and lobbies against legislation that would limit an individual's right to own guns. The American Civil Liberties Union defends individual rights and litigates against legislation that it believes threatens freedom of speech and other liberties guaranteed in the Constitution and the Bill of Rights. Tea Party groups advocate for conservative values in a countrywide movement (Skocpol and Williamson 2012).

Advocacy can be contentious work, as nonprofits may face direct and indirect opposition from other groups, business interests, and government agencies. Success for one cause may mean failure for another. For example, pro-choice organizations use public education, advocacy, and litigation to protect a woman's right to control her reproductive choices, while antichoice groups use the same tools to limit access to abortions based on their religious and ethical values. Each side perceives the other as undermining its core values and beliefs, often leading to rancorous public discourse and even violence.

While there is much talk of promoting social change among foundations, they are limited in their ability to directly affect political change. They may provide resources for some types of advocacy, lobbying, and litigation, but they are not permitted to lobby or be involved in partisan politics. Their influence is largely through other institutions, and, with a few exceptions, like Atlantic Philanthropies and the Haas Jr. Fund, they do not advance advocacy agendas.

Religious, Cultural, and Artistic Roles

The most deeply felt controversies over values are played out in the nonprofit sector—around religious beliefs, artistic expression, personal responsibility, individual rights, and the separation of church and state. Nonprofits express conflicts over competing values long before they reach the political system. These conflicts may be positive when they promote the dialogue and deliberation that are healthy for democracy. In extremely divisive cases like racial segregation and access to abortions, conflicts can involve legislative and judicial battles at the national, state, and local levels over long periods of time.

The impact of religion on American society is deep and enduring (Wuthnow 2011). Religious organizations serve the spiritual needs of their members and promote and preserve the group's religious doctrines and values. Sacramental activities and membership-serving activities such as childcare and counseling may be supplemented by social and health services, crisis care, and advocacy activities (Chaves 2002; Cnaan 1997; Hodgkinson and Weitzman 1993; Printz 1997; Wuthnow 2004). Religious congregations also impart civic skills to members who learn to organize and collaborate for common ends. Black churches, for example, are well known for their efforts to mobilize their members to vote and for their political work, particularly around ending segregation and promoting civil rights (Harris 1994). The IRS, however, in very limited ways has scrutinized political speech in religious organizations to determine if they are engaging in prohibited partisan campaign activities by using taxpayer-subsidized charitable contributions to endorse candidates who share their values.[13]

The separation of church and state in the United States involves an ongoing debate with a long evolution (Crimm and Winer 2011). Historically, however, the religious charities' receipt of government revenues for services provided to the general public is well established (Hall 1982). Government-funded social service provision by nonprofits affiliated with Catholic, Lutheran, and Jewish faiths, for example, has been widespread. When providing government-funded services, such groups have usually accepted limitations on proselytizing and on providing preferential services to their members.

Most religious entities fall outside of the government regulatory framework for nonprofit organizations (see chapter 4 by Brody and Cortes). Houses of worship and closely aligned entities enjoy the benefits of tax exemption and deductible contributions but are not required to register or report to the IRS; many do report however, and the number is increasing, partially in an effort to create a formal structure to qualify for faith-based funding initiatives. Government funding requires accountability, and some fear that monitoring contracts and performance will involve the government too deeply in the affairs of religious bodies. Like other charities, some simply lack sophisticated accounting and other skills that make compliance less onerous.

Congregations that desire government funding often set up separate charities to segregate finances, avoid potential conflicts, and protect their sacramental activities from government involvement.

The implementation of the Affordable Care Act, which requires employers to provide female employees access to insurance that covers contraception costs, still reveals the tension that arises from government regulation. Some businesses and religious organizations claim that even enabling such coverage operates as a mandate that violates their religious beliefs. Litigation has reached the Supreme Court.

Other values conversations are ongoing and are at times mediated by nonprofit organizations themselves. Government support of the arts raises a host of questions about the types of art that deserve public support, given that different standards of morality and decency may offend some people but not others (Wuthnow 2006). Arts and culture are embedded in community life and are reflected in worship, education, celebrations, and much more. Through arts and culture, we transmit group memory, celebrate ethnic and national identity, and interpret the past. The arts enhance our quality of life and generate economic benefits and much more for communities (Jackson 1998).

Service Roles

Nonprofits of all types provide services that may be offered to the whole community, to special populations, to members only, to governments, to businesses, and to other nonprofits. As service providers, nonprofits often overlap with business and government, for example, in education and medical care. They may be contractors for governments and businesses (providing preschool programs or drug abuse treatment), collaborators with governments (maintaining national and regional parks or preventing diseases), or act in lieu of government (accreditation or consumer protection). As the contracting out of government services has increased dramatically (see chapter 3 by Smith), the nonprofit share of the workforce has increased by roughly the amount that government employment has decreased (see chapter 2 by Steuerle et al.).

With more government money at stake, it is not surprising that nonprofits find themselves in competition with for-profit providers (US Congress 1996).[14] The effects, including the adoption of business practices, are felt not just internally but also by donors and clients. Nonprofits often find that competition means that they must market, actively attract clients, and report on their outcomes and impacts (see chapter 10 by Fyffe et al.). These changes can be positive, but may affect the way nonprofits are viewed by donors and experienced by clients. A pervasive bottom-line orientation may inadvertently affect even nonprofits that do not have government contracts or commercial revenues; the effort may increase efficiency and, at the same time, undermine charitable service missions and public trust.

Government may turn to nonprofits to undertake activities that require reaching local populations with culturally sensitive materials or to avoid hiring permanent staff for temporary projects. Nonprofits provide a way for governments to devolve programs either directly or through state and local authorities and provide services without incurring government salary scales and bureaucratic red tape, although nonprofits must then deal with government-imposed red tape and inefficiencies (Pettijohn and Boris 2013).

The use of nonprofits by governments to deliver services may separate governments from accepting responsibility for services funded, thus undermining popular support for public financing of programs or promoting cynicism toward nonprofits if programs fail. Nonprofits can provide a "cop out" for political leaders who wish to curtail government responsibilities. Nonprofits can also be used by wealthy communities to provide for their own needs, while neglecting to provide tax revenues for public education and other public health and human services for low-income residents.

Nonprofits also interact with and provide a variety of services directly and indirectly to the business sector (Cordes and Steuerle 2009). They collaborate with businesses in promoting quality of life in areas where firms operate. Donations to and contracts with cultural organizations and with childcare and recreation groups underwrite amenity services that attract and hold corporate employees, thereby helping to maintain the community's tax base. Environmental groups help to level the playing field for socially responsible behavior by demanding, for example, that all competitors within an industry clean up pollutants.

Nonprofit business associations provide information, research, and advocacy services for member corporations. They monitor the health of industries and the impact of legislation and regulation on corporate activities. They may provide low-cost insurance or cooperative buying opportunities. Nonprofit associations may provide similar types of services for groups of nonprofits, health-related nonprofits, philanthropic foundations, colleges and universities, symphonies, museums, and others.

State and local governments directly and indirectly fund nonprofits to provide services and also oversee the activities of nonprofits and their fundraising to ensure that the public is given accurate information and not misled by false claims and illegal operators (see chapter 5 by Lott and Fremont-Smith).

ECONOMIC IMPACTS

As mentioned earlier, nonprofits make significant contributions to the U.S. economy as employers and service providers. Their assets exceed $5 trillion, as Steuerle et al. report in chapter 2. Millions of people serve as volunteers, further expanding nonprofit resources. This economic role, however, is disproportionately concentrated in the largest organizations and in certain sectors, especially in hospitals, private universities, and multipurpose organizations like the American Red Cross, Catholic Charities, and others; over 40 percent of nonprofit employees work in hospitals.

Nonprofits provide the entry point into the labor force for many women and minorities. About two out of three workers in the nonprofit sector are women. Employment in the smaller nonprofits is often at lower-than-market wages and without health and retirement benefits. Major nonprofit hospitals and universities anchor whole inner-city neighborhoods or small towns with employment opportunities, services, and amenities like arts, culture, and recreation opportunities. They contribute to public coffers by paying payroll taxes, while employees pay both income and payroll taxes.

Because nonprofits generally do not pay property taxes or sales taxes, they may be perceived as a drain on the local economy (Brody 2002, 2010; Brody et al. 2012). Some local governments seek payments in lieu of taxes (PILOTs) and services in lieu of taxes (SILOTS) from nonprofits in their communities to help cover costs of services (Brody et al. 2012). These are generally not systematic efforts; they target the largest nonprofits and foundations. They are controversial but are becoming more prevalent. The Lincoln Institute of Land Policy reports that PILOTS have been used in 154 jurisdictions in 27 states (Brody et al. 2012; Kenyon et al. 2012), reflecting financial status of many localities, the cost to the community for providing services to the nonprofits, and an eroding concern for traditional local accommodations of nonprofit organizations.

To counter the view that nonprofits are a drain on communities, nonprofit associations and others have conducted or commissioned reports on the economic contributions of nonprofits. These economic impact studies are being used to grab the attention of policymakers as nonprofits attempt to negotiate for policy influence and revenues and deflect efforts to deny them tax benefits. A particularly comprehensive report on California finds that California nonprofits employ one million people, contribute 15 percent to the gross state product, and pay $37 billion in taxes (Deitrick et al. 2014).

INTERNATIONAL TRENDS

Many countries have long-standing, expansive nonprofit sectors that play economic, social, and political roles similar to those documented in the United States, but with variations reflecting the different cultural, historical, and economic contexts. Governments often provide extensive resources to nonprofits in their countries and may permit more or less advocacy than in the United States, or none at all. In many countries, the source of funds for most nonprofits, even churches, is government. Private contributions are almost universally a lower share of personal income than in the United States. The extensive scope of activities, giving, volunteering, and economic impact of nonprofit sectors around the world is being illuminated by increasing numbers of scholars, and notably through the Comparative Nonprofit Sector Program at Johns Hopkins University (Salamon 2006, 2014).

The US foundations and nonprofits that operate across national borders, as well as nonprofits that work within other countries, are growing both in numbers and influence. International nongovernmental organizations (INGOs) are active in human rights, economic development, disaster relief, disease prevention and treatment, environmental protection, conflict resolution, and many other fields. They often act in concert with national governments, and multinational and international institutions, although conflicts are also common. Contracts with governments are becoming more prevalent, and disaster relief and recovery have become high-profile issues. The Internet has transformed the ability of INGOs to collaborate, advocate, and raise money. They are linked in global networks that have huge potential to monitor and affect public policies.

As in the United States, social enterprises and hybrid organizational forms are growing in numbers and influence. So too is impact investing, involving governments, foundations, nonprofits, and businesses. In 2011, for example, the US Agency for International Development partnered with three foundations, Rockefeller, Gates, and Gatsby in the United Kingdom, as well as the investment bank JP Morgan Social Finance and a Uganda-based consultancy, Pearl Capital Partners, to create, fund, and manage a $25 million African Agriculture Capital Fund. This private investment fund, one example among many, is applying impact-investing techniques to spur agricultural development in Africa (Shah and Pease 2012; Salamon 2014).

Regulation and oversight of nonprofits and foundations around the world reflect many of the same concerns and tensions that we find in the United States, although issues of control differ because of the typically higher share of revenues from government, while repression is generally more intense in countries with weak or nonexistent democratic institutions. (See chapter 11 by Phillips and Blumberg for a comparative analysis of the regulatory systems in many countries).

CONCLUSION

The nonprofit sector continues to play critical roles in society both in collaboration and in conflict with government. Over time, changes within society and the nonprofit sector inevitably alter the dynamics of those relationships.

New philanthropic forms, investment vehicles, and hybrid structures arise, while demands for transparency and measurable impacts increase. Nonprofit organizations today are more visible than in the past. They are more likely to communicate and advocate online and via social media, and many operate locally, nationally, and globally. They are more likely to have diversified revenue streams that include fees for services, often from government, as well as businesslike enterprises. Financing relationships with government and business take new forms through joint investing and pay-for-success efforts. Donors have more choices in the ways they give and the vehicles and institutions they support, while many high net worth donors actively engage in philanthropic activities at younger ages, making significant gifts during their lifetimes rather than through their estates at death.

This dynamic picture contrasts with the more static nature of government oversight, which remains necessary for protecting donors and ensuring that dollars given for charitable purposes are spent for such purposes. Given their very limited resources, federal and state regulators are limited in their ability to coordinate activities, monitor nonprofit organizations, and keep up with the changes in the sector. More than ever, public oversight relies upon nonprofits and foundations to uphold the public trust; such efforts go well beyond deterring malfeasance to producing better outcomes and advancing society through charitable efforts. This oversight role requires both collaboration with and sometimes conflict between the sectors. The adequacy of this approach will be tested in the coming years.

We hope that this volume will increase understanding, provoke discussion, and perhaps even inspire some to find better ways to engage constructively in the ever-dynamic relationship between nonprofits and government. The chapters in this volume describe in detail the many dimensions of their ongoing and evolving interactions.

ACKNOWLEDGMENTS

The author is indebted to Gene Steuerle for his thoughtful comments on this chapter and for his contributions to this volume. Collaborating with Gene is a joy. Thanks also to Brice McKeever and Béatrice Leydier for contributions to and suggestions for this chapter, and to Ellen Steele for assistance with this volume.

NOTE ON DATA SOURCES

Data Sources. The data used in this chapter are compiled by the National Center for Charitable Statistics (NCCS) at the Urban Institute from government and private sources and are reported in annual updates (*Nonprofit Sector in Brief*) and in periodic editions of the *Nonprofit Almanac*. Data on the finances, types of nonprofits, and locations are derived from the Forms 990 that nonprofits are required to file with the IRS. The NCCS creates research data sets and summary tables from IRS data and provides them to researchers and the public at www.urban.nccs.org. IRS Forms 990 and 990 PF can be viewed at www.urban.nccs.org, www.guidestar.org, and www.foundationcenter.org.

Religious Congregations. Estimates of the number of religious congregations are from *U.S. Religion Census: Religious Congregations & Membership Study*, sponsored by the Association of Statisticians of American Religious Bodies.[15] Based on the data from the US Religion Census, this report estimates approximately 266,000 total religious congregations in 1998, 291,000 in 2003, 330,000 in 2008, and 368,000 in 2013. Estimates of 1998 are imputed using linear interpolation from 1990 and 2000 Religion Census numbers; 2003, 2008, and 2013 estimates were imputed using the 2000 and 2010 numbers. The number of estimated congregations registered with the IRS ranged from 96,000 in 1998 to 227,000 in 2013, based on an analysis of organizational purpose of the IRS Business Master File. The estimated numbers of organizations registered with the IRS were then subtracted from the US Religion Census numbers to get the final statistics this is reported in table I.2 as "Religious congregations not registered with the IRS."

NOTES

1. Forms 990 are public documents that provide financial data—assets, revenues, expenses, and so on. They are available for inspection on the websites of the National Center for Charitable Statistics (NCCS), GuideStar, and the Foundation Center. Research databases with financial information based on Forms 990 are available at NCCS.

2. For a thorough discussion of nonprofit accountability, see Kevin Kearns's "Accountability in the Nonprofit Sector" (Kearns 2012) and Evelyn Brody's "Sunshine and Shadows on Charity Governance: Public Disclosure as a Regulatory Tool" (Brody 2012).

3. See for example, Senate Finance Committee white paper: "Senate Finance Committee Staff Discussion Draft, Tax Exempt Governance Proposals." June 22, 2004. The proposals in this document led to a sector-wide effort to address the proposals and develop recommendations that nonprofits could live with. The Panel on the Nonprofit Sector, convened by the Independent Sector, formed working groups to draft and discuss recommendations for strengthening nonprofit transparency and governance. The results were published in *Strengthening Transparency, Governance, and Accountability of Charitable Organizations* (Panel on the Nonprofit Sector 2005).

4. The National Taxonomy of Exempt Entities (NTEE) was developed by the National Center for Charitable Statistics (NCCS) and is currently used by the IRS and

by many researchers to classify nonprofit organizations. See www.urban.nccs.org for a description of the categories.

5. The number of congregations in the United States is estimated at about 345,000, based on the 2010 U.S. Religion Census: Religious Congregations & Membership Study (Grammich 2012). About 227,000 register with the IRS, although they are not required to do so. See Note on Data Sources at the end of this chapter.

6. Most congregations are not included here because they are not required to report to the IRS, although many do. See table I.2 and figure I.1.

7. Charities with between $5,000 and $50,000 in gross receipts must register with the IRS, but they are not required to report their finances. In table I.2, they are under the heading "Nonreporting."

8. While 501(c)(4) organizations are commonly referred to as advocacy organizations because they are permitted greater freedom to lobby and conduct issue advocacy, and if they have members, they may issue partisan communications to their members (see chapter 6 by Colinvaux), but most are not advocates; organizations in this category include a mix of organizations that serve public purposes but are deemed not eligible for tax-deductible contributions.

9. *The New Nonprofit Almanac and Desk Reference* (Weitzman et al. 2002) defines the independent sector components to include all 501(c)(3) charities, including congregations, and 501(c)(4) social welfare groups; this convention continues.

10. Each of these tax benefits has a cost to government of revenues foregone, in effect a subsidy that in tight financial times may become a source of controversy. For example the Senate Finance Committee actions to limit the deductibility of car donations to the actual revenue realized by charities will cut government costs. Measuring the cost to the government and the benefit to nonprofits is possible; more difficult to measure is the benefit to society.

11. See the Foundation Center's "Foundation Stats" (2014) accessible at http://data.foundationcenter.org/#/foundations/all/nationwide/total/list/2014.

12. Chapter 4 argues that nonprofit tax exemption may be an attempt by government to respect the sovereignty of the nonprofit sector: government takes a hands-off approach to taxing, and nonprofits are required to be hands off in terms of advocating for government subvention.

13. To counter this limitation, Representative Walter Jones introduced a bill in the US House called the Houses of Worship Free Speech Restoration Act of 2005.

14. Todd J. Gillman. "Health Clubs Hit YMCAs' Tax Breaks," *Washington Post*, June 30, 1987.

15. Summary numbers for the US Religion Census (Grammich 2012) are available online at the Association of Religion Data Archives website, at http://www.thearda.com/rcms2010/r/u/rcms2010_99_US_name_2010.asp (accessed January 11, 2016).

REFERENCES

Abramson, Alan J., and Rachel McCarthy. 2012. "Infrastructure Organizations." *The State of Nonprofit America*, 2nd ed. Lester M. Salamon, eds. (pp. 423–458). Washington, DC: Brookings Institution Press.

Anheier, Helmut K., and David C. Hammack, eds. 2010. *American Foundations: Roles and Contributions*. Washington, DC: Brookings Institution Press.

Berry, Jeffrey M. 1984. *The Interest Group Society*. Boston: Little, Brown.

———. 1999. *The New Liberalism: The Rising Power of Citizen Groups*. Washington, DC: Brookings Institution Press.

Berry, Jeffrey M., and David F. Arons. 2003. *A Voice for Nonprofits*. Washington, DC: Brookings Institute Press.

Boris, Elizabeth T. 1999. "The Nonprofit Sector in the 1990s." *The Future of Philanthropy in a Changing America*. Charles Clotfelter and Thomas Erlich, eds. (pp. 1–33). New York, NY: The American Assembly, Columbia University.

Boris, Elizabeth T., and Jeff Krehely. 2002. "Civic Participation and Advocacy." *The State of Nonprofit America*, Lester M. Salamon, ed. (pp. 299–330). Washington, DC: Brookings Institute Press.

Boris, Elizabeth T., and Matthew Maronick. 2012. "Civic Participation and Advocacy." *The State of Nonprofit America*, 2nd ed. Lester M. Salamon, ed. (pp. 394–422). Washington, DC: Brookings Institution Press.

Brest, Paul. 2003. "Smart Money: General Operating Grants Can be Strategic—for Nonprofits and Foundations." *Stanford Social Innovation Review*.

Brody, Evelyn. 2010. "All Charities are Property-tax Exempt, but Some Charities are More Exempt than Others." *New England Law Review* 44(3): 621.

———, ed. 2002. *Property Tax Exemption for Charities*. Washington, DC: Urban Institute Press.

———. 2012. "Sunshine and Shadows on Charity Governance: Public Disclosure as a Regulatory Tool." *Florida Tax Review* 12(4): 183.

Brody, Evelyn, Mayra Marquez, and Katherine Toran. 2012. The Charitable Property-Tax Exemption and PILOTs. Washington, DC: Urban Institute.

Brown, Eleanor and James Ferris. 2007. "Social capital and Philanthropy: An analysis of the impact of social capital on individual giving and volunteering." *Nonprofit and Voluntary Sector Quarterly* 36 (March): 85–99.

Bureau of Labor Statistics. 2014. "Nonprofits Account for 11.4 Million Jobs, 10.3 percent of all Private Sector Employment." *The Economics Daily*. Washington, DC: U.S Department of Labor. Available online at http://www.bls.gov/opub/ted/2014/ted_20141021.htm, accessed January 11, 2016.

Chaves, Mark. 2002. "Religious Congregations." *The State of Nonprofit America*, Lester M. Salamon, ed. Washington, DC: Brookings Institution Press.

Clemens, Elisabeth. 2006. "The Constitution of Citizens: Political Theories of Nonprofit Organizations." *The Nonprofit Sector: A Research Handbook*, 2nd ed. Walter W. Powell and Richard Steinberg, eds. New Haven: Yale University Press.

Cnaan, Ram. 1997. "Social and Community Involvement of Local Religious Congregations: Findings from a Six-City Study." Paper presented at annual meeting of ARNOVA, Indianapolis, IN, December 4–6.

Cole, David. 2016. *Engines of Liberty: The Power of Citizen Activists to Make Constitutional Law*. New York, NY: Basic Books.

Colinvaux, Roger 2014. "Political Activity Limits and Tax Exemption: A Gordian's Knot." *Virginia Tax Review* 34(1).

Cordes, Joseph and C. Eugene Steuerle. 2009. "The Changing Economy and the Scope of Nonprofit-Like Activities." *Nonprofits and Business.* Joseph Cordes and C. Eugene Steuerle, eds. Washington, DC: Urban Institute.

Covington, Sally. 1997. "Moving A Public Policy Agenda: The Strategic Philanthropy of Conservative Foundations." Washington, DC: National Committee for Responsive Philanthropy.

Crimm, Nina J. 1952, and Laurence H. Winer. 2011. *Politics, Taxes, and the Pulpit: Provocative First Amendment Conflicts.* New York, NY: Oxford University Press.

Dees, J. Gregory. 1998. "Enterprising Nonprofits." *Harvard Business Review* (January–February): 55–67.

Deitrick, Laura, Jon Durnford, Andrew Narwold, Fred Galloway, and Mary Jo Schumann. 2014. *Causes Count: The Economic Power of California's Nonprofit Sector.* California, CA: CalNonprofits.

Etzioni, Amitai. 1993. *The Spirit of Community: Rights, Responsibilities, and the Communitarian Agenda.* New York, NY: Crown Publishers, Inc.

Fleishman, Joel L. 2007. *The Foundation: A Great American Secret: How Private Wealth is Changing the World.* New York, NY: Public Affairs.

Fremont-Smith, Marion. 2004. *Governing Nonprofit Organizations.* Cambridge: President and Fellows of Harvard College.

The Foundation Center. 2014. *Key Facts on U.S. Foundations, 2014 edition.* New York, NY: The Foundation Center.

Gillman, Todd J. 1987. "Health Clubs Hit YMCAs' Tax Breaks." *Washington Post*, June 30.

Goddeeris, John H., and Burton A. Weisbrod. 2006. "Ownership Forms, Conversions, and Public Policy." *Nonprofits & Government: Collaboration & Conflict*, 2nd ed. Elizabeth T. Boris and C. Eugene Steuerle, eds. (pp. 277–310). Washington, DC Urban Institute Press.

Grammich, Clifford A. Association of Statisticians of American Religious Bodies, and Church of the Nazarene. Global Ministry Center. 2012. *2010 U.S. Religion Census: Religious Congregations & Membership Study: An Enumeration by Nation, State, and County Based on Data Reported for 236 Religious Groups.* Kansas City, MO: Association of Statisticians of American Religious Bodies.

Grantmakers for Effective Organizations. 2007. *General Operating Support.* Washington, DC: Grantmakers for Effective Organizations.

Gray, Bradford H., and Mark Schlesinger. 2012. "Health Care." *The State of Nonprofit America,* 2nd ed. Lester M. Salamon, ed. (pp. 89–136). Washington, DC: Brookings Institute Press.

Grønbjerg, Kirsten A., Helen K. Liu, and Thomas H. Pollak. 2010. "Incorporated but not IRS-Registered: Exploring the (Dark) Grey Fringes of the Nonprofit Universe." *Nonprofit and Voluntary Sector Quarterly* 39(5): 925–945.

Gulati-Partee, Gita, and Lisa Ranghelli. 2009. "Strengthening Democracy, Increasing Opportunities: Impacts of Advocacy, Organizing, and Civic Engagement in Minnesota." Washington, DC: National Committee for Responsive Philanthropy.

Hall, Peter Dobkin. 1982. "Institutions, Autonomy, and National Networks." *Making the Nonprofit Sector in the United States*, David C. Hammack, ed. Bloomington: Indiana University Press.

Hansman, Henry. 1987. "Economic Theories of Nonprofit Organization." *The Nonprofit Sector: A Research Handbook*, Walter W. Powell, ed. New Haven: Yale University Press.

Harris, Frederick C. 1994. "Something Within: Religion as a Mobilizer of African-American Political Activism." *Journal of Politics* 56: 42–68.

Hess, Gary. 2003. "Waging the Cold War in the Third World: The Foundations and the Challenges of Development." *Charity, Philanthropy, and Civility in American History.* Lawrence J. Friedman and Mark D. McGarve, eds. New York, NY: Cambridge University Press.

Hodgkinson, Virginia and Murray Weitzman. 1993. *From Belief to Commitment: The Community Service Activities and Finances of Religious Congregations in the United States.* Washington, DC: Independent Sector.

Jackson, Maria-Rosario. 1998. "Arts and Culture Indicators in Community Building: Project Update." *Journal of Arts Management, Law and Society* 28(3): 201–205.

Jenkins, Craig J. 2006. "Nonprofit Organizations and Political Advocacy." *The Nonprofit Sector: A Research Handbook,* 2nd ed. Walter W. Powell and Richard Steinberg, eds. New Haven: Yale University Press.

Kania, John, Mark Kramer, and Patty Russell. 2014. "Strategic Philanthropy for a Complex World." *Stanford Social Innovation Review* 12(3): 26–37.

Kearns, Kevin P. 2012. "Accountability in the Nonprofit Sector." *The State of Nonprofit America*, 2nd ed. Lester M. Salamon, ed. (pp. 587–615). Brookings Institution Press.

Kenyon, Daphne A., Adam H. Langley, Bethany P. Paquin, and Lincoln Institute of Land Policy. 2012. *Rethinking Property Tax Incentives for Business.* Cambridge, MA: Lincoln Institute of Land Policy.

Kerlin, Janelle A. 2005. "Social Enterprise in the United States and Abroad: Learning from Our Differences." *Researching Social Entrepreneurship.* Rachel Mosher-Williams, ed. ARNOVA Occasional Paper Series, 1(3).

Kerlin, Janelle A., and Tom H. Pollak. 2011. "Nonprofit Commercial Revenue: A Replacement for Declining Government Grants and Private Contributions?" *The American Review of Public Administration* 41(6): 686–704.

Koulish, Jeremy. 2016. *From Camps to Campaign Funds: The History, Anatomy, and Activities of 501(c)(4) Organizations.* Washington, DC: Urban Institute.

Lohmann, Roger. 1992. *The Commons.* San Francisco, CA: Jossey-Bass Publishers.

———. 2003. "The Commons: Our mission if We Choose to Accept It." *Nonprofit and Voluntary Sector Quarterly* 10 (Summer 2003): 6–10.

Mayer, Jane. 2016. *Dark Money: The Hidden History of the Billionaires behind the Rise of the Radical Right.* New York, NY: Doubleday.

McCarthy, Kathleen. 2003. *American Creed: Philanthropy and the Rise of Civil Society 1700–1865.* Chicago: The University of Chicago Press.

McKeever, Brice. 2015. *The Nonprofit Sector in Brief 2015:* Public Charities, Giving and Volunteering. Washington, DC: Urban Institute

Morley, Elaine and Carol J. De Vita. 2007. *Providing Long-Term Services after Major Disasters.* Washington, DC: Urban Institute.

Moore, Alexander J. 2014. *The Food Fighters: DC Central Kitchen's First Twenty-Five Years on the Front Lines of Hunger and Poverty.* Bloomington Indiana: iUniverse.

National Center for Charitable Statistics. 2016. *Profiles of Individual Charitable Contributions by State, 2013.* Washington, DC: Urban Institute

O'Connell, Brian. 1997. *Powered By Coalition: The Story of Independent Sector.* San Francisco, CA: Jossey-Bass Publishers.

Ong, Paul, Silvia Jimenez, Bill Parent, and Elena Ong. 2014. *The State of Donations: Individual Charitable Giving in Los Angeles, The 2014 State of the Nonprofit Sector in Los Angeles Report.* Los Angeles: UCLA Luskin School of Public Affairs, Center for Civil Society.

Payton, Robert L. 1988. *Philanthropy: Voluntary Action for the Public Good.* New York, NY: American Council on Education/Macmillan Publishing Company.

Panel on the Nonprofit Sector. 2005. *Strengthening Transparency, Governance, Accountability of Charitable Organizations: A Final Report to Congress and the Nonprofit Sector.* Washington, DC: Independent Sector.

Pekkanen, Robert, Steven Rathgeb Smith, and Yutaka Tsujinaka, eds. 2014. *Nonprofits and Advocacy: Engaging Communities and Government in an Era of Retrenchment.* Baltimore: Johns Hopkins University Press.

Perks, Thomas and Michael Haan. 2011. "Youth Religious Involvement and Adult Community Participation: Do Levels of Youth Religious Involvement Matter?" *Nonprofit and Voluntary Sector Quarterly* 40 (February 2011): 107–129.

Pettijohn, Sarah L., and Boris, Elizabeth. 2013. *Contracts and Grants between Nonprofits and Government.* Washington, DC: Urban Institute.

Post, Stephen G. 2011. *The Hidden Gifts of Helping: How the Power of Giving, Compassion, and Hope Can Get Us through Hard Times.* San Francisco, CA: Jossey-Bass.

Printz, Tobi J. 1997. "Services and Capacity of Faith-Based Organizations in the Washington, DC, Metropolitan Area." Paper presented at annual meeting of ARNOVA, Indianapolis, IN, December 4–6.

Putnam, Robert D. 1993. *Making Democracy Work: Civic Traditions in Modern Italy.* Princeton: Princeton University Press.

———. 2000. *Bowling Alone: The Collapse and Revival of American Community.* New York, NY: Simon and Shuster.

Reid, Elizabeth J. 2003. "In the States, Across the Nation, and Beyond: Democratic and Constitutional Perspectives on Nonprofit Advocacy." Washington, DC: Urban Institute Press.

———. 2006. "Advocacy and the Challenges It Presents for Nonprofits." *Nonprofits & Government: Collaboration & Conflict,* 2nd ed. Elizabeth T. Boris and C. Eugene Steuerle, eds. (pp. 343–372). Washington, DC: Urban Institute Press.

Reid, Elizabeth J., and Janelle Kerlin. 2003. "More than Meets the Eye: Structuring and Financing Nonprofit Advocacy." A paper delivered at the American Political Science Association, Annual Conference, Philadelphia, Pennsylvania.

Rich, Andrew. 2004. *Think Tanks, Public Policy, and the Politics of Expertise.* Cambridge, United Kingdom: Cambridge University Press.

———. 2005. "War of Ideas." *Stanford Social Innovation Review* 3: 18–25.

Roeger, Katie L., Amy S. Blackwood, and Sarah L. Pettijohn. 2012. *The Nonprofit Almanac.* Washington, DC: Urban Institute Press.

Rotolo, Thomas and John Wilson. 2012. "State-level Differences in Volunteerism in the United States: Research Based on Demographic, Institutional, and Cultural Macrolevel Theories." *Nonprofit and Voluntary Sector Quarterly* 41 (June 2012): 452–473.

Salamon, Lester M. 1995. *Partners in Public Service: Government-Nonprofit Relations in the Modern Welfare State.* Baltimore: Johns Hopkins University Press.

———. 2006. *Nonprofits & Government: Collaboration & Conflict*, 2nd ed. Elizabeth T. Boris and C. Eugene Steuerle, eds. Washington, DC: Urban Institute Press.

———, ed. 2012. *The State of Nonprofit America.* Washington, DC: Brookings Institute Press.

———. 2014. *Leverage for good: An Introduction to the New Frontier of Philanthropy and Social Investment.* Oxford University Press.

Seligman, Martin E. P. 1991. *Learned Optimism: How to Change Your Mind and Your Life.* New York, NY: A. A. Knopf.

Shah, Sapna and Min Pease. 2012. "Diverse Perspectives, Shared Objective: Collaborating to Form the African Agricultural Capital Fund." Global Impact Investing Network, Case Studies.

Sievers, Bruce R. 2010. *Civil Society, Philanthropy, and the Fate of the Commons.* Medford, MA: Tufts University Press.

Skocpol, Theda. 1995. *Protecting Mothers and Soldiers: The Political Origins of Social Policy in the United States.* Cambridge: Harvard University Press.

Skocpol, Theda and Morris P. Fiorina. 1999. *Civic Engagement in American Democracy.* Washington, DC: Brookings Institution Press.

Skocpol, Theda and Vanessa Williamson. 2012. *The Tea Party and the Remaking of Republican Conservatism.* New York, NY: Oxford University Press.

Smith, David H., Helmut K. Anheier, Stefan Toepler, and Regina List. 2010. "Grassroots Associations." *International Encyclopedia of Civil Society* (pp. 804–810). New York, NY: Springer.

Stevenson, David R. 1997. *The National Taxonomy of Exempt Entities Manual.* Washington, DC and New York, NY: National Center for Charitable Statistics and Foundation Center.

U.S. Congress. 1996. House Committee on Small Business. *Government-Supported Unfair Competition with Small Business.* 104th Cong., 2d sess., July 19.

U. S. Congress, Senate Finance Committee, Staff of. 2004. Senate Finance Committee Staff Discussion Draft, Tax Exempt Governance Proposals." June 22. Available at http://www.finance.senate.gov/hearings/testimony/2004test/062204stfdis.pdf.

U.S. Congress. House. Committee on Ways and Means. H.R.235 - Houses of Worship Free Speech Restoration Act. 108th Congress (2003–2004). Rep. Jones, Walter B., Jr. [R-NC-3] (Introduced 01/08/2003). https://www.congress.gov/bill/108th-congress/house-bill/235

U.S. Supreme Court. *Obergefell v. Hodges.* 576 U.S. ___ (2015)

Verba, Sidney, Kay Lehman Schlozman, and Henry E. Brady. 1995. *Voice and Equality: Civic Voluntarism in American Politics.* Cambridge: Harvard University Press.

Walzer, Michael, ed. 1995. *Toward A Global Civil Society*. Providence, Rhode Island: Berghahn Books.

Warren, Mark. 2002. *Democracy and Association*. Princeton: Princeton University Press.

Weisbrod, Burton A. 1988. *The Nonprofit Economy*. Cambridge: Harvard University Press.

Weitzman, Murray S., Nadine T. Jalandoni, Linda M. Lampkin, and Thomas H. Pollak. 2002. *The New Nonprofit Almanac and Desk Reference*. New York, NY: Jossey-Bass.

Wolpert, Julian. 1993. "Patterns of Generosity in America: Who's Holding the Safety Net?" Twentieth Century Fund Paper. Twentieth Century Fund, New York.

Wuthnow, Robert, ed. 1991. *Between States and Markets: The Voluntary Sector in Comparative Perspective*. New Jersey, NJ: Princeton University Press.

Wuthnow, Robert. 2004. *Saving America*. New Jersey, NJ: Princeton University Press.

———. 2006. "Clash of Values: Government Funding for the Arts and Religion." *Nonprofits & Government: Collaboration & Conflict*, 2nd ed. Elizabeth T. Boris and C. Eugene Steuerle, eds. (pp. 311–342). Washington, DC: Urban Institute Press

———. 2011. *Red State Religion: Faith and Politics in America's Heartland*. Princeton: Princeton University Press.

Young, Dennis R., Lester M. Salamon, and Mary Clark Grinsfelder. 2012. "Commercialization, Social Ventures, and For-profit Competition." *The State of Nonprofit America*, 2nd ed. Lester M. Salamon, ed. (pp. 521–548). Washington, DC: Brookings Institution Press.

Zuckerman, Ethan. 2014. "New Media, New Civics?" *Policy & Internet* 6(2): 151–168.

Chapter 1

Supplementary, Complementary, or Adversarial?

Nonprofit-Government Relations

Dennis R. Young and John Casey

Policymakers and practitioners in the United States often take an oversimplified view of the nonprofit sector and its relationship with government. One narrative focuses on the service role of nonprofits. This narrative tends to be associated with a conservative (small government) agenda, but progressive boosters of nonprofits also champion the service role. Conservatives and progressives alike argue that these organizations are able to provide more agile and effective services than large bureaucratic government agencies (Anheier 2014; Smith 2012). In any case, governments continue to seek nonprofit subsidization of formerly publicly funded education, culture, and recreation activities (Murray 2010; Gazley 2015).

A second narrative focuses on the advocacy and rights-oriented role of nonprofits. There are advocacy organizations of all persuasions, and expressive activities are seen as an authentic and legitimate function of nonprofits. Nonetheless, commentators raise various issues: on the one hand, there is concern about the possible chilling effects of government service contracts through direct conditions restricting advocacy as well as self-censorship by organizations seeking to keep favor with government funders. Indeed, legislative calls to defund Planned Parenthood in various states serve as a cautionary example in this regard. Still many nonprofits may be overly cautious, and not be taking full advantage of their legal rights to lobby within specified limits (National Council on Nonprofits 2015). On the other hand, government (read Internal Revenue Service [IRS]) is criticized from both sides of the political spectrum with regard to the partisan use of 501(c)(4) organizations. Some protest that the IRS has disproportionately targeted right-wing groups, while others, including representatives of the nonprofit sector itself, complain that the IRS is insufficiently aggressive in policing the sector (see chapter 6 by Colinvaux, in this volume, for further discussion).

The duality between service and expressive orientations is enshrined in academic and industry classifications of nonprofits (Anheier 2014), including the National Taxonomy of Exempt Entities and the 501(c) section of the tax code. However, the reality of government-nonprofit sector relations in the United States is far richer and more complex. Nonprofit organizations interact with government in several different ways, and these patterns of interaction vary over time and among different fields of service. In various contexts, nonprofits have served as privately supported supplementary service providers of public goods, as complementary partners with government in public service provision, and as adversaries in the process of public policy formulation and implementation. Often, two or three of these roles are manifested simultaneously.

In this chapter, we consider the theoretical underpinnings of these three modes of government-nonprofit relations. Various strands of economic theory pertaining to nonprofit organizations illuminate the circumstances under which we can expect nonprofits to fulfill different roles vis-à-vis government—supplementary, complementary, and adversarial. These three theoretical modes of government-nonprofit relationships are first explained and then applied as conceptual screens for examining the history of government-nonprofit sector relationships in the United States. We show that each theoretical cut reveals new insights into the complex relationships between nonprofits and government and that no one view suffices for a full understanding.

Finally, we consider how alternative views of government-nonprofit relations can inform the present debate on the roles of government, nonprofits, and business in the United States. The shifting dynamics of recent decades, including governmental retrenchment and devolution, privatization of public services, restructuring in the business sector, commercialization in the nonprofit sector, demands for greater public accountability of nonprofit organizations, and the emergence of a new cohort of extremely wealthy, socially conscious philanthropists, social entrepreneurs, and new forms of social business, continue to transform government-nonprofit sector relationships. While government no longer takes comprehensive responsibility for social welfare, it has expanded its support and involvement in certain areas, notably health care, and clearly expects more from nonprofits. At the same time, corporations have become more narrowly strategic in their philanthropic programs; substantial new private wealth has been created among business entrepreneurs; nonprofit organizations have become more competitive and market-oriented and more aware of their need to be accountable to the public for their performance and behavior; and a growing social enterprise sector is pushing its claim as a solution to societal challenges. This shuffling of institutional conditions leaves open to question how the sectors will continue to divide responsibilities and work together toward solving social problems and meeting public needs in the future. Our review of the history of government-nonprofit relations through the three theoretical lenses suggests that a new social contract may be emerging, but we are yet to fully understand its nature and implications.

STRANDS OF THEORY

Different strands of economic theory support alternative notions of the nonprofit sector as supplementary, complementary, or adversarial to government. (This taxonomy is similar to that postulated by Najam [2000] for relations between government and nongovernmental organizations internationally. See also chapter 9 by Cordes et al., in this volume, for an examination of the resources of both nonprofits and government and how that leads them to serve as both complements and substitutes in the provision of services.) In the supplementary model, nonprofits are seen as fulfilling demand for public goods left unsatisfied by government. In this view, the private financing of public goods can be expected to have an inverse relationship with government expenditure. As government takes more responsibility for provision, less needs to be raised through voluntary collective means.

In the complementary view, nonprofits are seen as partners to government, helping to deliver public goods, and are largely financed by government. In this perspective, nonprofit and government expenditures have a direct relationship with one another. As government expenditures increase, they help finance increasing levels of activity by nonprofits.

In the adversarial view, nonprofits prod government to make changes in public policy and to maintain accountability to the public. Reciprocally, government attempts to influence the behavior of nonprofits by regulating their services and responding to advocacy initiatives. The adversarial view does not posit any specific relationship between the levels of nonprofit and governmental activity. For example, nonprofits can advocate for smaller or more efficient government operations or they can advocate for new programs and regulations that would increase government activity.

Figure 1.1 depicts the three views of government-nonprofit relations. As shown, the two sectors work separately, in parallel, in the supplementary mode. In the complementary mode, their activities are connected and coordinated with one another. In the adversarial mode, they oppose one another, each attempting to change the other.

The three modes are not mutually exclusive. Nonprofits may simultaneously finance and deliver services where the government does not deliver services financed or otherwise assisted by the government, advocate for changes in government policies and practices, and be affected by governmental

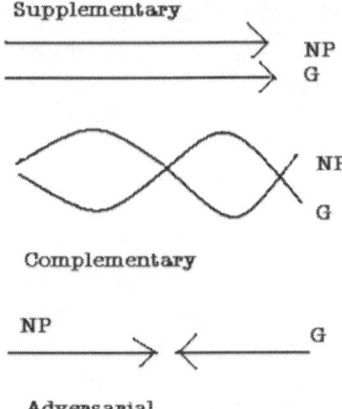

Figure 1.1 Three Modes of Government-Nonprofit Relations. *Note*: NP = nonprofit; G = government.

pressure and oversight. Kramer (1981) observed that nonprofits' reliance on public funds to deliver services does not always constrain their advocacy activity; later research has reinforced this conclusion (Chaves, Stephens, and Galaskiewicz 2004).

Also, the three modes frame the discussion of nonprofit-government relations as if nonprofits and government are clearly distinct entities, yet in fact the boundaries are often blurred. We acknowledged this drawback to our analytical framework when it was originally proposed in the first edition of this volume. Now, by the time of this third edition, the situation has become even more complex and the boundaries between the three modes of relationships and between the sectors have become even more blurred. New nonprofits have emerged with the specific goal of supporting government services, and governments sometimes contract out oversight to prime contractor nonprofits that then subcontract specific services to nonprofit or for-profit suppliers. Hybridized organizations sometimes establish both a for-profit company to raise capital and commercialize revenue-generating activities and a nonprofit to receive grants and donations. What outsiders may identify as a single nonprofit organization may in fact be a conglomerate of affiliated nonprofit and for-profit legal structures. Indeed, the reality is even more complex, with the emergence in many states of new for-profit forms of social purpose organizations such as Low-Profit Limited Liability Companies (L3Cs) and various types of benefit corporations. The new "social economy" now embraces parts of the for-profit sector itself as well as cooperatives and government-sanctioned nonprofits (see Mook et al. 2015).

However, we abstract from the messy detail of the real world in the following discussion and proceed under the assumption that government-nonprofit boundaries can be recognized without undue difficulty in most instances. In the same vein, we noted that while the three analytical views were derived primarily from rational choice models in the economics tradition, other social sciences including sociology, political science, policy analysis, and organizational theory also have much to contribute to the understanding of institutional relationships, as well as to an appreciation of the limitations of the economic approach (see the discussion in Casey 2016).

We recognize that other frameworks also inform research. In the context of industrialized democracies, commentators have focused on the tensions between the vertical dimension of relations (often expressed with terms such as "principal-agent model" and "control-command model") and the horizontal dimension (expressed as relational governance or partnership models); on the tendencies of governments to either embrace or constrain the work of nonprofits; and on the standing of nonprofits as either insiders or outsiders in policy processes. In the international context, scholars have focused on the impacts of political regimes, national scripts, and cultural conditions on the policy tools and instruments employed to regulate relations (Young 2000; Phillips and Smith 2014; Casey 2016).

Nonetheless we contend that our supplementary-complementary-adversarial model remains an essential element in any analysis of the nuances of government-nonprofit relations. Indeed, we would argue that supplementary, complementary, and adversarial relations are inherent elements in the other frameworks cited above. Most importantly, our model has withstood the test of time. Since the first edition of this volume, it continues to be a regularly cited benchmark for the analysis of government-nonprofit relationships in a wide range of research articles, conference papers, and textbooks on nonprofit theory, management, and policy.

Nonprofits as Supplements to Government

The thesis that nonprofit organizations provide collective goods on a voluntary basis was first advanced by Burton Weisbrod in his seminal work on government failure (Weisbrod 1977). The basic premise is that citizens have individual preferences about the levels, qualities, and types of public goods they desire and how much they are willing to pay for them. Governments decide on the level of public goods provided based on citizens' preferences and are constrained by equity considerations and bureaucratic procedures to tax and to offer public goods in a uniform way (Douglas 1987). Given democratic voting and policymaking procedures, governments follow preferences of the median voter or of a dominant political coalition (Buchanan and Tullock 1962) in choosing those uniform tax rules and levels, types, and qualities of services. If citizen preferences are not homogeneous, some citizens (e.g., those whose preferences vary substantially from the preferences of the median voter) will be left unsatisfied, either paying more and receiving more (of various) public goods than they want or paying less and receiving less than they want. Citizens in the latter group are presumed willing to provide additional (supplementary) levels of public goods for themselves and others by mobilizing on a voluntary collective basis through the nonprofit sector.

Weisbrod (1977) points out that nonprofits are not the only solution to the problem of public goods provision where the preferences of the citizenry are heterogeneous. Citizens may instead purchase various private market substitutes for public goods (e.g., guard dogs to supplement public policing). Moreover, where multiple local political jurisdictions exist, as they do in the United States, people may move to communities where tax rates and public goods best match their preferences (Tiebout 1956). However, these solutions all have limitations. Exercising mobility is costly. Political jurisdictions package multiple public goods together so citizens cannot make perfect matches between communities and personal preferences for services and taxes. And private goods are usually imperfect substitutes for public goods. Hence, substantial room is left for nonprofits to supplement government services.

In light of this theory, we can expect substantial variation in nonprofit sector-government relationships among fields of activity. In areas such as the arts, where citizens' preferences vary widely, private nonprofit provision can be expected to be substantial. In areas such as policing and defense, where preferences may be relatively homogeneous, we can expect the nonprofit role to be less substantial. In areas such as social services, where citizens' preferences can be volatile, we can expect nonprofit provision to respond to ebbs and flows of public sentiment and consensus. Supplementary provision is more likely to serve shifting or migrating population groups not well established within a particular governmental jurisdiction and for innovative services whose effectiveness is unproven. Nonprofits can be more nimble than government in responding to such circumstances and opportunities, perhaps showing the way for later governmental programming. However, nonprofits can view public decisions to expand the role of government in areas they traditionally serve as a threat (Bremner 1988).

Alternatively, the supplementary view illuminates the notion that private action is often intended to prod government into action, particularly by testing new intervention models. Innovation has long been seen as a fundamental role of nonprofits, and they are seen as the proving grounds to develop new projects and services as they are free of the constraints imposed by voters or shareholders (Kramer 1981). In the 1960s, the Ford Foundation's Public Affairs Program funded demonstration programs that became the models for many of the contemporary programs with poor and minority communities, and in the 1970s, the Robert Wood Johnson Foundation funded the first pilots of what would become the 911 emergency systems. In the last decades, contracting regimes have somewhat dampened innovation as nonprofits were funded to execute predesignated strategies and specific contracted outcomes. However, with new venture and impact funding models, some foundations have deliberately reintroduced innovation into their philanthropic portfolios, seeking projects with "transformative potential, exploring new solutions, and recognizing that innovation requires flexibility, iteration, and failure" (Kasper and Justin Marcoux 2014). In 2009, the Obama administration created the Office of Social Innovation and Civic Participation to cultivate "bottom up practices." The Social Innovation Fund, a program of the Corporation for National and Community Service, combines $241 million in federal grants and more than $516 million in nonfederal and private match commitments to fund foundations and frontline nonprofits (Office of Social Innovation and Civic Participation 2015).

Nonprofits and Government as Complements

Lester Salamon (1995, 2015) has been the principal advocate for the view that nonprofits and government are engaged primarily in a partnership or contractual relationship in which government finances public services and nonprofits deliver them. In this volume, Steuerle et al. show how much the government has increasingly contracted out to nonprofit institutions, affecting the relative employment in each sector over time. Aspects of the economic theories of public goods and of organizations help clarify the rationale behind this thesis. In the former category, the theory of collective action advanced by Mancur Olson (1965) highlights the phenomenon of "free riding" when people attempt to provide collective goods on a voluntary basis. Where the good is "nonrival" (i.e., can be consumed by one party without reducing the amount available to others) and "nonexcludable" (i.e., the good cannot be made available to one party without making it simultaneously available to others), people have the incentive to avoid contributing to its provision but to consume it once others provide it. As a result, a voluntary collective effort will not support such goods at efficient levels. Large groups with relatively homogeneous preferences (no one party is tempted to provide a good on its own) exacerbate the problem of free riding.

Solutions to the public goods problem include social pressure (e.g., appealing to conscience and peer-to-peer solicitations), tying together of private incentives with public goods support (e.g., bonuses given to members of public radio stations), and coercion (e.g., using the police power of the state to collect taxes). This last solution suggests government should finance public goods, either directly or through tax incentives, while not necessarily delivering them.

Economic theory of organizations, specifically aspects of the theory of the firm and transactions cost theory, helps illuminate why, in many instances, it may be more efficient for government to delegate delivery of services to private organizations (e.g., nonprofits) than to deliver those services itself. Simply stated, despite the costs of arranging and monitoring external contracts, it may be cheaper for governments to contract out for certain services than perform them internally (Grønbjerg 1997). Private suppliers may have lower labor costs if they are not unionized and may be better able to exploit economies of scale for certain services by producing them for more than one jurisdiction (Ferris 1993). The cost reduction argument helps explain why governments sometimes contract for service delivery with private suppliers. However, this explanation does not distinguish between nonprofit and for-profit contractors. Another aspect of transaction costs theory pertains to the information an organization requires in order to carry out a market transaction efficiently. In the case of public services, two aspects related to the quality of services delivered appear relevant. First, government may choose to contract out, not only because it is cheaper but because it may be unable to differentiate its services in response to the heterogeneous preferences of its citizens. There would be too much information to gather in order to do so. However, by contracting with nonprofits that are knowledgeable about the individual communities in which they are based, government can overcome the information problem and, within limits, allow those delivery agents to customize their services to local constituents.

To a certain extent, such differentiation would be possible if government contracted with for-profit businesses as well, so long as those businesses were community based or conscientious about monitoring their customers' preferences. However, without its own data, how could government verify such responsiveness? Here another aspect of the transaction cost literature comes into play in favor of nonprofits: nonprofits operate under different incentives than for-profits. In particular, they do not face the same imperatives to skimp on quality, renege on promised service, or lower the costs of production by homogenizing services in order to increase profits. Hence, government presumably faces lower monitoring and contract enforcement costs by contracting with nonprofits rather than with for-profits.

Steinberg (1997) points out that the arguments for nonprofits as less costly contractors for government are subject to a number of caveats and subtleties associated with donor reactions to government financing, the internal motivations of nonprofit agents, the level of competition, and the structure of the contracts themselves. Indeed, many nonprofits employ substantial paid staff who can be expected, as in any organization, to capture, in the form of additional wages or other benefits, some of the value added their organizations produce. Certainly, this is a concern of donors, government overseers, and nonprofit sector leaders (Jensen, Kerkman, and Moore 2005). Nonetheless,

Steinberg concludes that nonprofits deserve preferential treatment in bidding for contracts because of the transaction costs–related benefits they offer.

In all, the theory of public goods coupled with the theory of transaction costs provides a plausible explanation for why government and nonprofits often engage in a complementary relationship in which government finances and nonprofits deliver services. This relationship is more likely to be observed in areas such as social services and health care in low-income communities where free riding is a significant problem, where direct public production is likely to require a large bureaucratic operation, and where differences in local preferences favor some differentiation of services to alternative locales and consumer groups. At the same time, the complementary relationships are mediated by forces in increasingly mixed-form markets (Marwell and McInerney 2005) in which for-profits and nonprofits compete and government enjoys a monopsony position as the dominant "buyer." As a result, the complementary relationship between nonprofits and government can be substantially skewed in favor of government. Recent studies by the Urban Institute and the National Council of Nonprofits (2013) allude to the burdens often suffered by nonprofits in this regime.

Finally, a curious but historically important variation of government-nonprofit complementary relationships is where the government and nonprofit sector roles are reversed in terms of financing and service delivery. Interestingly, throughout US history, government has often been the recipient of private largesse for initiating, though seldom servicing over time, public projects, such as the construction of public monuments or the establishment of state or national parks. A theoretical explanation of such behavior seems more consistent with the supplementary than complementary view but with a slight twist: private parties raise funds for activities that public demand does not support. Moreover, the private givers find it more efficient (given the costs of private supply) to "contract" with government for their production rather than produce the goods themselves. (This occurs, for example, when the projects represent marginal additions to public sector operations, whereas private supply would have to start from scratch, or when the government is expected to assume a larger proportion of the costs eventually.) Additionally, the public values these activities, accepts implementation within the public domain, and may contribute to their financing; indeed, it often provides ongoing operational support. In this sense, private financing of governmental projects needs to be understood through both the supplementary and complementary lenses.

Nonprofits and Government as Adversaries

Economic theories in general have not explicitly addressed the advocacy role of nonprofits in public policy or the role of government in controlling nonprofits. To a certain extent, nonprofit advocacy and government pressure on nonprofits can be understood through the complementary lens of nonprofit-government relations. Often, nonprofit and government actors are collaborators in passing legislation or changing public attitudes. Similarly, government sometimes undertakes to encourage, prod, and stimulate private, voluntary activity in support of social goals. But advocacy activity suggests a third way of characterizing the relationship between nonprofit organizations and government—as adversaries in policymaking and service delivery. More precisely, government and the nonprofit sector are by no means homogeneous; indeed, multiple parties within government and within the nonprofit sector are engaged in various adversarial activities, often with diverse points of view, and sometimes collaborating across the sectors. In addition, adversarial activities can take various (more or less collaborative or acrimonious) forms, including the empowerment of citizens groups, direct confrontational activity such as lobbying and regulation, and educational programming in the form of research, forums, and the dissemination of information and data through public media.

Bits and pieces of economic theory help illuminate the adversarial relationship. On the issue of nonprofit advocacy, Weisbrod's (1977) theory of government failure is helpful again. In heterogeneous jurisdictions, where minority views are not well reflected in public policy, minorities will organize themselves on a voluntary collective basis not only to provide public services for themselves but also to press government to serve their interests and communities more adequately. In the basic Weisbrod model, government would have no incentive to respond since it simply follows the preferences of the majority. However, more nuanced analyses of public choice that allow for logrolling, vote trading, and the concentration of minority efforts on particular issues demonstrate that organized minorities can be effective in having their public policy concerns addressed (Buchanan and Tullock 1962). Such minorities mobilize through voluntary associations or interest groups, becoming an important component of the government-nonprofit sector constellation of relationships.

The Weisbrod model is also helpful for understanding how advocacy leads to new public services. Initially, only a minority of voters may favor proposals for new programs, which therefore are not immediately adopted by government. This minority may promote the idea through advocacy and demonstrate its efficacy with voluntary contributions. Nonprofit think tanks may also play a role in such efforts (e.g., see Hall 1994) or, as noted above, foundations may fund demonstration projects (e.g., see Bremner 1988). Such promotional efforts may secure pilot funding from government. Eventually, the concept may be proven and receive the support of a majority; then the government may undertake full-scale provision.

Economic theory is also helpful for understanding why government is moved to oversee nonprofit behavior and performance, and sometimes to press nonprofits to change. In particular, the theory of contract failure first developed by Henry Hansmann (1980) postulates that nonprofit organizations are chosen as efficient vehicles for delivering services where there is a condition of "information asymmetry" between consumers and producers that would allow a profitmaking firm to exploit consumer ignorance to its advantage. Nonprofits are seen to be more efficient in this circumstance because the nondistribution (of profits) constraint, as Hansmann argues, or the internal governance structure of nonprofit organizations, as Ben-Ner (1986) suggests, reduces the incentives and opportunities for nonprofits to cheat consumers; this makes them more "trustworthy."

Why then, if nonprofits are more trustworthy, does government need to regulate nonprofits? Two reasons are implicit in the theory of contract failure. First, the trustworthiness of nonprofit organizations depends in part on the credibility of the nondistribution constraint and the integrity of the nonprofit governance structure. These, in turn, must be policed, which is the government's role. Government must ensure that the nondistribution constraint is observed (see Young 1983, 2013) and, to ensure nonprofits' trustworthiness, that appropriate principles are followed for constituting governing boards. Otherwise, there remains the possibility that those in control of nonprofit organizations (e.g., management, staff, board members) will extract "rents" for their own benefit.

Second, contract failure may be seen as a broad phenomenon subject to a variety of approaches and solutions including licensure, accreditation, competition, and other means. Utilization of nonprofits is just one approach and not necessarily a perfect or complete solution to the problem. Nonprofits also violate the trust put in them on occasion, and some of the same oversight mechanisms that government uses to oversee for-profit providers in various markets can be applied to nonprofits as well. In general, government regulates nonprofits in order to protect consumers (see chapter 5 by Lott and Fremont-Smith, this volume) and enforce compliance with tax laws to ensure that contributions are used for charitable purposes (see chapter 4 by Brody and Cordes, this volume).

It is interesting to return to Weisbrod's (1977) model in the context of the nonprofit advocacy role and explore its implications for government behavior. If nonprofits advocate for minority positions in the policy arena, it follows that government may react by defending majority interests. One form that reaction may take is an attempted restriction of nonprofit advocacy. In the guise of regulation, government can become the adversary of nonprofits in the policy arena. The long history of government regulations to limit the use of government appropriations for influencing contracting or legislation can be partially understood in this light. The annual federal Health and Human Services appropriations act states that contract and grant funds cannot be used for activities seeking to influence legislation or appropriations pending before the Congress or any state legislature. But a recent report by the HHS inspector general (2014) notes the limited capacity of government to identify noncompliance.

Finally, it is worth observing that nonprofits and government may oppose one another for the simple reason that these parties independently pursue objectives whose impacts are felt differently by the two parties. For example, President Obama has sought to restrict charity and other tax breaks for wealthy people as a way to raise additional revenues almost exclusively from high-income earners, but these proposals have triggered fervent opposition by nonprofit trade associations (see Eisenberg 2011). Though popular support for this proposal was questionable, the Obama administration may still view this as an example of Weisbrod's model of decision-making in which the political process pursues a public good which a minority (some nonprofits) opposes as a public bad. Alternatively, some nonprofits may support public goods whose benefits are confined to the nonprofits' own narrow constituencies, such as sufferers of a rare disease, while government judges the opportunity costs of support (relative to other uses of funds) to be too high.

INTERACTIONS AND TRANSITIONS

We have recognized that government and nonprofits may relate to each other via all three modes simultaneously. In addition, government and nonprofits influence each other's behaviors in ways that involve more than one of these modes. An important example of this is tax policy. By decreasing income tax rates, for instance, government reduces revenues that might be available to finance nonprofit services in a complementary relationship. At the same time, the lower tax rates undermine giving, discouraging nonprofit activity in a supplementary mode, as well as increasing nonprofit adversarial activity aimed at restoring lost government financing. Alternatively, government can encourage private giving through the use of matching provisions in grant programs. The continuing "nonprofitization" of public goods (Nathan 1996; Salamon 2015) illustrates the subtle interplay of the modes of nonprofit-government relations. While it promises to expand the complementary relationship of government through outsourcing of service provision, widespread government cutbacks and retrenchments also lead to greater reliance on the supplementary form of nonprofit social service provision.

It is noteworthy also that changes in the political environment can lead to changes in the relationships between government and certain nonprofit organizations whose missions align differently with different political administrations. For example, faith-based institutions and pro-life advocacy organizations may move from supplementary or adversarial to complementary relationships with government when a conservative political regime comes to power, while other nonprofits, such as those in the arts, environmental conservation, and other areas, may shift in the reverse direction. Recent efforts by states to defund Planned Parenthood are a dramatic case in point. These changes help institutionalize the values of incoming administrations by bringing resources to activities and policy positions that the current governing coalition favors and drawing resources away from nonprofits associated with the previous regime (see Evans, Rueschemeyer, and Skocpol 1985).

It is also important to emphasize that the overlap and simultaneity of the three modes is not only observable at a sectoral level, but it is also evident in the work of any single organization. Table 1.1 provides examples of the possible activities of four hypothetical nonprofit organizations.

HISTORICAL PERSPECTIVES

The supplementary, complementary, and adversarial theories, taken as a cluster, show the complexity of nonprofit-government relationships. These are not mutually exclusive ways of understanding those relationships but rather overlapping models that each captures important elements. History may be examined in layers by asking sequentially, what does each model reveal about the nature of government-nonprofit relationships as they have evolved over time in the United States?

We proceed by reviewing, through each of the three theoretical lenses, the history of the nonprofit sector in the United States at various stages—colonial times, the early republic, after the Civil War, the late nineteenth and early twentieth centuries, and modern times—as documented by several contemporary nonprofit sector scholars. History is examined here in a necessarily cursory fashion through secondary and tertiary sources. This approach does not do justice to the work of serious nonprofit historians, but it does suggest researchers can use the proposed theoretical framework to understand government-nonprofit relations and how they change over time. We hope it partially addresses Hall's (1992: 109–110) complaint that "shortcomings in the social sciences stem from their 'ahistoricity.'"

Finally, it must be acknowledged that the concept of nonprofit as a sector is a modern construct that we must impose somewhat awkwardly to analyze earlier historical periods. Like the blurring of boundaries between sectors in the modern era, the ambiguity of institutional definitions requires a certain amount of license in making historical observations.

Table 1.1 Nonprofit Activities in the Three Modes

	Supplementary	Complementary	Adversarial
Family and Children Support Agency—501(c)(3) charitable organization	Tax-deductible charitable donations and earned income to support core administration and innovative charitable activities.	Government contracts and grants to provide a range of support programs for low-income families.	Advocacy for expanded support services, or policy changes to discourage abortions.
Environmental Advocacy Organization—501(c)(3) charitable organization and 501(c)(4) social welfare organization	Tax-deductible charitable donations to support volunteer program to clean and maintain various public spaces (parks, roads, wetlands, and woodlands). Nontax-deductible donations to (c)(4) support advocacy.	Partnering with government on waste reduction and recycling programs. CEO chair of government-sponsored environmental task force that then receives grants for education programs.	Advocacy for stronger environmental protections and simplification of industry regulation.
Affordable Housing Organization—501(c)(3) foundation and affiliated C-Corporation residential developments	Tax-deductible donations, tax credits, and subsidies fund new residential developments.	Government contracts to provide emergency accommodation and supported housing.	Advocacy for greater funding of affordable housing programs and conversion of public housing to housing vouchers.
Professional Association—501(c)(6) business league	Tax-deductible membership fees (deductible as business expenses not as charitable donations) to support professional certification programs and development of industry standards.	Partnering with government on a range of public awareness and education programs.	Advocacy for expanding role of profession and for the reduction of regulatory burdens.

History through the Supplementary Lens

Examining how nonprofits have attended to collective needs unaddressed by government helps us appreciate the roles of government and nonprofit organizations in the United States (Bremner 1988). While documentation is spotty, nonprofit activity supplementing government clearly predates the US republic. A review by Lohmann (1992) suggests that colonists brought with them religious-based traditions of mutual aid, including religious voluntary associations, charitable and mutual-aid societies, fire brigades, lodges, and professional societies. While religion and government were sometimes intertwined during the colonial period, specifically in New England and the South, O'Neill (1989) argues that the diversity of religious beliefs in the colonies ultimately made necessary the separation of church and state, hence reinforcing the development of the nonprofit sector as supplementary to government.

Bremner (1988) notes that in the early period of the republic, private initiative in higher education was a particularly important area of nonprofit activity as a supplement to government. O'Neill (1989) documents examples where privately based initiatives, such as the Quakers' founding of the first US psychiatric hospital, ultimately led to adoption by government in the first half of the nineteenth century. In the nineteenth and twentieth centuries, the traditions of self-help, both religious and secular but largely separate from government, continued to be very important. Lohmann (1992) observes that immigrants brought with them many associational practices and that fraternal organizations were an important means of social integration. Bremner (1988) observes that the years after the Civil War were notable for their philanthropic achievements, while Nielsen (1979) claims that the late nineteenth and early twentieth century was the period in which private initiative peaked in its prominence.

The surge of private, nonprofit initiative supplemental to government in this period was fueled by a combination of new and enormous private, concentrated industrial wealth and political progressivism stemming from industrialization, urbanization, and immigration. According to Hall (1992), this included the growth of universities, libraries, hospitals, museums, symphony orchestras, social welfare organizations, professional societies, and private clubs, underwritten by industry and private wealth, unions, fraternal organizations, settlement houses, and building and loan associations organized by middle and lower classes, as well as charitable organizations to address sickness, poverty, and societal reform. Andrew Carnegie's *Gospel of Wealth* was influential in this period and supportive of the concept of philanthropy as a substitute for government programming (Bremner 1988). The role of women was especially important in creating voluntary associations that addressed social needs in this era of weak government (McCarthy 1997).

Of great long-term significance in this period was the invention of the modern foundation, which institutionalized the ability of private interests to fund nonprofit sector activity in a focused manner, starting with the Russell Sage Foundation (Hall 1992). As Hall (1992) notes, the Russell Sage Foundation was followed by the major foundation initiatives of Andrew Carnegie, John D. Rockefeller, and other industrial giants. These initiatives were but one aspect of a broader strategy of "welfare capitalism" that allowed private initiative and wealth to underwrite a variety of programs supplemental to government's own efforts, including the YMCA, by the railroad industry. Other institutional innovations, including Community Foundations and Community Chests, also emanated from the era of business and private social activism in the late nineteenth and twentieth centuries, as means to coordinate the development and allocation of private resources to community needs.

While much of the twentieth century witnessed the growing role of government in the provision of public services of all varieties, supplemental provision by nonprofit sector institutions persisted and grew. One noteworthy development was the establishment of the federal income tax in 1913, which included an exemption for nonprofits from corporate taxation and the implementation of the charitable deduction as part of that system in 1917, creating the incentive for individuals to give to charity by reducing their tax liabilities (Rushton 2010). Early in the depression of the 1930s, for example, President Hoover put perhaps undue emphasis on charity as a substitute for potential government relief. Partially as a consequence, charity fell into some public disrepute between the 1930s and the 1960s (Bremner 1988). But measurements made since then (in the 1980s) of the size and scope of the sector reveal the substantial character and continued growth of churches, foundations, trade and professional associations, and other subsectors that support themselves without government help and that provide collective goods essentially supplemental to those of the government sector. Indeed, the number of foundations has grown rapidly over the course of the past four decades, along with the real value of assets they hold and the allocations they dispense (Foundation Center 2014). Moreover, the measured part of the supplemental nonprofit sector may represent only a fraction of the total picture. If David Horton Smith (1997a) is correct, quantitative research has missed a substantial fraction of the grassroots organizations that provide self-help, communal relief, and other services, essentially on a volunteer basis without significant exchange of funds, and supplemental to government. These organizations trace themselves back further than formal nonprofits and have been part of the American scene since the beginning (Smith 1997b).

Finally, the late twentieth and early twenty-first centuries seem to manifest a resurgence of the supplemental model, not just in the United States but internationally. Developments such as the growth of venture philanthropy by newly minted billionaires, the extraordinary public policy initiatives of modern-day Rockefellers and Carnegies, and the rapid growth of private foundations, donor-advised funds, and international nongovernmental organizations suggest an era when the supplemental mode of nonprofit-government relations may again become predominant. We appear to be entering a period of resurgence of the private provision of public goods. The most evident examples are the ways in which prominent philanthropists, including Michael Bloomberg, Bill Gates, George Soros and Mark Zuckerberg, are putting their personal stamp on public services, but there is also a notable broader trend. (Zuckerberg, however, has pledged the money through a hybrid institution that will not seek formal charitable status. See chapter 9 by Cordes et al. in this volume.) Gazley (2015) notes that government agencies are creating numerous new 501(c)(3) institutions to organize volunteers and donors to support their programs, indicating that the goal is a permanent fundraising and support infrastructure.

The supplementary lens identifies an important component of the history of nonprofit-government relations in the United States. In various contexts, private citizens, rich as well as poor, have often provided for themselves and for others. In some cases, such activity supplements government provision; in other cases, the nonprofit sector creates and supports new forms of collective activity not yet undertaken by government. History shows that such activity is undertaken by minorities, including ethnic and religious groups and business leaders with their own social preferences and agendas, often different from the political majority, in a manner that appears consistent with the supplemental theory of voluntary collective action.

Some scholars argue, however, that the supplemental mode of nonprofit-government relations is not usually the dominant stream. For example, Hall (1992) claims that voluntary associations were relatively sparse and subservient to government in the eighteenth and early nineteenth centuries. And Nielsen (1979) considers the period of private sector vigor in the late nineteenth and early twentieth centuries an aberration from the more pervasive mode of nonprofit sector-government interpenetration. However, government continues to exercise regulatory power and is a key influence on who enters the markets for public goods, through its expenditure and tax policies. Thus, the supplementary lens gives only a partial view, and we need to take another look through the complementary lens.

History through the Complementary Lens

Several scholars, including Hall (1992), Nielsen (1979), Bremner (1988), and Salamon (1987), have observed that governmental partnerships with private philanthropy and nonprofit organizations have been a part of the American scene from colonial times. Through the complementary lens, we see one sector engaging the other in order to get the public's business done together. No less prominent a figure than Benjamin Franklin was a proponent of public and private collaboration, including its role in the establishment of the Pennsylvania Hospital and the University of Pennsylvania (Bremner 1988).

The case of Harvard University is often cited as the earliest example of public support and nonprofit provision. Harvard was regarded as a public institution because most of its revenues came from legislative grants and from tuitions and fees (Hall 1992: 16–17). Parallel situations characterized Yale (Salamon 1987) and Williams College, Columbia, and the University of Pennsylvania (Nielsen 1979). Similar arrangements were also found in the health and social services in colonial and postrevolutionary times, including Pennsylvania Hospital which offered health care for indigent patients with their expenses paid by local or colonial governments and the Hartford (Ct.) Retreat and McLean Hospital in Boston which used state and local government funds to provide care for indigent mentally ill patients (Smith and Lipsky 1993).

Governmental involvement and financial support of private, nonprofit organizations providing higher education, hospital care, and social services, begun in the early republic, continued unabated through the nineteenth and twentieth centuries. For example, Nielsen (1979) cites Massachusetts General Hospital, Louisville General Hospital, University Hospital in Baltimore, and Natchez Charity Hospital as examples of private, nonprofit institutions established or supported with state government funds between 1820 and 1840. And Salamon (1987) observes that toward the end of the nineteenth and beginning of the twentieth centuries, government support of hospitals and nonprofit social service organizations was fairly common. Observers seem to agree, however, that governmental support of nonprofit organizations did not become extensive until the mid-twentieth century (Smith and Lipsky 1993).

In the 1930s, however, the federal Works Progress Administration promoted an especially important example of government-nonprofit collaboration in the arts, helping important institutions such as Chicago's Art Institute, the Cincinnati Museum, and New York's Metropolitan Museum survive financially (McCarthy 1994). The magnitude and scope of governmental support and contracting with nonprofits began to grow dramatically in the 1960s because of expansion in federal programs, especially in human services. Congress enacted the 1967 Amendments to the Social Security Act that specifically encouraged states to enter into purchase-of-service agreements with private agencies. By 1976, the expenditure for these agreements had risen to 49 percent of social services spending (Smith and Lipsky 1993).

In addition, in 1961, the establishment of the Combined Federal Campaign allowed certain charities to solicit charitable contributions from federal employees (Bremner 1988). In a study of 16 local communities in 1982, government reliance on nonprofit organizations to deliver public services was found to be extensive in social services, housing and community development, health care, and the arts. In each field, more than 40 percent of government expenditures were allocated to private, nonprofit organizations (Salamon 1987). In the arts, the creation of the National Endowment in 1965 was a particularly important element in the developing public-private partnership. According to Senator Claiborne Pell, who helped to draft the enabling legislation, the key to the proposal was the notion of using the Endowment "as a catalyst . . . [to] help spark nonfederal support" (McCarthy 1994: 15).

International relief was another area where public support of nonprofit efforts became important in the 1960s (Bremner 1988). While the expansion of contractual arrangements between government and nonprofits was dramatic in the 1960s and 1970s, it continued unabated, though modified in form, in the 1980s and 1990s and into the new century. In the social services, for example, Smith (2012) cites key developments including expanded use of Medicaid to support social services; new federal programs for at-risk youth, drug and alcohol treatment, community care, and prisoner reentry; welfare reform legislation that provided new funding for job training, welfare-to-work aid and child care; and innovations in the form of federal financing, including tax credits, loans, and tax exempt bonds. Contemporary thinking reflected in the "new public management" encouraged the contracting out of government services to lower costs and increase the effectiveness of government programs (Lane 2000).

The reverse model of private financing and public provision has also appeared throughout US history. In the early republic, there were bequests to the city of Philadelphia to improve streets and to the state of Pennsylvania to build canals, and later examples include James Smithson's gift to the federal government for what became the Smithsonian Institution, Andrew Mellon's gift of the National Gallery, and Andrew Carnegie's gifts of public libraries to many communities (Bremner 1988). This tradition is also reflected in various voluntary campaigns to raise charitable funds for government monuments, including building the Washington Monument and refurbishing the Statue of Liberty; funding drives during and after World Wars I and II; establishing the Sanitary Commission during the Civil War to improve conditions in military camps; and financially assisting government in wartime from revolutionary times to the present era. Indeed, the tradition has continued with philanthropy supporting public-private partnership by contributing to mainly tax-supported institutions such as state colleges and universities, public radio and television stations, and public or endowed museums, libraries, parks, zoos, and various public monuments (Bremner 1988).

Finally, the complementary relationships of government and nonprofits extend to more subtle instances where government has acted as an encourager and cheerleader of nonprofit sector efforts. In the early years of the Depression, for example, President Hoover "enlisted the services of one hundred leaders of business, industry, finance, and philanthropy" in the "task of mobilizing and coordinating the charitable resources of the country" (Bremner 1988: 139). National administrations made similar efforts during wartime, and since the 1990s, the federal government has put increased efforts into stimulating volunteerism and engaging business in solving social issues. They include the Points of Light program, initiated by President H. W. Bush; the President's Summit on Voluntarism under President Clinton; and President Obama's United We Serve initiative. Building on the historic volunteering programs such as VISTA, Americorps, and Senior Corps, President Obama in 2014 designated the Martin Luther King Jr. holiday as a Day of Service.

The early 1980s was a robust period for government and nonprofits to partner in funding the delivery of public services. Beginning with the Reagan administration, however, policy shifted temporarily toward cutting back government funding and encouraging private organizations to take up the slack not only in service delivery but in resource support (Nathan 1996). Moreover, devolution moved the action to the state and local levels where complementary relations between government and nonprofits, while historically significant, became even more important.

The complementary lens reveals a very different overlay of nonprofit-government relations than does the supplementary lens. At various times and places in American history, private philanthropy has been as a supportive force, helping finance government work. More generally, government has been the driver, looking to nonprofits as means of delivering mainstream public services under mandates of public policy. This orientation was particularly apparent in the post–World War II period when the federal government allocated massive new funding for social services, health care, education, and the arts, but largely resisted creating or expanding government bureaucracies to deliver those services. In terms of theory, the transactions and production costs associated with contracting, subsidizing, or creating nonprofits were apparently more reasonable than those associated with administering a greatly expanded governmental delivery system.

While efficacious for government, the partnership model, under which government finances and nonprofits deliver services, may have looked more ominous to nonprofits. As noted, this mode of government-nonprofit relations clearly gained prominence in the 1960s and 1970s. And it would appear nonprofits could hardly have resisted its momentum. Given mandates for expanded public services and facing internal fiscal problems, many nonprofits had the choice of joining the parade or being swept aside (Smith and Lipsky 1993).

The momentum of these tax revenue-based complementary relationships between government and nonprofits slowed in the early twenty-first century, as the fiscal outlook for all levels of government worsened, particularly after the fiscal crisis of 2008. There was some bounce in funding of nonprofits driven by the American Reinvestment and Recovery Act (the Obama administration's economic stimulus package), and employment in the nonprofit sector continued to grow, in contrast to the decline in the for-profit sector (Salamon, Geller, and Sokolowski 2012). But given the simultaneous emphasis on cutting taxes and addressing budget deficits, cutbacks, have been the order of the day, especially for discretionary programs. A result is a revival of the mix of supplementary and complementary relationships featuring reverse private funding of public services. This is perhaps best evidenced by the rise of the charter schools. In their zeal to "save" public education, foundations and private donors have rushed to fund the enhanced services of these schools which are publicly funded but privately operated as nonprofits (Fabricant and Fine 2012).

Some high-profile closures of prominent nonprofit organizations have highlighted weaknesses in both the contracting processes and the governance of organizations. In 2012, Hull House, a historic settlement house in Chicago, founded in 1889 by Jane Addams, the pioneer social worker and activist, filed for bankruptcy. In 2014, a similar fate befell Federation Employment Guidance Services (FEGS) in New York, which had been founded in 1934. Both had been among the largest nonprofit social welfare organizations in their respective cities (the FEGS annual budget in its last years was around $250 million), but they were apparently victims of their overdependency on large portfolios of government service contracts that did not support their core operating costs (also in the case of FEGS, of establishing for-profit subsidiaries which only generated more deficits). The "overhead debate" in which nonprofits decry the lack of funding for indirect administrative costs has been a continuing point of contention in government contracting. New federal Office of Management and Budget guidelines issued in 2013 clarify that indirect costs are legitimate expenses that need to be reimbursed in all contracts using federal funds. Although the guidelines apply to every federal agency as well as to pass through state and local agencies, they are not yet being applied consistently and they do not cover nonfederal funds, foundation grants, or other private contributions.

The issues surrounding contracting and overhead costs are one aspect of a more general uncertainty and discontent about contemporary nonprofit-government relations in the United States. Indeed, Grønbjerg and Salamon (2012) have recommended a new paradigm of government-nonprofit interaction in which nonprofits acknowledge the legitimate performance requirements of government, and government acknowledges the advocacy responsibilities of nonprofits and its own obligation to provide greater stability in public funding for nonprofits. Government and nonprofits continue to invoke collaborative language in policy documents and to seek to establish new institutional structures for cooperation (Casey 2015). The National Council of Nonprofits (2013) sponsors the Partnering for Impact project which urges policymakers who want to "reduce the cost of government, as well as improve services provided to constituents and return greater value to taxpayers," to create joint government-nonprofit task forces for contract reform.

History through the Adversarial Lens

Taking the long view, nonprofit organizations in the United States have been tremendously influential in the shaping of public policy and prodding government to change and to address critical social issues. Over time, social movements, manifested largely through voluntary organizations, have revolutionized public policy across a broad spectrum of issues including civil and human rights, peace, the environment, consumer protection, women's rights, and accountability of both government and business. This continues to be the case with such issues as immigration, gun safety, and social inequality. Nonetheless, the adversarial relationship has ebbed and flowed in both directions. Moreover, as noted above, the financial interplay of nonprofits and government has become central to these dynamics.

As nonprofit organizations became more dependent on government funding in the 1960s and 1970s, for example, government's propensity to shape and control contracted programs in the social services, outsource whole programs and create new providers, grew (Smith and Lipsky 1993). Another reaction took place in the arts, where government officials sought to censor artistic endeavors and restrict funding for controversial projects (McCarthy 1994).

While government oversight, regulation, and control of nonprofit sector services expanded considerably in the mid-twentieth century in the United States, it too has long historical roots. The earliest manifestations of government control of nonprofits predate the republic and center on the debate concerning the very existence of nonprofits as corporate entities. In colonial times, the status of nonprofits was unclear. For example, Harvard College was governed by a board composed of ministers and public officials (Hall 1992). In the early days of the republic, especially prior to the resolution of the Dartmouth College case, government-nonprofit relations differed by state, depending on the state's position on the issue of incorporation of private organizations (Hall 1992).

A crucial turning point was the Dartmouth College case (Hall 1992). In 1819, in the Supreme Court, Dartmouth College ultimately won its case against the state of New Hampshire to retain control on the grounds that the college's charter constituted a contract between trustees and donors that could not be violated without contravening the Constitution. This set the precedent that has allowed nonprofit corporations in the United States to maintain their corporate integrity without threat of arbitrary governmental intervention.

Still, government regulation of nonprofits continued to evolve. For example, at the time of the Civil War, the US Freedmen's Bureau attempted to discourage duplication in the efforts of voluntary societies devoted to the needs of freed slaves. Several states established state charity boards "to inspect, report upon, and make recommendations for improving public welfare institutions and such private ones as received state assistance" (Bremner 1988: 91).

National emergencies sometimes required unusually heavy control of nonprofits by government. Just prior to World War II, the Neutrality Act of 1939 required "voluntary agencies which wished to engage in civilian war relief in belligerent countries to register with and submit monthly reports to the Department of State" (Bremner 1988: 158). And during World War II, the Roosevelt administration established the War Relief Control Board to control solicitations for voluntary war relief. More recently, however, the nonprofit sector has been a less constrained and indeed critical source of resources and services, for example in weather emergencies such as Hurricane Katrina, stepping up where government efforts fell short.

In the 1970s, charitable solicitation gained prominence as an issue for state and local governmental regulation (Bremner 1988). Perhaps the most vociferous efforts at government regulation of nonprofits have been directed toward foundations. The government's concern centered on whether the public was receiving sufficient value for the tax benefits of the charitable deduction. A key issue, however, has been the concentration of private power under nonprofit auspices and the public influence of that power. These concerns were apparent in the Jeffersonian era and became prominent again in the late nineteenth and early twentieth centuries with the blossoming of large industrial enterprises and the concentration of private wealth in the foundations of Carnegie, Rockefeller, Ford, and others. It was no secret that these institutions intended to influence public affairs. Concerns about the power of foundations were expressed in the 1930s and 1940s, and the issue intensified in the 1950s with an investigation by the Select (Cox) Committee for the House of Representatives (Hall 1992).

A series of congressional inquiries into foundations picked up steam in the 1960s when foundations such as Field, Ford, and others were becoming particularly active on social issues like voter registration, school decentralization, and urban poverty. Additional scrutiny came from the US Treasury Department and the privately funded Filer and Peterson commissions (Brilliant 2001). Ultimately, the 1969 Tax Reform Act put new restrictions on foundations and other tax exempt organizations, largely to curb undesired behavior, such as low payout rates and control of large businesses, that might obscure their charitable purposes, but also to keep foundations out of politics and make them more open and accountable (O'Neill 1989).

Government efforts restricting foundations can be seen as part of a wider effort to limit advocacy by nonprofit organizations. Since the 1930s, there has been language in the Internal Revenue Code that indicates that no substantial part of the activities of 501(c)(3) nonprofits may be used for attempts to influence legislation, although administrative lobbying is less restricted and other categories of 501(c) have fewer restrictions. In the 1990s, conservatives in Congress made several attempts to pass the Istook amendment that would have banned any lobbying and political advocacy by any nonprofit organization receiving federal funding. This issue too has an historical pedigree dating back to the 1930s (Bremner 1988).

During the 1970s, the pressure from government to suppress advocacy cut a broad swath, extending to grantmaking under the Nixon administration (Bremner 1988). Nor was the Nixon administration the last in pressing to restrict nonprofit advocacy prior to the 1990s. In the 1980s, for instance, the Reagan administration worked to exclude advocacy organizations from the Combined Federal Campaign (Bremner 1988). In all, through regulations and restrictions, government seems periodically to attempt to restrict the activities of nonprofits and hold them accountable to the public. At the same time, reciprocal efforts of private interests, through the formation and development of voluntary associations, have held government accountable, influenced the direction of public policy, and ultimately protected the nonprofit sector from government attack.

O'Neill (1989) ties these developments back to religious diversity in the colonies and the early republic, leading to the First Amendment to the Constitution as a fundamental pillar of the nonprofit sector in its advocacy role. Since colonial times, social reformers have pushed government to take action or institute programs in such areas as prison reform, help for the poor and homeless, care of neglected children, opposition to slavery and assistance to freedmen, and improvement of schools. Such activity has extended to the improvement of governance itself. In the context of the settlement house movement of the late nineteenth and early twentieth centuries, Bremner (1988) observed that a host of voluntary associations were organizing to strengthen the social framework of democracy and to restore and extend the principles of self-government.

Women's movements have been a very important component of this strand of public policy advocacy (Robertson 1998). Overall, social action movements, manifested largely through voluntary organizations, have been aimed at changing public policy across a broad spectrum of issues including civil right, peace, the environment, consumer protection, women's rights, and accountability of both government and business (Nielsen 1979). The boundary between the "soft" advocacy and the structured "hard" service-oriented parts of the nonprofit sector has long been fuzzy. They are not two distinct segments, but instead are arranged as points along a spectrum according to the particular mix of service orientation and reformism which gives each its distinctive personality (Nielsen 1979). Still, the distinction is important because in it lies a fundamental tension in the contemporary nonprofit-government relationship: how much should organizations that receive tax benefits or direct governmental support be allowed to influence public policy?

This issue has become particularly fraught since the Citizens United decision in 2010 legitimized campaign funding by corporations, and subsequently 501(c)(4) social welfare organizations became one of the preferred institutional vehicles for channeling funds to support candidates. (These organizations are tax exempt but are not eligible for charitable deductions.) Unlike political committees, they are not required to disclose the identities of donors. This role of 501(c)(4)s is likely to expand in the near future. In 2013, reports surfaced that the IRS's increased attention to (c)(4)s was disproportionately targeting conservative groups applying for tax exempt status for additional scrutiny. Subsequently, good government groups have encouraged the IRS to develop clarifying guidelines for political activity (Bright Lines Project 2013), but final guidelines have not been issued. Provisions in the 2015 budget bill in effect blocked the IRS from creating rules to curb donations and to require disclosure.

Advocacy using social media and new technologies are potentially disrupting the convening functions of nonprofits. Interactive and participatory networking is enabling new forms of political engagement. Cheap computing and mobile technologies are creating virtual constituencies, "organizing without organizations" (Shirky 2008), and conferring political voice to a far wider range of people than the traditional bases of militancy. This additional blurring of nonprofit boundaries raises the question of whether these associational forms are just another part of a transformation of the traditional nonprofit sector. The challenge is to understand whether these technologies and social media organizing modes are generating new autonomous processes that will compete with, and ultimately displace, traditional nonprofit organizing, or whether they are simply tools that nonprofits more broadly defined will use to extend their reach and influence. Similarly, new protest dynamics such as Occupy Wall Street and Black Lives Matter that began in 2011 and 2013, respectively, purport to eschew traditional nonprofits and create less structured social movements (although leaders from existing organizations are prominent in these movements). Governments are playing catch-up in understanding how to regulate such advocacy activity when it is less clearly identified with specific organizations.

The congressional attack on foundations in the 1950s and 1960s galvanized foundations and other parts of the sector into unprecedented collective action, first through exercises of self-study via the Peterson and Filer commissions, and ultimately to the organization in 1980 of the nonprofit trade association Independent Sector. The Council on Foundations had existed since the 1940s to represent that subsector, but the establishment of the Independent Sector meant that a more comprehensive national umbrella organization had emerged to increase public understanding about the sector and to advocate for its interests at the national level. In 1990, the National Council on Nonprofit Organizations (now the National Council of Nonprofits) was formed to bring together the existing state nonprofit trade associations and to promote creation of new state associations. The first state association had been formed in New York in 1927, but when the National Council was established, only twelve existed. Federal devolution initiatives appear to be the same kind of catalyst for organizing nonprofits at the state level that congressional attacks on foundations in the 1960s were for galvanizing collective action by the sector at the national level, and now there are forty-three state associations in the Council membership.

These coordinating trade associations have given the sector a stronger voice in public policy deliberations. That voice has subsequently addressed major national policy initiatives in the 1980s, 1990s, and early twenty-first century, affecting the welfare of the sector, including the numerous waves of budget cuts, changes in the tax code such as above-the-line deductibility of contributions by non-itemizers, the proposed reductions in tax rates that would reduce incentives to give, the issue of intermediate sanctions for disciplining nonprofits in violation of federal law, restrictions on lobbying and advocacy by nonprofit organizations, and self-regulation of the sector. The 2016 Public Policy Agenda of the National Council of Nonprofits declares that it opposes arbitrary budget cuts and seeks to expand incentives for giving, strengthen employment in the nonprofit sector, strengthen dialogue on public-private partnerships, protect advocacy work, and maintain a "proper balance" between reasonable regulation to ensure public trust and regulatory burdens that impede or constrain independent action (National Council of Nonprofits 2015).

The adversarial relationship between the nonprofit sector and the federal government has continued to evolve. For example, concerns about corporate governance stemming from scandals in the corporate sector, which led to the Sarbanes-Oxley legislation to hold top management more responsible for corporate misconduct, have spilled over into discussions about the nonprofit sector. With this in mind, instances of nonprofit malfeasance and fraud led to new congressional hearings and a wide-ranging series of discussions in the nonprofit sector on nonprofit regulation and governance. Senate Finance Committee hearings in 2004 criticized perceived abuses in the sector, such as excessive compensation for top executives and board members, conflicts of interest, inappropriate uses of donor-advised funds, exploitation of charities as tax shelters, overvaluation of noncash contributions, and inappropriate expensing of travel and other costs. These led to a subsequent revision in 2006 of the Form 1023 *Application for Recognition of Exemption under Section 501(c)(3)*, and the introduction in 2008 of an expanded Form 990 tax return with additional questions about organizational governance. However, as noted in the report of the HHS Inspector General (2014), oversight of the work of nonprofits is patchy. The Taxpayer Advocate Service (2015) found that 37 percent of organizations granted 501(c)(3) status after completing the newer short version of the Form 1023 application in fact do not meet the eligibility tests for qualification. And with more money floating around the sector, more cases of significant malfeasance continue to appear.

Governments have also challenged nonprofits at the state and local level in recent years in connection with property tax exemptions. Since the 1990s, challenges to property tax exemptions have been pursued in many states and cities, and there is increasing pressure on nonprofits, particularly large health and education organizations to provide some form of payments in lieu of taxes (known by the acronym PILOTs) to offset the costs to government of providing basic services (Grønbjerg and McGiverin-Bohan 2015). Moreover, state attorneys general are becoming increasingly active in regulating the fundraising and other practices of charities in their states, although their future capacity for oversight continues to be hostage to changes in federal regulations and structures (Fremont-Smith 2013). State regulatory resources are also quite minimal (see chapter 5 by Lott and Fremont-Smith, this volume).

Conscious that the first decades of the twenty-first century are witnessing a return to a national debate on accountability of nonprofit organizations, the sector has also expanded efforts to police itself and to assure government and the public of the sector's integrity through education and training, as well as through the peer review and accreditation standards and procedures of organizations such as Charity Navigator and the Better Business Bureau Wise Giving Alliance.

A NEW SOCIAL CONTRACT?

While each conceptual lens offers substantial insight, different views of the nonprofit sector-government relationship have prevailed at different periods of time. The adversarial lens is especially helpful in understanding the early republic, when public and private spheres of autonomy were first being sorted out, and the mid- to late twentieth century, with its debates over tax subsidy of lobbying or advocacy. Recent controversy over the use of 501(c)(4) social welfare organizations for political purposes is just the latest manifestation of this issue. The supplementary lens helps illuminate the late nineteenth and early twentieth centuries, when private interests asserted themselves in providing for social needs. The complementary lens helps to explain the post–World War II era, when government sought to address social needs by building social welfare programs without unduly expanding bureaucracy.

In each period, there was an implicit, though dynamic, general understanding of the roles of government, business, and the nonprofit sector in addressing the overall needs of society. Before the period of rapid industrial growth, the social contract divided responsibilities between modest government efforts to provide for basic public goods like defense, justice, and transportation, often leaving social needs to be met by multiple, autonomous private nonprofit efforts, primarily through faith-based organizations and mutual associations. With massive changes following the Civil War, including industrialization and immigration, the private sector—through new social welfare associations and the underwriting of welfare capitalism by the business sector—assumed new levels of responsibility for collective needs. In the mid-twentieth century, an American version of the welfare state emerged when government partnered with nonprofit organizations to provide for public needs, not only in human services but also in the arts, education, health, environment, and other fields.

Since the 1980s, another significant change has been under way. The complementary mode remains robust, especially in health care. However, government support in other areas such as social services and the arts have been constrained by fiscal conservatism. Thus, there is a new emphasis on the supplementary mode of government-nonprofit relations wherein the private and nonprofit sectors are expected to step up with new levels of charitable funding and volunteering. Certainly, as in the late nineteenth and early twentieth centuries, impressive new industrial enterprises have emerged, especially in the technology and communications areas. But while corporate titans have given massive gifts, these have been relatively isolated instances and reflective of individual predilections as much as corporate ones; corporate philanthropy generally remains an exercise in strategic marketing and employee morale building as much as social investment. Moreover, tax reform policy initiatives, such as tax code simplification, lowering tax rates, and eliminating the estate tax, while maintaining various tax loopholes, threaten to undermine rather than strengthen incentives for charitable giving (see Steinberg 1996). Nonetheless, the growing number of the "super-rich" in America may yet lead to a critical mass of philanthropists who could breathe new vigor into private initiatives that supplement government provision.

In the complementary mode, the rules are being rewritten as a result of both the privatizing of public goods and the growing market orientation of nonprofits. The boundary between supplementary and complementary is increasingly blurred as governments retrench and outsource, while nonprofits find supplementary revenues through entrepreneurial activities, partnerships with the business sector, and increased donations. Meanwhile nonprofits are held to stricter standards in governance and performance by government contractors and private donors leading to fears that the sector is losing its way, increasingly populated by bureaucratic and depoliticized organizations responding primarily to government and donor agendas.

Viewed through the adversarial lens, the shifting social contract is also troubling. While extolling the virtues of private, charitable initiatives, government seems more willing now to question the tax exemptions and to constrain the voices of charitable nonprofits, while at the same time permitting the exploitation of advocacy organizations for partisan political purposes. Criticized from all sides of the political spectrum, IRS scrutiny of nonprofit activity has been substantially constrained in recent years, leading even representatives of the sector itself to call for more resources for IRS oversight.

While the current changes derive from various political agendas and economic forces, the shifting social contract may be more a matter of inattention than ill intention. Examining the contemporary scene through the three lenses reveals gaps and inconsistencies, raising questions that beg resolution through some holistic concept of what the new contract ought to be. What are the relative roles of nonprofits, government, business, and private wealth? If nonprofits are to assume new levels of public responsibility, how can the resources be mobilized for them to do so? How can they do so if government limits tax incentives that encourage giving, questions the legitimacy of nonprofit commercial enterprise, and discourages nonprofits' voice in the public policy arena? And if private wealth is to drive new levels of voluntary initiative, how can that wealth be mobilized and directed to meet the needs of the most marginalized? Are businesses and individuals likely to contribute at levels commensurate with governmental reluctance to directly allocate resources to these challenges? Are we destined to live in a society in which great inequalities of wealth and welfare, social problems such as chronic poverty, homelessness, and differential access to basic human services persist, and remain hostage to market forces and the whims of social and business entrepreneurs?

Contemporary government policy toward the nonprofit sector is inconsistent, at once encouraging voluntarism and private initiative, and limiting its resource base and voice in various ways. And the role of the economy's dominant sector—business—remains anomalous. While business continues to be instrumental in its philanthropic efforts and strategic partnerships with nonprofits, segments of the business community object to the expansion of nonprofits into commercial arenas, while businesses continue to expand into areas of health care, social services, and education that once were the more exclusive domains of nonprofits. Overall, the role of business remains in flux and is not clearly articulated as part of an overall consensual social arrangement.

The three conceptual lenses—supplementary, complementary, and adversarial—provide a useful springboard for examining relations between nonprofits and government and indirectly between nonprofits and business as well. But they are at best the starting point for understanding the complex dances of intersectoral relations and their continually shifting dynamics.

ACKNOWLEDGMENTS

The authors would like to thank Robert Wuthnow, Kathleen McCarthy, and Waldemar Nielsen for their comments and suggestions on the first edition of this chapter; Elizabeth Boris, Eugene Steuerle, and Betsy Reid for their overall guidance in framing and refining the discussion; and Gardener Neeley for his assistance in checking citations. We thank Gene Steuerle and Teresa Derrick-Mills for their comments on the current text. And we congratulate Elizabeth Boris on the completion of her successful tenure as director of the Center on Nonprofits and Philanthropy at the Urban Institute and her stewardship in maintaining the study of nonprofits and government through this third edition.

REFERENCES

Abramson, Alan J., and Lester M. Salamon. 2005. "The Nonprofit Sector and the Federal Budget: Fiscal Year 2006 and Beyond." Nonprofit Sector Research Fund, Working Paper Series. Washington, DC: The Aspen Institute.

Anheier, Helmut K. 2014. *Nonprofit Organizations: Theory, Management, and Policy*, 2nd ed. London and New York, NY: Routledge.

Ben-Ner, Avner. 1986. "Nonprofit Organizations: Why Do They Exist in a Market Economy?" *The Economics of Nonprofit Institutions*. Susan Rose-Ackerman, ed. (pp. 94–113). New York, NY: Oxford University Press.

Bremner, Robert H. 1988. *American Philanthropy*, 2nd ed. Chicago: University of Chicago Press.

Bright Lines Project. 2013. History of the Bright Lines Project. Washington, DC: Public Citizen. http://www.brightlinesproject.org/about-us/history/.

Brilliant, Eleanor L. 2001. *Private Charity and Public Inquiry.* Indianapolis: Indiana University Press.

Buchanan, James M., and Gordon Tullock. 1962. *The Calculus of Consent.* Ann Arbor: University of Michigan Press.

Burlingame, Dwight F., and Dennis R. Young. 1996. *Corporate Philanthropy at the Crossroads.* Indianapolis: Indiana University Press.

Casey, John. 2015. "Tsars, Task Forces and Standards: The New 'IRS'"? *Nonprofit Policy Forum.* Published Online: 07/29/2015. http://www.degruyter.com/view/j/npf.ahead-of-print/npf-2015-0036/npf-2015-0036.xml.

———. 2016. *The Nonprofit World: Civil Society and the Rise of the Nonprofit Sector.* Boulder, CO: Kumarian Press, Lynne Rienner Publishers.

Chaves, Mark, Laura Stephens, and Joseph Galaskiewicz. 2004. "Does Government Funding Suppress Nonprofits' Political Activity?" *American Sociological Review* 69 (April): 292–316.

Douglas, James. 1987. "Political Theories of Nonprofit Organizations." *The Nonprofit Sector: A Research Handbook.* Walter W. Powell, ed. (pp. 43–54). New Haven: Yale University Press.

Eisenberg, Pablo. 2011. "Nonprofits Need to Put Aside Self-Interest in Tax Debate." *Chronicle of Philanthropy.* http://philanthropy.com/article/Nonprofits-Need-to-Put-Aside/129378.

Evans, Peter B., Dietrich Rueschemeyer, and Theda Skocpol. 1985. *Bringing the State Back In.* Cambridge: Cambridge University Press.

Fabricant, Michael and Michelle Fine. 2012. *Charter Schools and the Corporate Makeover of Public Education: What's at Stake?* New York, NY: Teachers College Press.

Ferris, James M. 1993. "The Double-Edged Sword of Social Service Contracting: Public Accountability versus Nonprofit Autonomy." *Nonprofit Management and Leadership* 3(4): 363–376.

The Foundation Center. 2014. *Key Facts on U.S. Foundations.* New York, NY: The Foundation Center.

Fremont-Smith, Marion R. 2013. The Future of State Regulation of Charities. New York, NY: Columbia University National State Attorneys General Program. http://academiccommons.columbia.edu/catalog/ac:171162.

Gazley, B. 2015. "How Philanthropy Props Up Public Services and Why We Should Care." *The Nonprofit Quarterly,* Spring 2015. https://nonprofitquarterly.org/2015/03/27/how-philanthropy-props-up-public-services-and-why-we-should-care/.

Grønbjerg, Kirsten A. 1997. "Transaction Costs in Social Services Contracting: Lessons from the U.S.A." *The Contract Culture in Public Services.* Jeremy Kendall, ed. (pp. 99–118). London: Ashgate Publishing Limited.

Grønbjerg, Kirsten and Lester M. Salamon. 2012. "Devolution, Marketization, and the Changing Shape of Government-Nonprofit Relations." *The State of Nonprofit America,* 2nd ed. Lester M. Salamon, ed. (pp. 549–586). Washington, DC: The Brookings Institution.

Grønbjerg, Kirsten and Kellie McGiverin-Bohan. 2015. Local Government Interest in and Justifications for Collecting Payments-in-Lieu of (Property) Taxes from

Charities. *Nonprofit Policy Forum.* Published Online: 10/20/2015. http://www.degruyter.com/view/j/npf.ahead-of-print/npf-2015-0043/npf-2015-0043.xml.

Hall, Peter Dobkin. 1992. *Inventing the Nonprofit Sector.* Baltimore: The Johns Hopkins University Press.

———. 1994. "Historical Perspectives on Nonprofit Organizations." *The Jossey-Bass Handbook of Nonprofit Leadership and Management.* Robert D. Herman and Associates, eds. (pp. 3–43). San Francisco, CA: Jossey Bass Publishers.

Hansmann, Henry. 1980. "The Role of Nonprofit Enterprise." *Yale Law Journal* 89(3): 835–901.

HHS Inspector General. 2014. *Laws Prohibit the use of HHS Grant Funds for Lobbying, But Limited Methods Exist to Identify Noncompliance.* Report 07-12-00620. Washington, DC. Department of Health and Human Services. http://oig.hhs.gov/oei/reports/oei-07-12-00620.pdf.

Jensen, Brennan, Leak Kerkman, and Cassie J. Moore. 2005. "Pay Raises for Charity Leaders Keep Pace with Inflation." *The Chronicle of Philanthropy* 17(24).

Kasper, Gabriel and Justin Marcoux. 2014. "The Re-Emerging Art of Funding Innovation." *Stanford Social Innovation Review,* Spring 2014. http://ssir.org/articles/entry/the_re_emerging_art_of_funding_innovation

Kramer, Ralph M. 1981. *Voluntary Agencies in the Welfare State.* Berkeley: University of California Press.

Lane, Jan-Erik. 2000. *New Public Management.* London: Routledge.

Lohmann, Roger. 1992. *The Commons.* San Francisco, CA: Jossey-Bass.

McCarthy, Kathleen D. 1994. "Twentieth Century Cultural Patronage." *Alternative Futures: Challenging Designs for Arts Philanthropy.* Andrew Patner, ed. (pp. 1–22). Washington, DC: Grantmakers in the Arts.

———. 1997. "Women, Politics, Philanthropy: Some Historical Origins of the Welfare State." *The Liberal Persuasion: Arthur J. Schlesinger, Jr. and the Challenge of the American Past.* John Patrick Diggins, ed. (pp. 142–150). Princeton: Princeton University Press.

Marwell, Nicole P., and Paul-Brian McInerney. 2005. "The Nonprofit/For-Profit Continuum: Theorizing the Dynamics of Mixed-Form Markets." *Nonprofit and Voluntary Sector Quarterly,* 34(1): 7–28.

Mook, Laurie, John R. Whitman, Jack Quarter, and Ann Armstrong. 2015. *Understanding the Social Economy of the United States.* Toronto: University of Toronto Press.

Murray, Michael F. 2010. "Private Management of Public Spaces: Nonprofit Organizations and Urban Parks." *Harvard Environmental Law Review* 34: 179–255.

Najam, Adil. 2000. "The Four-C's of Third Sector-Government Relations: Cooperation, Confrontation, Complementarity, and Co-optation." *Nonprofit Management and Leadership* 10(4): 375–396.

Nathan, Richard P. 1996. "The 'Nonprofitization Movement' as a Form of Devolution." *Capacity for Change?* Dwight F. Burlingame, William A. Diaz, Warren F. Ilchman, and associates, eds. (pp. 23–55). Indianapolis: Indiana University Center on Philanthropy.

National Council of Nonprofits. 2013. *Partnering for Impact: Government-Nonprofit Contracting Task Forces Produce Results for Taxpayers.* Washington, DC:

National Council of Nonprofits. https://www.councilofnonprofits.org/sites/default/files/documents/streamlining-report-partnering-for-impact.pdf

National Council of Nonprofits. 2015. Policy Agenda 2016. https://www.councilofnonprofits.org/public-policy-agenda.

Nielsen, Waldemar A. 1979. *The Endangered Sector*. New York, NY: Columbia University Press.

Niskanen, William A. 1971. *Bureaucracy and Representative Government*. Chicago: Aldine-Atherton.

Office of Social Innovation and Civic Participation. 2015. *Social Innovation Fund*. https://www.whitehouse.gov/administration/eop/sicp/initiatives/social-innovation-fund.

Olson, Mancur. 1965. *The Logic of Collective Action*. Cambridge: Harvard University Press.

O'Neill, Michael. 1989. *The Third America*. San Francisco, CA: Jossey-Bass.

Phillips, Susan and Steven Rathgeb Smith. 2014. *A Dawn of Convergence?: Third Sector Policy Regimes in the 'Anglo-Saxon' Cluster* 1(8): 1141–1163.

Reisch, Michael and David Sommerfeld. 2003. "Welfare Reform and the Future of Nonprofit Organizations." *Nonprofit Management and Leadership* 14(1): 19–46.

Robertson, Nancy M. 1998. "Kindness or Justice? Women's Associations and the Politics of Race and History." *Private Action and the Public Good*. Walter W. Powell and Elisabeth S. Clemens, eds. (pp. 193–205). New Haven: Yale University Press.

Roelofs, Joan. 2003. *Foundations and Public Policy: The Mask of Pluralism*. New York, NY: SUNY Press.

Rushton, Michael. 2010. "Federal Tax Policy". Chapter 20 in *Handbook of Research on Nonprofit Economics and Management*. Bruce A. Seaman and Dennis R. Young, eds. (pp. 291–302). Northampton, MA: Edward Elgar Publishing.

Salamon, Lester M. 1987. "Partners in Public Service: The Scope and Theory of Government-Nonprofit Relations." *The Nonprofit Sector: A Research Handbook*. Walter W. Powell, ed. (pp. 99–117). New Haven: Yale University Press.

———. 1995. *Partners in Public Service*. Baltimore: Johns Hopkins University Press.

———. 2015. "The Nonprofitization of the Welfare State." *Voluntas* 26(6): 2147–2154.

Salamon, Lester M., Stephanie L. Geller, and S. Wojciech Sokolowski. 2012. *Holding the Fort: Nonprofit Employment during a Decade of Turmoil*. Nonprofit Economic Data Bulletin. Baltimore MD: John Hopkins University. http://ccss.jhu.edu/publications-findings?did=369.

Shirky, Clay. 2008. *Here Comes Everybody: The Power of Organizing Without Organizations*. New York, NY: Penguin Press.

Smith, David Horton. 1997a. "Grassroots Associations Are Important: Some Theory and a Review of the Impact Literature." *Nonprofit and Voluntary Sector Quarterly* 26(3): 269–306.

———. 1997b. "The International History of Grassroots Associations." *International Journal of Comparative Sociology* 27: 3–4.

Smith, Steven Rathgeb. 2012. "Social Services." *The State of Nonprofit America*, 2nd ed. Lester M. Salamon, ed. (pp. 192–228). Washington, DC: Brookings Institution Press.

Smith, Steven Rathgeb and Michael Lipsky. 1993. *Nonprofit for Hire.* Cambridge: Harvard University Press.

Steinberg, Richard. 1996. "Can Individual Donations Replace Cutbacks in Federal Social Welfare Spending?" *Capacity for Change?* Dwight F. Burlingame, William A. Diaz, Warren F. Ilchman, and associates, eds. (pp. 57–79). Indianapolis: Indiana University Center on Philanthropy.

———. 1997. "Competition in Contracted Markets." *The Contract Culture in Public Services.* Jeremy Kendall, ed. (pp. 161–79). London: Ashgate Publishing Limited.

Taxpayers Advocate Service. 2015. *Study Of Taxpayers That Obtained Recognition as IRC § 501(c)(3) Organizations on The Basis of Form 1023-EZ.* Washington, DC: Taxpayer Advocate Service.

Tiebout, Charles. 1956. "A Pure Theory of Public Expenditure." *Journal of Political Economy* 64(October): 416–424.

U.S. Congress, House Committee on Ways and Means. 1995. "Contract with America: Overview: Hearings before the Committee on Ways and Means." Washington, DC: U.S. Government Print Office.

Weisbrod, Burton A. 1977. *The Voluntary Nonprofit Sector.* Lexington: D.C. Heath and Company.

———. 1997. "The Future of the Nonprofit Sector: Its Entwining with Private Enterprise and Government." *Journal of Policy Analysis and Management* 16(4): 541–555.

Williams, Grant. 2005. "Tax Agency Offers Guidance to Disaster-Relief Charities." *Chronicle of Philanthropy* 16(19).

Young, Dennis R. 1983, 2013. *If Not for Profit, For What?* Lexington: D.C. Heath and Company. 30th Anniversary Digital Reissue with new front matter and commentaries by leading scholars Georgia State University Library Digital Archive, 2013. http://scholarworks.gsu.edu/facbooks2013/1/.

———. 2000. "Alternative Models of Government–Nonprofit Relations: Theoretical and International Perspectives." *Nonprofit and Voluntary Sector Quarterly* 29(1): 149–172.

Chapter 2

Meeting Social Needs through Charitable and Government Resources

C. Eugene Steuerle, Alan J. Abramson, Ellen Steele, and Virginia Hodgkinson

Both the nonprofit and government sectors attempt to provide social benefits on a wide scale to the public. Because their roles often overlap, many debates arise as to which sector should assume greater responsibility for tackling various public problems, which has the greater capability, and how politics should intertwine with charitable, religious, and other nonprofit missions. One perennial debate is over whether growth in government tends to displace the nonprofit sector, or vice versa.

Addressing these issues requires understanding the resources for meeting social needs that are available in the nonprofit sector relative to government. But it also involves examination of the interdependency of the two sectors, especially the way that government spending—and changes in this spending—affects nonprofit organizations. To this end, this chapter also includes an analysis of the impact of federal spending changes on both the demand or need for nonprofit services and nonprofits' ability to provide these services. Rather dramatic changes have occurred in the extent to which the federal government has put money toward areas of interest to nonprofits such as health and international assistance, whether directly or channeled through nonprofit organizations. (See also chapter 1 by Young and Casey, this volume, for a discussion of the theories about how the sectors should relate to each other.)

Our focus will center on nonprofit "charities" that qualify under section 501(c)(3) of the Internal Revenue Code for a tax deduction because they are devoted to religious, educational, charitable, scientific, cultural, health, and similar purposes. We will follow convention and often use the term "nonprofits" when we refer mainly to charities, though the nonprofit sector also includes other nonprofit organizations such as social welfare organizations, labor unions, clubs, and other mutual benefit societies.

Social needs here refer to such social welfare functions as health, welfare, and education that both nonprofit organizations and the government have traditionally supported. In the not very distant past, government spent only small proportions of its revenue on social welfare. Today, the majority of public expenditures fall into this category (Steuerle et al. 2008). In recent decades, the percentage of total government spending directed toward social welfare has continued to rise as spending on the "physical" side of government—defense, highways, energy, buildings—declined in relative importance (figure 2.1). Defense itself has declined from about 60 percent of federal spending in the mid-1950s to less than 20 percent today. Of course, that percentage can only decline so far, and it has witnessed several cycles that included increases in spending for wars such as in Iraq.

Over time, the evolution of government activity has dramatically influenced the character of nonprofits. Many debates focus on whether government cutbacks have put more pressures on the nonprofit sector, or whether its growth has displaced nonprofit activity. Whether government was waxing or waning,

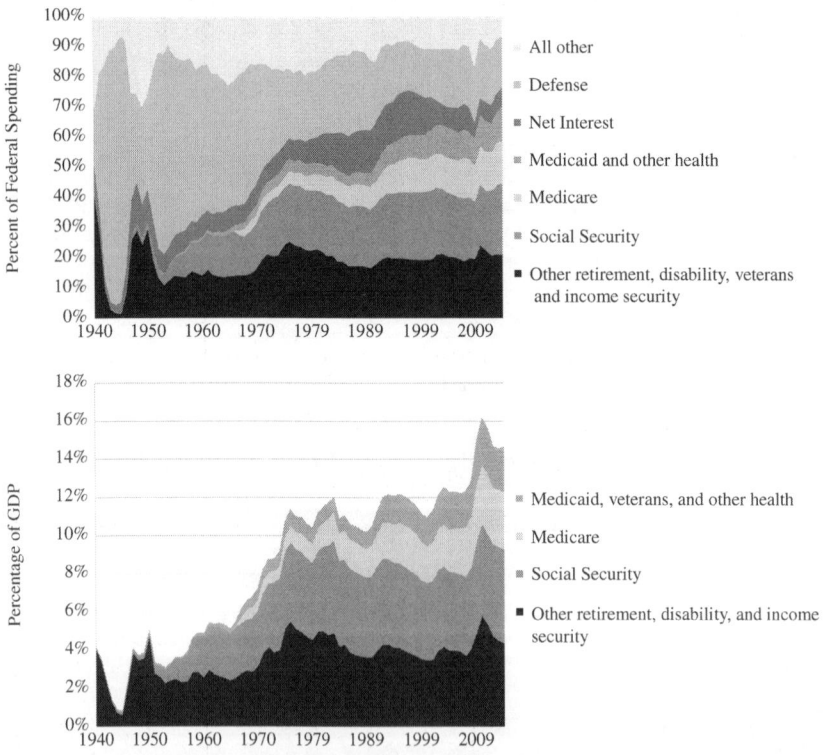

Figure 2.1 Trends in Federal Spending. *Source*: Office of Management and Budget Historical Tables 3.1, 2015.

however, devolution of service provision to the nonprofit sector has been occurring for decades at federal and state levels. A driving force behind many recent changes in the size and scope of the nonprofit sector has been the use of charities and nonprofit institutions as intermediaries or contractors in providing the services government finances, particularly in health and higher education. More on this later, but since the early 1980s, federal spending on programs relevant to nonprofits' areas of concern has grown, but much of the growth occurred in Medicare, Medicaid, and elderly support programs. Among many other programs of interest to the nonprofit sector, federal support fell.

Here we will focus on resources of the two sectors as a way to trace their evolution. In so doing, we do not pretend to provide more than a statistical snapshot of the complex relative roles of government and nonprofits. Government enforces order and contracts, while nonprofit organizations provide individuals and communities with a voice and a means for participation. Those and many other important activities cannot be measured adequately by a simple focus on quantifiable resources such as budget outlays, contributions, and volunteer time. Nonetheless, examining trends in resources reveals much about how much the public relies on these sectors to meet a range of different social needs, how priorities have changed over time, and the degree to which the two sectors exert control over the delivery of social services. By comparing the resources government and nonprofits provide, we can also roughly assess how much their activities complement or substitute for each other.

THE INEVITABLE INADEQUACY OF BOTH SECTORS

Any discussion of resources must recognize that both the nonprofit and the government sectors face limits on their ability to satisfy social needs. Economic scarcity is unavoidable; needs are infinite, but the resources available to satisfy those needs are not. No single nonprofit organization, group of organizations, or government agency can prevent all death, suffering, and pain, or educate each one of us to our full potential. Moreover, nonprofit organizations and the government are merely two institutional means through which individuals act to address a variety of social needs. Despite all the power of institutions, individual efforts at being good parents, neighbors, spouses, friends—and yes, citizens of the state and participants in nonprofit efforts—form the base on which a "civil society" is built.

As noted above, this chapter explores the capacity—measured in terms of physical and budgetary resources—of nonprofits and the government to meet social needs. It is not a philosophical essay on the attributes of a good society. Nonetheless, only by considering the total scope of what they do can we place in perspective the activities of government and the nonprofits, and their relationship to each other.

What we accomplish through government and nonprofits is moderate when compared to what we accomplish as individuals, in our households and our workplaces. Why is this important to our inquiry? It is at home and at work that we spend and make use of most of our time, money, and physical resources. Hundreds of billions of dollars' worth of resources may flow through the nonprofit and public sectors, but as important as those resources are, they are moderate relative to the economy at large. Moreover, the sum of measured economic activity includes only activities taking place through formal exchanges in the marketplace: measures such as gross domestic product (GDP) do not include, for example, home-provided childcare, cooking, repairs, teaching, cash gifts, and other services produced for oneself or given to family and friends. Thus, the resource snapshot we present is limited to formal exchanges, plus some adjustments for volunteer activity through charitable and government institutions.

That the activities of nonprofits and the government are embedded in a larger web of economic and other activities has an important implication. When government expands, it is at least as likely to divert resources from the household and business sectors as it is from the nonprofit sector. Why? There is simply greater room for substitution from sectors with the most resources. Similarly, when the nonprofit sector expands, it often substitutes for activities undertaken in the home or by businesses instead of government. For example, as formal schooling and childcare arrangements have expanded, government and the nonprofit sector have increased their efforts simultaneously. They together substituted for labor that otherwise might have been employed in private business or in home-provided education and childcare.

A corollary is that if substitution can take place elsewhere, then the nonprofit sector and government often complement rather than substitute for each other. Expanded or changing government services may create a demand for more nonprofit organizations to act as intermediaries, and conversely, a larger nonprofit sector may demand more government services and resources.

Nonprofit organizations, therefore, alternate between complementing and substituting for what government does, depending upon the social needs to be met. Government programs may displace private cash assistance for old age, for instance, and they may increase the use of nonprofit nursing homes which provide elderly care through expanded government health care dollars.

In any event, we should expect the size of the nonprofit sector and government—whether measured by income-produced, assets, workers, or other attributes—to change over time not only relative to each other but also relative to the business and household sectors. The relative "size" will vary in no small part according to the efficacy with which nonprofits and government achieve various goals, including those of greater equity and well-being for parts of the population. Large swings in the relative importance of the nonprofit and government sectors can come about through an expansion of defense needs or of government contracts to nonprofits, through tax revolts, or through the transformation of large nonprofits into profit-making institutions. There is, therefore, no basis for a simplistic view that an ever-growing or ever-declining government or nonprofit sector is somehow good or bad. Swings in relative size may represent either gains or losses to society but are not inherently bad or good because there is no unchanging ideal size for these sectors.

Constraints on Both Sectors

If the challenges of meeting infinite needs with finite resources were not enough, government and nonprofits also face significant constraints on their ability to collect and use resources. Government does not obtain its resources in the same way as nonprofit organizations. Individuals make relatively few direct contributions of money or volunteer time to government, although there are exceptions, as in the case of purchases of war bonds and volunteering in public schools. It may appear that government raises resources more easily than do nonprofits because of its legal power to tax. Yet the ability to tax is limited because taxation exacts a variety of costs. Most visibly, taxes reduce the income that people and businesses have to spend. Less visible but equally important, taxes are costly to administer and enforce, as well as distort people's economic decisions about working and saving. And, of course, voters themselves constrain the extent to which revenues can be raised.

The need to treat individuals fairly—which is essential when compulsory forces of the state are at play—can also have the unintended consequence of discouraging experimentation and limiting flexibility in government programs. Norms of fair taxation and equitable distribution of benefits tend to push government toward uniform treatment of citizens in equal situations. But that may also make it administratively difficult to respond to the particular needs of individuals (Douglas 1987; Steuerle et al. 1998).

In contrast, the nonprofit sector can often better respond to individual situations, but seldom in any uniform manner.[1] People often express their generosity through a community or church or other voluntary or citizen association in which they are involved, leaving aside other communities and groups that may have equal or greater needs. The definition of community and church, just like tribe or nation, is at once both inclusive (it encourages identity and mission) and exclusive (it excludes those who do not belong and ignores issues not connected to the organizational mission) (Sacks 2015). Nonprofit organizations often distribute services on the basis of membership or geography because the organizations lack resources to determine need (see, for instance, Clerkin and Grønbjerg 2007). Also, their responses depend upon the nature of the organizations and the cohesion of community, with a lower density of nonprofit human service organizations working in low-income and under-resourced communities (Allard 2009).

Even when individuals give beyond the immediate family, much of their giving is to relatives and friends. In 2014, for instance, 26 percent of respondents in a national survey indicated that their household gave a median of $1,000 to assist relatives and friends outside of their immediate family (Pew Charitable Trusts 2016). Meanwhile, average giving per household in the United States was about $2,200 in 2014, nearly a third of which went to religious congregations (*Giving USA* 2015).

MAJOR FINDINGS

With this background, we now provide some data on the size, capacity, and employment of the nonprofit sector, often comparing it with the government sector or with wider measures of economic output. We start with two caveats. First, one should avoid the temptation to project the future based on the recent past. Some trends we will discuss are sustainable, some are not, and some measures themselves are affected by the interaction between government and the nonprofit sector, especially when the former pays the latter to carry out its functions.

Second, one should not confuse statistical measures of resources with "importance." Resources such as revenues often are counted twice. For example, $1 of government spending through a contract with the nonprofit sector may result in only $1 of output to the economy, despite being counted in both sectors' revenues and expenditures.

By the same token, measures of resources can understate the impact of the activities of government and nonprofits. Regardless of size, the presence of a well-functioning government allows individuals to act without fear of repression or anarchy and with trust that legal obligations will be fulfilled. Nonprofits can provide unity within diversity, enhance goodwill in society, and encourage a "civil society," in which social interaction more easily transpires among individuals and with their government. Some measures of resources are also incomplete; for example, there is no easy way to account for the added output made possible when individuals work for nonprofits at below-market wages.

With those cautionary notes, the following broad conclusions can be drawn about the resources of the nonprofits.

The Nonprofit Sector in Relation to the Economy

The nonprofit sector is a large part of the American economy:

- It produces 5.4 percent of national income (excluding the value of labor of volunteers).

- Its assets are valued at over $5 trillion.
- It employs nearly 9 percent of the labor force (excluding volunteers).[2]

Figure 2.2 displays these three measures of the size of the nonprofit sector and relates them to other sectors of the economy. As might be expected, the nonprofit sector is much smaller than the business sector, which dominates the production of goods and services. When calculations of output are made, they reflect mainly where production occurs, not who finances it. Thus, federal, state, and local government production in figure 2.2 is much lower than the taxes government collected or expenditures made, which are more than one-third of personal income. Even that one-third figure understates government activity because it excludes those tax subsidies, such as some earned income tax credits and special treatment of employer-provided health insurance, administered by the Internal Revenue Service (IRS) (Marron and Toder 2012).

Of course, government makes both direct transfers through programs that involve very little outright production, such as Social Security, and indirect transfers by purchasing services, such as health care, from other sectors credited with production. Over the past few decades, government has increasingly spent larger shares of its expenditures and revenues on transfers and produced less goods and services within the formal government sector itself.

The nonprofit sector now holds about $5.2 trillion in assets as of 2013, an increase of 68 percent since 2003 (McKeever 2015). There are many valuation problems that on net probably cause that estimate to be low; for instance, figure 2.2 shows totals for nonprofits that file Form 990 with the IRS, which exclude the assets of churches and some small organizations.[3]

Employment by the nonprofit sector, excluding volunteers, is about 8.7 percent of total employment in the United States. That figure is higher than the sector's share of gross national product (GNP), at least partly because of how national income is measured. It values the output of many services according to what consumers pay or what is paid to workers, lenders, and owners. Consider a childcare center in which paid workers might earn less than they could in other jobs. As one consequence, charges for the services of the center will also be lower than they might otherwise be. In effect, the value of the below-market wages accrues to the children and families using the center. But that value will not be counted in national income.[4] The services of a childcare worker making $10,000 a year who could make $30,000 elsewhere will be counted as $10,000, not $30,000. However, the case should not be overstated. There is some evidence that workers in nonprofit hospitals and private higher education earn as much and sometimes more per hour of work than they would by working in government or business (Butler 2009).

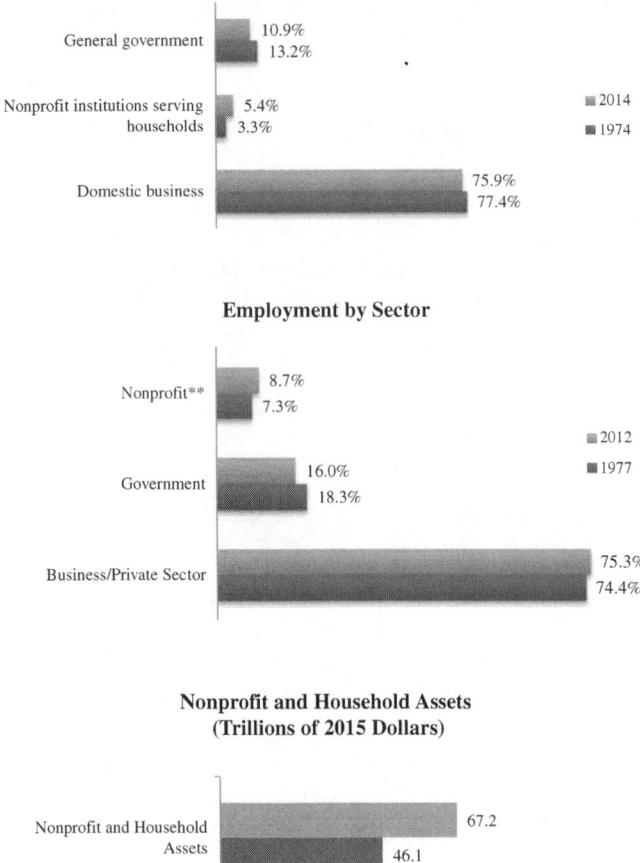

Figure 2.2 The Nonprofit Sector in the U.S. Economy. *Sources*: The Urban Institute, 2016; Bureau of Labor Statistics, 2015; Bureau of Economic Analysis, NIPA table 1.13, August 2015; *Nonprofit Sector in Brief 2015*; Board of Governors of the Federal Reserve System, Flow of Funds Accounts of the United States, L.100 and L.100.a, 2005 and 2015; Quarterly Census of Employment and Wages and Research Data on the Nonprofit Sector, National NAICS 2-digit and 3-digit Industry Data 2012 annual averages. *Note*: Assets exclude liabilities. Non-filers include most churches. The share of employment by the nonprofit sector differs from table 2.2 because this table only includes employees covered under Unemployment Insurance, whereas table 2.2 includes all of the labor force. See endnote 3.**Includes full- and part-time nonfarm employment for the nonprofit sector.

Relative Size of Monetary Contributions to Nonprofits

Although the charitable sector is economically important, charitable contributions are a small share of total income and are dwarfed by the government's social welfare spending. The charitable sector receives about 2 percent of personal income as contributions, about one-twelfth of the government's social welfare spending.

Figure 2.3 shows that charitable contributions are (and, for some time, have been) about 2 percent, perhaps a little less, of personal income. That can be contrasted to social welfare spending supported by government at all levels, which has been in excess of 20 percent of personal income since the early 1970s and has surpassed 25 percent since the beginning of the twenty-first century. By far, the largest part of that spending is on retirement assistance and health care (social insurance) for the near elderly and elderly, followed by education and public aid.

Outright charitable giving of money has always been moderate relative to households' total monetary resources and assets and relative to the economy's

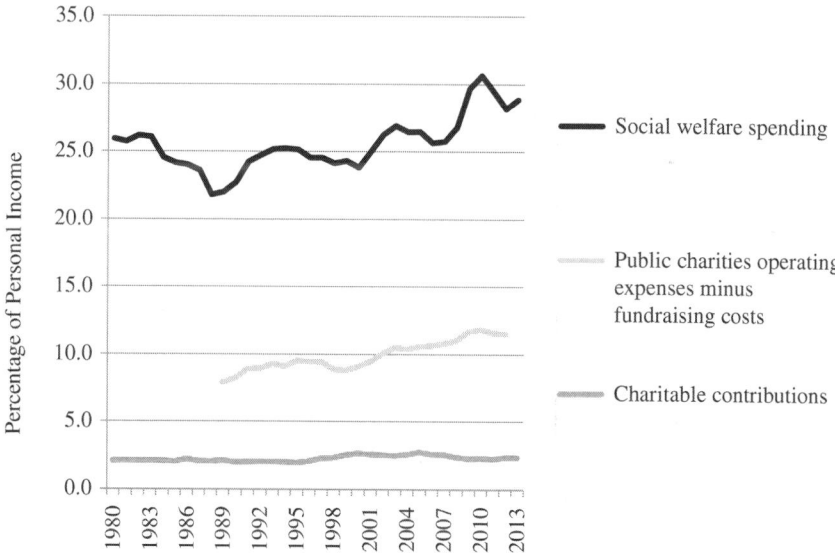

Figure 2.3 Government Social Welfare Spending and Charitable Contributions (1980–2013). *Source*: Urban Institute 2016. Based on data from Office of Management and Budget Historical Table 3.1, 3.12, 3.16, and Tax Expenditures, 2015; the Bureau of Economic Analysis NIPA Tables 2.1; the Congressional Budget Office's The Budget and Economic Outlook: 2016–2026; Giving USA 2015; and the NCCS Core File Public Charities, 1989–2013.

output. For better or worse, that is one reason why government has stepped in to provide many social welfare benefits. Some argue that relying on government distorts behavior and reduces welfare because of the costs associated with enforced taxation and other government actions. Others, however, argue that only government can raise adequate revenues and ensure that people who would otherwise ride free—that is, benefit from others' efforts without sharing the cost—pay their "fair share."

No matter who is right, individuals have shown more willingness to pay higher taxes than to contribute voluntarily out of their own pockets. That calls into question how much charity could displace government. It might be nice to hope that voluntary effort could rise to that level—very few individuals do give a substantial portion of their income to charity—but no historical precedent for such widespread generosity exists, no matter how much the nation's various religions and mores might espouse the values associated with giving. It is highly doubtful, therefore, that the nonprofit sector could, in the foreseeable future, rely on voluntary giving to take over all or even a large share of social welfare functions, such as providing health care or minimum cash benefits to the elderly, universal education for the young, or widespread opportunity for college attendance.

Growth in Public Welfare Spending

Public social welfare spending, which affects much of the nonprofits, has grown rapidly in the postwar period. Since 1960 the share of personal income devoted to public sector social welfare spending rose quite dramatically from about one-eighth of GDP, settling between about 20 to 30 percent of GDP after 1980 (figure 2.3).

Especially worth noting is the large and significant growth in domestic spending between the mid-1960s and mid-1970s and then again in the first decade of the twenty-first century (Bixby 1990; Quakenbush and Steuerle 2016). Indeed, over the nation's history, domestic spending as a share of GDP increased mainly under Republican presidents, including Nixon and George W. Bush (Steuerle 2014). Public social welfare spending relative to national income fell in the early 1980s, then resumed its growth in the late 1980s and early 1990s, leveled out, perhaps declined in the late 1990s, and then grew again significantly from 2000 to 2005—with much of the trend due to cycles in the growth of health care spending. It grew temporarily in the Great Recession, though it then settled back down some during the recovery period. Much of that growth at the federal level was accomplished without increases in average tax rates. Peace dividends and the corresponding decline in defense's share of the budget had allowed many of these shifts toward social welfare spending (see figure 2.1) (Steuerle 2014).

Of course, within each period, the story is more complex. At the end of the twentieth century, a stalemate between a Republican Congress and a Democratic president led to little new legislation. Revenues increased with a stock market bubble, defense spending continued to decline, and health care spending was temporarily restrained. At the beginning of the twenty-first century, each of these items reversed. While revenues declined with the stock market bust, a small recession, and a tax cut, spending on war, health care, and almost every domestic spending category increased as a percentage of GDP. It was an unusual and unsustainable period when taxes went down and almost every major spending category went up as a percentage of GDP. Then the Great Recession intervened, with increases in both automatic (e.g., unemployment insurance) and discretionary (e.g., a stimulus package) stabilizers. As the nation moved into recovery, however, the beginning of the baby boom generation's retirement, health cost growth, and the high levels of debt remaining from the Great Recession of 2007–2009 added to the pressures on discretionary spending, much for other social welfare functions.

State and local governments expanded significantly after the traumas of the Depression and World War II ended. These governments also suffered from the revenue boom-bust cycles accompanying the late twentieth-century stock market bubble, the 2001 recession, and the Great Recession. They, too, face pressures to spend relatively more on the needs of an aging population and relatively less on other social welfare functions.

In the post–World War II period, some state and local funding growth may have been induced by federal matching grant formulas, which might lead one to speculate that state and local growth in welfare spending could slow in the future if enough federal matching grants are converted into block grants. As Steuerle and Mermin (1997) note, devolution of "welfare" to the states (the conversion of welfare from Aid to Families with Dependent Children [AFDC] to Temporary Assistance for Needy Families [TANF]) initially increased federalization of the financing of cash welfare; that is, the federal government took on a bigger share of the total financing.

However, the incentives for states to spend additional money were thereby reduced since under the new formula the state bore 100 percent rather than only a fraction of the cost of additional spending.[5] Over time, as one consequence, there has been a downward trend at both federal and state levels in spending on cash welfare as a percentage of personal income.

In health care, the story is quite complex. Under Medicaid and a related health support program for children (S-CHIP), as well as the Affordable Care Act or Obamacare, the federal government has increased spending. Its sharing formulas often require minimum or zero sharing of new costs with the states, which traditionally would have led to rising shares of GDP spent on health care. However, as part of the opposition in Republican-led states to the

Affordable Care Act, many states refused to expand Medicaid even with 90 or 100 percent federal support.

Constancy of Private Giving

In contrast to rising public social welfare spending, private contributions have been almost constant as a percentage of personal income. The share of income given to health organizations appears to have declined slightly over the past twenty years, and religious institutions have claimed a declining income share for a longer period of time.

In 2014, charitable giving was estimated at 2.0 percent of personal income, a slight increase from its early postrecessionary rates of 1.8 to 1.9 percent (*Giving USA* 2015). One needs to be careful here, as there are problems of overreporting and underreporting contributions on tax returns and surveys. Further, changes in survey techniques or audit practices of the IRS could produce different types of errors over time.

Individuals make most donations (figure 2.4). When one adds up all sources of private contributions from 1989 to 2014, the annual rate of growth in real (inflation adjusted) private contributions equals 2.6 percent (figure 2.5). Giving, however, has shifted among subsectors. Over the same period, private giving to religious groups grew just 0.9 percent per year; thus, its share of the total declined. Contributions to several other types of organizations have grown more quickly than the total.

Giving by high income and wealthy taxpayers follows its own cycle (see table 2.1). The gifts of a few people can dominate this giving, as when billionaires decide to give sizable shares of their wealth away before death. The activity of this group can also be influenced by changes in the tax law, including lower marginal tax rates in the 1980s and 1990s, and then higher rates during President Obama's administration. The top tax rate dropped from 70 to 50 percent in 1981, to 28 or 33 percent in 1988, back up to about 41 percent from 1993 to 2000, and then fell again to about 35 percent through legislation passed between 2001 and 2003. Today the top statutory marginal tax rate is 39.6 percent (see chapter 4), though it can go higher through other provisions such as the alternative minimum tax (AMT).

Given changes in rates of taxation, the relative constancy of giving out of personal income might be considered surprising in two respects. First, periods of decline in tax rates significantly increased the net cost of charitable giving, which might lead one to expect a sharp drop in private giving (see chapter 4). Second, if government spending on social needs displaces private charity, one might have expected the substantial increase in public spending described above to have displaced more private giving than it appears to have displaced.

Table 2.1 Giving and Income of the Top 1 Percent of Taxpayers, 1979–2013

Variable	1979	1984	1991	1994	1999
Number of returns	872,011	950,556	1,033,202	1,063,600	1,155,386
Income	143,712	258,091	437,722	530,634	980,019
Charitable deductions	4,848	8,535	13,054	17,332	37,337
Giving as % of income	3.6	3.1	3.1	3.3	3.8
Top 1% share of total income	9.4	11.2	12.8	13.7	19.3
Top 1% share of charitable deductions	14.0	14.1	14.1	16.6	31.4
	2004	2007	2009	2013	
Number of returns	1,225,046	1,431,539	1,326,138	1,383,071	
Income	1,057,207	1,441,879	999,462	1,272,321	
Charitable deductions	42,312	51,900	33,882	51,191	
Giving as % of income	4.0	3.6	3.4	4.0	
Top 1% share of total income	18.9	23.3	17.2	19.0	
Top 1% share of charitable deductions	28.7	35.8	26.5	32.9	

Notes: Income is a constant-law definition of adjusted gross income (AGI) plus most adjustments based on tax laws after 1986. Contributions are the deductions claimed, which includes carryovers from prior years and excludes nondeductible contributions in excess of percentage limitations. Dollar amounts are mean values.

Source: Internal Revenue Service, Statistics of Income as reported in Gerald Auten, Charles Clotfelter and Richard Schmalbeck, "Taxes and Philanthropy Among the Wealthy," in Joel Slemrod, editor, Does Atlas Shrug? The Economic Consequences of Taxing the Rich, (Russell Sage and Harvard University Press: New York and Cambridge, 2000). Updated March 2016 by Gerald Auten.

One needs to be cautious when interpreting data from any particular period. Individuals adjust their behavior only gradually in response to a change such as an increase in the after-tax cost of giving. For example, when tax rates change, individuals may take years to fully respond. Randolph (1995) finds that people are much more likely to adjust the timing of their giving up or down in response to what they believe are temporary changes in their tax rates, and hence in the after-tax cost of giving, than to changes they believe are permanent.[6]

Apart from changes in tax rates, a further complication is that the greater inequality in income after the mid-1970s has been attributed to a variety of factors that may separately influence giving. These include an increase in the number of two-earner couples where both spouses earn significant incomes and, at very high incomes, the appearance of a "winner-take-all" economy. Piketty (2014) wrote a popular but controversial book that argued that economic forces were leading the wealthy to get wealthier because of increases in the rate of return to capital.

Giving is responsive not just to incentives, but to the needs of the public and the intermediary charitable institutions. The needs of churches, research

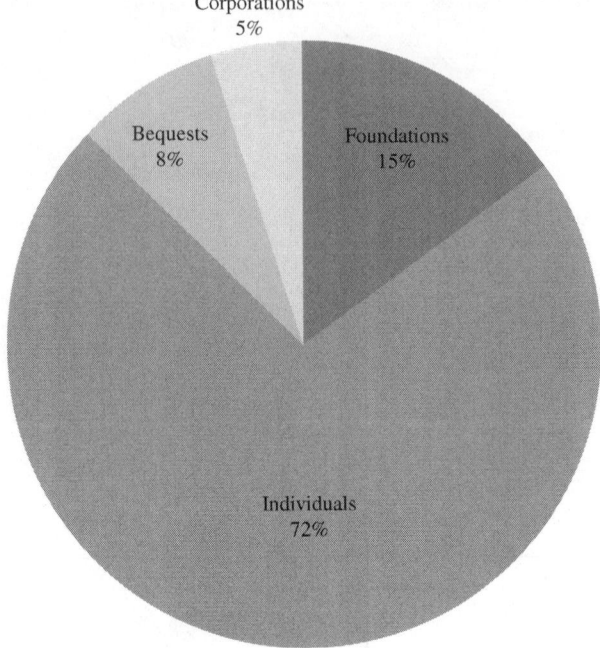

Figure 2.4 2014 Charitable Contributions by Source. *Source*: The Urban Institute (2016). Based on data from *Giving USA* (2015).

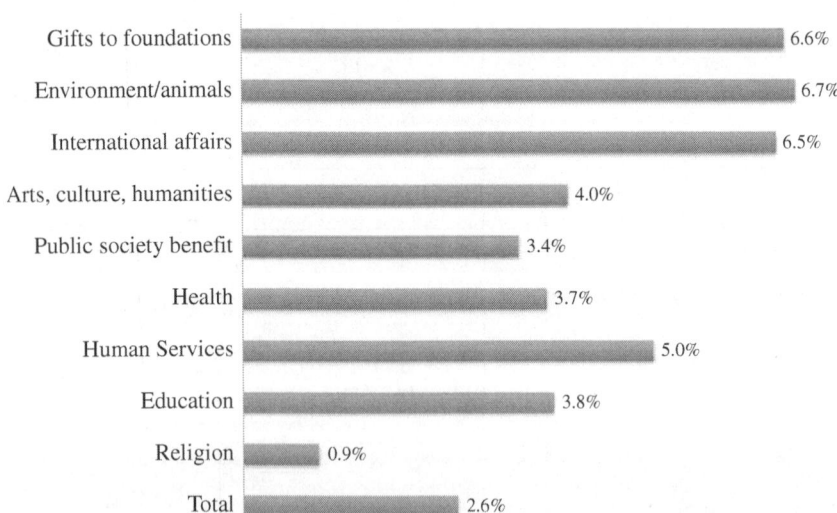

Figure 2.5 Average Annual Rates of Change in Private Contributions, 1989–2014. *Source*: The Urban Institute (2016). Based on data from *Giving USA* (2015).

and educational institutions, and other charities may be invariant (inelastic in economic terms). In effect, if taxpayers respond to lower incentives by giving less, then the demand for giving becomes more pressing and offsets some of the decline in the supply of giving that might otherwise occur. That would explain how changes in incentives might shift who gives, while resulting in little or no changes in total giving. Kent Smetters was the first to develop a formal model that predicts behaviors consistent with some patterns we currently see in the data.[7]

If one were to compare the growth in the government's social welfare spending as a share of income over recent decades with the relative constancy of charitable giving as a share of income, it would imply that almost no displacement took place. That is consistent with Richard Steinberg's 1996 estimate that the rate of displacement ranges from 1 to 10 percent (Steinberg 1996). But there's a catch. An estimate on aggregate giving does not tell us what may have happened over time by subsector, or by charity. If government activity displaces one type of charitable effort but enhances another, for instance, the combined effect may show up as no net displacement of total charitable activity even though the effect on each effort may be substantial. People may give less to the poor elderly today, for instance, because there are relatively fewer of them, but they may still give equal shares of their income to poorer classes of society. The decline in giving to health organizations already noted may well be one consequence of the large government presence in that sector.

Volunteer Time

Contributions of volunteer time significantly leverage the resources available to the nonprofits (see table 2.2). In 2014, 62.8 million people volunteered an estimated 8.7 billion hours, conservatively valued at $179.2 billion (McKeever 2015). When contributions of time and foregone earnings are added, donations made to the nonprofits are much larger than they appear when only monetary contributions are taken into account.

That is not to imply that the government does not receive volunteer support. For example, educational or youth service volunteering, much of which is spent at public schools, accounted for 25.5 percent of volunteering in 2015 (Bureau of Labor Statistics 2016). Still, the vast bulk of volunteer effort—about 70 percent—is transmitted through nonprofits (Weitzman et al. 2002). One complication with volunteering data is that it depends upon involvement with formal institutions. For example, while the Bureau of Labor Statistics estimates that in 2015, whites volunteered at a rate of 26.4 percent; blacks, 19.3 percent; Asians, 17.9 percent; and Hispanics, 15.5 percent, those differentials may well reflect the greater presence of nonprofits in some

Table 2.2 Employment and Volunteering in the Nonprofit Sector

	1977	1987	1992	1997	2002	2008	2012
Paid employees, full time and part time (percent of labor force)	5.3	5.7	6.6	6.4	6.4	7.0	7.4
Volunteers, full-time employee equivalent (percent of labor force)	3.1	3.9	4.0	4.7*	4.5	3.0	3.2

*Figure is for 1998.
Note: The volunteer data are based on several different sources and may not be completely comparable throughout all years. The results for paid employees as a percentage of the labor force differ from Figure 2.2 because the labor force here includes workers not covered by unemployment insurance, whereas Figure 2.2 does. See footnote 3.
Sources: Weitzman et al. 2002; Economic Census, 1977, 1987, 1992, 1997, 2002, 2008, and 2013; Current Population Survey; *Monthly Labor Review*, August 2003 and authors estimates; Giving and Volunteering in the United States, 2001, Independent Sector; *Nonprofit Sector in Brief 2015*.

communities than in others and the degree of family, rather than institutional, involvement (Bureau of Labor Statistics 2016). Volunteering has also varied over history (see chapter 1 by Young and Casey, this volume).[8]

Comparability of the Two Sectors in Terms of Spending

Measuring resources in terms of total spending rather than individual transfers of money brings the relative size of the nonprofit sector and government closer together.

- Spending by nonprofits and government appears more comparable in size, in part because the nonprofit sector is a major contractor or intermediary for both government and for businesses.
- Due partly to this contracting, employment by the nonprofit sector as a share of total employment increased by almost exactly the amount as the decline in government employment from 1974 to 2014.

As opposed to spending financed by private contributions versus taxes, total spending by the nonprofit sector comes somewhat closer in size to that of government (see figure 2.3). What accounts for this magnified measure of nonprofit sector activity? The nonprofit sector does not finance all or even a majority of its activities exclusively from charitable donations of money and time; it also charges for many of its activities, especially in such areas as health, education, and social services. In turn, the government often works through other sectors to achieve its goals. Perhaps the best examples of government money flowing through nonprofit organizations are grants for nonprofit institutions of higher education and payments for Medicare and Medicaid services through nonprofit hospitals.

One of the more interesting and telling recent institutional changes has been the growth in nonprofit sector employment, from 7.3 to 8.7 percent of all employment covered by unemployment insurance between 1977 and 2012 (see figure 2.2). Interestingly, that growth is almost of the same order of magnitude as the decline in the government sector from 18.3 to 16.0 percent of all employment. Many government officials like to proclaim their success at reducing the government's size and point in particular to the decline in the direct employment of individuals. In truth, what has occurred in large part is that the government has increasingly paid others to perform the work it finances.

Outsourcing or contracting for services has not simply been a result of "reinvention" of government—for example, finding private garbage disposal companies to displace public employees. Instead, the large growth in government spending for services, particularly health care, that were always "contracted out" dominates the figures. Doctors, nurses, and others increasingly have had to view themselves as service providers for government insurance payments. Their work for the government has in a sense displaced others' work in areas where government activity has declined—defense being the most obvious example for the post–World War II period, despite temporary increases during Vietnam, the second Iraqi conflict, and other conflicts.

Table 2.3 shows the size and growth of revenue sources for various subsectors of operating charities from 1989 to 2012. As the table shows, program service revenues, including fee-for-service revenues, dominate, particularly in health but also in education and social services. Approximately 89 percent of total revenues, including investment income, for health organizations came from program service revenues. By contrast, program service revenues are relatively unimportant in international affairs, religion-related programs (that report to the IRS), environment, public and societal benefit, and arts and culture. For these organizations combined, just 24 percent of total revenues were from program services. The table also shows that government grants have grown at about the pace of private sector contributions.[9]

It is hard to determine the extent to which these past trends and relationships will continue. The amount that can be produced under government contracts must, by its nature, be less than the total production in the economy, so the government's contract growth rate depends upon the economy's growth rate, the corresponding growth rate in government revenues, and the share of those revenues government distributes through contracts.

THE IMPACT OF FEDERAL SPENDING CHANGES ON NONPROFIT ORGANIZATIONS

Federal spending has two kinds of impacts on nonprofits, affecting both the *demand* for nonprofit services and the ability of nonprofits to *supply*

Table 2.3 Government Grants, Private Sector Contributions, and Program Service Revenues by Nonprofit Subsector (In Billions of 2015 Dollars)

	Government Grants			Program Service Revenue			Private Sector Contributions		
	1989	2012	% Change	1989	2012	% Change	1989	2012	% Change
Arts, culture, and humanities	3	5	88	5	12	146	6	14	151
Education	17	47	172	73	214	191	21	49	137
Environment	0.3	2	761	1	5	286	2	8	362
Health	10	29	183	326	919	181	13	27	112
Human services	19	48	148	33	122	268	12	39	225
International	3	13	410	1	5	226	4	18	312
Mutual benefit	0.0	0.1	167	12	2	−84	0.1	0.1	0
Public and societal benefit	5	16	218	10	22	126	13	39	213
Religion	0.0	0.1	2209	2	3	91	3	7	155
Unknown	0.1	0.0	−100	0.2	0.0	−97	0.0	0.0	−100
Total	57	160	179	464	1302	181	73	203	178

Sources: IRS Statistics of Income Division Exempt Organizations Sample for Public Charities, 1989 and 2012. The Urban Institute, NCCS National Nonprofit Research Database, Special 2003 Research Version; Bureau of Economic Analysis, NIPA Table 1.1.9, August 2015.

these services. The demand effects result from the fact that federal spending affects the level of unmet need in society. For instance, at any given level of need, when federal spending for the Supplemental Nutrition Assistance Program (SNAP, formerly the Food Stamp program) declines, more needy individuals are likely to turn to nonprofit soup kitchens for assistance. We can refer to these as the *indirect* effects of federal budget decisions on nonprofit organizations.

However, because the federal government often finances delivery of services directly through nonprofits, the same budget cuts that increase the need for nonprofit services can also decrease the ability of these organizations to meet this need. We refer to these as the *direct* effects of federal budget decisions on nonprofit organizations. Because only a portion of federal spending in most fields flows through nonprofit organizations, the indirect effects are likely to be larger in overall size than the direct effects, but both are important and will be examined here.

To assess these effects, we have analyzed federal spending on more than 100 programs in fields where nonprofit organizations are active, such as social services, health, education, income assistance, international development, and the arts. Our analysis considered both overall spending in these programs—which affects the need for nonprofit services (i.e., the indirect effect)—as well as program spending that flowed to nonprofit organizations to deliver assistance through these programs—which affects the ability of nonprofits to supply services (i.e., the direct effect). In this section, we examine both of these effects, in historical perspective going back to 1980 as well as in terms of possible future trends over the next several years. Underlying the analysis are several caveats:

- First, the focus is on spending policies only and not on the broader array of impacts that government has on the nonprofit sector through its regulatory, credit, tax expenditure, and other programs.
- Second, our focus here is on federal government policies only and not those of state and local governments, though we do track the flow of federal funds through state and local governments and on to nonprofit organizations. One reason for this restricted focus is the absence of comprehensive data on combined state and local spending and its effects on nonprofit organizations. Even to assess the flow of federal support to nonprofit organizations, we have had to develop our own estimates based on detailed scrutiny of program records and other sources.[10]
- Third, we use FY 1980 as the "base year" for this analysis even though it was far from the high point of federal spending for many programs of interest to nonprofit organizations. As the year prior to the onset of a significant round of deficit reduction agreements, 1980 seemed an appropriate

basis for comparison, though meaningful budget paring in many budget programs began prior to 1980.
- Fourth, the analysis in these pages uses federal spending data at the level of "budget functions." Overall, the federal budget is divided into twenty major functions. Included in this analysis are the functions covering international affairs (150); community and regional development (450); education, training, employment, and social services (500); health (550); Medicare (570); and income security (600). Program-level information was also obtained from federal budget documents for federal Medicaid spending. An adjustment was made to add back in to Medicare outlays the deduction that the budget records for Medicare premiums payments.
- Fifth, all spending amounts are adjusted for inflation and expressed in constant FY 2015 dollars. The GDP deflator is used for all programs except health programs for which we used the CPI-U medical care.
- Finally, no independent attempt is made here to assess the changing level of societal needs during the period. Obviously, if needs decline, reductions in government spending may be justified, whereas if they grow, reductions may be problematic.

Federal Spending and the Need for Nonprofit Services: The "Demand Effect"

As reflected in table 2.4, when expressed in FY 2015 dollars, federal spending on the major programs of interest to nonprofit organizations accounted for outlays of $713.4 billion as of FY 1980.[11] By comparison, total federal expenditures in that year amounted to $1.8 trillion after adjusting for inflation. In other words, slightly less than 40 percent of all federal expenditures in FY 1980 went to programs identified here as being especially relevant to nonprofit organizations.

Of this $713.4 billion in spending, approximately half consisted of health care expenditures, chiefly for Medicare and Medicaid, the large federal health finance programs for the elderly and the poor, respectively. Another 30 percent represented income assistance payments, including SNAP (Food Stamps), housing vouchers, and welfare aid. Spending for education, training, employment, and social services accounted for another 10 percent. Outlays for international aid and community and regional development made up the remaining 10 percent.

Aggregate Changes, FY 1980 to FY 2015. Between FY 1980 and FY 2015, overall federal spending on these programs of interest to nonprofits increased from $713.4 billion in FY 1980 to $1.8 trillion in FY 2015. Over the thirty-five-year period, FY 1981–2015, inflation-adjusted spending was

Table 2.4 Federal Spending in Program Areas where Nonprofits Are Active, FY 1980–2015 (In Billions of Constant FY 2015 Dollars)

			Excluding Medicare and Medicaid		Excluding Medicare, Medicaid, and Income Assistance		Federal Spending as % of GDP
	All programs		Change from FY 1980		Change from FY 1980		
Fiscal year	Outlays	Change from FY 1980	Amount	Percent	Amount	Percent	FY 1980 = 100
1980	713						100
1981	742	29	1	0	(11)	−6	92
1982	718	5	(32)	−8	(46)	−23	74
1983	733	19	(24)	−6	(59)	−30	67
1984	718	5	(46)	−11	(53)	−27	66
1985	766	53	(23)	−5	(53)	−27	64
1986	738	25	(51)	−12	(60)	−30	59
1987	735	21	(59)	−14	(69)	−35	52
1988	746	33	(54)	−13	(68)	−35	51
1989	762	48	(51)	−12	(69)	−35	49
1990	812	98	(24)	−6	(52)	−26	55
1991	859	146	11	3	(47)	−24	58
1992	942	228	51	12	(43)	−22	58
1993	982	268	71	17	(32)	−16	62
1994	1,004	291	68	16	(38)	−19	57
1995	1,043	330	80	19	(29)	−15	59
1996	1,050	336	72	17	(39)	−20	54
1997	1,075	361	76	18	(37)	−19	52
1998	1,071	358	74	18	(39)	−20	50
1999	1,072	358	84	20	(31)	−16	50
2000	1,094	381	99	24	(24)	−12	50
2001	1,148	435	123	29	(14)	−7	52
2002	1,255	542	204	49	17	9	61
2003	1,332	619	255	61	48	24	69
2004	1,359	646	252	61	58	29	69
2005	1,422	708	287	69	89	45	76
2006	1,489	775	327	79	135	69	86
2007	1,479	765	266	64	70	35	68
2008	1,541	828	321	77	61	31	65
2009	1,733	1,019	429	103	62	31	68
2010	1,914	1,201	588	142	129	66	85
2011	1,857	1,144	513	123	94	48	75
2012	1,701	988	427	103	78	40	70
2013	1,690	976	391	94	57	29	64
2014	1,709	995	376	90	74	38	67
2015	1,812	1,099	417	100	127	64	78
TOTAL	41,103	16,132	5,500	38	186	3	66

Source: U.S. Office of Management and Budget, 2016. *Budget of the United States Government: Fiscal Year 2017, Historical Tables.* Washington, DC: OMB.
GDP = gross domestic product.

a cumulative total of $16.1 trillion above what it would have been had FY 1980 levels been maintained for each of those thirty-five years (see table 2.4). However, this aggregate picture is somewhat misleading because it is heavily affected by the inclusion of the two large federal health programs, Medicare and Medicaid, which grew significantly through this period. Outside of Medicare and Medicaid, the cumulative gain was a much smaller $5.5 trillion. And if income assistance, comprised mostly of entitlement programs, is also excluded, the remaining programs experienced a cumulative thirty-five-year gain of only $185.7 billion, or roughly 3 percent.

Much of the increase in federal spending outside of Medicare and Medicaid took place, moreover, only in the latter part of the period after 2000. Prior to this, federal spending on these programs, after adjusting for inflation, remained below or only modestly above FY 1980 levels. In fact, outside of the major entitlement programs in health and income assistance, federal spending did not return to its FY 1980 level in real terms until FY 2002, as indicated in table 2.4.

Because the country's GDP was rising during this period, federal spending on programs of interest to nonprofit organizations outside of Medicare, Medicaid, and income assistance fell through much of this period as a share of the country's GDP, ending up as of FY 2015 at only 78 percent of its FY 1980 value, as table 2.4 also shows.

Breakdown by Functional Areas. As shown in table 2.5, the direction and level of federal spending changes between FY 1980 and FY 2015 varied considerably by program area:

- The *community and regional development* area absorbed the heaviest reductions in federal spending during this period. Spending in this field remained well below the FY 1980 baseline level of $28.4 billion for much of the FY 1981–2015 period. In fact, the value of federal spending in this area was a cumulative total of $294.4 billion lower over the thirty-five years, FY 1981–2015, than it would have been had FY 1980 spending levels been maintained. Measured as a share of GDP, federal spending in this area as of FY 2015 was only 29 percent as great as it was in FY 1980.
- Federal spending on *international assistance* programs grew by 51 percent between FY 1980 and FY 2015. However, during much of the period spending was below FY 1980 levels, so that international assistance programs actually experienced a cumulative loss of $61.2 billion over the thirty-five-year period. Moreover, expressed as a share of GDP, international assistance spending as of FY 2015 was just 60 percent of what it was in FY 1980.
- Federal outlays for *education, training, employment, and social services* increased from $80.4 billion in FY 1980 to $122.1 billion in FY 2015.

Table 2.5 Federal Outlays by Program Area, 1980 and 2015 (In Billions of Constant FY 2015 Dollars)

Program Area	Outlays FY 1980	Outlays FY 2015	Change, FY 2015 vs. FY 1980 Amount	Change, FY 2015 vs. FY 1980 Percent	Cumulative Change, FY 1981–2015 vs. FY 1980 Level	FY 2015 Outlays as a Percent of GDP (FY 1980 = 100)
International assistance	32	49	16.4	51	−61	60
Community and regional development	28	21	−7.8	−27	−294	29
Education, training, employment, and social service	80	122	41.6	52	26	60
Health	354	1,112	758.4	214	11,148	300
Income assistance	219	509	290.1	133	5,314	92
TOTAL	713	1,812	1,098.8	154	16,132	142
TOTAL, excluding Medicare and Medicaid	416	833	416.9	100	5,500	86
TOTAL, excluding Medicare, Medicaid, and income assistance	197	324	126.8	64	186	78

Source: U.S. Office of Management and Budget, 2016. *Budget of the United States Government: Fiscal Year 2017, Historical Tables.* Washington, DC: OMB.
GDP = gross domestic product.

However, because of spending reductions between FY 1980 and FY 2015, outlays in this area rose by only a cumulative total of $25.6 billion over the thirty-five-year period. As of FY 2015, spending was only 60 percent of what it was in FY 1980 when expressed as a percent of GDP.
- In contrast, spending for *health* and *income assistance* programs increased significantly during FY 1981–2015 over FY 1980 levels. Spending for Medicaid quadrupled between FY 1980 and FY 2015; spending for Medicare tripled; and spending for other health programs and income assistance activities more than doubled. However, despite the increases in income assistance programs, FY 2015 outlays for these programs were still only 92 percent of what they were in FY 1980 when expressed as a percent of GDP.

In sum, federal spending in program areas of concern to nonprofits declined or grew modestly in the 1980s and 1990s but subsequently recovered, so that by FY 2015 combined federal outlays in these areas were 154 percent above FY 1980 levels. However, this overall trend hides the very different spending histories of the various program fields. Medicare, Medicaid, and some other health and income assistance programs expanded rapidly throughout much of the FY 1981–2015 period. However, excluding Medicare, Medicaid, and income assistance programs, spending for the many other programs of interest to nonprofits lost significant ground, especially as a share of GDP, while even income assistance did not keep fully apace. This suggests increased pressures on many nonprofit organizations during this period to respond to social and economic needs, especially in program areas where federal resources were withdrawn.

Federal Spending and Support for Nonprofit Organizations: The "Supply Effect"

Changes in overall federal spending during FY 1981–2015 in programs of interest to nonprofits affect not only the need for nonprofit services but also the revenues these organizations receive from federal programs and hence their ability to meet this need.

As reported in table 2.6 overall, federal support of private nonprofit organizations grew both in absolute terms and as a share of GDP between FY 1980 and FY 2015.[12] As of FY 2015, federal support of nonprofit organizations was 187 percent higher than it was in FY 1980 after adjusting for inflation. Measured as a share of GDP, such support as of FY 2015 was moderately higher at 114 percent of what it had been in FY 1980.

However, these aggregate data mask two strikingly different trends in federal support—one for health and health-related institutions and the other for all other types of nonprofit organizations.

So far as health institutions are concerned, growth in federal Medicare, Medicaid, and other health spending significantly boosted federal support.

Table 2.6 Spending by the Nonprofit Sector, 1980 and 2015 (In Billions of Constant FY 2015 Dollars)

Program Area	Amount		Change, FY 2015 vs. FY 1980		Cumulative Change, FY 1981–2015 vs. FY 1980 Level	FY 2015 Support as a Percent of GDP (FY 1980 = 100)
	FY 1980	FY 2015	Amount	Percent		
International assistance	2	3	1	51	−4	60
Community and regional development	2	1	−1	−27	−21	29
Education, training, employment, and social services	22	33	11	52	7	60
Health	148	460	312	243	4,679	297
TOTAL	174	497	324	187	4,662	114
TOTAL, excluding Medicare and Medicaid	45	82	38	84	158	73

Source: U.S. Office of Management and Budget. 2015. *Budget of the United States Government: Fiscal Year 2017, Historical Tables*. Washington, DC: OMB; and authors' calculations.

Between FY 1980 and FY 2015, federal support to nonprofit organizations in the health field multiplied enough that it more than doubled as a share of GDP.

Outside of the health field, however, federal funding of nonprofit organizations grew much less robustly during FY 1981–2015. In fact, for the first two decades of this period, such support remained below its FY 1980 level and only surpassed it after FY 2000. By FY 2015, support for nonprofit organizations through these other programs stood 84 percent above its FY 1980 level. Even so, measured as a share of GDP, such support was still only 73 percent of its FY 1980 level as of FY 2015. Reflecting the long period of budget constraint, nonprofit revenues from federal international assistance; community and regional development; and education, training, employment, and social services programs experienced cumulative losses or only modest gains during the thirty-five years, FY 1981–2015.

Federal Spending and Nonprofit Organizations: Outlook for the Future

The first decade of the 2000s saw substantial increases in federal spending in fields where nonprofit organizations are active and in federal support to nonprofit organizations after twenty years of cuts or modest growth, at least outside of health and income assistance. However, as noted in previous sections, recent years have seen a return to some measure of fiscal stringency outside of areas like health and retirement. And it has occurred among both political parties. For instance, President Obama's FY 2017 budget proposals would reduce inflation-adjusted federal spending on programs of interest to nonprofit organizations outside of health and income assistance by 35 percent between FY 2015 and FY 2021, without taking into account unallocated cuts in nonsecurity spending that would be required to meet budget caps. This would cut $10.2 billion out of the revenue stream that these organizations would receive over the period FY 2016–2021 if FY 2015 spending levels were maintained.

DIVERSITY OF THE NONPROFIT SECTOR

Measures of resources available to all nonprofit organizations disguise the great diversity of the nonprofit sector.

The nonprofit sector is diverse and heterogeneous; its characteristics are sometimes hidden when viewing figures on aggregate size, which are dominated by the large health and education subsectors and, within each subsector, by the largest organizations. Among public charities that reported information about their finances and operations on the IRS Form 990 in

2013, organizations with more than $10 million in expenses make up a mere 4 percent of total organizations but have 82 percent of the total assets and 87 percent of the expenses. Correspondingly, 74 percent of organizations (those with less than $500,000 in expenses) had less than 2 percent of the total expenses and 4 percent of the total assets. Indeed, much nonprofit activity may not be reflected here at all. If a group of volunteers organizes and has little or no financing, it may not even establish itself as a legal organization, much less file with any government agency. Note also that subsectors with larger institutions, such as the higher education and hospital sectors, show up with smaller percentages of total organizations than their percentages of total expenses and assets, whereas other subsectors, such as arts and culture or social services, have a much larger share of total organizations than they do of total expenses or assets (see figure I.2).

There are a variety of ways of disaggregating to get a better view of the nonprofit sector's component parts. Figure 2.6 shows the distribution revenues by different subsectors of the charitable sector. In 2013, health services garnered about 59 percent of revenues, including assets and public support. The international and foreign affairs subsector is relatively small relative to health or higher education, but it has the greatest relative dependence on private sector contributions (table 2.3).

As we just read, when examining changes in federal financing in areas of interest to nonprofits, researchers must be careful to distinguish claims made about the entire sector from claims about its various subsectors. What may happen to social services, for example, may be very different from what happens to health services.

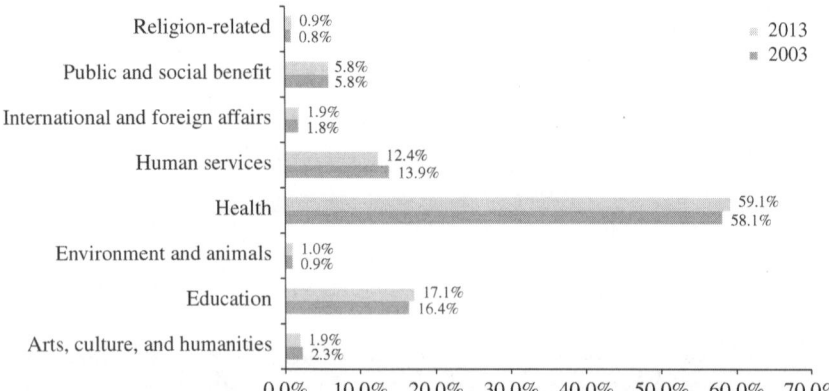

Figure 2.6 Share of Total Funds for Selected Public Charity Subsectors (percent). *Note*: Subtotals may not sum to totals because of rounding. *Source*: Urban Institute, National Center for Charitable Statistics, Core Files (Public Charities, 2003 and 2013).

Trends in government and nonprofit spending on health care demonstrate the different ways in which shifts in government policy can affect nonprofit organizations. Consider the ways that Medicare and Medicaid growth are projected to continue to dominate almost all uses of new government revenues (Steuerle 2014). Those payments go not only to nonprofit organizations (mainly nonprofit hospitals, but increasingly to other types of nonprofits) but also to profit-making organizations such as doctors' offices. Government recently has put larger shares of its money into doctor services not provided in hospital settings (e.g., by putting money into Medicare Part B, rather than Hospital Insurance or Medicare Part A). It is motivated both to save money (e.g., by discouraging expensive hospital stays) and to obscure revenue flows to meet arbitrary budget accounting standard rules. For example, Medicare hospital payments are paid out of a fund that depends on Social Security Health Insurance taxes and thus is threatened with a shortfall, while Medicare outpatient care is paid mainly out of general revenues, for which no shortfall is measured; switching the location of payment thus allows the trust fund to appear to be more in balance.

One consequence of a simple shift to outpatient care, even if the same services and personnel are involved, is that fewer funds flow through nonprofit hospitals and more funds flow directly through doctors' offices. Another shift can occur when hospitals move to profit-making status. It does not follow, however, that there will be a net loss in "charitable" activity simply because fewer receipts flow through nonprofit hospitals. Such activity could fall if the charitable contributions or free care given to low-income patients decline when services move out of hospitals into doctors' offices or other settings defined as "profit-making."

CONCLUSION

In recent decades, the government and the nonprofit sectors have often acted more as complements than substitutes in many activities. When one considers the relatively constant rate of charitable contributions out of personal income and the growth in shares of total output and employment by the nonprofit sector—all of which occurred during a period of rising social welfare spending (including Medicare and Medicaid) by government—it is hard to argue that increased government activity has displaced private nonprofit activity in any aggregate sense. Indeed, one of the most important aspects of the modern relationship between the sectors is the way that the government has increasingly turned to the nonprofit sector to serve as an intermediary or contractor in providing many public services (see chapter 3 by Steven Rathgeb Smith).

Although more government social welfare spending does not appear to have crowded out nonprofit activity in the aggregate, there has nonetheless been both significant displacement and reorientation of specific nonprofit activities over time. For example, the very large government role in health and retirement programs for the elderly probably has displaced much cash or housing assistance to the old that would have otherwise occurred. The movement toward foster care helped reduce the use of orphanages. Large government subsidies for health care have probably reduced charitable contributions to hospitals. The expansion of public schooling coincided historically with the decline in the percentage of children attending religious schools. In each of those cases, of course, other factors are also at play, but, clearly, when government meets a need, private efforts often shift focus within the nonprofit sector. At the same time, the decline in federal efforts in many areas outside of health and retirement may well have "crowded in" higher levels of activity by nonprofits.

In effect, what is observed can be better described as "replacement" rather than "displacement." A relatively constant share of income earmarked for contributions implies that the activities such contributions finance will rise at about the rate of growth in the economy. Since the nature of charitable activities is changing, the further implication is that the public will "replace" support for some "old" activities with support for "new" efforts. In other words, a decrease in the rate of giving to one activity often means an increase in rate of giving to another.

Returning to a point made at the start of this chapter, one should not be surprised to find that what looks like a "crowding out" of nonprofits may represent shifting priorities. Recall that theoretically there is no *a priori* reason why government activity should necessarily displace nonprofit activity. The two sectors merely satisfy a range of social needs, acting as both substitutes and complements in fulfilling those needs. More government spending on education, for instance, could either substitute for private and nonprofit spending or add to the demand for scholarship funds. In the United States, as well, the long social history of complementary efforts (chapter 1 by Young and Casey, this volume) has a powerful effect on how the sectors evolve together; such patterns likely differ in other countries, particularly those with a weaker history of voluntary activity and greater dependence upon government to lead.

To think that all past trends, whether short or long, will continue would be a mistake. For example, the federal government's social welfare budget may continue to grow faster than the economy, but social security and health care are scheduled to garner the lion's share of that growth. Yet, even within health care, there are significant pressures to subsidize organizations with better cost controls, which could over time include or exclude the nonprofit portion of the sector. If there is less emphasis on hospitals and more on outpatient care, contracts may shift more into profit-making settings. The latter movement could also reduce the relative size of nonprofit hospitals simply because more dollars flow directly to doctors or profit-making hospitals.

At the same time, we have seen how federal spending in other program areas of interest to many nonprofits has declined significantly as a share of the economy. Remember that government social welfare spending is well in excess of ten times charitable contributions, and a significant portion of it is paid out in the form of fees and program service revenues to nonprofits. A government shift in what it finances, therefore, may well crowd in and crowd out where private contributors put their money, but there is no way that donors will replace any large decline in government funding.

No matter how measured, the growth of the nonprofit sector and of many of its program areas is likely to vary over time relative to the growth in government and the economy. Whether the consequence is positive or negative cannot be determined without a specific examination of each change, a broad concept of social welfare, and an examination of the combined changes in all sectors—nonprofit, government, business, and household.

NOTES

1. Admittedly, government often makes exceptions to a uniformity standard, but only at the cost of inequity and a disgruntled citizenry. For example, queues, which define who is the "next" eligible beneficiary in a precise legal fashion, are used in housing and other programs even though this process is applied arbitrarily.

2. The share of the nation's labor force employed by the nonprofit sector can be measured several different ways. Here, we consider the Census Bureau's analysis of employment in the nonprofit sector, which includes only employees covered by unemployment insurance. Later in this chapter, we consider the entire labor force, including those workers not covered by unemployment insurance, which adds over 20 million workers, most of whom are self-employed, members of the armed services, or agricultural workers, putting the share of nonprofit employment in the labor force at 7.4 percent. The *Nonprofit Alamanac 2012*, a publication of the Center for Nonprofits and Philanthropy, considered the number of nonprofit employees using tax, census, and Department of Labor data to place nonprofit employees at 10.6 percent of the workforce in 2010, with workforce defined as nonfarm employees.

3. The Federal Reserve's flow of funds data in figure 2.2 does not separate nonprofits' assets from households' assets. Measures of assets do not incorporate liabilities.

4. In general, national income accounts exclude the value of all services and goods produced in the home and not sold in the market.

5. These changes in incentives are not examined here in any depth. On the one hand, removing matching grants may make states more efficient in spending their

money. With no match, when they spend a dollar, it costs them a dollar. On the other hand, some argue that fear of having too high a tax rate relative to neighboring states creates a "race to the bottom" where states bow out of providing much social welfare. Still another issue is whether any federal minimum—such as the earned income tax credit, food stamps, and Medicaid might provide—might not already deal with many of these interstate equity and efficiency issues.

6. The expected difference in response is similar to how people might be expected to act if, say, Macy's announced it would offer a 50 percent discount on all purchases made between Christmas and New Year's but offered no discount thereafter. Shoppers could be expected to respond to this "once in a lifetime" chance by shifting purchases of goods they might have made in future years to the "sale year." That would magnify their spending in the sale year and cut into sales in subsequent years. Economists believe that people will respond to temporary changes in tax incentives in a similar fashion. For example, if people have tax rates that in one year are likely to be unusually high, their tax accountants would advise them to shift charitable contributions and other deductions to that year. That produces an exaggerated increase in charitable contributions in the year in which the tax rate is temporarily high (and hence when the net cost of giving is temporarily low).

7. Kent Smetters, "A Free-Rider Explanation of the Charitable Giving Puzzles of the 1980s and an Application to Fundamental Tax Reform," unpublished paper.

8. Longer-term forces affect the availability of volunteers. For example, not too long ago, a nation of farmers had limited time and resources to gather in formal volunteer activity even though interfamily cooperation may have been intensive. With urbanization came many demands, often met by generous increases in the volunteer efforts of women who were not always working at paid jobs, but worked instead through the home and volunteer associations (see, e.g., McCarthy 1982; Scott 1992). On the other hand, recent decades have seen a greater concentration of work, especially by women, in the formal marketplace and a lesser concentration of work among the many near-elderly and elderly who now typically retire almost two decades before their expected year of death.

9. Congregations and aligned organizations are not required to report to the IRS, although some do. Government grants are as reported on Form 990. Finally, note that private contributions include corporate and corporate foundation gifts.

10. These estimates were based on detailed examination of programmatic data, scrutiny of existing program evaluations, and extensive discussions with program managers at the federal, state, and local levels. Our estimates of federal support flowing to nonprofits include funds that flow directly from the federal government to nonprofit organizations, as well as federal funds that flow indirectly through state and local government or other entities to nonprofits.

11. We focus here on "outlays" as our measure of spending even though when Congress allocates money to a program, it formally makes an "appropriation" or grant of "budget authority" to the program. Ultimately, however, it is not the grant of budget authority but the actual outlays of money that make the difference on the ground. Also, it often takes well over a year for changes in budget authority to show up as changes in outlays.

12. See Salamon and Abramson (1981) for more detail on the procedure for estimating nonprofit revenues from federal programs.

REFERENCES

Allard, Scott W. 2009. *Out of Reach: Place, Poverty, and the New American Welfare State*. New Haven, CT: Yale University Press.
Auten, Gerald E., Charles Clotfelter, and Richard Schmalbeck. 2000. "Taxes and Philanthropy Among the Wealthy." *Does Atlas Shrug? The Economic Consequences of Taxing the Rich*. Joel Slemrod, ed. (pp. 392–424). Cambridge, MA: Harvard University Press.
Bixby, Ann Kallman. 1990. "Public social welfare expenditures, fiscal years 1965–87." *Social Security Bulletin* 53: 10.
Butler, Amy. 2009. "Wages in the Nonprofit Sector: Healthcare, Personal Care, and Social Service Occupations." Washington, DC: Bureau of Labor Statistics.
Bureau of Labor Statistics. 2016. "Volunteering in the United States–2015." Washington, DC: Bureau of Labor Statistics.
Clerkin, Richard M., and Kirsten A. Grønbjerg. 2007. "The Capacities and Challenges of Faith-Based Human Service Organizations." *Public Administration Review* 67(1): 115–126.
Douglas, James. 1987. "Political Theories of Nonprofit Organization." *The Nonprofit Sector: A Research Handbook*. Walter Powell, ed. (pp. 43–54). New Haven, CT: Yale University Press.
Giving USA Foundation. 2015. *Giving USA: The Annual Report on Philanthropy for the Year 2014*. Chicago: Giving USA Foundation.
Marron, Donald and Eric Toder. 2012. "How Big is the Federal Government?" Washington, DC: Urban-Brookings Tax Policy Center.
McCarthy, Kathleen. 1982. *Noblesse Oblige*. Chicago: University of Chicago Press.
McKeever, Brice. 2015. "The Nonprofit Sector in Brief 2015: Public Charities, Giving, and Volunteering." Washington, DC: Urban Institute.
Pew Charitable Trusts. 2016. "Extended Family Support and Household Balance Sheets." Washington, DC: The Pew Charitable Trusts.
Piketty, Thomas. 2014. *Capital in the Twenty-First Century*. Cambridge, MA: Harvard University Press.
Quakenbush, Caleb and C. Eugene Steuerle. 2016. "Social Welfare Spending in the United States." Washington, DC: Urban Institute.
Randolph, William. 1995. "Dynamic Income, Progressive Taxes, and the Timing of Charitable Contributions." *Journal of Political Economy* 103(4): 709–738.
Roeger, Katie L., Amy S. Blackwood, and Sarah L. Pettijohn. 2012. *The Nonprofit Almanac 2012*. Washington, DC: The Urban Institute Press.
Sacks, Jonathan. 2015. *Not in God's Name: Confronting Religious Violence*. New York: Knopf Doubleday Publishing Group.
Scott, Ann Firor. 1992. *Natural Allies: Women's Associations in American History*. Urbana, IL: University of Illinois Press.

Steinberg, Richard. 1996. "Can Individual Donations Replace Cutbacks in Federal Social Welfare Spending?" in *Capacity for Change: The Nonprofit World in an Age of Devolution.* Dwight F. Burlingame, William A. Diaz, Warren F. Ilchman, and Associates, ed. (pp. 57–79). Indianapolis: Indiana Center on Philanthropy.

Steuerle, C. Eugene, Edward N. Gramlich, Hugh Heclo, and Demetra Smith Nightingale. 1998. *The Government We Deserve: Responsive Democracy and Changing Expectations.* Washington, DC: Urban Institute Press.

Steuerle, C. Eugene, Gillian Reynolds, and Adam Carasso. 2008. "How Much Does the Federal Government Spend to Promote Economic Mobility and For Whom?" Washington, DC: Economic Mobility Project, an initiative of the Pew Charitable Trusts.

Steuerle, C. Eugene. 2014. *Dead Men Ruling.* New York: The Century Foundation Press.

Weitzman, Murray, Nadine Jalandoni, Linda Lampkin, and Thomas Pollack. 2002. *The New Nonprofit Almanac and Desk Reference.* San Francisco: Jossey-Bass Publishers.

Wolpert, Julian. 1993. "Patterns of Generosity in America: Who's Holding the Safety Net?" New York: The Twentieth Century Fund Press.

Chapter 3

Cross-Sector Nonprofit-Government Financing

Steven Rathgeb Smith

Since the 1990s, major shifts have occurred in government financing of nonprofit organizations. Governments have adopted market-based policies emphasizing greater choice of service providers by government and citizens, leading to more contracting with nonprofits and increased utilization of other funding tools including vouchers and tax credits. The recession of 2008 led to widespread cutbacks in government funding for nonprofit organizations, with many agencies forced to reduce staff and programs. While funding has recovered in many states and localities, many nonprofits find a drastically altered funding landscape marked by competition, greater regulation, and a heightened focus on accountability and performance. At the same time, community-based nonprofits in education and health care find rising funding and support due to the expansion of charter schools and the implementation of the Affordable Care Act (ACA). The recession and its aftermath also abetted a marked shift in the structure of government funding for health and social service nonprofits, with more emphasis on individual-level subsidies including Medicaid, vouchers, and tax credits.

Great differences among policy fields also remain in the extent of government funding of nonprofits; thus, health and social service agencies are far more reliant on government funding, either direct or indirect, than arts or environmental nonprofits. Further, significant differences exist among different policy fields in the tools of government financing, so the arts, for example, rely more on grants and various tax credits and deductions in comparison to social, educational, or health nonprofits. Different financing tools then also affect the structure of the relationship between government and nonprofits, affecting the extent to which government and nonprofits engage in collaborative or conflictual behavior.

Government financing of nonprofits has also been profoundly influenced by the widespread interest in "social innovation"—a broad term typically referring to new programmatic strategies that integrate market principles and an outcome orientation. The Obama administration established a Social Innovation Fund (SIF) in partnership with leading national foundations to support promising social programs around the country. Many leading nonprofits including Teach for America, Roberts Enterprise Development Foundation (REDF), the Harlem Children's Zone, YouthBuild, and Nurse Family Partnership are regarded as good examples of effective social innovations. Many social innovations rely upon a mix of government funding, earned income through fees, and private philanthropy; thus, they are often complex public-private partnerships with multiple funding streams. In the process, the distinctive niche for government funding has eroded as public grants are pooled with philanthropic funds to support promising new programmatic initiatives by nonprofits. Indeed, recent developments in government financing would seem to challenge prevailing frameworks of the government-nonprofit relationship, particularly as they pertain to the independence and autonomy of nonprofits. Increasingly, philanthropic funds, as exemplified by SIF, reflect public priorities, and nonprofits are receiving support from a complex mix of public funds that require nonprofits to adapt their operations to new, less predictable funding streams.

This chapter focuses on the transformation of government financing of nonprofits in the last twenty-five years, including the growth of performance contracting and more direct and indirect subsidies to individuals who use nonprofit services. The management and policy implications of these important financing trends are also detailed and examined. In addition, the shifts in government financing are placed in the context of the development of the American welfare state and changes under way in the role of government. Recommended management and governance strategies for nonprofits to adopt in this increasingly turbulent environment are also discussed.

BACKGROUND

Government financial support of nonprofit organizations has a long tradition in the United States, dating to the colonial period when nonprofit institutions such as Harvard University received public subsidies (Smith and Lipsky 1993). Nonetheless, government funding of nonprofits remained very modest and targeted throughout the nineteenth century and into the twentieth century. It could also be temporary, as was evident in the 1930s when government funding of nonprofit relief organizations rose sharply, only to decline sharply after the Depression. The clear break in this historical pattern occurred in the 1960s. Fueled by extensive federal spending on many new social and health programs, government funding of nonprofit organizations across a range of policy fields—from child welfare to social services to the arts—rose sharply. A plethora of new nonprofit community organizations were established largely with federal funds, especially in the fields of social and health services, at least initially. These organizations included community action agencies, community mental health centers, neighborhood health centers, substance abuse treatment programs, battered women's shelters, rape crisis programs, and emergency shelters for runaway youth. Also, new federal health programs including Medicaid and Medicare were created.

In the early 1980s, the Reagan administration switched course and substantially reduced funding for many federal social programs (Bawden and Palmer 1984, p. 185; Bixby 1990, p. 14), including many grant programs funding nonprofits. Nonetheless, government funding for nonprofits eventually recovered and continued to grow, albeit unevenly, during the 1980s and 1990s. Many states and localities substituted their own funds for lost federal money, refinanced their contracts with nonprofit agencies, or reconfigured programs to maximize federal assistance by taking advantage of federal programs with increasing budgets. This shift is particularly apparent in such policy areas as mental health, developmental disabilities, child welfare, home health, and counseling, where state government increasingly tapped Medicaid to fund services previously funded through federal, state, and local categorical grant programs (Allard and Smith 2014).

In addition, federal funding for child care, immigrant assistance, and community development rose during this period as well. Nonprofit low-income housing agencies proliferated throughout the country, spurred in part by the federal Low-Income Housing Tax Credit (LIHTC) program enacted in 1986. Welfare reform enacted in 1996 by the Clinton administration also, at least initially, led to a rise in federal funding of services (as well as sharp declines in income support for welfare recipients [Gais, Dadayan, and Bae 2009; Falk 2014]). Many nonprofit social welfare agencies expanded their services in the late 1990s and early 2000s to provide an array of workforce-related services to welfare recipients. Overall, federal and state spending for social and health programs offered by nonprofit organizations increased during this period. Subsequently, many federal programs including Medicare, Medicaid, the Earned Income Tax Credit, and the Supplemental Nutrition Assistance Program (SNAP) have grown substantially (Falk 2014; Spar 2011). But many nonhealth programs of particular funding relevance to nonprofit organizations such as the Social Services Block Grant (SSBG) have declined or been essentially level funded, especially in recent years (Lynch 2014). Federal funding for child welfare services has also declined (DeVooght,

Fletcher, and Cooper 2014, p. 2). In addition, state government funding of key social programs declined during the 2000s after a period of sharp growth in the mid- to late 1990s (Gais, Dadayan, and Bae 2009). With the onset of the recession of 2008, many state governments dramatically cut funding for social programs, resulting in often sharp cutbacks in staffing and services by community-based nonprofit agencies (Krauskopf et al. 2009; National Council of Nonprofits 2010; Harrison, Eleveld, and Ahern 2011; Boris et al. 2010). As the economy has recovered, states have been able to replace some of the lost funding; nonetheless, the recovery has been very uneven with many states still struggling to fund their social and health programs (see, e.g., Palmer and Robertson 2016).

Unlike general social and health programs, government funding of nonprofits in other subfields, including cultural policy, health care, and education, has been flat or rising. Regarding the arts, public funding—which goes disproportionately to nonprofit arts organizations—increased between 1995 and 2015 by 26 percent in nominal dollars to $1.33 billion; yet, this figure represents a 15 percent decline adjusted for inflation (Stubbs and Clapp 2015; also see Lewis and Rushton 2007). More specifically, federal funding of the arts, primarily through the National Endowment of the Arts, has been essentially flat at $146 million after deep cuts in the mid-1990s. State government appropriations however were far higher at $349 million in FY 2014. But the biggest public funder of the arts is actually county and municipal government at $840 million (Stubbs and Clapp 2015). This local funding is often tied to economic development and tourism. Many municipalities have funded the renovation and expansion of local arts organizations throughout the country. Nonetheless, public funding remains a relatively small percentage of the operating budgets of most nonprofit arts organizations, unlike other policy fields such as social services (see Gronbjerg and Smith 2015). In addition, many local nonprofit arts agencies have faced sharp reductions in their public grants and subsidies due to the recession of 2008 and its aftermath. Total revenues for nonprofit arts and cultural organizations have declined in inflation-adjusted terms since 2008 (McKeever 2015).

Growth in Funding for Nonprofit Health Care and Education Organizations

Two notable exceptions exist to the overall trend of declining government funding support for nonprofit organizations. First, public health care spending has continued to rise in inflation-adjusted terms through the two major government health care programs: Medicare and Medicaid (Mitchell 2015; Falk 2014). Most funding is directed to acute care in nonprofit (and for-profit) hospitals. To a limited degree, Medicare also funds long-term care services, and it is the primary funder of hospice care (which is dominated by for-profit providers). Medicaid is the primary government funder of long-term care including nursing homes (Mitchell 2015). Most nursing homes are for-profit but nonprofits including national and regional chains remain a significant part of the nursing home market. Overall, the nonprofit subfield in nursing homes has continued to grow substantially in terms of revenues since 2003, despite the recession of 2008 (McKeever 2015); government revenues are a big factor in the continued growth of this field.

Less visibly, though, Medicaid has emerged as a central funder for community-based, nonprofit social service programs—a trend that dates to the 1980s. Cutbacks in federal and state funding programs like SSBG have accelerated this shift, particularly for services for the mentally ill, developmentally disabled, and at-risk youth. Medicaid expansion under ACA also provides very strong incentives to tap Medicaid since state governments can shift the cost of services largely to the federal government as the federal government will pay for up to 100 percent of the cost of expansion, at least initially (Snyder et al. 2016). For instance, in 1980, most public funding for services for the developmentally disabled came from state dollars, but because of Medicaid's Home and Community-Based Services waiver program, federal dollars (and the state match) through Medicaid are currently the primary funder for these services (Allard and Smith 2014; Braddock et al. 2015; Ng et al. 2015; Andrews et al. 2015). At the street level, this reliance on Medicaid for services to the developmentally disabled is vividly illustrated by the nonprofit agency, Banchero Disability Partners (BDP) based in Edmonds, Washington, and founded in 1971 by students at the University of Washington. This agency provides in-home case management and support services for the developmentally disabled. Currently, BDP receives almost 95 percent of its funding from state government. This funding is almost entirely through fee income from Medicaid. Many child welfare agencies providing foster care services have experienced a similar shift from reliance on state (and philanthropic dollars) to Medicaid since 1980. In general, the growth of Medicaid as a funder of social services is an important reason for the continued increase in total revenues for the nonprofit social services sector in recent years (see McKeever 2015).

Medicaid funding for community nonprofit health agencies has also increased sharply in the last few years because of the implementation of the ACA. The high-profile legislation offers significant federal subsidies to states that decide to expand eligibility for Medicaid. As of 2015, over half of the states have taken advantage of these subsidies and increased eligibility and services for low-income and disabled individuals (Snyder and Rudowitz 2015). This effort has in turn led to sharp rises in federal funding of community health centers and other related community health programs such as substance abuse clinics. More generally, the expansion of Medicaid has blurred the boundaries between health and social services. That is, community-based nonprofit social programs are now often quite reliant on funding from Medicaid and subject to their rules and regulations; many state governments require community social service programs to be Medicaid certified in order to receive state government grants and contracts. To be sure, the future of ACA is quite uncertain, especially given the polarized state of American politics; many states remain opposed to Medicaid expansion, for example. However, given the pressure for community-based health care programming, including community health centers, the importance of nonprofit community programs is likely to continue in the coming years.

The second policy field with growth in government financing of nonprofit organizations is education. Higher education institutions rely heavily upon indirect government subsidies such as student loans and bond financing. However, K-12 education has experienced a marked change in the mix of public, nonprofit, and for-profit institutions, albeit quite variably by state. As states have changed their laws to allow charter schools and, in some cases, indirect or direct subsidies of private schools, the number of charter schools—largely financed by government—has risen from 1542 in 1999–2000 to 6440 in 2013–2014 (Public Agenda 2014), although the number of students enrolled in charter schools is still less than 5 percent of all students (NCES 2015). Many of these charter schools are independent nonprofit schools, while over 30 percent of the total number of charter schools are managed by management companies including large nonprofit management entities like KIPP (Miron and Gulosino 2013). Importantly, the growth in nonprofit charters has occurred in the context of falling overall funding for K-12 education in many states (Leachman et al. 2016). The result for local nonprofits including charter schools is often underfunding and intense competition for resources.

In short, total government funding has been quite variable: continued growth in some programs, dramatic swings in funding due to the recession and its aftermath, and incremental spending increases (or decreases) in many other programs. This variability also masks the difficult straits of many nonprofits who have suffered severe cutbacks and funding reversals. Moreover, significant changes have been under way in the form of government funding via the diversification of the tools of government funding, with profound effects on the management of nonprofit organizations and their relationship to government and their communities. The next section focuses on this diversification.

THE DIVERSIFICATION OF GOVERNMENT FINANCING IN AN ERA OF ACCOUNTABILITY AND PERFORMANCE MANAGEMENT

Government financing of nonprofits began its big buildup in the 1960s with an explosion in grants and contracts to many community agencies and a big rise in fees for service in nonprofit hospitals and health care institutions. Significantly, though, government funding for nonprofit community agencies has shifted away from direct grants and contracts to a diverse array of grants, contracts, fees for service including Medicaid, voucher payments, tax credits, and new forms of capital financing including tax exempt bonds and social impact bonds (SIBs). This restructuring of the tools of government (Salamon 2002) funding of nonprofits reflects several important trends in public administration and nonprofit management (Phillips and Smith 2011): the increased attention to performance and accountability; the continued expansion of health financing programs such as Medicaid and Medicare; and widespread interest in social enterprise and innovation. These new tools of financing have in turn profoundly changed the landscape of nonprofit organizations and their relationship to government.

DIRECT GRANTS AND CONTRACTS

Before the 1960s, government funding of nonprofit agencies other than hospitals and higher education was relatively limited and restricted to services such as child welfare or high-profile institutions like the Metropolitan Museum of Art. Typically, public subsidies to nonprofit agencies were provided with relatively minimal accountability requirements; nonprofit agencies were assumed to use the money wisely and efficiently, partly because many nonprofits were part of a web of relationships that included the local chapter of the United Way, which offered legitimacy and some measure of accountability to government. Also, state and local governments—the primary source of government funding—had scant capacity to monitor nonprofit grantees. As a result, formal detailed contracts were quite rare.

The buildup of government funding of nonprofit agencies in the 1960s and 1970s went hand in hand with the growth of an array of new grant programs. For some federal programs, federal grants such as Title XX grants for social services would be distributed to the states and then the states would use the funds to contract with local community agencies. Other federal agencies such as the National Endowment of the Arts or community development grants were given directly to local agencies. Despite the sharp rise of federal government funding, detailed contracts with specific outcome measures or expectations remained relatively unusual.

Performance Management and Government Funding

Over time, the management of government grants and contracts changed to emphasize accountability and performance (Gronbjerg 1993; Smith and Lipsky 1993; Smith 2012). The substantive content of this shift has varied by subfield and even by geographic region. Initially, the increased focus on accountability was reflected in increased regulation of the grant and contract management including reporting on the expenditure of government funds such as number of service units or users. Through greater financial oversight, nonprofit agencies were increasingly required to provide detailed accounting for their grants and contracts.

Beginning in the 1990s, government agencies began to more stringently regulate the programmatic content of nonprofits. This trend was particularly apparent in social services and health care. To varying degrees depending upon the jurisdiction, many key social service contracts, including welfare-to-work, mental health, workforce development, and child welfare, are now performance based wherein agencies are reimbursed for services only if they meet specific performance targets (Desai, Garabedian, and Snyder 2012; Smith 2012; Fraser and Whitehill 2014; Freundlich and McCullough 2012). (Indeed, many private funders such as local United Way chapters and national foundations such as the Edna McConnell Clark Foundation are also tying their grants to an outcome orientation and expectation of meeting specific performance targets.)

More broadly, performance-based contracts are part of a broader movement affecting public and nonprofit management called "pay for success" (PFS) (Corporation for National and Community Service 2015; In the Public Interest 2015; Roman et al. 2014). In brief, PFS seeks to link payment for services to the success of the intervention for clients and the broader community.

Social Impact Bonds

Recently, "social impact bonds" (SIBs), a form of PFS tools, have achieved wide attention in the United States and abroad as an innovative strategy to achieve greater social impact. SIBs are complicated initiatives that depend upon private investors assuming the risk of social programs, with the government paying off those investments if and when the outcome goals are met. Private investors loan money to an intermediary (usually a nonprofit) which then subcontracts with service providers (nonprofit and for-profit), who then deliver services with specific performance targets. The project is evaluated by independent researchers, and government repays the loan with interest to investors if the performance targets are met. Despite widespread publicity to SIBs, they remain quite limited in terms of their impact on services in part because of their complexity and high transaction costs. Nonetheless, SIBs illustrate the ongoing shift in contracting with local community agencies toward greater emphasis on outcome measures and evaluation.

SIBs also illustrate the enthusiasm among government policymakers and many nonprofit leaders for "evidence-based practices and decision-making," so government contracts with nonprofits are guided by the latest research on program effectiveness (Metz, Blasé, and Bowie 2007; Johnson and Austin 2008). Meanwhile, though, many nonprofit agencies are voluntarily adopting these practices in response to evolving professional norms and expectations and encouragement by public and private funders.

The Importance of Intermediary Organizations

The advent of SIBs is also consistent with the greater reliance on intermediaries in the contracting relationship between government and nonprofits. In the early years of widespread contracting, most contracts entailed a direct relationship between government and the nonprofit agency such as a direct contract between state or federal government and a local nonprofit social service agency. But this relationship has evolved significantly through the involvement of a wide variety of intermediary organizations. Managed-care organizations (MCOs) are one prominent example in health and social services. In particular, many states contract with MCOs for their Medicaid spending; these MCOs then contract with local nonprofit and for-profit service providers. The managed-care model has also been used in child welfare services in many states whereupon the state child welfare agency replaced direct contracts with local service providers with a large capitated contract with an MCO that in turn contracted with community agencies on a performance-contracting basis (McBeath and Meezan 2010; also, Courtney 2000).

Managed care in the context of government contracting for social and health services presents complicated policy tradeoffs. MCOs in their contracts with local nonprofit (and for-profit) providers may allow greater opportunity to focus on client and program outcomes and introduce efficiencies into the delivery of contract services. Yet, managed care tends to create financial and programmatic uncertainty, since service providers now depend on managed-care firms, instead of government, for client referrals. Further, managed-care contracts typically have strong incentives for efficiency, unlike many previous contracts with government; indeed, over half the states with MCOs include various forms of pay-for-performance contracts (Gifford et al. 2011, p. 3). The implementation of the ACA, including Medicaid expansion, will further abet this shift to MCOs with resulting effects on nonprofit social and health agencies.

The increase in intermediary relationships is also evident in various public-private partnerships that have become more common in the last twenty-five years. For example, the Gates Foundation collaborates with numerous public, for-profit and nonprofit entities throughout the world in support of their initiatives. A nationwide initiative called Funders Together to End Homelessness strives to bring together the resources and expertise of multiple funders in order to develop a more coordinated and effective strategy to end homelessness (Wertheimer 2011). In Washington state, Thrive by Five was formed as a collaborative effort of several private foundations, corporate funders and the state of Washington to support early childhood education. In Minnesota, the Itasca Area Schools Collaborative is a joint project of local schools and the Blandin Foundation to support better opportunities for improved success in school for all students regardless of income or background (Bielefeld 2015). These new intermediary initiatives can help promote the greater integration of services, but they also can create contract uncertainty for local nonprofits.

In sum, contracting between government and nonprofit agencies continues to be a very important tool of government financing for the nonprofit sector. Yet, the structure of contracting has undergone important shifts. Contracts are much more performance oriented, including the PFS models and SIBs. A greater performance orientation, combined with continued budget austerity, has intensified the competition among nonprofits for government contracts. Pressure from government to contain costs also means that the value of the contract often does not cover all of the agency's costs, especially administrative expenses. Contracts tend to be more detailed and project focused, limiting the ability of agencies to cross-subsidized parts of their operations. Consequently, larger organizations with access to other sources of revenue including private philanthropic funds, earned income, or private capital have an advantage in this competitive fiscal environment. This fiscal dynamic has also given for-profit organizations in many subfields such as human services an organizational advantage since they have access to private capital. Indeed, the for-profit share of human services has been rising in recent years. For example, the for-profit market share of social services and related services like mental health counseling rose from 47.8 percent in 2002 to 53.8 percent in 2012. In the sizable subfield of individual and family services, the for-profit share has increased from 21.9 to 37 percent during the same period (US Census Bureau 2014).

FEES FOR SERVICE

The restructuring of government grants and contracting is also reflected in the growing role of fee-for-service revenue received by nonprofits that is directly or indirectly government funding. Fees have always been a part of the nonprofit revenue mix. Universities have historically been very dependent upon tuition revenue. Museums rely heavily upon admission fees and special event ticket sales. And many long-standing child welfare agencies received per diem payments from government and private individuals from the nineteenth century through the post–World War II period; only the advent of federal funding in the 1960s substantially decreased the reliance of these agencies on fee income.

Today "fees" has become an umbrella term for diverse revenue collected from individuals and organizations and can include rent payments from residents in community housing programs, reimbursement from public and private health insurance programs, direct payments from clients, income from technical assistance services, tuition, the sale of goods (such as meals from a café), and special event ticket sales.

For social and health organizations, the consequential shift in the past twenty years has been the increase in fee income directly or indirectly from government funds, especially from Medicaid and, to a lesser extent, Medicare. For instance, Catholic Community Services of Western Washington (CCSWW) had total revenue of $134 million in FY 2014 (more than double its revenue in 2004 of $63 million). It receives approximately $104 million in fees and grants from government with over $70 million from Medicaid for a wide array of important services for its poor and disadvantaged clientele, including foster care, home care for the disabled and elderly, and mental health services and counseling. CCSWW is quite typical of many larger nonprofit social service agencies that have grown larger despite the competition for government funds and fiscal scarcity of state and local governments: their large size and diversified revenue base have given them advantages not enjoyed by smaller, financially vulnerable community agencies, and they are providing many Medicaid eligible services, so they have been able to tap this revenue source even as more traditional sources of federal social services funding such as SSBG have declined.

Government can also contribute to the fee income of nonprofits by agreeing to use nonprofits' goods and services. Three examples illustrate this point. First, an agency to help the homeless may operate a restaurant staffed by the homeless to earn income and provide training opportunities for agency clients. Government might agree to use the restaurant to cater functions as a way of boosting the agency's earned income. Second, the government (or a private company) might contract with this agency to provide staff for certain purposes and pay fees for these workers' services. (Private companies that hire disadvantaged workers may be eligible for tax credits as well.) And third, a service program for the disabled might produce certain goods that government could buy.

The Diversity of Fee Income

The diversification in government financing has also contributed to the increase in fee income for nonprofits. The Child Care and Dependent tax credit (CDCTC), for example, subsidizes the fees paid to caregivers for services provided. Government voucher payments are another form of fee income. Section 8 housing vouchers, for instance, provide vouchers to low-income individuals to offset the cost of rent payments. Many nonprofit organizations with housing programs will collect voucher payments from their residents to support the operations of their programs. The federal Child Care/Voucher program also provides direct subsidies to nonprofit providers to support the child care of eligible low-income parents. Educational vouchers remain quite limited, but charter schools typically receive payments from local governments based upon their attendance numbers; this funding is received by the nonprofit charter school providers as fee income. Medicaid has introduced "Self-Directed Services" which offer individual Medicaid recipients some control over the expenditure of funds for their own care. For example, a senior citizen in need of various types of home care might have control over a "budget" of Medicaid funds that can be directed to different local providers (Center for Medicare and Medicaid Services 2016). These personal budgets have been widely used in the United Kingdom and elsewhere to provide more individual control and choice in the selection of local agencies. Many nonprofit agencies with residential programs also may collect fee income in the form of rent from their residents. For disabled residents, Supplemental Security Income (SSI) may be used to pay for the rental charges, either directly from the resident or essentially assigned to the nonprofit. For some residents, the rent payment may also include Section 8 voucher income.

The increased reliance on fee income also represents the enthusiasm for social enterprise, social innovation, and earned income by nonprofits, as well as for some a desire to diversify sources of funds. In brief, social enterprise generally refers to organizations with a social mission that mixes nonprofit and for-profit elements such as market income (Dees 1998). FareStart, a nonprofit agency for the homeless, established a restaurant staffed by previously homeless individuals to help them learn job-ready skills. The federal SIF has supported many nonprofit social enterprises, including local nonprofits that have mix of government contracts and earned income; typically, SIF projects are also based upon the best practices and credible research proving the effectiveness of the social enterprise. One good example of an SIF initiative is a social enterprise program operated by REDF, a nonprofit based in San Francisco. They have multiple programs, but the SIF funds have been used to support the scaling of a social enterprise program using creative and effective strategies to advance employment opportunities for the disabled and disadvantaged (Thornley, Anderson, and Dixon 2015; REDF 2016). In Seattle, a nonprofit architectural design firm serving other nonprofits such as child care agencies called Environmental Works (EW) was started with a federal grant in the 1970s at a time when over 270 similar nonprofits were created around the country. Over time, though, EW shifted from a reliance on federal and state grants and contracts to fee income from other nonprofits for various design services. Since many of the clients of EW are nonprofits with substantial reliance on government funding, EW's fee income is often government contract or grant income that the nonprofit uses to purchase needed design services.

Effects of Shift to Fee Income

The shift toward fee income from grants and contracts leads to several consequences.

- First, fee income such as Medicaid, vouchers, and market income from a restaurant employing the disadvantaged embeds nonprofits in a more competitive market situation for the acquisition of resources than historically was the case for contracts. To be sure, government contracts are now more difficult to acquire and retain than the past; nonetheless, a reliance on fee income can expose nonprofits to significant market forces. This pressure can be positive since it encourages a focus on efficiency and customer service. However, the risk is that market exposure can shift a nonprofit away from its social mission.
- Second, fee income provides an incentive for growth because the more individuals or eligible users, the more income the agency receives. Further, the money is generally unrestricted so the revenue can be used by the nonprofit to cross-subsidize administrative infrastructure and other cost centers. This revenue situation is quite different from traditional contracts which were typically on a cost-reimbursement basis with a fixed contract amount; thus, the agency would have little financial incentive to serve individuals other than specified in the contract. The incentive for growth embodied in fees also tends to give a competitive edge to larger nonprofit and for-profit service organizations with access to capital and a willingness to grow.
- Third, the rising importance of fees, broadly defined as a revenue source for nonprofits, further obscures the role of government in supporting local service provided by nonprofits. In an era of direct government programs, citizens, at least in theory, know who to hold accountable for any failure in public programs. Contracting can and often does make this direct link between government and private citizens less direct. So many citizens may use the services of a local nonprofit such as a local Headstart program and

be unaware of the reliance of the nonprofit on federal funds (Smith 1993). Fees create further complexity for citizens in terms of understanding government's funding and regulatory role in the operations of the local agency.

Potentially, fees can also increase the engagement between citizens and nonprofit agencies. For example, voucher payments are conceptualized as a strategy of encouraging individual citizens to investigate the cost and quality of local services and purchase the services with the "best" value; in the process, local nonprofit such as charter schools will also develop stronger community connections as part of their outreach strategy to woo citizens to their organization. Self-directed services require that individuals obtain information on local agencies and their services; potentially, the incentives embedded in self-directed services and vouchers for example, could promote more engagement of citizens with nonprofit service providers and more broadly their communities (see also, Bovaird 2007).

TAX DEDUCTIONS AND EXEMPTIONS

Tax deductions and exemptions are a central tool of government support of nonprofit activity. Individuals and corporations can receive a deduction from their income taxes for cash and in-kind contributions to nonprofit organizations. Through the tax deduction, government is indirectly subsidizing nonprofits and encouraging individuals and corporations to give money to them. In FY 2011, the charitable deduction reduced federal government revenues by about $40 billion. However, equally important to the nonprofit sector—especially large institutions like universities and museums—is the tax exemption of earnings from assets. For instance, university endowments can grow tax free; it is estimated that in FY 2011, this tax benefit cost the treasury approximately $50 billion (Gravelle and Sherlock 2013). Property tax exemptions cost state and local governments untold millions of dollars especially in many urban areas with a concentration of large tax exempt institutions such as hospitals and universities.

The substantial cost of property tax exemptions has then led to calls by state and local governments to restrict the exemption to certain types of nonprofits such as agencies serving the poor. Also, many states and localities have increasingly sought to levy "payments in lieu of taxes" (PILOTs) to offset the cost of the tax exemption. A typical example of a PILOT is the contribution of a university to a municipality for the cost of fire and police services (see Brody 2010).

PILOTs and the pressure on tax exemption also illustrate the ongoing tension between the autonomy of nonprofit organizations and their public purposes (Brody and Tyler 2010). Tax exemptions are a government subsidy that raises at least the possibility that the government can use the subsidy as a justification for regulating or restricting the operations of nonprofits. Foundations, for example, have faced restrictions on their international grantmaking in order to avoid inadvertent grants to overseas organizations with ties to terrorist groups. The fiscal pressure on the federal government has also led to calls for limitations on the charitable deductions by policymakers including President Obama, especially since wealthy individuals receive a disproportionate amount of the benefits of the charitable deduction.

CAPITAL FINANCING

Nonprofit organizations face a special challenge in raising private capital because, unlike for-profit organizations, certain forms of raising capital, for example, selling equity shares, become quite cumbersome without the creation, say, of private partners. Although faced with an absence of private capital, nonprofits can have some advantage when they can build capital through donations from individuals, corporations, and foundation grants (Miller 2003). Direct government grants for capital expenses tend to be relatively unusual, and government contracts are usually for ongoing operational expenses. However, government has an increasingly diverse menu of other financing options for capital expenses. The most widely known and used government subsidy for capital expenses are tax exempt bonds (see Calabrese and Ely 2015). Large nonprofit institutions such as hospitals and universities (as well as for-profits) have taken advantage of tax exempt bonds for decades. These bonds help nonprofit organizations finance the cost of capital improvements such as a new construction or renovation. What is new is the growing use of tax exempt bonds by smaller nonprofit organizations such as housing development organizations, child welfare agencies, and mental health centers. This increase in tax exempt bond financing reflects in part the steady rise in the number of nonprofit organizations, especially smaller community-based organizations who are often woefully undercapitalized. To address this problem, state housing finance agencies have issued tax exempt bonds on behalf of a wide variety of social, health, and educational nonprofits, including some relatively small community organizations. Tax exempt bonds are an especially attractive financing option for nonprofits because they can obtain sizable financing for their capital needs at a much lower interest rate than obtaining a comparable bank loan. These bonds can finance a wide variety of projects: the purchase of the agency's office building, refinancing of existing debt, and new building projects. The amounts can range from small

$1 million building purchases to $35 million or more (for Washington state, see Washington State Housing Finance Commission 2016).

Low-Income Housing Tax Credit

One specialized form of government financing of the capital needs of nonprofits comes through tax credits. In particular, the LIHTC enacted by Congress in 1986 provides funding for the development costs of low-income housing by allowing private investors to receive a tax credit for investments in eligible nonprofit projects by nonprofit (and for-profit) housing developers (Keightley 2013). Congress allocates the LIHTC to the states based upon a formula; the states then issue requests for proposals for the allocated tax credits. After an award, a nonprofit housing agency can use the credits to tap private capital for development expenses. The LIHTC also has a set-aside for nonprofit housing developers in the federal regulations governing the allocations of tax credits by the states.

Underscoring the complexity of government financing, many housing agencies also package a variety of government financing mechanisms including grants, Section 8 vouchers, other federal and local tax credit programs (including the Historic Tax Credit program), and contracts to support other capital and programmatic costs of a housing project (See National Trust for Historic Preservation 2014; Keightley 2013). Further, LIHTC financing has had a number of important implications for the organization and management of local nonprofit housing and community development agencies. First, tax credit financing has pushed (and forced) nonprofits to create hybrid nonprofit-for-profit structures, typically by creating an affiliated for-profit limited partnership (so the private investors can receive their tax credits). Sometimes, the limited partnership is effectively owned by the nonprofit; in other cases, the nonprofit may be a minority partner. These hybrid structures also tend to unintentionally obfuscate the actual revenue and expenses of a housing development since public and private money is flowing through more than one entity. Second, tax credit deals are very complicated and require the specialized services of accountants, lawyers, investment bankers, equity funds, and consultants, though the LIHTC was designed specifically to make the subsidy amount explicit so that the government subsidy would be more likely to flow through to the ultimate renters and consumers. Still, this complexity makes it difficult for small agencies to participate and tends to give an edge to skilled professionals with the detailed knowledge of the program, rather than community members or laypeople who may have an interest in developing more affordable housing. Third, tax credit financing—like fee income—pushes an agency to be entrepreneurial and to keep building. A child welfare agency with contracts with state government can often depend upon a certain number of children every year and a predictable stream of funding, barring any major budget or program quality problems; little direct incentive exists for growth. By contrast, tax credits are allocated on a project-by-project basis; competition is fierce, and the tax credit package only finances a portion of the total development and operational costs. Further, the tax credit deals typically do not provide sufficient revenue for ongoing property maintenance, thus necessitating new revenue streams or new building projects (with a portion devoted to infrastructure costs).

After the recession of 2008, the market for the LIHTC collapsed because of the credit crunch. It has slowly recovered, but the environment for the LIHTC remains challenging. Indeed, many smaller providers are being squeezed because they find it difficult to effectively compete for new tax credit deals against larger nonprofit (and for-profit) developers, and they do not have the size to adequately manage their existing properties. A good example of this dynamic is a nonprofit housing agency in Seattle called Lutheran Alliance To Create Housing (LATCH), founded in 1990 by a group of Lutheran churches to develop and provide affordable housing opportunities in the Puget Sound region. Over time, LATCH successfully developed several housing projects using the LIHTC program, at least in part. But the 2008 recession and the increasingly scarce resources for affordable housing projects forced LATCH to eventually merge with a much larger nonprofit housing organization, Compass Housing Alliance; this merger has allowed the creation of a more financially robust organization and the potential for a broader base of community support.

The challenges faced by nonprofits in raising capital are also leading to innovation and experimentation in organizational form and delivery. Most notable, perhaps, is the widespread interest in hybrid organizations that are for-profit organizations (and thus able to tap private capital markets) but also have a clear social mission (see Strom 2011; Reiser 2013; chapter 9 by Cordes et al., this volume). These new entities include low-profit limited liability companies (or L3Cs), community interest companies (CICs), and the benefit corporation. These different organizational forms are subject to state regulation and have received extensive attention as an option for social entrepreneurs interested in social change and addressing public problems. However, these different forms—sometimes called the fourth sector (Sabeti 2009) because of the blurred sectoral boundaries—remain far outnumbered by the more traditional 501(c)(3) public charity.

MANAGING GOVERNMENT FINANCING

The diversification of government funding of nonprofits and the different subfields of nonprofit activity such as human services and the arts means that the mix of direct and indirect government funding will vary substantially depending upon the specific type of nonprofit (Gronbjerg and Smith 2015). Arts organizations reliant on local subsidies, tax exempt bonds, occasional federal and state grants, and private philanthropy will have a different relationship to government than child welfare agencies primarily dependent upon performance-based government contracts. Nonetheless, certain characteristics of government financing are common across policy fields within the nonprofit sector. First, government and nonprofits tend to have different norms guiding their decisions about services and their target audience. Nonprofits emerge out of a desire of a group of like-minded "community" of people to address a problem or social need. Examples include battered women shelters, neighborhood drop-in centers for youth, interfaith homeless shelters, community health centers, and Lutheran Social Services. All of these organizations represent a "community," and as such, in their ideal type, feel a special obligation to their community of interest. Battered women shelters may view their obligation as primarily to any abused women in a given locality; community health centers may want to serve anyone in a community regardless of their specific problem; and a drop-in center may serve any adolescent who self-identifies himself or herself as troubled and in need of help. Responsiveness to a particular community is the guiding norm (Smith and Lipsky 1993).

Government, by contrast, tends to approach services and clients from the norm of equity. The ever-present problem facing government officials charged with distributing funds or services is to justify why they provide services to one group rather than another, since government does not have the resources to serve everyone in need. In a democracy, groups can seek redress if they feel they are being unfairly treated; government officials are accountable to these groups and to the citizenry in general for their policy choices. Equity is a norm consistent with the need of government officials to treat groups and individuals fairly, which includes notions of both "equal justice under the law" and progressively helping those most in need. Equity can be interpreted in a variety of ways, but it usually means defining need in order to allocate resources by criteria deemed to be fair—for example, income, geographic location, and severity of need.

Because of their emphasis on responsiveness, nonprofit agencies may clash with government over policy matters relating to services, clients, and staff. For instance, a program for troubled youth may prefer to serve any adolescent in the community; but government officials may believe its funds should only serve the neediest clients, by some definition. Indeed, government staff may accuse the program of "creaming"—or taking only the easiest cases and neglecting the so-called tough cases. Nonprofit agencies often respond to the creaming charge by arguing that they are only providing services within their mission, and in any case their services were never designed to serve difficult and expensive clients such as troubled youth. This same basic disagreement between government and nonprofits can occur when nonprofit agencies favor certain groups such as coreligionists or local neighborhood children. Many contemporary disputes between government and nonprofits—from admission policies at charter schools to the practices of emergency shelters—exemplify this difference in guiding norms.

The clash of norms may not be apparent with some types of nonprofits that are oriented toward government from the beginning, especially through sizable government contracts and funding; thus, the organizational changes characteristic of agencies with roots in the community may not be as evident. For instance, an entrepreneurial individual interested in helping youth might have close connections with government contracting authorities; the latter encourage the social entrepreneur to submit a proposal for a contract to serve at-risk youth. The subsequent contract will likely reflect government priorities from the outset since the founding social entrepreneur did not have a preexisting community of interest prior to the contract. Some of these social entrepreneurs may also have previously worked for the government, further reinforcing the shared norms and values. In addition, nonprofits dependent upon largely private philanthropy and fees such as arts organizations may be less susceptible to direct government influence as well. Nonetheless, small arts organizations dependent upon volunteers and donations that receive a sizable government grant or contract may also experience the same mission-related issues as social and health organizations. For instance, the government contract is likely to be for specific programmatic goals connected to government priorities such as serving specific types of clients such as people with low incomes.

The differences are also evident in the faith-related organizations receiving government contracts. Nonprofit agencies such as CCSWW, LATCH, and Compass Housing are connected to specific denominations and thus have a religious community of interest. But their government contracts require them to offer a secular service on a nondiscrimination basis. In general, faith-related agencies offering a religiously based service including proselytizing and bible study are ineligible for government contracts. Thus, faith-related agencies offering an intensive religious experience as part of their service such as the Salvation Army are primarily reliant on private donations and earned income. Recently, controversy has erupted over the requirements of ACA that mandate health facilities offer reproductive services. This requirement has in turn spawned lawsuits challenging the requirement by Catholic health care organizations. While the dispute is specific to ACA, it is ultimately rooted in different norms and expectations by government and nonprofits that arise in the context of government financing and accompanying regulation.

Effect of Government Financing on Staff Costs and Professionalization

Yet, government financing affects nonprofits in other related ways, even if the funding is indirect through tax credit subsidies such as the LIHTC. Nonprofits started through community initiative often lack, at least initially, a highly trained professional or administrative staff. Some of these agencies originally emerge from an unincorporated group of like-minded people concerned about a social problem. A clear separation between the board and staff is absent, and many of these agencies do not have full-time executive directors. Government funding means more accountability, which often requires these agencies to adopt new administrative procedures, add professionals, institute new financial management practices, and, in some cases, even modify existing physical structures. Thus, government funding can significantly increase the overhead costs of these agencies, requiring the agencies to raise much larger sums of money to fund their basic operations from both public and private sources. LATCH and other nonprofit developers have to meet exacting reporting standards for their tax credits (and other government subsidies); the costs of ongoing compliance (and the initial financial and legal consultants) are substantial.

Yet, the impact of government financing goes beyond the need for investments in administrative infrastructure and technical expertise. Government funding for nonprofits tends to encourage professionalization of the organization, both directly through regulation and more subtly through the ripple effects on an agency's operations (Hwang and Powell 2009; Smith and Lipsky 1993). As noted, government funding through grants and contracts is now accompanied by expectations for programmatic outcomes, to varying degrees, including programmatic standards informed by "evidence-based" practice and decision making. Indeed, new "professions" may emerge and be accredited, especially given the widespread interest in "evidence-based practice" in social work and related fields (Metz, Blasé, and Bowie 2007; Johnson and Austin 2008)—even as interest in coproduction remains on the policy agenda.

In turn, capable professionals may increasingly be mobile, with organization- and sector-jumping more common and accepted, making wages more competitive for some, and probably depressed for those less adaptable. This development also places smaller providers at a disadvantage in the competition for talent, especially since many smaller providers do not have a lot of upward mobility for staff. To the extent that professionalization and sector hopping becomes more frequent, staff turnover could also increase, particularly among smaller providers, thus negatively affecting the quality of services and the ability of providers to develop long-term community networks

THE OLYMPIC SCULPTURE PARK

One excellent example of these compliance pressures is the development of the Olympic Sculpture Park (OSP) by the Seattle Art Museum (SAM) in the early 2000s. The OSP evolved from the joint efforts of SAM, private donors, a large oil company, Unocal, and the nonprofit Trust for Public Land (TPL). Unocal offered to sell a stunning site on the Seattle waterfront to the TPL for $16 million, although it was appraised for $24 million (taking a tax deduction for the difference). TPL, working with SAM, raised the money for the purchase price from private donors.

TPL then transferred title of the land to the Museum Development Authority, a public development authority, or PDA—a quasi-public institution with more financing flexibility than a traditional nonprofit, including the capacity to issue bonds. The role of TPL underscores the importance of intermediary organizations in supporting public-nonprofit financing partnerships as well as the growth of innovative financing through different organizational forms.

But the acquisition of the site was only the beginning: the total project cost is projected to be $80 million including site acquisition costs, $40 million for the design, construction, and project management, and $20 million for an endowment for the future maintenance of the park. Consequently, the successful development of OSP requires extensive public and private fundraising and creativity on the part of SAM staff from private gifts, public grants and contracts from a variety of federal, state, and local agencies, and tax exempt bonds issued by the state of Washington. This multifaceted effort required extensive staff and volunteer resources over period of several years, putting this type of public-private partnership out of reach for most small arts organizations.

and support. Government agencies will need to work closely with state and local nonprofit associations and with professional bodies to anticipate and support relevant training programs, especially for smaller providers. However, in the competition for talent, smaller providers may be able to leverage their attractiveness as organizations in which to develop and grow professionally (Smith and Phillips 2016).

Importantly, professionalization occurs at both the managerial and programmatic levels. That is, government funding has in recent years often failed to adequately cover the full cost of service in nonprofits. This shortfall, combined with the frequently intense competition for public and private funding, has pushed nonprofits to be more entrepreneurial and more bottom-line oriented, encouraging the adoption of a "managerialist" orientation. The sector hopping of nonprofit managers also encourages this managerialism because many nonprofit managers, especially in fields such as health care and community care, have experience in the for-profit sector. The professionalization of nonprofit management is also facilitated by the sharp growth in the hiring of managers with professional graduate degrees in public and nonprofit management and business administration.

Managerialism in nonprofits can create tension between nonprofit executives and their program staff, even as the latter become more highly skilled (Hwang and Powell 2009). For example, a hallmark of professionalization is decision-making autonomy guided by professional norms and standards; but the shift toward performance contracting, PFS models, and outcome measurement has the effect of constraining professional autonomy. The social worker who wants to offer intensive counseling to a welfare recipient will be forced to emphasize job placement and skill development due to the structure of the performance contracts in welfare-to-work programs (Desai, Garabedian, and Snyder 2012). The nonprofit housing professional will only be able to serve certain types of individuals in the residences developed through LIHTC financing.

In an era of professional managers, mission-based programming that operates at a loss may be susceptible to cutback or elimination even if it has significant social impact and a devoted professional cadre of individuals in the agency. The diversification of government funding has further contributed to this shift since noncontract income such as fee-for-service and tax exempt bonds tends to reward organizational and service growth as well as sizable scale. Further, important services such as community outreach or advocacy with no specific standards and a lack of easily measured outcomes are also vulnerable in the current funding and political environment.

The Implications of Government Financing on Nonprofit Governance

The emphasis on impact (and entrepreneurship) also has consequences for the governance of nonprofits. As noted, nonprofits often start due to the passion and interest of a group of interested community members interested in social issues such as education or promoting local arts programming. The leadership and boards of these nonprofits are often friends and neighbors who work together to create and build the organization. When the initial nonprofit becomes incorporated, these friends often form the core of the new board of directors overseeing the new nonprofit. Government financing, over time, can change the incentive structure for the nonprofit in terms of board leadership, especially in the current context of funding scarcity and competition. In particular, nonprofits are encouraged to appoint individuals to the board who can assist with resource acquisition, including government contracts and private donations. To be sure, some nonprofits have devised novel approaches to restructuring their governance structures including the appointment of advisory committees and relying upon new board members who have long volunteer service in the organization. Nonetheless, the changes in governance can be quite challenging, especially for nonprofits facing fiscal difficulties or staff upheaval.

These potential changes in governance also underscore another important consequence of government financing of nonprofits on the relationship between agency governance and its community. As agencies grow and become more dependent upon government financing, a natural tendency of the agency board and its staff leadership is to look upward to their government agencies for support and feedback on operation. This orientation is reinforced by the implementation of more stringent performance regimes which tend to be based upon standards outside of local communities. The unfortunate consequence for many nonprofits is that they may lack strong community ties (except for a small number of community members on their board). In the current environment, this absence of strong community ties can be a serious liability when an agency is threatened with reductions in their government funding or the imposition of inappropriate programmatic regulations. Larger agencies with diverse boards, affiliated advisory committees, and strong connections to local political elites are better positioned to organize and sustain community engagement in support of the organizations and its funding and programmatic goals.

Part of community support for a nonprofit can also entail advocacy in support of the organization and its priorities. In particular, government financing tends to encourage nonprofits to engage in lobbying and advocacy to retain funding and obtain more funding if possible; thus, it tends to focus on advocacy in support of organizational maintenance, rather than on larger policy goals (Smith and Lipsky 1993; Mosley 2014). This advocacy can be direct contact by the nonprofit's leadership with policymakers or more indirect outreach through intermediary organizations such as coalitions and associations of nonprofits. Indeed, as the fiscal pressure on nonprofits has risen, these coalitions have become more important tools for nonprofit advocacy to preserve their government funding.

Government financing can also seriously constrain a nonprofit's advocacy activity. Nonprofits may be afraid that advocacy on behalf of their government grants and contracts might undermine their existing relationship with government and, indeed, it can conflict at times. Even advocacy on other matters, unrelated to their government contracts, could potentially impair their relations with policymakers. In addition, government contracts generally prevent agencies from using government funding to undertake advocacy, so nonprofits must find other sources of revenue to fund their advocacy. This task is unlikely to be a problem for large agencies, but many smaller agencies may struggle with finding adequate nongovernmental revenues to undertake advocacy (Pekkanen, Smith, and Tsujinaka 2014).

LOOKING AHEAD

In the 1960s, the advent of significant government funding of new social programs and of nonprofits was accompanied by widespread interest on community agencies, voluntarism, and the expansion of services—from social and health services to the arts to education. Since then, the nonprofit charitable sector has expanded over fivefold and now tops one million organizations; the rise in direct and indirect government funding encouraged this growth. Yet, unlike the earlier era, the government-nonprofit relationship has become increasingly occupied with issues of impact, social innovation, and greater transparency and accountability. Moreover, the 2008 economic crisis and its aftermath have exposed the vulnerabilities of nonprofit agencies in a devolved political system. Federal financing has either declined or stagnated for a range of important programs; health care through Medicaid and Medicare is the one prominent exception. Consequently, nonprofits reliant on government financing are dependent, at least in part, on the condition of state and local finances. Moreover, nonprofits are also dependent upon favorable state and local political support, as exemplified when many governors and legislatures refused to expand Medicaid in the early years after passage of ACA. In addition, the budgetary and fiscal problems of government at all levels can compromise the capacity of government to effectively monitor and support nonprofit organizations receiving government funding. This lack of government administrative and funding capacity in turn undermines the capacity of nonprofits and their ability to provide quality programming and adequate representation.

Given this political and economic context, nonprofits need to practice good "risk management" by taking steps to manage the risks now inherent in government funding—whether it is contracts, grants, fees for service, or tax exempt bonds. Important strategies can include a diversification of revenue, which can entail developing private philanthropic support and earned income streams to complement government funding or developing a capacity for multiple government contracts and grants from different public agencies. Nonprofits also need to invest in their own infrastructure and capacity in order to effectively compete for government funds; this effort requires adequate administrative expertise and program staff who fully understand government performance expectations. Furthermore, nonprofits need a governance structure that responds flexibly and quickly to emergent developments in government policy. An advocacy policy designed to strengthen and sustain community and political support for a nonprofit is also essential.

In the coming years, the stakes are likely to be high for nonprofits as they strive to manage a highly turbulent funding environment. The ongoing emphasis of government on accountability and performance means that the distinctive advantage nonprofits enjoyed in many fields such as human services is eroding as policymakers increasingly look to for-profit firms and larger nonprofits to provide human services, community care, or early childhood education. In order to tap local public funds, nonprofits, including cultural organizations and social service agencies, will need to build community and political support. The limitations faced by nonprofits in raising capital will continue to encourage policymakers and nonprofits to explore alternative organizational forms like SIBs or L3Cs and tax exempt bond financing.

Finally, the changes underway in government financing of nonprofits also illustrate the ongoing evolution of the American welfare state. Nonprofits funded by government are increasingly vital as providers of important public services. Further, the changes in government financing, including the continued expansion of government health care programs such as Medicaid, are remaking local community services and blurring the boundary between health and social services. Important social programs including welfare and retirement have been reformed and changed in the last twenty-five years to place more responsibility on individuals for their economic security—what Jacob Hacker called the "great risk shift" (Hacker 2006). Similarly, the growth of new tools of government financing such as tax credits and fees for service place greater responsibility on nonprofits to find money to cover the full cost of services and to implement satisfactory performance regimes. Greater competition and higher performance expectations are pushing nonprofits—from hospitals to home health agencies to residential programs for the disabled—to be more entrepreneurial and grow their organizations, especially through new fee income (and private philanthropy). But, even larger agencies are at risk for failure or serious problems, given low payment rates and the difficulty of adequately investing in agency infrastructure (See Wing and Hager 2004; Human Services Council 2015). To ensure the provision of high-quality services by nonprofits, government needs to provide more robust funding and cover the full cost of services; nonprofits, for their part, need to develop broad-based support, transparency in their governance and operations, and sustained investment in their organizational infrastructure.

ACKNOWLEDGMENT

The author is indebted to many individuals for their assistance during the preparation of this chapter. Special thanks to Putnam Barber, Peter Bernauer, Elizabeth Boris, CaraLee Cook, Mark Rosenman, and C. Eugene Steuerle for their comments and input. Thanks also go to Meghan McConaughey, who provided excellent research assistance.

REFERENCES

Allard, Scott W., and Steven Rathgeb Smith. 2014. "Unforeseen Consequences: Medicaid and the Funding of Nonprofit Social Services," *Journal of Health Politics, Policy and Law*, 39, 6 (December): 1135–1172.
Andrews, Christina, Colleen Grogan, Marianne Brennan, and Harold A. Pollock. 2015. "Lessons from Medicaid's Divergent Paths on Mental Health and Addiction Services," *Health Affairs*, 34, 7: 1131–1138.
Bawden, D. Lee and John L. Palmer. 1984. "Social Policy: Challenging the Welfare State," In *The Reagan Record*. John L. Palmer and Isabel V. Sawhill, eds. (pp. 177–215). Washington, DC: Urban Institute.
Bielefeld, Wolfgang. 2014. *Using Collective Impact to Improve Student Success*. The Hubert Project. Minneapolis, MN: University of Minnesota. http://www.hubertproject.org/hubert-material/345/.
Bixby, Anne Kallman. 1990. "Public Social Welfare Expenditures, Fiscal Year 1965-87," *Social Security Bulletin*, 53, 2 (February): 10–26. https://www.ssa.gov/policy/docs/ssb/v53n2/v53n2p10.pdf.
Boris, Elizabeth T., Erwin de Leon, Katie L. Roeger, and Milena Nikolova. 2010. *Human Service Nonprofits and Government Collaboration: Findings from the 2010 National Survey of Nonprofit Government Contracting and Grants*. Washington, DC: Urban Institute.http://www.urban.org/sites/default/files/alfresco/publication-pdfs/412228-Human-Service-Nonprofits-and-Government-Collaboration-Findings-from-the-National-Survey-of-Nonprofit-Government-Contracting-and-Grants.PDF.
Bovaird, Tony. 2007. "Beyond Engagement and Participation: User and Community Coproduction of Public Services," *Public Administration Review*, 67, 5 (September/October): 846–860.
Braddock, David L., Richard E. Hemp, Mary C. Rizzolo, Emily Shea Tanis, Laura Haffer, and Jiang Wu. 2015. *State of the States in Intellectual and Developmental Disabilities* Tenth Edition. Washington, DC: AAIDD. http://www.stateofthestates.org/documents/UnitedStates.pdf.
Brody, Evelyn. 2010. "All Charities are Property-tax Exempt, But Some Charities are More Exempt Than Others," *New England Law Review*, 44, 621.
Brody, Evelyn and John Tyler. 2010. "Respecting Foundations and Charity Autonomy: How Public is Private Philanthropy," *Chicago-Kent Law Review*, 85, 571.
Calabrese, Thad D., and Todd L. Ely. 2015. "Borrowing for the Public Good: The Growing Importance of Tax-Exempt Bonds for Public Charities," *Nonprofit and Voluntary Sector Quarterly*. on-line. pp. 1–20.
Center for Medicare and Medicaid Services (CMS). 2016. *Self Directed Services*. Washington, DC: CMS. https://www.medicaid.gov/Medicaid-CHIP-Program-Information/By-Topics/Delivery-Systems/Self-Directed-Services.html.
Corporation for National and Community Service, Office of Research and Evaluation. 2015. *State of the Pay for Success Field: Opportunities, Trends, and Recommendations*. Washington, DC: author.
Courtney, Mark E. 2000: "Managed Care and Child Welfare Services: What are the Issues?" *Children and Youth Services Review*, 22, 2: 87–91.

Dees, J. Gregory. 1998. "Enterprising Nonprofits." *Harvard Business Review* 76(1): 54–67.

Desai, Swati, Lisa Garabedian, and Karl Snyder. 2012. *Performance Based Contracts in New York City: Lessons Learned from Welfare-to-Work*. Albany, NY: Rockefeller Institute of Government. http://www.rockinst.org/pdf/workforce_welfare_and_social_services/2012-06-Performance-Based_Contracts.pdf.

DeVooght, Kerry, Meghan Fletcher, Hope Cooper. 2014. *Federal, State, and Local Spending to Address Child Abuse and Neglect in SFY 2012*. http://www.childtrends.org/wp-content/uploads/2014/09/2014-47ChildWelfareSpending2012.pdf.

Falk, Gene. 2014. *Low-Income Assistance Programs: Trends in Federal Spending*. Washington, DC: Congressional Research Service. http://greenbook.waysandmeans.house.gov/sites/greenbook.waysandmeans.house.gov/files/R41823_gb.pdf.

Fraser, Jeffrey and Evelyn Whitehill. 2014. *Introducing Performance-Based Contracts: A Comparison of Implementation Models*. Pittsburgh, PA: Allegheny County Department of Human Services.

Freundlich, Madelyn and Charlotte McCullough. 2012. *Privatization of Child Welfare Services: A Guide for State Advocates*. State Policy Advocacy and Reform Center and First Focus. http://childwelfaresparc.org/wp-content/uploads/2014/07/17-Privatization-of-Child-Welfare-Services-A-Guide-for-State-Advocates.pdf.

Gais, Thomas, Lucy Dadayan, and Suho Bae. 2009. *The Decline of States in Financing the U.S. Safety Net: Retrenchment in State and Local Social Welfare Spending, 1977–2007*. Albany, NY: Rockefeller Institute of Government. http://www.rockinst.org/pdf/workforce_welfare_and_social_services/sws.pdf.

Gifford, Kathleen, Vernon K. Smith, Dyke Snipes, and Julia Paradise. 2011. *A Profile of Medicaid Managed Care Programs in 2010: Findings from a 50-State Survey*. Washington, DC: Kaiser Commission on Medicaid and the Uninsured. https://kaiserfamilyfoundation.files.wordpress.com/2013/01/8220.pdf.

Gravelle, Jane G., and Molly F. Sherlock. 2013. *Tax Issues Relating to Charitable Contributions and Organizations. Congressional Research Service Report*. RL34608. http://www.pgdc.com/pgdc/crs-reports-tax-issues-relating-charitable-contributions-and-organizations.

Gronbjerg, Kirsten. 1993. *Understanding Nonprofit Funding*. San Francisco: Jossey-Bass.

Grønbjerg, Kirsten and Steven Rathgeb Smith. 2015. "The Changing Dynamic of the Government-Nonprofit Relationship." Unpublished paper.

Hacker, Jacob S. 2006. *The Great Risk Shift: The New Economic Insecurity and the Decline of the American Dream*. New York: Oxford University Press.

Harrison, David S., Julita Eleveld, and Paul Ahern. 2011. *Resilient Nonprofits: How Western Washington Nonprofits Have Been Coping with the Impact of the Economic Downturn*. Seattle, WA: Nancy Bell Evans Center on Nonprofits and Philanthropy, Evans School of Public Affairs, University of Washington. http://evans.uw.edu/sites/default/files/public/ResilientNonprofits2011_0.pdf.

Human Services Council. 2015. *New York Nonprofits in the Aftermath of FEGS: A Call to Action*. New York: Human Services Council. http://www.capitalnewyork.com/sites/default/files/Nonprofits%20in%20the%20Aftermath%20of%20FEGS%202016.pdf.

Hwang, Hokyu and Walter W. Powell. 2009. "The Rationalization of Charity: The Influences of Professionalism on the Nonprofit Sector," *Administrative Science Quarterly*, 54: 268–298.

In the Public Interest. 2015. *A Guide to Evaluating Pay for Success Programs and Social Impact Bonds*. Washington, DC: In the Public Interest. http://www.inthepublicinterest.org/wp-content/uploads/ITPI-Pay-for-Success-Guide-Dec-2015.pdf.

Johnson, M., and Michael E. Austin. 2008. "Evidence-Based Practice in the Social Services: Implications for Organizational Change," *Journal of Evidence Based Social Work*, 5, (1–2): 239–269.

Keightley, Mark P. 2013. *An Introduction to the Low-Income Housing Tax Credit*. Washington, DC: Congressional Research Service. Report #RS22389. https://www.fas.org/sgp/crs/misc/RS22389.pdf.

Krauskopf, Jack, Micheline Blum, Romuald Litwin, Jennifer Hughes, and Alexis Browne. 2009. *The Helpers Need Help: New York City's Nonprofit Human Service Organizations Persevering in Uncertain Times*. New York: School of Public Affairs, Baruch College. https://www.baruch.cuny.edu/spa/centers-and-institutes/center-for-nonprofit-strategy-and-management/documents/CNSM_HelpersNeedHelpReport.pdf.

Leachman, Michael, Nick Albares, Kathleen Masterson, and Marlana Wallace. 2016. *Most States Have Cut School Funding, and Some Continue Cutting*. Washington, DC: Center for Budget and Policy Priorities. http://www.cbpp.org/sites/default/files/atoms/files/12-10-15sfp.pdf.

Lewis, Gregory B. and Michael Rushton. 2007. "Understanding State Spending on the Arts, 1976-1979," *State and Local Government Review*, 39, 2: 107–114.

Lynch, Karen, E. 2014. *Social Services Block Grant: Background and Funding*. Washington, DC: Congressional Research Service. https://greenbook.waysandmeans.house.gov/sites/greenbook.waysandmeans.house.gov/files/CH%2010%2094-953_gb_0.pdf.

McBeath, Bowen and William Meezan. 2010. "Governance in Motion: Service Provision and Child Welfare Outcomes in Performance-Based, Managed Care Contracting Environment," *Journal of Public Administration Research and Theory*. Vol. 20, Supplement 1: The State of Agents: A Special Issue (January): i101–i123.

McKeever, Brice S. 2015. *The Nonprofit Sector in Brief 2015: Public Charities, Giving, and Volunteering*. Washington, DC: Urban Institute. http://www.urban.org/sites/default/files/alfresco/publication-pdfs/2000497-The-Nonprofit-Sector-in-Brief-2015-Public-Charities-Giving-and-Volunteering.pdf.

Metz, Allison J. R., Karen Blasé, and Lillian Bowie. 2007. *Implementing Evidence-Based Practices: Six Drivers of Success*. Part 3 in a Series on Fostering the Adoption of Evidence-Based Practices in Out-Of-School Time Programs. Child Trends. 2007. http://www.childtrends.org/wp-content/uploads/2013/07/2007-29EVPSuccess.pdf

Miller, Clara. 2003. "Hidden in Plain Sight: Understanding Nonprofit Capital Structure," *The Nonprofit Quarterly* 10, 1: 16–23. http://www.nonprofitfinancefund.org/sites/default/files/docs/2010/NPQSpring03.pdf.

Miron, Gary and Charisse Gulosino. 2013. *Profiles of For-Profit and Nonprofit Education Management Organizations*. Fourteenth Edition—2011–2012.

Boulder, CO: National Education Policy Center. http://nepc.colorado.edu/files/emo-profiles-11-12.pdf.

Mitchell, Alison. 2015. *Medicaid Financing and Expenditures.* Washington, DC: Congressional Research Service. https://www.fas.org/sgp/crs/misc/R42640.pdf.

Mosley, Jennifer. 2014. "From Skid Row to the Statehouse: How Nonprofit Homeless Service Providers Overcome Barriers to Policy Advocacy Involvement." In *Nonprofits and Advocacy: Engaging Communities and Governments in an Era of Retrenchment.* Pekkanen, Robert J., Steven Rathgeb Smith, and Yutaka Tsujinaka, eds. (pp. 107–134). Baltimore, MD: Johns Hopkins University Press.

National Center for Education Statistics (NCES). 2015. "Charter School Enrollment," in The Condition of Education. Washington, DC: NCES. http://nces.ed.gov/programs/coe/pdf/coe_cgb.pdf.

National Council of Nonprofits. 2010. *State Budget Crises: Ripping the Safety Net Held by Nonprofits.* Washington, DC: National Council of Nonprofits. https://www.councilofnonprofits.org/sites/default/files/documents/Special-Report-State-Budget-Crises-Ripping-the-Safety-Net-Held-by-Nonprofits.pdf.

National Trust for Historic Preservation. 2014. *Catalyst for Change. The Federal Historic Tax Credit: Transforming Communities.* Washington, DC: NTHP. http://www.preservationnation.org/take-action/advocacy-center/policy-resources/Catalytic-Study-Final-Version-June-2014.pdf.

Ng, Terence, Charlene Harrington, MaryBeth Musumeci, and Erica L. Reaves. 2015. *Medicaid Home and Community-Based Services Program: 2012 Data Update.* Kaiser Family Foundation. http://kff.org/medicaid/report/medicaid-home-and-community-based-services-programs-2012-data-update/.

Palmer, Emily and Campbell Robertson. 2016. Mississippi Fights to Keep Control of Its Beleaguered Child Welfare System," *The New York Times.* 17 January. http://www.nytimes.com/2016/01/18/us/mississippi-fights-to-keep-control-of-itsbeleaguered-child-welfare-system.html.

Pekkanen, Robert J., Steven Rathgeb Smith, and Yutaka Tsujinaka, eds. 2014. *Nonprofits and Advocacy: Engaging Communities and Governments in an Era of Retrenchment.* Baltimore, MD: Johns Hopkins University Press.

Phillips, Susan D., and Steven Rathgeb Smith, eds. 2011. *Governance and Regulation of the Third Sector: International Perspectives.* London: Routledge.

Public Agenda. 2014. *Charter Schools in Perspective.* Spencer Foundation and Public Agenda. http://www.in-perspective.org/.

REDF. 2016. *REDF Collaborates with the Federal Social Innovation Fund to Expand Jobs and Opportunities across America.* http://redf.org/wordpress/wp-content/uploads/2016/02/SIF-REDF-Press-Release-2_9_16.pdf.

Reiser, Dana Brakman. 2013. "Theorizing Forms of Social Enterprise," *Emory Law Journal,* 62: 681.

Roman, John K., Kelly A. Walsh, Sam Bieler, and Samuel Taxy. 2014. *Pay for Success and Social Impact Bonds: Funding the Infrastructure for Evidence-Based Change.* Washington, DC: Urban Institute. http://www.urban.org/sites/default/files/alfresco/publication-pdfs/413150-Pay-for-Success-and-Social-Impact-Bonds-Funding-the-Infrastructure-for-Evidence-Based.PDF.

Sabeti, Heerad. 2009. *The Emerging Fourth Sector: Executive Summary*. Fourth Sector Network. http://www.fourthsector.net/attachments/39/original/The_Emerging_Fourth_Sector_-_Exec_Summary.pdf?1253667714.

Salamon, Lester M., ed. 2002. *The Tools of Government*. New York: Oxford University Press.

Smith, Steven Rathgeb. 1993. "The New Politics of Contracting: Citizenship and the Nonprofit Role." In *Public Policy for Democracy*. Helen Ingram and Steven Rathgeb Smith, eds. (pp. 198–221). Washington, DC: Brookings Institution Press.

Smith, Steven Rathgeb. 2012. "Social Services." In *State of Nonprofit America*, 2nd ed. Lester M. Salamon, ed. (pp. 192–228). Washington, DC: Brookings.

Smith, Steven Rathgeb and Michael Lipsky. 1993. *Nonprofits for Hire: The Welfare State in the Age of Contracting*. Cambridge, MA: Harvard University Press.

Smith, Steven Rathgeb and Susan D. Phillips. 2016. "The Changing and Challenging Environment of Nonprofit Human Services: Implications for Governance and Program Implementation," *Nonprofit Policy Forum*, 7, (1): 63–76.

Snyder, Laura and Robin Rudowitz. 2015. *Medicaid Financing: How Does It Work and What are the Implications?* Kaiser Family Foundation. http://files.kff.org/attachment/issue-brief-medicaid-financing-how-does-it-work-and-what-are-the-implications.

Snyder, Laura, Katherine Young, Robin Rudowitz, and Rachel Garfield. 2016. *Medicaid Expansion Spending and Enrollment in Context: An Early Look at CMS Claims Data for 2014*. Menlo Park, CA: Kaiser Family Foundation. http://files.kff.org/attachment/issue-brief-medicaid-expansion-spending-and-enrollment-in-context-an-early-look-at-cms-claims-data-for-2014.

Spar, Karen. 2011. *Federal Benefits and Services for People with Low Income: Programs, Policy, and Spending, FY2008-FY2009*. Washington, DC: Congressional Research Service. http://greenbook.waysandmeans.house.gov/sites/greenbook.waysandmeans.house.gov/files/RL41625_gb.pdf.

Strom, Stephanie. 2011. "A Quest for Hybrid Companies That Profit, but Can Tap Charity," *The New York Times*. October 12, 2011.

Stubbs, Ryan and Henry Clapp. 2015. "Public Funding for the Arts: 2015 Update", *GIA Reader*, 26, 3 (Fall). Grantmakers in the Arts. http://www.giarts.org/article/public-funding-arts-2015-update.

Thornley, Ben, Jacquelyn Anderson, and Lauren Dixon. 2015. *Impact to Last: Lessons from the Front Lines of Social Enterprise*. San Francisco: REDF. https://redfworkshop.org/wp-content/uploads/2015/09/Impact-to-Last.pdf.

US Census Bureau. 2014. *Economic Census*. Services Report. Washington, DC.

Washington State Housing Finance Commission. 2016. *Nonprofit Facilities: Buy, Build, Renovate—Even Refinance*. Seattle, WA: Washington State Housing Finance Commission. http://www.wshfc.org/facilities/npfBrochure.pdf.

Wertheimer, David. 2011. "Maximizing the Impact and Amplifying the Voice of Philanthropy," *Responsive Philanthropy* (Fall): 1-6. http://www.ncrp.org/files/rp-articles/Responsive%20Philanthropy_Fall11_Homelessness.pdf.

Wing, Kenneth and Mark A. Hager. 2004. *Getting What We Pay For: Low Overhead Limits Nonprofit Effectiveness*. Washington, DC: The Urban Institute. http://www.urban.org/sites/default/files/alfresco/publication-pdfs/311044-Getting-What-We-Pay-For.PDF.

Chapter 4

Tax Treatment of Nonprofit Organizations

A Two-Edged Sword?

Evelyn Brody and Joseph J. Cordes

Nonprofit organizations have come to rely on a variety of special tax rules to secure an important portion of the resources needed to support their various activities. As a result, charitable organizations have benefited from preferential tax treatment. In some cases, however, these benefits come with a price in the form of constraints on what nonprofits are allowed to do. Providing financial support to the nonprofit sector through the tax code also makes the sector dependent on the vicissitudes of tax policy.

At least since Joseph's proclamation of a land law in Egypt that "Pharaoh should have the fifth part; except the land of priests only, which become not Pharaoh's" (Gen. 47:26), societies have acknowledged the presence of a nontaxable sector. In modern America, the nexus between the government and the nontaxable sector is myriad and complex. Multiple levels of government lay claim to different sources of tax revenue. State and local governments rely primarily on property and sales taxes; the federal government relies primarily on personal and corporate income taxes and payroll taxes. The nonprofit sector embraces a range of mutual, donative, and commercial enterprises, not all of which qualify for exemption under one or more of the foregoing taxes. The government provides supply-side tax subsidies for two specific forms of support for charity: donations and borrowing through bond finance. Both government direct expenditures (see chapter 2) and demand-side tax expenditures (see chapter 3) provide billions of dollars of additional support to social service charities. While the state attorney generals enforce the substantive nonprofit laws, Congress gives the Internal Revenue Service (IRS) an increasing role in regulating the nonprofit-government border and the nonprofit-commercial border (Simon, Dale, and Chisolm 2006), as well as the financial arrangement between charities and their insiders (Brody 1998a).

A few words on terminology will help focus the following discussion. The public often conflates the terms "nonprofit" and "tax exempt." Nonprofit entities fall loosely into two categories: charities (including churches, schools, hospitals, and social service organizations) and mutual-benefit organizations (including labor unions, trade associations, and social clubs). While exemption from federal, state, and local taxes is available to most corporations and trusts organized as nonprofit enterprises under state law, so central is the federal tax law's role that nonprofits have come to be known by their designation in the Internal Revenue Code. For example, charities are referred to as "section 501(c)(3)" organizations. Importantly, most of the special tax treatments discussed in this chapter (notably, deductibility of contributions and property tax and sales tax exemptions) extend only to charities, while mutual-benefit nonprofits generally enjoy only income tax exemption. Similarly, "action" organizations (which engage in substantial lobbying) generally qualify for exemption only as section 501(c)(4) social welfare organizations, which cannot offer tax deductibility to their donors. Because of its focus on the tax benefits for charities, this chapter sometimes uses the term "nonprofit" interchangeably with "charity."

Tax exemption confers financial advantages on nonprofit organizations that other providers of goods and services do not enjoy. Tax exemption allows nonprofits to keep much, if not all, of the surplus earned from a range of income-producing activities. In addition, charities have access to several unique sources of revenue: at the federal level, tax-deductible charitable contributions and the ability to issue tax exempt bonds; at the state level, property tax exemption and sales tax exemption on purchases.

But what the government provides it can also take away—or at least regulate. Tax exemption casts the government in the role not just of benefactor but also of certifying the legitimacy of nonprofit organizations through requirements for tax exempt status and regulation of what nonprofits can and cannot do to retain their tax-preferred status.

The special tax treatment of nonprofit organizations and the accompanying tax regulations make up a major set of government policies for the nonprofit sector. As a result, changes in tax policy can be as important to the nonprofit sector as the ebb and flow of government spending. Thus, after summarizing the main tax benefits nonprofit organizations enjoy, we consider a number of questions raised by the tax treatment of nonprofit organizations:

- What is the economic importance of nontaxable status to nonprofit organizations?
- What policy judgments does the current tax treatment of nonprofits reflect?
- What strings are attached to receipt of the nonprofit tax exemption?

- How does the existing web of tax provisions and regulations shape the behavior of donors and nonprofit organizations?
- What does the future hold for the tax treatment of nonprofit organizations?

TAX POLICY TOWARD NONPROFIT ORGANIZATIONS

The government acts as a benefactor of the nonprofit sector through the tax code in two broad ways. First, allowing individuals and corporations to deduct the value of charitable contributions against income and estate taxes provides an important economic incentive for private donors to provide financial support to a wide range of philanthropies. It is widely recognized that allowing such deductions effectively reduces the out-of-pocket cost of supporting nonprofit organizations by an amount that depends on the donor's tax rate. For example, if the tax rate is 25 percent, allowing a tax deduction for charitable contributions cuts the net cost of contributing from $1.00 to $0.75 because the taxpayer gets back a tax deduction that saves $0.25 in tax for every dollar contributed. A deduction has the upside-down effect of having a greater subsidy value to those in the highest tax brackets; moreover, only those who itemize their personal deductions may claim deductions for charitable contributions. The price of giving falls further for gifts of appreciated property, by the capital gains tax that would have been paid had the donated property been sold.[1] Charitable gifts may not, generally, reduce adjusted gross income by more than 50 percent.

In addition to deductions that may be taken against income for charitable contributions, the tax code also allows charitable contributions to be deducted against the taxable value of estates. Although this provision is relevant only for a relatively small number of estates that are taxable in 2016 (a married couple enjoys a federal estate tax exclusion of $10.9 million), in those cases where estate taxes are due, the deduction lowers the after-tax cost of leaving bequests to charities by up to 40 cents on the dollar.

The federal tax code allows nonprofit organizations to devote more financial resources to support their philanthropic missions by exempting them from the obligation of paying corporate or trust income taxes. In addition to the charitable contribution deduction and entity-level exemption, the federal tax system subsidizes charities by granting them the ability to issue section 501(c)(3) bonds, the interest income of which is exempt from tax. Similarly, states typically exempt nonprofits from state income tax and exempt charities from local property taxes (as well as sales taxes on purchases). Entity-level tax exemption, though quite broad, does not extend to any and all income earned or property owned by a nonprofit organization. In particular, the income must be earned from activities deemed related to the organization's exempt purpose. Since the 1950s, nonprofit organizations have been subject to a federal "unrelated business income tax," which is meant to tax nonprofits on the same basis as for-profit corporations on income earned in a trade or business that is regularly carried on and not substantially related to the nonprofit's exempt purposes (Hansmann 1989; Simon, Dale, and Chisolm 2006; Brody 2009). States that levy corporate income taxes usually follow the federal government's lead in this area by imposing their own unrelated business income taxes, and most states require that property be used for an exempt purpose to qualify for property tax exemptions (Brody 2002).

ECONOMIC VALUE OF THE CHARITABLE DEDUCTION, TAX EXEMPTION, AND TAX EXEMPT BONDS

What is the economic importance of special tax treatment to charities? The accompanying tables provide data bearing on this question.

Charitable Deduction

Each year the Joint Committee on Taxation estimates the cost to taxpayers, in forgone tax revenue, of providing tax incentives to individuals and corporations for contributing to charitable activities (JCT 2006). As shown in table 4.1, the five-year cost (for fiscal years 2015–2019) of this "tax expenditure" is estimated at $260.1 billion.

From the perspective of nonprofit organizations, what matters, however, is not the budgetary cost of tax incentives for charitable deductions, but the importance of charitable contributions as a financial resource and how much additional giving these tax incentives encourage. That is, taking the 2015–2019 numbers in table 4.1, the charitable contribution deduction could increase donations by more or less than the $260 billion in forgone taxes over the next five years, depending on how responsive donors are to the tax incentive.

Charitable deductions vary in importance as a resource for supporting nonprofit activities, as set forth in table 4.2. On the one hand, some nonprofits,

Table 4.1   Charitable Tax Expenditures (2015–2019)

	Estimated Budgetary Cost of Tax Deductions for Charitable Contributions		
Charitable Activity	Corporate Tax Expenditure ($Billions)	Individual Tax Expenditure ($Billions)	Total ($Billions)
Education	1.9	33.1	35.0
Health	9.9	16.8	26.7
Social services (i.e., other)	5.41	193.0	198.4

Source: US Congress, Joint Committee on Taxation (2015).

such as those in health care (most notably hospitals), depend relatively little on charitable gifts. While for others, such as education, charitable gifts are a more important source of revenue. Overall, notwithstanding growth in alternative sources of funding, private contributions remain a significant financial resource for most philanthropic organizations.

How much lower would private contributions be if donations to charity were not deductible? In the case of giving by individuals, which account for more than three-fourths of private contributions (Center on Philanthropy at Indiana University 2015), there is fairly broad empirical consensus among economists who have studied private giving that individual donors are at least somewhat sensitive to the after-tax cost of giving, although there is a range of sensitivity estimates. The higher end of the range suggests that increasing (decreasing) the cost of giving by 10 percent decreases (increases) contributions by at least 10 percent. The lower end of the range implies considerably more modest responses, with a (permanent) 10 percent increase (decrease) in the cost of giving leading to only a 5 percent decrease (increase) in contributions (Gravelle and Sherlock 2009).

The responsiveness of corporate donors and of bequests to changes in the after-tax cost of giving has not been studied as intensively as the price sensitivity of private giving. Estimates of the determinants of corporate giving suggest that the responses of corporations to changes in the after-tax cost of giving are similar to the range of estimates reported above for individual giving (Joulfaian 1991). In the case of bequests, some research suggests that a 10 percent decrease (increase) in the cost of making a bequest would increase (decrease) bequests by just over 20 percent (Bakija and Gale 2003a, 2003b), although other research again shows a wide variance (Joulfaian 2004, 2005a, 2005b).

Table 4.2 Private Contributions as a Percentage of Nonprofit Revenue (2011)

Subsector	Median Percent (%)	Mean Percent (%)
Total	33.2	41.0
Arts and culture	40.6	44.5
Public and societal benefits	42.1	45.3
Education	14.1	32.2
Environment and animals	65.9	58.3
Health	11.3	33.1
Human services	18.4	34.8
International affairs	96.7	74.6
Religion related	95.7	74.0
Unknown	78.0	58.4

Source: Tabulations based on digitized IRS 990 data for the fiscal year 2011 from the National Center on Charitable Statistics 2016.

Table 4.3 Effect of Tax Deductions on Financial Resources of Charities

NTEE Group	Total Private Contributions ($Billions)	Predicted Change in Contributions ($Billions)	Predicted Change as a Percent of Financial Resources (%)
Arts and Culture	12.2	3.7	13.4
Education	31.8	9.5	9.7
Environment and animals	6.5	2.0	17.4
Health	23.4	7.0	9.9
Human services	35.3	10.6	10.2
International foreign affairs	18.8	5.6	22.4
Public and societal benefits	9.4	2.8	13.6
Religion related	7.5	2.3	22.2
Unknown	0.5	0.15	17.5

Source: Tabulations based on digitized IRS 990 data for the fiscal year 2011 from the National Center on Charitable Statistics 2016 and on author calculations.

Table 4.3 presents some rough estimates of the effect of charitable tax deductions for the case in which donations are assumed to be fairly responsive to changes in the after-tax cost of giving. The estimates are based on applying a factor to total private contributions that assumes that in the case of private donors a 1 percent increase (decrease) in the after-tax cost of giving would result in a 1 percent decrease (increase) in giving by individuals and corporations. In addition, we assume that individual contributions enjoy an average combined federal-state tax subsidy of 30 percent. Taken together, these assumptions imply that if contributions were not tax deductible, individual contributions would decline by approximately 30 percent. Applying that factor to the contribution levels shown in table 4.3, one can roughly estimate the decrease in financial resources that nonprofit organizations would experience if charitable contributions were not tax deductible. These estimates suggest that absent charitable tax deductions, the financial resources of nonprofit organizations would fall by amounts ranging from just under 10 percent to just over 20 percent.

At the same time, as noted in the previous two chapters and as discussed below, charitable giving did not drop as sharply in the 1980s as these calculations would portend when the price of giving rose, which has led some analysts to favor using a lower price sensitivity factor for charitable giving. In this case, eliminating charitable tax deductions would cut the total financial resources of nonprofit organizations by between roughly 4.9 and 11.2 percent.[2]

Exemption from Corporate Income Taxes

Data tabulated from Form 990 returns (National Center for Charitable Statistics 2005 [see references for Q]) show that in 2011 the charities

Table 4.4 Total Surplus by NTEE Group, 2011 (Billions of $)

NTEE Group	Total Surplus ($Billions)
Arts and culture	3.4
Education	28.0
Environment and animals	1.0
Health	31.6
Human services	7.6
International foreign affairs	0.9
Public and societal benefits	4.2
Religion related	0.9
Unknown	0.02

Source: Tabulations based on digitized IRS 990 data for the fiscal year 2011 from the National Center on Charitable Statistics 2016.

listed in table 4.4 reported surpluses ranging from $3.4 billion to $30.6 billion.

The size of such nonprofit surpluses is sometimes viewed as an indicator of the economic importance of the corporate income tax exemption (CBO 1997). The reader should bear in mind, however, that the residual between income and expense that is measured by the *surplus* of a nonprofit organization is not a measure of *profit* as accountants and economists would understand the term. For example, in computing a nonprofit's surplus, donations are appropriately treated as a source of funds. Although donations could, in theory, be counted as a taxable receipt for determining taxable profit, given the stated rationale for organizing as a nonprofit organization, this seems rather unlikely. Similarly, for policy reasons, one might choose not to count "below-market" fees received for providing mission-related services to clients as a taxable receipt. Moreover, as a recent Congressional Budget Office (CBO) report points out, if the nonprofit surplus were to become subject to tax, nonprofits (and other tax exempt organizations) might react by reducing their taxable income by, for example, lowering fees charged for services provided or increasing staff salaries (CBO 2005).

A more reasonable measure of what might be termed the "potentially taxable income" of nonprofit organizations would be the income earned from investments plus profit earned on activities undertaken with the specific intent of earning income to support mission-related activities. This amount is not directly observable from the financial data that nonprofit organizations provide. An estimate of this magnitude can be inferred by adding together an organization's interest, dividend, and net rental income plus capital gains from sales of securities and other assets plus its gross profit on sales of goods (Cordes 2004; Halperin 2011).

These estimates of nonprofit organizations' potentially taxable income are presented in table 4.5. If one were to apply the current 34 percent federal

Table 4.5 Potentially Taxable Income of Public Charities, 2011

NTEE Group	Estimated Potentially Taxable Income ($Billions)	Estimated Income Tax Savings ($Billions)	Tax Saving as a Percent of Total Revenue (%)
Arts and culture	3.4	1.2	3.7
Education	28.0	9.5	3.6
Environment and animals	1.0	0.3	2.5
Health	31.67.6	10.7	1.2
Human services	7.6	2.61.4	1.2
International foreign affairs	0.90	0.3	0.9
Public and societal benefits	4.2	1.4	2.8
Religion related	0.9	0.3	2.6
Unknown	0.02	0.005	0.2
Total	77.6	26.4	1.7

Source: Tabulations based on digitized IRS 990 data for the fiscal year 2011 from the National Center on Charitable Statistics 2016.

rate that applies to all but the highest-income corporations, tax exemption is estimated to increase the resources of charitable nonprofit organizations by roughly $27 billion in the aggregate.[3]

Exemption from Property Taxes

Table 4.6 presents data showing the value of the tax exemption from local property taxes. Because of the myriad of local property tax rates, it is extremely difficult to place a precise value on the aggregate value of the property tax exemption. table 4.6 presents estimates of the financial impact of the nonprofit property tax exemption drawn from Cordes (2011).

Ability to Issue Tax Exempt Bonds

According to data from the IRS Statistics of Income Division, section 501(c)(3) organizations reported over $392 billion in outstanding tax exempt bonds in 2011 (Arnsberger 2015, table 1). This amount represents an explosion in tax exempt borrowing. Note that after the Tax Reform Act of 1986 and until the Taxpayer Relief Act of 1997, a charity other than a nonprofit hospital could not have outstanding more than $150 million of section 501(c)(3) bonds. A 1996 study (JCT 1996) reported that in 1992 hospitals issued $13.152 billion in section 501(c)(3) bonds, and nonhospitals (mainly private universities) issued $9.745 billion. The Joint Committee's revenue estimate (for the 1997 Taxpayer Relief Act provision repealing the non-hospital cap) totaled $798 million over the ten-year-period 1997–2006 (JCT 1997). The Joint Committee's latest tax expenditure budget separately reports the value,

Table 4.6 Estimated Financial Effect of State and Local Property Tax Exemption

Organization Type	Percent with Taxable Property	Estimated Tax Saving as a Percent of Total Revenue of Organizations with Taxable Real Property ($)		Estimated Tax Savings of Organizations with Taxable Real Property ($)	
		Mean	Median	Mean	Median
Higher education	75.6	4.0	1.6	2,865,423	430,402
Hospitals	76.4	3.1	0.7	3,724,043	1,371,685
Human service—multipurpose	26.7	3.7	1.1	107,156	21,890
Housing and shelter	52.8	12.1	5.0	76,111	69,624
Arts	13.7	5.8	1.9	219,305	19,195
Public benefit—performing arts	9.0	1.8	0.4	170,720	12,377
International affairs	6.6	2.0	0.2	83,082	11,611
All organizations	19.2	5.7	1.3	280,616	21,276

Source: Cordes (2012).

for the five-year period 2006–2010, of the exclusion of interest on state and local governments bonds at $13.1 billion for private nonprofit and qualified public educational facilities and at $19.1 billion for private nonprofit health facilities (JCT 2015).

Indirect Value of Other Tax Preferences

Of growing importance to charities is the indirect benefit from a host of tax preferences that, deliberately or incidentally, stimulate demand for the services that charities provide (see chapter 3). The exclusion from workers' income of employer-provided health insurance has long been one of the largest tax expenditures; while doctors and other proprietary firms benefit, so do the hospitals, which are mostly nonprofit (U.S. General Accounting Office 2003). The Bill-Clinton-era education tax credits, designed to help keep college affordable for the middle class, immediately made the list of top-20 tax expenditures; many education experts believe that colleges and universities capture the credits' value by charging higher tuition or granting lower internal aid (Brody 1999a; Turner 2011). Nonprofit day care providers benefit from the dependent care credit. Nonprofit housing developers benefit from the low-income housing tax credit. Although the nonprofits' share of these subsidies cannot be easily quantified, for the period 2005 to 2009 the Joint Committee on Taxation's (2005a) estimates by budget function peg the cost of tax expenditures—aside from the charitable contribution deduction—at $62.1 billion for education, $21.6 billion for social services (ignoring $231.7 billion for the child credit), and a staggering $609.9 billion for health.

SUBSIDY OR TAX BASE DEFINING?
A SOVEREIGNTY PERSPECTIVE

As the above-mentioned tables show, special tax treatments for charities increase the resources available to nonprofit organizations for their philanthropic missions.[4] It is tempting to treat these features of the federal and state tax systems as a quid pro quo in recognition of the goods and services provided. As Brody (1998b) has argued elsewhere, however, the underlying tax policy rationale for the nonprofit sector may be better characterized as involving some mix of (1) an attempt to properly measure the tax base and (2) an explicit intent to subsidize nonprofit organizations. Moreover, both of these approaches seem influenced by a historic desire to respect the sovereign boundaries between the nonprofit and public sectors rather than to ascertain the appropriate ability to pay off a taxpayer (either the entity or its donors or beneficiaries).

Charitable Deduction

Although a charitable contribution did not appear in the 1913 enactment of the income tax, Congress was concerned that the high marginal tax rates enacted to finance World War I would deter private philanthropy, and so it permitted individuals to reduce up to 15 percent of their net taxable income by charitable contributions. The scope of the deduction steadily expanded—broadening the range of eligible charitable activities, extending to corporate contributions, and increasing the percentage of taxable income (later, adjusted gross income) that could be deducted annually. Legislative histories reflect a clear subsidy motivation. In the Tax Reform Act of 1969, for example, Congress declared that raising the contribution limit from 30 percent of adjusted gross income to 50 percent (for cash contributions to public charities) would "strengthen the incentive effect of the charitable contribution deduction" (JCT 1970).

That policymakers view the charitable contribution deduction as a subsidy suggested by its treatment as a tax expenditure by both the Treasury Department and the Joint Committee on Taxation. Tax expenditures—as distinct from provisions that properly measure the tax base—include special income tax provisions "analogous to direct outlay programs and may be considered alternative means of accomplishing similar budget policy objectives" (JCT 2015).

As discussed more fully below, the subsidy view of the charitable contribution deduction remains firmly embedded in debates about fundamental tax reform. Some proposals retain, as an express recognition of the desirability of the subsidy, deductions for charitable contributions, while those proposals that eliminate the deduction do so deliberately to measure the donor's tax base more accurately and not to provide a subsidy.

Income Tax Exemption

In contrast to the charitable contribution deduction, the impetus for the entity's income tax or exemption appears not to have been to provide an economic subsidy to nonprofits. Rather, tax exemption appears to reflect an attempt to properly define the corporate income tax base, overlain with a historical desire (at least in the Anglo-Saxon tradition) to avoid government intrusion into a sphere of activities believed to belong to the church and its secular philanthropic successors. Thus, notwithstanding its economic value to nonprofit organizations, the nonprofit income tax exemption for "related" business activities is not treated as a tax expenditure: "In general, the imputed income derived from nonbusiness activities conducted by individuals or collectively by certain nonprofit organizations is outside the normal income tax base" (JCT 2015). In other words, tax exemption is not a tax subsidy when income never rises to the level of taxable in the first place. (The Joint Committee distinguishes exemptions from the unrelated business income tax, which are treated as tax expenditures.)

This explanation, however, begs the question of why nonprofit enterprises' "related" business income should fall outside of the normal tax base. Notably, why should fee-reliant charities such as hospitals and universities be treated differently than their for-profit counterparts providing similar goods and services (JCT 2015 mentions these examples)? As the proprietary sector makes further incursions into traditionally nonprofit industries, and as charities expand their search for related sources of revenue, pressures on the definition of a normal tax base increase (see Ben-Ner and Gui 1993; Brody 1996). See Brody (2009) for discussion of a failed legislative proposal to shift exemption from a relatedness test to a commerciality test.

In addition, the US Senate Finance Committee has raised questions and concerns about the exemption of income received by nonprofit hospitals and by colleges and universities. The broad issue raised has to do with how the financial benefits of the tax exemption of income received by nonprofit "meds and eds" are used. For example, do nonprofit hospitals use the exemption to provide charitable care, and do universities with large endowments that generate substantial tax exempt income use endowment income to provide financial aid to needy students? In the case of hospitals, these concerns led Congress, in 2006, to add subsection (r) to section 501, setting forth community benefit requirements for hospitals exempt under section 501(c)(3). In the case of private universities, the chairpersons of the House Ways and Means Committee, and the Senate Finance Committee, have recently sent letters to the presidents of universities with endowments of $1 billion or more asking them to describe how such endowments are used (Sherlock et al. 2015; Rosenbaum et al. 2015).

Even if tax exemption represents a subsidy, exemption makes for a blunt and inefficient form of subsidy. Interestingly, the tax treatment of the nonprofit sector resembles federal tax rules that respect the sovereignty of state and local governments. (Even JCT [1996] lumped nonprofits together with state and local governments, without commenting on the juxtaposition.) The federal income tax excludes from gross income "income derived from any public utility or the exercise of any essential governmental function and accruing to a State or any political subdivision thereof" (IRC sec. 115(a)). States and municipalities that borrow generally may issue bonds whose interest is tax exempt in the hands of the bondholders. Payments of state and local income and property taxes are deductible from income, but user fees paid to the government are treated as nondeductible payments for services. As already described, each of these inter-government tax treatments finds an analogue in the tax treatment of charities. Although no one would argue that the nonprofit sector enjoys true co-sovereignty with the public sector (because the nonprofit sector lacks the compulsory powers that inhere in a sovereign), this tax framework carries with it a sense of leaving the nonprofit sector inviolate and self-governing, while generally obligating charities to stay out of the business of petitioning government for subvention (see chapter 6 by Colinvaux).

HOW TAX EXEMPT STATUS AFFECTS THE RANGE AND SCOPE OF CHARITABLE ACTIVITIES

Despite the subsidy motive that seems to explain the rationale for the charitable contribution deduction, the government has not, as a matter of policy, tried to target the subsidy to particular uses. (For example, both a pro-life nonprofit and a pro-choice nonprofit can qualify for the tax treatment for charities.) Some might argue that open-endedness follows logically from using the tax code to provide the subsidy, because tax subsidies are harder to target than direct subsidies. Yet, many tax expenditures do come with eligibility rules that try to distinguish between activities that merit subsidy and those that don't. (The tax credit for research and experimentation is a particularly good example.) In the case of the charitable deduction, the only real rule is that a nonprofit be recognized as a 501(c)(3) organization. For discussion of the rules policing the charity and government border—that is, the restrictions on lobbying and the prohibition on electioneering—see chapter 6, by Colinvaux. Similarly, rules that determine which commercial activities will be granted tax exemption can be viewed as attempting to police the borders between nonprofit and for-profit organizations (see chapter 9; Simon, Dale, and Chisolm 2006; Brody 2009).

Moreover, Congress' choice of particular tax tools can affect behavior. The decision to subsidize charitable contributions through a tax deduction, instead of some other means, implicitly favors some philanthropic activities over others. Moreover, because of its close link to the tax system, the magnitude of the nonprofit subsidy will be sensitive to broader changes in tax policy (see Brody 1999a).

CHARITABLE CONTRIBUTION DEDUCTION

By its terms, the charitable contribution deduction is not directly targeted to any particular set of charitable activities. In practice, however, the deduction affords high-bracket donors (affluent individuals and corporations) with the greatest incentive to give. As a threshold matter, lower-income taxpayers typically do not itemize deductions and hence are not eligible to claim a deduction for charitable contributions. In addition, among itemizers, the benefit of the deduction increases with the taxpayer's marginal tax rate.

If higher-income donors had preferences for giving that broadly reflect those of the population at large, then providing an incentive to contribute that increased with a taxpayer's income would not tend to favor one type of charitable activity over others. Indeed, in the parlance of "optimal tax theory," one might argue that targeting the subsidy in this manner would be a cost-efficient way of encouraging giving, because the subsidy would be aimed at taxpayers who, some studies have shown, are more likely to respond to a reduction in the price of giving.

But there is considerable evidence that higher-income donors tend to channel their giving to charities in the arts and, particularly, education (Center on Philanthropy at Indiana University 2007). Thus, providing the benefit in the form of an uncapped itemized deduction skews the contributions toward charities such as arts and education and away from churches and social service organizations with low-income clienteles (Cordes 2011). To offset this tendency, the Obama administration has repeatedly, although unsuccessfully, proposed to cap value of itemized deductions (including the charitable contribution deduction) at a rate of 28 percent. Recently, the concern over the tax policy toward the philanthropy of the wealthy has also shifted to whether "donor advised funds" should be treated more like private foundations, subject to ongoing payout requirements and closer policing of private benefit.

EXEMPTION AND THE UNRELATED BUSINESS INCOME TAX

The attempt to draw boundaries between exempt and commercial activity can lead to suboptimal social policy. Notably, nonprofit hospitals are entitled to section 501(c)(3) tax exemption, but the returns to capital that nonprofit physician practices earn are not (of course, the government taxes wages earned from both for-profit and nonprofit hospitals). The IRS has struggled with the appropriate limits on "whole hospital joint ventures" and "joint operating agreements" with proprietary partners (Rev. Rul. 98–15, 1998–1 *Cum. Bull.* 718; Rev. Rul. 2004–51, 2004–1 *Cum. Bull.* 974). However, to the extent it makes economic sense for health care to be provided earlier (e.g., preventive care rather than treatment), we inefficiently constrain provision of preventive health care by denying charity exemption.

Moreover, the income tax exemption can cause nonprofit organizations to become more commercial, but the mechanism through which this happens is a subtle one. If nonprofits act as if a tension exists between earning income to finance their primary mission and undertaking their primary mission, then they will only pursue commercial activities when they can earn a premium return. Income tax exemption, though initially granted to respect the sovereignty of the nonprofit sector, creates opportunities for not-for-profits to earn such premium returns (Steuerle 1988).[5]

Limiting the exemption to related activities probably reinforces internal incentives that nonprofits already have to limit their commercial pursuits to areas where excess returns are likely to exist, which involve cost complementarities between the primary mission-related activity and the secondary commercial activities (Cordes and Weisbrod 1998).

The requirement that nonprofit organizations pay taxes on income earned from unrelated business activities appears, on its face, to be quite strict. However, the practical operation of the regime can be slippery. First, a particular activity is exempt or taxable depending on the purposes of the entity engaged in it.

Second, nonprofit organizations have sought out perfectly legal ways of shifting costs from their tax exempt activities to taxable activities to reduce, if not eliminate, tax liability. Because it is easier to shift costs from tax exempt activities to taxable activities when these activities are complements in production, nonprofit organizations appear to have been somewhat selective in the types of unrelated business activities they have chosen to undertake (Cordes and Weisbrod 1998; Hines 1999; Sansing 1998; Yetman 2001, 2005; Yetman and Yetman, 2009). Because many un-related businesses accordingly make use of assets used in or employees devoted to exempt activities, the allocation of dual-use expenses to the taxable activity can minimize net income. Indeed, in many years most unrelated business income tax returns have reported net losses. Jackson (2014) has reported that for the tax year 2010, exempt organizations reported $11 billion in total gross unrelated business income received, as well as aggregate deductions of $10.8 billion; about half of all Form 990-T filers paid UBIT. The IRS's own regulations limit its ability to reallocate deductions under current law.[6]

In some cases, the combination of tax rules inadvertently solves problems. For example, if a charity has issued tax exempt bond financing to build a facility, the charity may not use more than 5 percent of the proceeds for a taxable activity; accordingly, to preserve the exempt status of its bond financing, the charity will be loath to over-allocate the costs of dual-use assets away from the exempt activity. Moreover, nonprofits might have nontax reasons to conduct what would otherwise qualify as exempt activities in taxable form (Steuerle 2001).

EXEMPTION FROM PROPERTY TAXES

State property tax exemption does not automatically follow from Internal Revenue Code section 501(c)(3) status, but rather must be independently obtained. Many property tax statutes are less developed than the federal income tax regime, but typically require that the property must be both owned by a charity and used for a charitable purpose. In some states, charities can forfeit property tax exemption by using the property, even in part, for an unrelated business, while in other states, the exemption is apportioned. Similarly, in some, but not all states, exemption does not extend to property rented out to commercial tenants. Finally, many states adopt various acreage limits for exempt property held by particular types of organizations (see Brody 2007, 2010, 2016). Separately, as described below, in some localities, agreements by exempt owners to make "payments in lieu of taxes" have modified the statutory exemption.

REMOVING THE CAP ON TAX EXEMPT BORROWING

The ability of charities to issue tax exempt debt favors charities that generate a revenue stream sufficiently predictable to support an acceptable bond rating. The ability to issue low-rate debt while earning a market return on investment assets proves irresistible to well-endowed colleges and universities (even some private foundations are using bond financing, most often for offices); the arbitrage profits need not be returned to the federal government unless the bond is actually secured by the endowment or investment assets (Brody 1997). The most recently available Form 990 of Harvard University (admittedly an extreme example) reports, as of June 30, 2014, almost $3.3 billion in tax exempt debt—and almost $50 billion in investment assets.

RELYING ON THE TAX CODE: A NOT-SO-MIGHTY FORTRESS

Because most government subsidies to nonprofit organizations arrive in the form of tax incentives, changes in the tax code can affect their financial value. Important recent examples include changes in tax rates, the tax treatment of estates, and the tax treatment of capital income; attempts to better target charitable incentives; and proposals for fundamental reform of the income tax.

Changing Tax Rates

Changes in marginal (e.g., last dollar) income tax rates directly affect the subsidy value of the charitable contribution deduction. Legislation enacted in the 1980s slashed the top individual tax rate from 70 to 50 percent (in 1981) and 28 percent (in 1986). The top rate subsequently increased, to 31 percent in 1990 and to 39.6 percent in 1993. The 2003 Bush tax rate cuts reduced the top rate to 35 percent, but the 2013 "Fiscal Cliff" deal brought back the 39.6 percent top rate. Taxpayers subject to the alternative minimum tax, however, see the value of the charitable deduction set by the 28 percent (or the lower 26 percent) alternative minimum tax rate.

The Estate Tax

Studies have also been made of the impact on giving of reducing or eliminating the estate tax, now applicable only to the very largest estates. Repealing the estate tax altogether would have offsetting effects on charitable bequests. On the one hand, estates that were previously taxable would have more assets that could be distributed to both heirs and charities; this "wealth effect" would tend to increase charitable bequests. On the other hand, estate tax repeal would increase the cost of making a bequest from the current average of $0.40–$1.00. This "price effect" would have the opposite effect, reducing bequests. The empirical evidence indicates that the price effect would be stronger than the wealth effect, so that one estimate is that the net effect of abolishing the estate tax would be to reduce bequests by between 22 and 37 percent or by between $3.6 billion and $6 billion per year (Bakija, Gale, and Slemrod 2003; see also CBO 2004.)

Tax Treatment of Capital Income

Changes in the effective income tax rate on capital income can also affect the relative value of the nonprofit income tax exemption. After all, subsidies to private businesses in the form of tax credits can have unintended effects on nonprofits. In the 1980s, for example, in the first wave of tax reform under President Ronald Reagan, certain sectors of the business community actually enjoyed *negative* income tax rates through the combination of accelerated depreciation and investment tax credits on new equipment (JCT 1982). In this setting, the relative advantage resulting from the *zero* tax rate conferred by the nonprofit exemption was eroded. During this period, nonprofits had less incentive than before (or after) to seek out related commercial ventures as a source of income. Some might be pleased that nonprofits should so be discouraged from expanding their financial resources by undertaking businesslike activities. Yet, the relative reduction in the value of the corporate income tax exemption also may have caused nonprofits to avoid pursuing some legitimate opportunities for exploiting cost complementarities between their primary activity and ancillary profit-making activities. Nonprofits should also have found it financially more attractive to engage in nonexempt income-producing activities that benefited from investment tax incentives.

Lastly, from colonial times, the states have also granted exemptions to infant business industries,[7] a practice enjoying a resurgence as states deliberately choose the tool of property tax exemption to entice business relocation. As with negative tax rates, such property tax abatement programs have the effect of reducing the relative advantage that charitable nonprofits enjoy from the local property tax exemption. In addition to the extent that such tax abatement programs shrink the local property tax base, local governments may seek to limit the nonprofit property tax exemption. Nonprofits might contend that removing exemption will encourage mobile nonprofit organizations to move, thereby costing jobs. But the fact that charitable nonprofit organizations do not pay other taxes (e.g., sales on their purchases), as for-profit businesses do, may somewhat undermine the persuasiveness of that argument.

Targeting the Tax Subsidy

The fact that tax incentives for charitable giving tend to favor certain charities over others has also not been lost on policymakers. In the late 1990s, Republican proposals to grant additional tax credits for contribution to charities that primarily serve the poor attempted to better target the tax subsidy that the charitable deduction is intended to provide. The charities, however, closed rank, thwarting the attempt to treat antipoverty philanthropy as more worthy of public support by asserting that they do not know the income levels of their beneficiaries. In addition, Congress might selectively repeal tax exemption for particular institutions, such as hospitals, continuing the trend to identify overly commercial activities as candidates for taxation (see Brody 2009).

As a separate matter, the Joint Committee on Taxation (2005b) described three alternative proposals to limit the deduction for donations of appreciated property: (1) allowing a deduction for the contributor's basis only (or fair market value, if less); (2) allowing a fair market value deduction only for publicly traded securities; and (3) allowing a fair market value deduction for both publicly traded securities and assets used in the charity's conduct of its exempt purpose. Notably, the Joint Committee raised an additional efficiency concern: that, other things being equal, a charity would prefer a gift of cash to a gift of property to be sold.[8] A similar basis-only deduction rule that existed temporarily under the alternative minimum tax suggests how costly such targeted rules could be to charities.[9]

Some Recent Proposals for Change

In 2013, as part of the "fiscal cliff deal," Congress increased the top marginal individual income tax rates, and at year-end 2015, Congress made permanent the IRA Charitable Rollover (which allows individuals who have reached age 70½ to donate up to $100,000 to charitable organizations directly from their individual retirement account without treating the distribution as taxable income). Otherwise, there have been few major changes in the tax provisions impacting affecting nonprofits. There have, however, been a number of proposals made that, if enacted, would have led to potentially major changes in the charitable deduction.

These proposals are encapsulated in the draft Tax Reform Act of 2014 released by then-House Ways and Means Committee chairman Dave Camp (R-MI), which would have affected tax incentives for charitable giving both directly and indirectly. Most significantly, the Camp plan would have greatly reduced the number of taxpayers who itemize, and those who still did would have faced generally lower statutory tax rates. As noted by Rosenberg et al. (2014), the impacts of the Camp proposal can be grouped into four categories:

- *Group 1: Rate structure.* This group included changes to statutory individual income tax rates, the 10 percent surtax rate, repealing the individual alternative minimum tax, the treatment of capital gains and qualified dividends, and the phaseout of the 10 percent bracket.
- *Group 2: Standard deduction and other nonitemized deduction provisions.* This group included the increased standard deduction, repeal of personal exemptions, phaseout of the standard and itemized deduction, phaseout of the child tax credit, and other provisions.
- *Group 3: Itemized deductions other than charity.* This group included eliminating the deduction for medical expenses and state and local taxes paid, and the limitation on the deduction for mortgage interest.
- *Group 4: Charitable deduction.* This group included adding a 2 percent adjusted gross income (AGI) floor to the charitable deduction and a combined 40 percent of AGI limit.[5]

The total impact of the Camp plan is estimated to reduce individual giving in the range of 7 to 14 percent, which corresponds to a reduction of between $17 and $34 billion based on 2013 giving levels. The wide range reflects uncertainty in the responsiveness of individuals to the tax incentive provided by the charitable deduction. Provisions that directly affect the charitable deduction account for less than half of the total effect. The provisions included in groups 2 and 3—including the larger standard deduction and the elimination of most other itemized deductions—would dramatically reduce the number of taxpayers who elect to itemize deductions and by themselves would reduce giving by an estimated $5 billion to $10 billion. The lower statutory rates under the Camp bill (a $2–$5 billion effect) and interactions between provisions (a $2–$5 billion effect) account for the remaining decline.

Some candidates for the 2016 Republican presidential nomination have also proposed replacing the current income tax with a consumption-based flat tax. The treatment of charitable contributions under such a tax would be similar to those under an income tax. However, the consumption tax treatment of business enterprises under such plans would essentially eliminate the benefits of the nonprofit income tax exemption because the profits of many for-profit corporations would effectively be exempt from tax.

To the extent that the personal income tax was to be replaced with a personal consumption tax, one important policy issue would be whether to retain the charitable contribution deduction. Unlike the mortgage interest deduction, which is economically incompatible with the "correct" definition of the tax bases under a consumption tax, the charitable deduction could be retained as an explicit means of encouraging a particular desired type of consumption.[10] By retaining the charitable deduction, the Republican proposals come down on the side of retaining the charitable incentive for giving.

Finally, discussion continues about the potential for a value-added tax in the United States. If, for example, federal income taxes were scrapped altogether and replaced by a value-added tax, the most visible effect would be to eliminate the charitable contribution deduction. Moreover, because all capital income would face a zero federal tax rate, much of the relative advantage of the nonprofit tax exemption would be eroded, as would the advantage associated with being able to issue tax exempt bonds. (If all interest income is excluded from the tax base, then all bonds are tax exempt.) The proposals that would apply tax to inputs purchased by charities would remove exemption from all but their "value added" to goods and services and would require complex accounting and filing obligations to boot. Reform would also eliminate the tax-free treatment of fringe benefits, including health insurance, provided to workers. Finally, the proposals would in general collect a single level of tax on a host of commercial charitable services, notably health care.

It seems unlikely, however, that a value-added tax would be introduced as a complete replacement of existing federal income taxes. More plausibly, future budget deficit pressures might create a political environment in which a VAT would be enacted as a revenue source to supplement federal taxes. In that event, the current individual tax incentives for charitable giving would likely remain intact. Nonprofit organizations would, however, face issues of complying with a value-added tax of the sort discussed above.

STATE AND LOCAL INITIATIVES TO LIMIT THE NONPROFIT PROPERTY TAX EXEMPTION

Three features characterize the current property tax exemption for charities (see Brody 2002). First, the data, although sparse, suggest that exemptions granted to nonprofit organizations constitute only a small fraction of total exemptions (the largest category of exempt property belongs to governments). Second, municipal demands for voluntary payments in lieu of taxes (PILOTs)[11] occur only sporadically, and even where PILOT programs exist, they raise comparatively little revenue. Third, the press treats the charity exemption as front-page news. This is not, it turns out, the paradox it appears.

If "all politics is local," then no tax system is more local than the property tax. Property tax exemptions are enacted at the state level, often in the state constitution. However, property ownership by charities tends to cluster in center cities. Because property tax units are local (municipal, county, or special districts, such as school districts), the burden of exemption is distributed unevenly throughout the state. Worse, the same municipalities that host a disproportionately high share of nonprofit property often suffer a disproportionately high demand for public expenditures. Thus, averages mask the widely varying impact of exemptions on particular communities and of taxes or PILOTs on particular nonprofits. Moreover, the benefits of a particular charity's activities might be enjoyed more broadly than the narrowly defined community that bears the cost of the exemption. Finally, as charities engage in a wider range of activities, including some very commercial ones, public support for exemption crumbles. Much to the nonprofit sector's consternation, tax exemption has come to be viewed as a government subsidy rather than an inherent entitlement of the organizational form. In applying PILOTs, the charities that look most attractive to local governments are those (1) that have income (excluding, in general, only donations) and (2) whose income comes primarily from patrons outside the taxing jurisdiction. Accordingly, taxing the nonprofit can be viewed as a proxy for taxing the nonresident patrons of the organization. Currently, the practice of challenging exemption or seeking PILOTs focuses on hospitals, institutions of higher education, and, in some cases, foundations. Under the same theory, municipalities could extend this policy to museums and performing arts organizations—and even to break-even social service nonprofits, thus passing their costs on to government funders, state and federal. (Such a theory might provide a nonconstitutional explanation of why municipalities have not sought to tax churches, which rely primarily on donations, and whose benefits are primarily local.)

Recently, lawsuits and proposed legislation asserting tighter state and local definitions for exemption reflect a growing divergence of federal and state policies on tax exemption and a growing acceptance by the states of a quid pro quo rationale, particularly for health care and other income-generating organizations (see Brody 2007, 2010, 2016).

USING THE TAX CODE TO IMPROVE NONPROFIT GOVERNANCE

Increasingly, the federal tax regime affects the governance of nonprofit organizations (see Brody 1999b). Currently, the influence is largely passive, taking the form of mandated public disclosures that, in theory, spur good governance (see Brody 2012). Few substantive restrictions apply to charities other than private foundations: Notable exceptions include the fair-market-value requirements for insider transactions and the prohibition on political campaign activity and limits on legislative lobbying (see chapter 6).[12]

Although the IRS Form 990 is currently the most widely available uniform document on individual charity finances, it is not a complete window into nonprofit operations. Because of exemptions, it can be difficult, if not impossible, to obtain information on churches and on charities with less than $50,000 in gross receipts. Moreover, many of the forms as filed contain errors, some materially misleading. Some noncompliance is because of ignorance, some because of a desire to hide costs of fundraising and administrative expenses relative to program expenditures, and some intentional. Substantively, because the Form 990 focuses on finances, it does not provide much insight into the nature and quality of charity activities.

Separately, the US Treasury Department (2014) maintains a set of resources, including voluntary best practices, advising charities on how to avoid being used to advance terrorism.

FUTURE POLICY DIRECTIONS

As noted at the beginning of this chapter, tax exemption defines an important nexus between government and nonprofit organizations in the United States. Symbolically, in the public's eye, conferral of tax exempt status is seen as legitimating the activities of individual nonprofit organizations. At a more practical level, tax exemption expands the financial resources of nonprofit organizations in a variety of important ways.

Charities are vulnerable to—or would benefit from—four different types of changes in federal tax law. First, change could come head on, if Congress were to deliberately alter the eligibility rules; for example, Congress might repeal the tax exemption of nonprofit hospitals or impose a payout requirement on university endowments.[13] Second, change could come indirectly as a result of overall reform of the tax structure that affects the value of the charitable contribution deduction or of the income tax exemption; for example, Congress might alter the tax burden on individuals (thus indirectly altering the income tax or estate tax price of giving) or on businesses (thus directly altering the relative tax benefit of income tax exemption). Third, change could come incidentally through simplifying the tax code of rules that happen to fuel demand for the types of services charities provide; for example, Congress might strip away the tuition tax credits or eliminate the exclusion from workers' income for the value of employer-provided health insurance. The fourth potential change could come from a major federalization of the regulation of nonprofit governance.

Their reliance on tax subsidies suggests that nonprofits would not give them up without a fight. Viewing nonprofits as above the political fray was always probably an idealized image, and the growing talk of tax reform is already bringing forth educational efforts by charities. The increasingly political visibility of nonprofits will, in turn, likely put increased pressure on the current loose lobbying restrictions. In the process of defending against fundamental threats to their tax subsidies, charities risk appearing like any other special interest—and they could forfeit special claim to subsidies in the process.

Both this chapter and others suggest that the effects of eliminating all or some of the tax provisions that currently benefit nonprofit organizations would certainly not be uniform. For example, nonprofit organizations that depend on charitable contributions for a large portion of their financial resources have more reason for concern about tax changes that raise the after-tax cost of giving than do nonprofits that depend for their financing on fees-for-service paid out of government spending. Similarly, nonprofit organizations that rely on subsidies for specific social services that are provided through tax credits are more apt to be affected by changes in these provisions than are their counterparts that depend on charitable contributions.

Lastly, anytime two different tax regimes could apply to the same economic activity, the opportunity for tax arbitrage exists. There is some evidence that nonprofits have become increasingly aware of these opportunities and sophisticated at exploiting them. For example, some nonprofits use unrelated business activities to earn additional revenue and then shelter that income from tax by over-allocating to the taxable activity the expenses of dual-use assets. Yet, the desire of policymakers to preserve not only the political boundaries between nonprofit organizations and the government but also the economic boundaries between nonprofit organizations and for-profit enterprises may impose limits on this trend. As charities grow more sophisticated in operating both exempt and taxable enterprises, Congress might be unwilling to maintain the existing flexible tax regime. Short of replacing the income tax with a consumption tax, should it prove too hard to define taxable income for nonprofits, Congress could instead simply impose a (probably low-level) tax on investment income, making all nonprofit organizations potentially taxable.

NOTES

1. Under the complicated rate structure now in effect, donors have an incentive to donate "collectibles": Tax on the appreciation is saved at a 28 percent rate instead of the general 15 percent rate on long-term capital gains.

2. This result is obtained by replacing the assumed value of −1.0 for the price elasticity of giving in the calculation described in note 5 with a value of −0.50.

3. Churches are not required to file IRS Form 990. Hence the public charities listed in table 4.5 do not include the churches listed in table 4.2.

4. To use an accounting framework sketched out by Steuerle (1998), the charitable deduction increases the amount of charitable contributions of money and assets, and tax exemption allows nonprofits to capture a higher return on their net assets. Tax exempt bond financing allows nonprofits to earn arbitrage profits on their investments, and property tax exemption reduces the cost of real-property inputs to charitable activity.

5. Such premium returns become available to nonprofits because market competition drives up the return that taxable corporations earn before taxes in part to compensate for the corporate taxes. Because nonprofits do not need to pay corporate taxes on related business activities and can easily avoid even unrelated business income taxes, it is possible for nonprofit organizations to capture this premium as additional revenue. For a discussion of this mechanism, see Cordes and Weisbrod (1998), Rose-Ackerman (1982), and Steuerle (1988). It should also be noted that the exemption from property taxes as distinct from income taxes provides a different kind of financial benefit to nonprofits. See Cordes, Gantz, and Pollak (2002).

6. In *Rensselaer Polytechnic Institute*, the Internal Revenue Service lost an attempt to allow the university deductions only for the marginal costs of renting out a hockey stadium (*Rensselaer Polytechnic Inst. v. Commissioner*, 732 F.2d 1058 [2d Cir. 1984]). The Treasury regulations permit an allocation of dual-use expenses on "a reasonable basis." Treas. Reg. sec. 1.512(a)–1(c).

7. Note that early state governments made no sectoral distinctions in bestowing or withholding tax subsidies. New England canal, turnpike, bridge, and manufacturing companies enjoyed the same tax exemption extended to eleemosynary institutions such as Yale College (Hall 1992).

8. And things are not always equal: Following a study showing an alarming gap between the claimed value of some donated cars and the amounts that ultimately went to the charity, Congress in 2004 limited the deduction for donated cars to the amount realized by the charity upon resale (IRC sec. 170(f)(12)).

9. The price of giving also increased in 1986 for gifts of appreciated property when the unrealized appreciation became an item of tax preference under the alternative minimum tax (Auten, Cilke, and Randolph 1992). This rule was modified in 1990 and repealed in 1993. Table 7 in Auten, Cilke, and Randolph (2005, 280) shows that between 1979 and 1989, the average contribution (in 1991 dollars) by taxpayers with pretax income of $1 million or more dropped from $133,837 to $82,113, and by taxpayers with between $200,000 and $1 million in income dropped from $11,104 to $8,476.

10. Deducting interest expense is inconsistent with the proper definition of a true consumption tax base, under which interest income is untaxed.

11. The term has long been in use to refer to payments made to affected municipalities by the federal government. See Advisory Commission on Intergovernmental Relations (1981). States also pay PILOTs to affected municipalities, but payments often fall short of amounts due. See, for example, Brody (2016, 274), discussing Bostob's revamped PILOT program, as evaluated by Lustig (2015, 11).

12. For private foundations, Congress enacted specific penalty taxes not just for self-dealing but also for failure to distribute a minimum payout for charitable purposes, maintenance of excess business holdings, and jeopardizing investments.

13. See Sherlock (CRS) 2015. Such a payout proposal raises many difficult design issues, many of which are addressed in the private foundation payout context. Entities covered: all 501(c)(3) organizations, all public charities, only colleges and universities (and what if the university has a hospital)—and what about assets held by supporting organizations or affiliated entities, such as alumni associations? The base: "endowment" in the financial reporting sense or all surplus from investment assets? On all assets or just those acquired after date of enactment? Exclusions for set-asides? The calculation of tax: a fixed rate or a range? Based on last year's numbers or a moving average? Carrybacks and carryforwards of excesses? Qualifying the payout: what expenses count—management and overhead as well as tuition reduction? Restricted endowed gifts (say for the library or for faculty) that cannot be used for tuition—does that increase the expenditure requirement on other funds, or is the requirement fund by fund? The consequences: an excise tax or loss of exemption? See Brody 2008.

REFERENCES

Advisory Commission on Intergovernmental Relations. 1981. *Payments in Lieu of Taxes on Federal Real Property*. Washington, DC, Advisory Commission on Intergovernmental Relations, September.

Arnsberger, Paul. 2015. "Charities and Other Tax-Exempt Organizations, 2011." *Statistics of Income Bulletin* (Spring). https://www.irs.gov/pub/irs-soi/soi-a-npco-id1508.pdf.

Bakija, Joh M. "Tax Policy and Philanthropy: A Primer on the Empirical Evidence for the U.S. and its Implications" *Social Research* 80(2): 557–584.

Bakija, Jon M., and William G. Gale. 2003a. "Charitable Giving and the Estate Tax." *Tax Notes* 101 (December 8), 1233.

———. 2003b. "Effects of Estate Tax Reform on Charitable Giving." Washington, DC: The Urban Institute. *Tax Policy Issues and Options* Brief 6.

Bakija, Jon, William Gale, and Joel Slemrod. 2003. "Charitable Bequests and Taxes on Inheritance and Estates: Aggregate Evidence from Across States and Time." *American Economic Review* 93(2): 366–370.

Barry, John S. 1996. "How a Flat Tax Would Affect Charitable Contributions." Washington, DC: Heritage Foundation *Backgrounder*, (November 7).

Ben-Ner, Avner and Benedetto Gui, eds. 1993. *The Nonprofit Sector in the Mixed Economy*. Ann Arbor, MI: University of Michigan Press.

Bickley, James M. 2005. "Flat Tax Proposals and Fundamental Tax Reform: An Overview." Washington, DC: Congressional Research Service, Library of Congress. CRS Issue Brief IB95060.

Bradford, David S., and U.S. Treasury Tax Policy Staff. 1984. *Blueprints for Basic Tax Reform*, 2nd ed. Washington, DC: Tax Analysts.

Brody, Evelyn. 1996. "Institutional Dissonance in the Nonprofit Sector." *Villanova Law Review* 41(2): 433–504.

———. 1997. "Charitable Endowments and the Democratization of Dynasty." *Arizona Law Review* 39(3): 873–948.

———. 1998a. "The Limits of Charity Fiduciary Law." *Maryland Law Review* 56(4): 1400–1501.

———. 1998b. "Of Sovereignty and Subsidy: Conceptualizing the Charity Tax Exemption." *Journal of Corporation Law* 23(4): 585–629.

———. 1999a. "Charities in Tax Reform: Threats to Subsidies Overt and Covert." *Tennessee Law Review* 66(3): 687–763.

———. 1999b. "A Taxing Time for the Bishop Estate: What Is the I.R.S. Role in Charity Governance?" *University of Hawaii Law Review* 21(2): 537–591.

———, ed. 2002. *Property-Tax Exemption for Charities: Mapping the Battlefield*. Washington, DC: Urban Institute Press.

———. 2007. "The States' Growing Use of a Quid-Pro-Quo Rationale for the Charity Property Tax Exemption." *Exempt Organization Tax Review* 56(June): 269–288.

———. 2008. Comments at Panel on "A Technical Look at Endowment Spending: Policies, Filing, Accounting and Possible Legislation." In Transcript of the May 9, 2008 ABA Tax Section Exempt Organizations Committee Meeting. *Exempt Organization Tax Review* 61(July): 19.

———. 2009. "Business Activities of Nonprofit Organizations: Legal Boundary Problems." In *Nonprofits and Business*. C. Eugene Steuerle and Joseph J. Cordes, eds. (pp. 83–127). Washington, DC: Urban Institute Press.

———. 2010. "All Charities Are Property-Tax Exempt, But Some Charities Are More Exempt than Others." *New England Law Review* 44(3): 621–732.

———. 2012. "Sunshine and Shadows on Charity Governance: Public Disclosure as a Regulatory Tool." *Florida Tax Review* 12(4): 183–234.

_____. 2016. "The 21st Century Fight Over Who Sets the Terms of the Charity Property-Tax Exemption." *Exempt Organization Tax Review* 77(4) (April): 259–277.

CBO. See U.S. Congress, Congressional Budget Office.

Center on Philanthropy at Indiana University, 2007. Patterns of Charitable Giving by Income Group: 2005. Prepared for Google.

_____. 2015. *Giving USA 2014*. Glenview, IL: Giving USA Foundation.

Clotfelter, Charles T. 1990. "The Impact of Tax Reform on Charitable Giving: A 1989 Perspective." In *Do Taxes Matter? The Impact of the Tax Reform Act of 1986*. Joel Slemrod, ed. (pp. 203–235). Cambridge, MA: MIT Press.

Clotfelter, Charles T., and Richard L. Schmalbeck. 1996. "The Impact of Fundamental Tax Reform on Nonprofit Organizations." In *Economic Effects of Fundamental Tax Reform*. Henry Aaron and William Gale, eds. (pp. 211–246). Washington, DC: Brookings Institution.

Commonwealth of Massachusetts, Auditor of the Commonwealth, Div. of Local Mandates. 1994. *A Review of the Financial Impact of the C.58 Payments-in-Lieu-of-Taxes (PILOT) Program on Massachusetts Cities and Towns*, October 27. Boston: Commonwealth of Massachusetts.

Cordes, Joseph J. 2004. "The Partially Subsidized Muse: Estimating the Value and Incidence of Public Support Received by Nonprofit Arts Organizations." In *City Taxes, City Spending: Essays in Honor of Dick Netzer*. Amy Ellen Schwartz, ed. (pp. 198–241). Northampton, MA: Edward Elgar Publishing.

_____. 2011. "Re-Thinking the Deduction for Charitable Contributions: Evaluating the Effects of Deficit Reduction Proposals." *National Tax Journal* 64(4): 1001–1024.

_____. 2012. "Assessing the Nonprofit Property Tax Exemption: Should Nonprofit Entities be Taxed for Using Local Public Goods?" In *Value Capture and Land Policies*. Gregory K. Ingram and Yu-Hung Hong, eds. Cambridge, MA: Lincoln Institute of Land Policy.

Cordes, Joseph J., and Burton A. Weisbrod. 1998. "Differential Taxation of Nonprofits and the Commercialization of Nonprofit Revenues." In *To Profit or Not to Profit: The Commercial Transformation of the Nonprofit Sector*. Burton A. Weisbrod, ed. (pp. 83–105). Cambridge, England: Cambridge University Press.

Cordes, Joseph J., John O'Hare, and C. Eugene Steuerle. 2000. "Extending the Charitable Deduction to Non-Itemizers: Policy Issues." Washington, DC: The Urban Institute. *Charting Civil Society* Brief 7.

Enrich, Peter D. 1996. "Saving the States from Themselves: Commerce Clause Constraints on State Tax Incentives for Business." *Harvard Law Review* 110(2): 377–468.

Feldstein, Martin and Charles Clotfelter. 1976. "Tax Incentives and Charitable Contributions in the U.S.: A Microeconomic Analysis." *Journal of Public Economics* 5: 1–26.

Galper, Harvey and Eric Toder. 1983. "Owning or Leasing: Bennington College, and the U.S. Tax System." *National Tax Journal* 36(2): 257–261.

Graetz, Michael J. 1991. "Statement of Michael J. Graetz, Dept. Assistant Secretary (Tax Policy), Dept. of the Treasury before the Comm. on Ways and Means" (July 10), available (with LEXIS subscription) as *Treasury Official Testifies on*

Tax-Exempt Status of Hospitals. *Tax Notes Today* File 91 TNT 146-10, July 11. Lexis, Fedtax Library.

Gravelle, Jane and Sherlock, Molly. 2009. *An Overview of the Nonprofit and Charitable Sector.* Congressional Research Service, Washington, DC.

Hall, Peter Dobkin. 1992. *Inventing the Nonprofit Sector.* Baltimore, MD: Johns Hopkins University Press.

Hall, Robert E., and Alvin Rabushka. 1995. *The Flat Tax,* 2nd ed. Stanford, CA: Hoover Institution Press.

———. 1989. "Unfair Competition and the Unrelated Business Income Tax." *Virginia Law Review* 75: 605–635.

Halperin, Daniel. 2011. "Is Income Tax Exemption for Charities a Subsidy?" *Tax Law Review* 64: 283–312.

Hellerstein, Walter and Dan T. Coenen. 1996. "Commerce Clause Restraints on State Business Development Incentives." *Cornell Law Review* 81: 789–878.

Hines, James R. 1999. "Nonprofit Business Activity and the Unrelated Business Income Tax." In *Tax Policy and the Economy,* vol. 13. James M. Poterba, ed. (pp. 57–84). Cambridge, MA: MIT Press.

Jackson, Jael. 2014. "Unrelated Business Income Tax Returns, 2010." Internal Revenue Service Statistics of Income Bulletin (Winter). https://www.irs.gov/pub/irs-soi/soi-a-eoub-id1403.pdf.

JCT. See U.S. Congress, Joint Committee on Taxation.

Joulfaian, David, 1991. "Charitable Bequests and Estate Taxes." *National Tax Journal* 44(2): 169–180.

———. 2004. "Gift Taxes and Lifetime Transfers: Time Series Evidence." *Journal of Public Economics* 88(9–10): 1917–1929.

———. 2005a. "Estate Taxes and Charitable Bequests: Evidence from Two Tax Regimes." OTA Paper 92. Washington, DC: Office of Tax Analysis, U.S. Department of the Treasury. https://www.treasury.gov/resource-center/tax-policy/tax-analysis/Documents/ota92.pdf

———. 2005b. "Basic Facts on Charitable Giving." OTA Paper 95. Washington, DC: Office of Tax Analysis, U.S. Department of the Treasury. https://www.treasury.gov/resource-center/tax-policy/tax-analysis/Documents/ota95.pdf.

Lustig, Eric A. 2015. "A Continuing Look at Boston's Revised Payment in Lieu of Taxes (PILOT) Program: Update Version 2.0," 50 New Eng. L. Rev. On Remand 1 (2015), at https:// newenglrev.com/on-remand-2/volume-50-on-remand/lustig-a-continuing-look-at-bostons-revised-payment-in-lieu-of-taxes- pilot-program/.

National Center for Charitable Statistics. 2016. http://nccs.urban.org.

Price Waterhouse LLP and Caplin & Drysdale, Chartered. 1997. "Impact of Restructuring on Tax-Exempt Organizations." *Tax Notes Today* file 97 TNT 83-21, April 30, 1997. Lexis, Fedtax Library.

Randolph, William C. 1995. "Dynamic Income, Progressive Taxes, and the Timing of Charitable Contributions." *Journal of Political Economy* 103(4): 709–738.

———. 2005. "Charitable Deductions." In *The Encyclopedia of Taxation and Tax Policy,* 2nd ed. Joseph J. Cordes, Robert D. Bell, and Jane G. Gravelle, eds. (pp. 51–53). Washington, DC: Urban Institute Press.

Rose-Ackerman, Susan 1982. "Unfair Competition and Corporate Income Taxation." *Stanford Law Review* 34: 1017–1036.

Rosenbaum, et al. 2015. "The Value of the Nonprofit Hospital Tax Exemption Was 24.6 Billion in 2011." *Health Affairs* 34(7): 1225–1233.

Rosenberg, Joseph, C. Eugene Steuerle, Ellen Steele, and Amanda Eng. 2014. "Preliminary Estimates of the Impact of the Camp Tax Reform Plan on Charitable Giving." Washington, DC: Urban Institute. http://www.urban.org/research/publication/preliminary-estimates-impact-camp-tax-reform-plan-charitable-giving/view/full_report

Salamon, Lester M. 1995. *Partners in Public Service: Government-Nonprofit Relations in the Modern Welfare State*. Baltimore, MD: Johns Hopkins University Press.

Sansing, Richard. 1998. "The Unrelated Business Income Tax, Cost Allocation, and Productive Efficiency." *National Tax Journal* 51(2): 291–302.

Schiff, Jerald. 1990. *Charitable Giving and Government Policy*. New York: Greenwood Press.

Simon, John G., Harvey Dale, and Laura B. Chisolm. 2006. "The Tax Treatment of Nonprofit Organizations: A Review of Federal and State Policies." In *The Nonprofit Sector: A Research Handbook*, 2nd ed. Walter W. Powell and Richard Steinberg, eds. New Haven, CT: Yale University Press.

Sherlock, Molly F., Jane G. Gravelle, Margot L. Crandall-Hollick, and Jeffrey M. Stupak. 2015. "College and University Endowments: Overview and Tax Policy Options." Washington, DC: Congressional Research Service (7-5700 www.crs.gov R44293). At https://www.fas.org/sgp/crs/misc/R44293.pdf.

Steuerle, C. Eugene. 1988. "Current Federal Policy Issues for the Nonprofit Sector." Working Paper 88–10. Durham, NC: Duke University Center for the Study of Philanthropy and Voluntarism.

———. 1998. *Just What Do Nonprofits Provide?* Washington, DC: The Urban Institute. http://www.urban.org/sites/default/files/alfresco/publication-pdfs/1000102-Just-What-Do-Nonprofits-Provide-.pdf.

———. 2005. "A Win-Win Option for Charity and Tax Policy." *Tax Notes* 107(April 18): 361.

Turner, Nick. 2012. "Who Benefits from Student Aid? The Economic Incidence of Tax-Based Federal Student Aid." *Economics of Education Review* 31(4): 463–481.

U.S. Congress, Congressional Budget Office. 1997. "The Potential Effects of Tax Restructuring on Nonprofit Institutions." *CBO Papers* (February) Washington, DC: CBO.

———. 2002. "Effects of Allowing Nonitemizers to Deduct Charitable Contributions." *CBO Papers* (December). https://www.cbo.gov/sites/default/files/107th-congress-2001-2002/reports/12-13-charitablegiving.pdf.

———. 2004. "The Estate Tax and Charitable Giving." *CBO* Papers (July). https://www.cbo.gov/sites/default/files/108th-congress-2003-2004/reports/07-15-charitablegiving.pdf

———. 2005. "Taxing the Untaxed Business Sector." *CBO Background Paper* (July). https://www.cbo.gov/sites/default/files/109th-congress-2005-2006/reports/07-21-untaxedbus.pdf

U.S. Congress, Joint Committee on Taxation. 1970. *General Explanation of the Tax Reform Act of 1969.* JCS-16-70 (December 3). https://www.jct.gov/publications.html?func=startdown&id=2406.

———. 1982. *General Explanation of the Revenue Provisions of the Tax Equity and Fiscal Responsibility Act of 1982,* 97th Congress, 2nd Session, H.R. Rep. 97-4961. http://www.jct.gov/jcs-38-82.pdf.

———. 1996. *Impact on State and Local Governments and Tax-Exempt Organizations of Replacing the Federal Income Tax.* JCS-4-96. http://www.jct.gov/s-4-96.pdf

———. 1997. *General Explanation of Tax Legislation Enacted in 1997.* Washington, DC: Joint Committee on Taxation. https://www.jct.gov/publications.html?func=startdown&id=1215.

———. 2005a. *Historical Development and Present Law of the Federal Tax Exemption for Charities and Other Tax-Exempt Organizations.* JCX-29-05. http://www.jct.gov/x-29-05.pdf.

———. 2005b. *Options to Improve Tax Compliance and Reform Tax Expenditures.* JCS-2-05. http://www.jct.gov/s-2-05.pdf.

———. 2015. *Estimates of Federal Tax Expenditures for Fiscal Years 2015–2019.* JCX-141R-15. https://www.jct.gov/publications.html?func=startdown&id=4857.

U.S. General Accountability Office. 2005. Nonprofit, For-Profit, and Government Hospitals: Uncompensated Care and Other Community Benefits. Washington, DC

U.S. Treasury Department. 20014 *Protecting Charitable Organizations.* https://www.treasury.gov/resource-center/terrorist-illicit-finance/Pages/protecting-index.aspx.

Yetman, Robert. 2001. "Tax-Motivated Expense Allocations by Nonprofit Organizations." *Accounting Review* 76: 297–311.

———. 2005. "Causes and Consequences of the Unrelated Business Income Tax." Paper presented at the National Tax Association Conference, Miami 2005.

Yetman, Michelle and Robert Yetman. 2009. "Determinants of the Taxable Activities of Nonprofit Organizations." *Journal of Accounting and Public Policy* 28: 495–509.

Chapter 5

State Regulatory and Legal Framework

Cindy M. Lott and Marion Fremont-Smith

STATE REGULATION OF CHARITIES[1]

State governments have a direct impact on nonprofit charities in several ways: they regulate them, they exempt them from major taxes, and they use them as vehicles to deliver publicly funded services.[2] This chapter, which addresses state regulation of charities, has three parts. The first section explores the common law basis of the power of the state attorneys general to police charities, and it reviews state efforts to assure the proper administration of charitable organizations under the direction of state attorneys general. This section includes regulation of charitable solicitations, powers that are exercised by the attorney general in some states and by the secretary of state or other state officer in others. The second section describes briefly some recent developments in state laws regulating charities and their fiduciaries that are designed to improve the regulatory regime and the governance and administration of charities. The final section gives a brief overview of efforts among sector stakeholders to promote self-regulation through the development of industry standards and guidelines.

STATE CHARITY OFFICIALS: NATURE, SCOPE OF AUTHORITY, AND SECTOR RELATIONSHIPS

Regulatory Authority

Although they have long had the role of protecting charitable assets to be used for charitable purposes, state charity officials have recently become more visible and vocal in the sector, despite the constraints imposed by a historical and continuing lack of financial, technological, and human resources. Almost 40 percent of state attorney general's offices dedicated less than one (or the equivalent of one) full-time employee to charity regulation for the entire state. Only eight states had ten or more full-time employees for charity enforcement (Lott et al. 2016). Despite these figures, state attorneys general play a dominant role and have become increasingly engaged in reviewing and modernizing state nonprofit laws,[3] although various other state agencies such as secretaries of state, the state agriculture departments, and state departments of commerce also participate in some enforcement actions. Since the 1970s, these state officials have worked in tandem, and many times cooperated, through the National Association of State Charity Officials (NASCO) (National Association of State Charity Officials 2016a).

State charity officials work independently and with local and federal law enforcement agencies in their capacity as both regulators and legal enforcers of the charitable sector. With these "dual" hats, state charity officials are on the front line as the primary regulatory and law enforcement personnel safeguarding charitable assets for their intended use.[4] Due to low numbers of state charity regulators and lack of resources to proactively police the field, whistleblower complaints remain the chief source of initial complaints in the nonprofit sector, with journalists increasingly playing a role as well. The last decade has seen major cases brought at the state-level addressing board governance by high-profile foundations (Office of Consumer Protection, Montana Department of Justice 2012; California Office of the Attorney General 2006; Connecticut Office of the Attorney General 2015), fraudulent fundraising activity leading to prison sentences (*State v. Cody* 2015; Tampa Bay Times 2016) and a lifetime ban on fundraising in a state (New York Office of the Attorney General 2013a).

With hundreds of years' history of charity regulation and enforcement, all state attorneys general have some form of jurisdiction and authority to enforce common law and/or statutory law regarding charitable assets. Although the authority of attorneys general initially arose from common law (which remains as an active source of jurisdiction in most states), this authority is now codified in almost all states and territories (Myers 2013: 27, 33).[5] Common law imposes upon all fiduciaries dealing with charitable assets the concomitant duties of care and loyalty (Fremont-Smith 2004, chapter 4). Enforcement of these duties is manifested in various substantive legal areas: board governance, interpretation of provisions establishing charities in wills, trusts and governing documents of charitable corporations, solicitation and registration compliance, conservation easements, corporate transactions within the life cycle of a nonprofit, and even criminal law. Attorneys general enforce these duties in myriad ways, including telephone inquiries, injunctions, board removal, and litigation, both civil and criminal (Carlson 2013: 204; Lott et al. 2016).

In most states, the attorney general shares regulatory authority over different aspects of the charitable and nonprofit sector with another state agency office (most commonly the secretary of state); this is called a "bifurcated" jurisdiction.[6] Depending on the jurisdictional divisions within the states, one of the offices will maintain registries of various charitable entities, with registration requirements varying state to state (Lott et al. 2016).[7]

Charitable Solicitation

State regulation of charitable fundraising is a separate aspect of government regulation of charities. In some states it is a part of the regulation of charitable fiduciary duties, whereas in others it is a component of the attorney general's consumer protection programs or under the jurisdiction of a state official other than the attorney general altogether (Lott et al. 2016). Substantive state laws governing charitable solicitations are directed at preventing fraud and misrepresentations and apply not just to charities but also to for-profit entities that claim they are charitable.

Regulation of charitable solicitation is achieved in the first instance through laws that mandate registration and financial reporting by charities that solicit funds from the general public as well as by individuals and corporations that conduct fundraising activities on a for-profit basis. The statutes may also extend to "commercial co-venturers"—business organizations that agree publicly to donate a certain percentage of their sales or services to named charities, prohibiting them from undertaking such ventures without a written contract with the charity (National Council of Nonprofits 2016a). The statutes specifically define prohibited deceptive acts or practices (Fremont-Smith 2004: 373). Charities are required to register with a state office, file certain prescribed information on their proposed activities, and obtain a license to solicit (315–317). State officials do not have discretion to deny a license so long as the required information is provided, and it indicates that the charity's intended activities will not violate the law.

There are both criminal and civil sanctions for violation of these laws. The agency assigned the duty of enforcement has broad powers to conduct investigations, subpoena witnesses, and demand documents. In addition, the courts have equity powers to issue injunctions, revoke certain transactions, and ultimately remove fiduciaries and appoint receivers (Fremont-Smith 2004: 302).

State officials charged with regulating charitable solicitation regularly attempt to improve public understanding of charities so that donors may make informed decisions. The websites for states that have active enforcement programs provide a summary of the state laws and information to assist in compliance (New York Office of the Attorney General 2016). A number of states publish annual reports on the costs of certain fundraising efforts, such as those by telemarketers or professional fundraisers (Multi-State Filer Project 2016). In addition, charity watchdog groups such as the Wise Giving Alliance at the Better Business Bureau (BBB Wise Giving Alliance 2016) or Charity Navigator (Charity Navigator 2016) provide current information on charities, and more and more information is available through GuideStar (certain data are free, others require paid subscription), as well as new online platforms such as Cause IQ (Guidestar 2016; Cause IQ 2016).

In 1999, at the annual NASCO meeting, state charity regulators attempted to deal collectively with the problems created by the rapid proliferation of solicitations on what was then a novel technological innovation, the Internet. The result was a definition of the circumstances under which charities soliciting funds on the Internet would be required to register and report in a state in which they were not domiciled. The "Charleston Principles," discussed further in section E.1.b, below, require registration if the charity specifically targets individuals in a particular state or receives substantial contributions from persons in that state on a repeated and ongoing basis through its Internet solicitations. In the last decade, charitable solicitation practices have experienced an evolutionary leap due to the Internet and mobile giving ("text to give"). Although state charity regulators continue to try to keep pace with these changes, many stakeholders in the sector find the regulations addressing solicitations lagging in applicability to contemporary industry practices (National Association of State Charity Officials 2001).

Recent Changes at the IRS: Impact on the Sector, Impact on State Regulation, and Enforcement

In the 100-plus years since the Revenue Act of 1913 (*Revenue Act of Oct. 3, 1913*; Fremont-Smith 2004: 56–62), an act that afforded certain organizations exemption from the federal income tax, the Internal Revenue Service (IRS) has had an outsized regulatory footprint in the collective mind of the sector. Congress has delegated to the IRS the power to recognize organizations entitled to tax exemption and, for a charitable subset of nonprofit organizations, qualification to receive gifts that qualify for deductions for their donors from income, estate, and gift tax. The IRS thus can have a profound influence on the viability of an organization while it is pursuing its mission. The actions or inactions by the IRS Exempt Organizations Division on any given issue create a ripple effect for both the state regulators and the sector as a whole.

Within the "interlocking" jurisdiction of the IRS and state charity regulators, exercised at different points in the life cycle of a nonprofit, the IRS is the chief determinant for (1) initial and ongoing tax exempt status, applied first through the Form 1023, and (2) collecting baseline information on the operations of an entity, primarily through requirements to file variants of the IRS Form 990 or 990 PF (for private foundations). Both the actions of the IRS, through the exemption determinations process as well as the information gathering executed through the Form 990, impact nonprofits and the state enforcement endeavors (Fishman 2013).[8] Combined, the required Form 1023 and the Form 990 serve as the foundation of much of the information publicly available on charities, information utilized by policymakers, the enforcement community, researchers, and practitioners. Changes in the use or content of these documents by the IRS impact the entire nonprofit sector, as discussed in the two sections below. This occurred in both 2007 and 2014, after the revision of these two important forms used by the IRS to determine eligibility for tax exemption and to obtain information annually on the activities and financial status of the larger tax exempt organizations.

The Redesign of the Form 990

A decade ago, the IRS Exempt Organizations Division was in an expansive mode. In 2007, the IRS determined that it would redesign Form 990, the annual information reporting form for larger exempt organizations, for the first time in almost thirty years, believing that such a redesign would address "the increased demand for transparency and accountability" of the time (Ferraro 2008). This followed a "Good Governance" initiative, begun in 2002, that the IRS announced was due to a perceived increase in media and public scrutiny of the sector. The IRS announced three guiding principles: "[e]nhancing transparency to provide the IRS and the public with a realistic picture of the organization; [p]romoting compliance by accurately reflecting the organization's operations so the IRS may efficiently assess the risk of noncompliance; and [m]inimizing the burden on filing organizations" (Internal Revenue Service 2007b). The redesign of the Form 990 was intended to be an iteration of that Good Governance initiative.

The IRS utilized its Advisory Committee on Tax Exempt and Government Entities (the ACT) subcommittee on tax exempt organizations to help recommend how best to revise the form. Notably, one of the recommendations acknowledged that the state regulators have their own need for the federal data on the Form 990 and that the IRS should continue to accommodate the needs of the states as long as they do not adversely affect the IRS's primary mission or unduly burden filers (Advisory Committee on Tax Exempt and Government Entities 2006).

The IRS recognized that the Form 990 provides meaningful data for a diverse group of reviewers and researchers, including state regulators. The IRS also recognized inherent difficulties in overhauling the Form 990. These difficulties included a variety of data users with competing priorities and budgetary constraints (Advisory Committee on Tax Exempt and Government Entities 2006: 1). These concerns are likely to continue for the foreseeable future.

On the theory that "a well governed organization is more likely to be tax-compliant" (Goff 2007: 4), the discussion draft of the revised Form 990 released on June 14, 2007 included new sections on governance, management, and financial reporting. The IRS stated overtly that such information, reported in a transparent fashion for public inspection, was necessary to ensure that the organizations were using their assets in ways that were consistent with their tax exempt purposes. Notably, however, such information was not required explicitly by federal tax law (Internal Revenue Service 2011).

The draft generated over 700 public comments (Internal Revenue Service 2007b; Internal Revenue Service 2007c). In a background paper regarding the Form 990 redesign process, the IRS summarized the bulk of these comments, many of which reflect both the strengths and the limitations of the form for its many users (Internal Revenue Service 2007d). Experts continued the debate. The "governance-focused" part of the Form 990 was hailed by Steve Miller, the then commissioner of the Tax Exempt and Government Entities (TE and GE) Division, as "the crown jewel" of the IRS's progress in the nonprofit governance area. It proved "somewhat controversial" (Brody 2012: 200)[9] in part due to a perceived incursion into review of governance issues, a regulatory function based in state jurisdiction.

Introduction of the Form 1023-EZ

In 2014, the IRS developed a new, more expedited version of the Form 1023, the application for tax exemption used by those organizations that wished to have their exempt status recognized. Although the new Form 1023-EZ drastically reduced the waiting time for applicants, the form collects only a fraction of the information about the applicant entity compared to the full Form 1023. Because state regulators, as well as grantmaking organizations, rely on the information collected in the Form 1023 for information and data on tax exempt organizations, NASCO as well as other major nonprofit membership organizations such as the National Council of Nonprofits (Delaney 2014; Wyland 2014) publicly objected to the adoption of the Form 1023-EZ:

> State charities regulators use the same vital information collected on Forms 1023 to ensure compliance with federal tax regulations to carry out our respective state regulatory duties to protect charitable assets from fraud and abuse.... We believe that the Form 1023-EZ will increase opportunity for fraud and heighten the burden on state regulators to compensate for the reduced standards that will be required of the organization to meet federal tax exemption requirements.... Both IRS and state charities regulator enforcement capabilities are already stretched thin. (Gardenswartz 2014)

The concern of the nonprofit sector, of course, is that a weakened regulatory environment enables fraud. Additionally, little or no data track the extent of fraud, thus a "before and after" comparison regarding the utilization and impact of the Form 1023-EZ will be impossible. Research that tracks the new organizations that complete the Form 1023-EZ could be done; thus far, however, the only statistics available on these organizations are from the IRS itself, which noted that 95 percent of all Form 1023-EZ applications are approved, compared to 77 percent when the fuller documentation of the Form 1023 was provided. In addition, in one research study of twenty states, 37 percent of the applicants approved did not meet the basic organizational qualifications as a Section 501(c)(3) organization (Internal Revenue Service 2016a).

Although the IRS has determined as a policy matter that it will rely not on prophylactic measures but instead on the auditing function to ferret out noncompliant entities, the reality is that the former, more comprehensive Form 1023 application gave substantive information that states and the sector needed, far more information than the current, reduced number of audits will make available. As a result of the reduction of staff in the Exempt Organizations Division over the last several years, within the short time span of 2011–2013, the examination rate through audits fell from 0.81 to 0.71 percent, well below the examination rate for individuals (1.0 percent) or corporations (1.4 percent) (US Government Accountability Office 2014).

Statutory Prohibition on Information Sharing between IRS and State Regulators

A major unresolved issue that impacts enforcement efforts in the nonprofit sector lies squarely in the jurisdiction of Congress: a provision of the Pension Protection Act of 2006 that, inadvertently, made information sharing between the IRS and state charities regulators so burdensome so as to be tantamount to a prohibition. Violations of certain provisions are criminal in nature and put state charities regulators in an untenable position for processing information received from the IRS. Although these prohibitions are appropriate for protecting individual (private) taxpayer information, they are inapt when applied to nonprofits that file publicly available Forms 990 information returns (Brody 2012: 223–224; *Pension Protection Act of 2006*).

In 2011, 43 state attorneys general signed a letter to Senators Baucus and Hatch of the Senate Finance Committee, requesting that Congress remedy the situation. Under the current law, the attorneys general have noted unworkable legal and ethical conflicts for the states trying to share information with the IRS (National Association of Attorneys General 2011). As of 2016, those states that had vaulted the arduous hurdles to enter into an information-sharing agreement with the IRS per current law have withdrawn from those agreements, as procedures had become unduly burdensome for the limited resources of state offices (Jones 2015).

Electronic Filing and Dissemination of IRS Information

In order for the nonprofit sector and regulators to have verifiable and usable data on the operations of nonprofits, digitized data from Forms 990 must be available. Electronic filing of nonprofit information returns and electronic dissemination of these returns to the public are two sides of the same transparency coin (Jones 2013; Duncan 2015). For years academics and researchers have made efforts to encourage electronic filing by nonprofits, beginning with the long-standing efforts of the National Center for Charitable Statistics at Urban Institute (National Center for Charitable Statistics 2016). In 2013, a research study supported by the Aspen Institute and the Gates Foundation went so far as to make the case for federal legislation that would require electronic filing (Noveck and Goroff 2013). Mandatory e-filing was also included in President Obama's FY 2016 budget, as well as Representative Dave Camp's Tax Reform Act of 2014. Organizations that advocate for mandatory e-filing, such as the Aspen Institute's Program on Philanthropy and Social Innovation, argue that if all nonprofits were required to electronically file their Forms 990 and the IRS were required to release all Form 990 data in an electronically accessible format, the sector would see many benefits, including an increase in transparency, a reduction in fraud, and an increase in the accuracy of the data collected (Aspen Institute 2016).

As the states move forward with their own platform for collecting and making available electronic data (see *infra* section I.E.1.a), a major assist will come when the IRS releases in electronic form all Form 990 data that were submitted electronically. The Government Accountability Office (GAO) overtly supports this next, technologically enabled step toward transparency (US Government Accountability Office 2014).[10]

An announcement to that end came at the end of 2015 by the IRS (Ripperda 2015), and it was a welcome step toward universal electronic availability. This decision by the IRS, although made on its own terms and timeline, was triggered by a lawsuit filed by a plaintiff seeking the production of nine Form 990s for specific entities that had filed electronically with the IRS. Shortly after the federal court ruled against the IRS, requiring the IRS to produce the forms electronically (*Public.Resource.org v. United States Internal Revenue Serv.* 2015), the IRS announced that it intended to release in digitized form all Form 990s filed electronically beginning in 2016 (Perry 2015). Once implemented, these digitized data will serve as an invaluable trove for researchers, regulators, and the public.

The IRS Advisory Committee on Tax Exempt and Government Entities

In 2001, the IRS established the Advisory Committee on Tax Exempt and Government Entities, an entity which was intended to serve as a liaison between the IRS and the public (Internal Revenue Service 2015a). Since its first yearly report in 2001 (Herman 2001), the ACT has provided pro bono expertise to the IRS about current and proposed IRS policies, programs, and procedures and suggested improvements through five subcommittees (Internal Revenue Service 2016b). As a general rule, one of the members of the ACT Exempt Organizations subcommittee is grounded in the perspective of state charity regulators and serves as a liaison between the IRS and state regulators.

In addition to advising on the need for and challenges of redesigning the Form 990 in 2006, the Exempt Organizations subcommittee of the ACT tackled many issues of importance to the sector, relying not only on its members' expertise but also on original research involving hundreds of interviews in the field and, in the instance of the 2015 ACT report on e-filing, surveys of thousands of nonprofit entities. Previous ACT reports have addressed topics ranging from the determinations process, compliance efforts, Form 990 revisions, international grantmaking, executive compensation, and mandatory e-filing (Internal Revenue Service 2015b). Over the years through the ACT, the IRS received voluntary input from thousands of experts and in-the-trenches nonprofit professionals.

As is well known in the sector, a pronounced shift occurred at the IRS beginning in 2013, when political controversy enveloped the Exempt Organizations Division of the IRS. Full-blown congressional hearings took place, with IRS management testifying under oath as to administrative actions undertaken at the IRS in the application and exempt status recognition process. Although ultimately poor management and not criminal activity accounted for controversial events (Kadzik 2015), as a result of the intense scrutiny of the division and overall debate about funding, management practices, and mission, the Exempt Organizations Division experienced budget and staffing reductions and a reorganization and realignment of reporting lines within the division.[11] The IRS Exempt Organizations Division is experiencing a realignment of priorities and duties, and the ACT was not exempt from those changes.

In January 2016, the IRS announced that it would make a major shift in the structure and purposes of the ACT, which included reducing the number of members from twenty-one to fifteen and shifting the focus to "tax administration issues in general."[12] This new focus revealed the most formative change to the ACT's charge: as of 2017, there will no longer be five individual subcommittees producing written comments and recommendations on their individual substantive areas of expertise, and likely, this channel for communicating issues of state concern will be restricted (Internal Revenue Service 2016c).[13] These changes engendered observation that the IRS Exempt Organizations Division was losing not only internal expertise due to shifting priorities and a lack of both political and financial support, but was now shedding one of the last open channels for public input on specific substantive areas often overlooked in the past within the IRS, including issues relevant to state charities regulation.

Increased Interaction among State Charity Regulators, the Sector, and the Public

As discussed earlier, the growth of the nonprofit sector in the United States continues apace, despite the 2008–2013 recession and its lingering effects. In the decade between 2003 and 2013, the number of registered nonprofits in the United States rose by 2.8 percent; in 2013, approximately 1.41 million nonprofits were registered with the IRS (McKeever 2015: 3). The sector should be concerned, however, that state charity enforcement capacity is insufficient to oversee such a large and valuable portion of the US economy.

The good news was that for the five-year time span of the 2008 recession, approximately 355 state charity regulators and enforcers, including all attorneys and investigators, remained fairly stable, despite slashed state budgets that required shrinking staff, furloughs, and no-replacement policies for staff attrition.[14] In fact, roughly 30 percent of state charity offices experienced an increase in staffing at some level during this time period, with the largest offices, unsurprisingly, seeing the most gains (Lott et al. 2016).[15] Nonetheless, the unfortunate reality is that as the nonprofit sector grew in numbers, dollars, and stature, regulatory and enforcement resources did not keep pace.

Despite the low absolute numbers of state charity officials in the United States in the late 2010s, a new relationship began between regulators and the nonprofit sector. First, state regulators became more visible about their role in the nonprofit sector. NASCO, their membership organization, revamped its annual conference in order to engage the public, sector leadership, and other regulators in both the conference itself and its planning. NASCO turned its attention to its internal structure, as well, to provide greater continuity in leadership and accessibility to both its members and to the sector. NASCO members represent state perspectives on charitable regulation at conferences and meetings more frequently than ever before, illuminating their role in the sector and learning firsthand from sector leadership about issues that are of concern to the overall health of the nonprofit sector. In addition, in 2015, the National Association of Attorneys General (NAAG) added a Special Charities Committee to its roster of subcommittees, reflecting an emphasis on individual and multi-state enforcement efforts within the state regulatory and enforcement community never before seen.

Second, this increased interest in regulation of nonprofits is bearing fruit through a nascent research movement. Although to date the most thorough, overarching research on state regulation in the nonprofit sector has been Marion Fremont-Smith's treatise, *Governing Nonprofit Organizations: Federal and State Law and Regulation* (Fremont-Smith 2004), the research and commentary mantle is being taken up by a number of academics, practitioners, and even regulators themselves as they attempt to illuminate some of the inner workings of this sector. Of note is Urban Institute's new Regulation of Nonprofits and Philanthropy program within the Center on Nonprofits and Philanthropy, the latter of which for nearly twenty years has made available the most robust of all data on state-level statistics for the nonprofit sector (Urban Institute 2016).

A catalyst for research on state-level regulatory matters of the sector, the Columbia Law School Charities Regulation and Oversight Project for almost a decade provided trainings and conferences focused on the intersection of state regulation of charities, soliciting papers from an array of regulators, academics, and practitioners on a spectrum of topics (Columbia Law School 2016), and eventually undertaking the first-ever empirical research on state charity regulators, in conjunction with Urban Institute (Lott et al. 2016). Individual academics are exploring more research topics on regulation of the sector, beyond tax policy, and the Association of Research on Voluntary and Nonprofit Associations (ARNOVA) increased the number of sessions on state-based research, as well as a "policy day" grounded in state-based issues. As a national force in advocacy and policy at the state and federal levels, the National Council of Nonprofits has stepped up its research and involvement in many aspects of the sector in the last years.

Trends in Enforcement

Impact of Technology

The impact of technology on the nonprofit sector and its regulators cannot be overstated. Stakeholders in the sector are continually challenged to keep up with technology's newest tools; opportunists intent upon defrauding the system exploit these same technologies that afford anonymity and lightning fast transactions, particularly in fundraising.

Multi-state Registration and the "Single Portal" Project

As discussed in Section I.B., above, registration across the dozens of states with different registration requirements, both for registration of charities as well as solicitors, has been a lingering problem in day-to-day operations for nonprofits and fundraisers. The most pervasive complaint about state regulation of solicitation is the lack of uniformity in statutory coverage and the consequent burden of meeting numerous, varying filing and disclosure requirements (National Association of State Charity Officials 2016b). For many years, complaints have routinely surfaced of the inefficiency inherent in various states' multiple and often duplicative requirements, which, in turn, often duplicate the IRS Form 990.[16]

Efforts by state charities regulators to help alleviate these burdens began formally in 1997, with the NAAG and NASCO Standardized Reporting Project, which developed a "Uniform Registration Statement" (URS) for charities that solicit funds from the general public and for private solicitors.[17] Although no longer the definitive guide to all states' registration requirements (Multi-State Filer Project 2016), for many years the URS was the most the regulators offered to the sector to ease multi-state registration. The URS was not a technology-enabled platform for users, nor did it afford state regulators a platform to compare and share data about regulatory or enforcement data on any individual nonprofit entity. In 2016, to the chagrin of many stakeholders in the sector, many state charities regulators still rely primarily on paper registration filings, both for intake and for storage. Without electronic sharing of data among states, large-scale patterns of activity cannot be efficiently discerned or analyzed. However, even with constrained resources, both human and technological, NASCO is now beginning to harness the most current technologies available to begin resolving this dilemma that impacts both regulators and the regulated entities (Multi-state Registration & Filing Portal, Inc. 2016; National Association of State Charity Officials 2016b).

With the advent of cell phone technology, apps, and more sophisticated online platforms, NASCO realized that the opportunity exists to create efficiencies for both the sector and the regulators through a "Single Portal" for all registration requirements (charities as well as their professional fundraisers) and data sharing. Aided by the Urban Institute and the Columbia University State Charities Regulation and Oversight Project, state regulators currently are attempting to alleviate many of these burdens through their Multi-state Registration and Filing Portal project, which will create a single, online platform for charities to file required documentation in all states, automatically querying for all data required by every state in which the charity must register. Through the Single Portal platform, state regulators will be able to share data through a regulator-only "back page." In addition, the platform will retrieve information for a charity automatically from the Form 990, populate the Single Portal with that data, and allow easy and efficient updates by users year to year. All interactive data from this platform that is not confidential will be available to researchers, academics, and the public for review and use

(Multi-state Registration & Filing Portal, Inc. 2016; National Association of State Charity Officials 2016b).

For a sector that benefits from public inquiry and watchdog activities, transparency and accessibility of data are critical. The Single Portal project, currently scheduled to come online in 2016, will be revolutionary for multi-state registration, data collection, and regulatory capacity in the sector. It will be designed to be an interoperable platform to share with other government entities, both federal and state. This initiative will serve the regulators' need for data sharing and analytics that will enable the preservation of donor dollars and help ensure the integrity of the nonprofit sector (National Association of State Charity Officials 2016b).[18]

Charleston Principles Governing Interstate Solicitation of Charitable Funds

With the nascent Internet in the 1990s, nonprofits increasingly expanded the scope of their activities, including fundraising, across state lines. What society now takes for granted in instantaneous, multijurisdictional communications was an impetus to all commerce across the globe as the Internet took hold. The nonprofit sector was not immune to these opportunities, nor to the regulatory challenges inherent in them.[19]

Although common law has long embraced the notion of "long arm jurisdiction," with various legal tests to determine whether or not a commercial entity is deemed to be "doing business" in a jurisdiction beyond that of its incorporation, the Internet truly raised novel issues of jurisdictional reach, particularly as to fundraising and marketing. Such new issues were contemplated at the NASCO annual conference in 2001 in Charleston, South Carolina. There, the state charities regulators created and agreed to disseminate a set of guidelines for the charitable sector, the "Charleston Principles." These guidelines were intended to be elastic principles to state the legal framework in which new technologies, enabling interstate and global reach of charitable activity and solicitation, could fit (National Association of State Charity Officials 2001). More than a decade later, questions remain about the continuing efficacy of the Charleston Principles in an age of routine, technologically enabled interstate commerce.

Multi-state Enforcement

In 2015, a milestone in state enforcement occurred in the charitable sector, with the filing of a lawsuit against four related cancer charities that were soliciting funds throughout the United States. A total of fifty-eight state enforcement offices, including state attorneys general, secretaries of state, and other agencies, filed suit on behalf of all fifty states, the District of

Columbia (DC), and the Federal Trade Commission (FTC) (Missouri Office of the Attorney General 2015; Federal Trade Commission 2015). This suit is the first time that all states, DC, and the federal government have joined forces in a single enforcement matter.

The government alleged that over $180 million of charitable funds had been misused by the nonprofits and the individuals who controlled them, and that the entities were sham charities utilizing their charitable status as a façade for for-profit activities. Importantly, the states and the FTC made clear that severe governance issues may constitute actual deception and fraud (Missouri Office of the Attorney General 2015; Federal Trade Commission 2015). The complaint by the plaintiffs provides a virtual primer on the variations in jurisdiction among states, between attorneys general's offices and other state offices, and between state offices and the FTC (*FTC, 50 States, and D.C. v. Cancer Fund of America, Inc., et al.*).

This suit is notable not only for the sheer amount of the fraud alleged, but because the government offices worked for years to present a unified front on a case of such significance. Working without a shared electronic database such as that anticipated in the Single Portal project, described above in section I.E.1.a, it took the states almost four years to gather the information needed for filing the complaint, illustrating the current unwieldy and inefficient system of data and information sharing among states.[20]

Hybrid and Mixed Mission Entities

As of 2016, state charity regulators were grappling with questions as to the oversight of "hybrid" or "mixed mission" entities, legal entities that had both a for-profit or low-profit purpose in addition to a charitable or social purpose. First enacted in Vermont in 2006, some permutation of these statutes has been adopted by state legislatures, with almost twenty states allowing for some corporate form of a hybrid entity, known by various names.[21] Major issues with these entities from a regulatory perspective include the legitimacy of state regulation, transparency, governance, false marketing, confusion with co-venture relationships, and definitional concerns of which activities constitute "charitable" activity, thus triggering oversight by state charities regulators. See chapter 9 for examination of these developments and the economic forces behind them, while recognizing here the new demands they may possibly place on regulators.

NEW STATE LAWS AND GUIDANCE FOR THE SECTOR

In addition to changes in enforcement initiatives at the IRS and in the states during the decade between 2006 and 2016, there were a number of changes in state laws that govern nonprofit organizations, as well as initiatives by lawyers, legal scholars, and members of the judiciary to draft laws that would serve as models for adoption by state legislatures.[22] These efforts resulted in passage of laws that describe the manner in which charitable corporations and trusts are established and governed, including how they invest their funds, as well as the manner in which the state attorneys general and the courts regulate charities.

The Uniform Law Commission and the American Bar Association

The impetus for new laws or amendment of existing ones comes from two principal sources: the Uniform Law Commission, and the American Bar Association.

The purpose of the Uniform Law Commission is to determine which areas of the law should be uniform among the states and then work through committees to draft legislation suitable for adoption in each state (Uniform Law Commission 2016a). Following adoption by the Commission, attorneys and state bar associations in some states will then introduce the acts and lobby to have them adopted by the state legislature.

Examples of the influence of the Commission in regard to charities include the Uniform Prudent Management of Institutional Funds Act that was approved by the Commission in 2006. This act, which contains new standards for investment and distributions from endowment funds, applies to almost every charity in a state and has been enacted in every state except Pennsylvania (Uniform Law Commission 2016b). The Uniform Trust Code, which contains a number of important provisions governing the administration of charitable trusts, was originally completed in the year 2000 and by the start of 2016 had been adopted in thirty states (Uniform Law Commission 2016c). A third act, the Uniform Prudent Investor Act, completed in 1994, governs the manner in which charities invest their funds and had by 2016 been enacted in 41 states (Uniform Law Commission 2016d). In 2011, the Commissioners adopted a Model Protection of Charitable Assets Act designed to unify the powers of the state attorneys general to regulate charities operating in their respective states (Uniform Law Commission 2016e). It is similar to acts in effect in California, Illinois, Michigan, and Ohio.[23] It was adopted in Maryland in 2014 (Maryland Code Annotated, Business Regulation §§ 6.5-101 – 6.5-105).

The Business Law Section of the American Bar Association (ABA) has had the greatest influence on the laws governing nonprofit corporations, including charities (American Bar Association 2016a). This Section first adopted a Model Nonprofit Corporation Act in 1952 (American Bar Association 2016b), and its 1987 amended version, referred to as the Revised Model Nonprofit Corporation Act (Fremont-Smith 2004: 52–53), is now in effect in more than half of the states. In 2015, the ABA approved yet another amended version of the Model Nonprofit Corporation Act; this act sets forth procedures for creating and governing nonprofit corporations and for their merger, dissolution, or termination (American Bar Association 2016b). Accordingly, the provisions in the newest Model Act can be expected to have a substantial influence on the laws dealing with nonprofit corporations in years to come.[24]

The American Law Institute Restatement of the Law of Charitable Nonprofit Organizations

The American Law Institute (ALI), established in 1923, has, among its purposes, "to encourage and carry on scholarly and scientific legal work" (American Law Institute 2016a). The members of the Institute, elected by its board, comprise lawyers, judges, and legal scholars (American Law Institute 2016b). Since its inception, it has sponsored the preparation and dissemination of Restatements of the Law on almost every major legal subject conceivable (American Law Institute 2016c). All of these publications are used by judges, practitioners, and scholars, often as their first source when conducting research on a given field of law. The ALI has had a project on nonprofit organizations since 2000 (Fremont-Smith 2007: 612). In 2014, the board designated the project a Restatement of the Law of Charitable Nonprofit Organizations (American Law Institute 2016d). It will be the first Restatement on this subject. In May 2016, at its Annual Meeting, the ALI members approved Tentative Draft No. 1, that contains sections in the first three chapters: Definition, Legal Forms, and Charities with Members; Governance; and changes to Purpose and Organization (American Law Institute 2016d). The Draft is available from the American Law Institute for public dissemination.

CONTINUING EFFORTS BY THE SECTOR TOWARD IMPROVED LEGAL AND ETHICAL COMPLIANCE

The challenges and complexities of charitable regulation in the United States are shared among both regulators and the regulated charities. As with all sectors, the charitable sector provides guidance for its own constituents in the form of published guiding principles, industry standards, and accreditation programs. Major membership organizations have produced sophisticated and influential guidance for their members and the sector at large.

In the last decade, Independent Sector, the nonprofit organization that represents the largest number of charities in the United States, published "Principles for Good Governance and Ethical Practice, A Guide for Charities and Foundations" (Independent Sector 2015). This publication represented the final report of a Panel on the Nonprofit Sector, formed by Independent Sector at the encouragement of the US Senate Finance Committee, the members of which were considering ways to improve the oversight and governance of charitable organizations (Independent Sector 2016b). These principles became the focus of Independent Sector's efforts to improve the governance and operations of nonprofit charitable organizations and were widely disseminated. In 2014, Independent Sector convened a new panel of representatives of the sector to reconsider the principles and recommend changes that reflected changes in the law since 2007 and new circumstances in which the sector functions, as well as new relationships within and between the sectors (Independent Sector 2015). Importantly, the revised principles addressed a number of cutting-edge issues important to the sector, including: ethics and whistleblower policies; risk tolerance and mitigation in response to technology advances; nonprofits taking up new business or earned income opportunities; the tension between increasing transparency and protecting privacy; executive compensation; overhead costs; and fundraising.[25] The revision and dissemination of these principles highlighted the ethical standards in the sector and meshed with the IRS's recent efforts to focus on governance issues, as required through the 2007 revisions to the Form 990 described above.

Independent Sector is not alone in its efforts to raise the bar on legal compliance and ethical standards. Other major stakeholders throughout the nonprofit sector have developed their own standards to be used by their respective memberships, some including accreditation, others promulgating ethical standards. The National Council of Nonprofits provides links to some of the standards promoted within each state on its website. "[M]any state associations of nonprofits promote 'best practices'—whether described as 'guiding practices,' 'principles and practices,' or 'standards'—to encourage legal, ethical, accountable, and transparent practices by all charitable nonprofits and boards of directors" (National Council of Nonprofits 2016b). The Standards for Excellence Institute developed the "Standards for Excellence: An Ethics and Accountability Code for the Nonprofit Sector" "to promote the highest standards of ethics, effectiveness, and accountability in nonprofit governance, management, and operations" (Standards for Excellence Institute 2016).[26] The Community Foundations National Standards Board, a supporting organization of the Council on Foundations, developed and administers "National Standards for U.S. Community Foundations," an accreditation program (National Council on Foundations 2016; Community Foundations National Standards Board 2016).[27] The Association of Fundraising Professionals has also developed both a Code of Ethical Standards for fundraisers and a statement of principles for charities that solicit contributions, both designed to promote ethical standards and maintain public trust (Association of Nonprofit Professionals 2016a, 2016b).[28]

Taken together, formal government regulation and the sector's own efforts to promote principles and standards for ethical behavior appear to have had an important impact on regulators and the members of the charitable sector. Despite budget and staffing cuts in the last several years, the IRS continued its efforts to heighten awareness of good governance practices. The increasing attention of state regulators to charities regulation, the multi-state efforts of those regulators, and their use of current technologies to create efficiencies for their offices and for the regulated entities, should bring improvement in the ability of charities to carry out their purposes.

NOTES

1. Marion R. Fremont-Smith explores the issues discussed in this section in detail in her books *Governing Nonprofit Organizations: Federal and State Law and Regulation* (2004) and *Foundations and Government: State and Federal Law Supervision* (1965).

2. Property tax exemption and publicly funded services are described in more detail in chapter 4.

3. In 2013, New York passed the Non-Profit Revitalization Act, making significant changes to its Not-for-Profit Corporation Law (Attea and Marks 2014: 28; Halper 2013). Delaware overhauled its nonprofit laws in 2010 (Zeberkiewicz and Rohrbacher 2011: 271). The District of Columbia also made significant updates to its nonprofit laws in 2012 (Kingsley 2012: 16).

4. Although states routinely refer cases to the IRS, unfortunately, this is a "one-way valve"; virtually no information flows from the IRS to the state attorneys general regarding evidence of exemption application denials. See *infra* section I.C.3.

5. As Myers notes, "[t]he common law is the origin of the attorney general's authority to represent, defend, and enforce the legal interests of state government and the public. . . . The constitutions of 44 states establish an office of attorney general, and many of these constitutions direct the attorney general to perform duties 'prescribed by law.'"

6. According to the research report forthcoming from Lott, Boris, et al.: "In twenty-three jurisdictions, the authority to regulate public fundraising campaigns by and on behalf of charities is shared by the Attorney General and another state-level office, usually the office of the Secretary of State, whose authority is conferred by state charitable solicitation statutes."

7. *Ibid*: "The statutory authority that gives these other state offices jurisdiction typically requires (1) soliciting charities and their professional fundraisers to register prior to solicitation activity in the state and to file annual reports; (2) the state charity office to maintain a registry of such filings, and (3) the office to enforce registration and reporting requirements."

8. Fishman notes that although governance issues reside in the jurisdiction of the states, the states did not object when the IRS added several governance questions to the Form 990 in 2008.

9. Professor Jim Fishman went so far as to assert that the entire Form 990 governance section is "stealth preemption," and he was not alone in this stance (Fishman 2010, 586, 588–589) ("The Service's corporate governance initiative preempts traditional state sources of nonprofit corporate law, eroding a traditional area of state interest, expertise, and control. . . . The governance recommendations are not in Service's area of expertise. Nor is there any empirical validation that they will improve tax compliance"). Marcus S. Owens has also noted that "[c]learly, an argument can be made that the IRS has exceeded its authority by incorporating questions on governance and other matters that, by its own admission, are not required by the code" (Owens 2008).

10. As Noveck and Goroff also noted, "information contained in the 990s could potentially be far more useful if it were not only public but 'open' data. Open data are data that are available to all, free of charge, in a standard format, published without proprietary conditions, and available online as a bulk download rather than only through single-entry lookup. Making the Form 990 data truly open in this sense would not only make it easier to use for the organizations that already process it, but would also make it useful to researchers, advocates, entrepreneurs, technologists, and nonprofits that do not have the resources to use the data in its current form. We argue that open 990 data may increase transparency for nonprofit organizations, making it easier for state and federal authorities to detect fraud, spur innovation in the nonprofit sector and, above all, help us to understand the potential value of the 990 data" (Noveck and Goroff 2013).

11. According to the US Government Accountability Office (GAO), "Internal Revenue Service (IRS) total appropriations declined from a high of $12.1 billion in fiscal year 2010 to $11.3 billion in fiscal year 2014, a reduction of about 7 percent" (US Government Accountability Office 2015).

12. Noting that the priorities were being shifted to more closely align with the new priorities of the Tax Exempt and Government Entities Division: "TE/GE's five key priorities going forward are: continuous improvement, knowledge management, risk management, data-driven decision-making and employee engagement" (Internal Revenue Service 2016c).

13. Beginning in 2017, the ACT will operate as a single committee on topics to be chosen by the IRS annually, focusing on issues of administration of tax laws, rather than the substantive areas previously defined.

14. "Survey respondents reported that staff size in most offices (53 percent) has been the same since the onset of the recession in 2008" (Lott et al. 2016).

15. "Thirty-one percent of survey respondent offices indicated an increase in staff, while 13 percent said staff size decreased. In general, most small offices (less than 1 FTE) were likely to report no change in staff; large offices (10+ FTEs) were somewhat more likely to report an increase."

16. As one example, in 2015 the New York office of the Attorney General began the process of reviewing its own required filings in order to determine necessity of data requested and efficiencies in filing, the first major state to undertake such a formal review (Sheehan 2015).

17. "The most recent version of the URS is v. 4.02, which was released in March 2014. Version 4.02 supports 37 jurisdictions (36 states and the District of Columbia),

and requires (and includes) supplemental forms for 13 jurisdictions" (Multi-State Filer Project 2016).

18. According to NASCO's website, their "goal is to maximize efficiency, data transparency, and information sharing by enabling compliance with registration and reporting requirements for any state, or any combination of multiple states, without duplication of data entry, at the single portal, and then making the collected registration data from all states available to the public in a searchable and interactive format. Academics, policy makers and interested members of the public will be able to conduct their own inquiries. Availability of the data in electronic format (rather than in paper or static pdf format), will enable analytics that will lead to better understanding of charitable resources, better targeting of law enforcement and fraud prevention resources, and better policy making for protection of charitable resources" (National Association of State Charity Officials 2016b).

19. For an early view from a state attorney general's perspective on enforcement challenges in general commerce brought by the Internet, see Modisett and Lott 2000.

20. For a summary of the challenges to state regulators in bringing such a large-scale suit against a number of charities, see former Tennessee Attorney General Robert Cooper's article, Why Taking Legal Action Against Charity Fraud Is So Hard (Cooper 2015).

21. The Independent Sector notes that nine states recognize low-profit limited liability companies (L3Cs), fourteen states recognize benefit corporations, and one state recognizes flexible purpose corporations (Independent Sector 2016a). John Tyler and others have written that "[s]ince 2008 over half of the states in the U.S. have enacted one or more statutes that authorize formation of hybrid forms of business organization" (Tyler et al. 2015: 237). See also Brewer 2015.

22. New York is an example of a state in which the legislature recently did a complete overhaul of its laws governing nonprofit organizations. In December 2010, New York adopted a Non-Profit Revitalization Act, effective July 1, 2014, which attempted to reduce outdated regulatory burdens on nonprofit organizations, and applied a number of internal procedures to charitable trusts (New York State Senate 2016). The law clarifies the powers of the attorney general to regulate nonprofit organizations in the state, while making it easier for individuals to create nonprofit organizations and govern them more effectively. Development of the law reflects the efforts of members of the New York bar associations, the Charity Officials in the Office of the Attorney General, legislators, and members of the nonprofit community. The Act likely will have a large influence outside of the state, in light of the critical mass of charities located in New York and thorough its leadership in the state charitable regulation scheme (Dale et al. 2014). In addition to rewriting the laws applicable to nonprofit corporations in New York, certain of its sections were made applicable to charitable trusts, notably those addressing related party transactions, mandatory conflict of interest, and whistleblower policies and audit oversight (New York Office of the Attorney General 2013b).

23. Susan N. Gary noted that "[t]welve states (California, Illinois, Massachusetts, Michigan, Minnesota, New Hampshire, New York, Ohio, Oregon, Pennsylvania,

Rhode Island, and Washington [now repealed]) already have registration statutes for charities, separate from statutes related to solicitation. These states typically require charities to register and file annual reports, and the statutes apply broadly to charities organized or operating in those states. Thus, the idea of a registration and reporting statute is not new. Indeed, the Act is based on a 1954 uniform act, the Uniform Supervision of Trustees for Charitable Purposes Act, and some of the state statutes are based on that act." (Gary 2012).

24. In 2012, the District of Columbia enacted a form of the Model Nonprofit Corporation Act, and with the 2015 amended version, a number of other states are also debating adoption of the act (Kingsley 2012).

25. Overall, there are thirty-three principles in the 2015 revised configuration organized under four categories: legal compliance and public disclosure; effective governance; strong financial oversight; and responsible fundraising (Independent Sector 2015).

26. "The Standards for Excellence Institute is a national initiative established to promote the highest standards of ethics, effectiveness, and accountability in nonprofit governance, management, and operations, and to help all nonprofit organizations meet these high benchmarks. Our program is a system of nonprofit sector self-regulation and replicated by state, regional, and national associations and support organizations" (Standards for Excellence Institute 2016).

27. National Council on Foundations, in describing the National Standards for US Community Foundations, says "[c]ommunity foundation leaders take seriously their role and commitment to serve and support their communities. To demonstrate this to lawmakers and the people in their communities, they came together, over ten years ago in the late 1990s, to create a peer-driven, accreditation program. Executed with rigor and expertise, this program was designed to demonstrate the willingness of community foundations to go above and beyond what the law requires to ensure accountability and compliance with legal requirements and to avoid legislation that would require further regulation and oversight by a body that had difficulty distinguishing the important nuances of community foundation work." The Community Foundations National Standards Board says, "[w]e create standards for operationally and legally sound community foundations . . . [and w]e lead community foundation staff and boards through the process of achieving operational excellence" (Community Foundations National Standards Board 2016).

28. The Association of Nonprofit Professionals describes their Code of Ethical Standards on their website: "The Association of Fundraising Professionals believes that ethical behavior fosters the development and growth of fundraising professionals and the fundraising profession and enhances philanthropy and volunteerism. AFP Members recognize their responsibility to ethically generate or support ethical generation of philanthropic support. Violation of the standards may subject the member to disciplinary sanctions as provided in the AFP Ethics Enforcement Procedures. AFP members, both individual and business, agree to abide (and ensure, to the best of their ability, that all members of their staff abide) by the AFP standards" (Association of Nonprofit Professionals 2016a). "The Accountable Nonprofit Organization is a statement of principles to guide charities. It outlines the operations and procedures

a nonprofit undertakes to show it is accountable to donors, the people it serves, and the general public" (Association of Nonprofit Professionals 2016b).

REFERENCES

Advisory Committee on Tax Exempt and Government Entities. 2006. "General Report: Policies and Guidelines for Form 990 Revision." *Internal Revenue Service.* Last modified June 7, 2006. https://www.irs.gov/pub/irs-tege/tege_act_rpt5.pdf.

American Bar Association. 2016a. "About the American Bar Association." *American Bar Association.* Accessed February 29, 2016. http://www.americanbar.org/about_the_aba.html.

———. 2016b. "Model Nonprofit Corporation Act, Third Edition." *American Bar Association.* Accessed February 29, 2016. http://shop.americanbar.org/ebus/store/productdetails.aspx?productid=213949

American Law Institute. 2016a. "Creation." *American Law Institute.* Accessed February 29, 2016. https://www.ali.org/about-ali/creation/ (last visited).

———. 2016b. "Members." *American Law Institute.* Accessed February 29, 2016. https://www.ali.org/members/.

———. 2016c. "Institute Projects." *American Law Institute.* Accessed February 29, 2016. https://www.ali.org/about-ali/institute-projects/.

———. 2016d. "Restatement of the Law, Charitable Nonprofit Organizations." *American Law Institute.* Accessed February 29, 2016. https://www.ali.org/projects/show/charitable-nonprofit-organizations/.

Aspen Institute. "Transparency, Accuracy, and Innovation: Electronic-Filing of IRS Forms 990 for Open Data." *Aspen Institute.* Accessed March 14, 2016. http://www.aspeninstitute.org/sites/default/files/content/images/Form%20990%20E-filing%20One%20Pager%207-31-15.pdf.

Association of Nonprofit Professionals. 2016a. "Code of Ethical Standards." *Association of Nonprofit Professionals.* Accessed March 4, 2016. https://www.afpnet.org/Ethics/EnforcementDetail.cfm?ItemNumber=3261.

———. 2016b. The Accountable Nonprofit Organization, *Association of Nonprofit Professionals.* Accessed March 4, 2016. https://www.afpnet.org/Ethics/EnforcementDetail.cfm?ItemNumber=3262.

Attea, Frederick G., and Kelly E. Marks. 2014. "The New York Non-Profit Revitalization Act: A Summary and Analysis." *New York State Bar Association Journal* 86(4): 28–34.

BBB Wise Giving Alliance. "BBB Wise Giving Alliance—give.org." *BBB Wise Giving Alliance.* Accessed March 14, 2016. http://give.org.

Boris, Elizabeth T., and C. Eugene Steuerle. 2006. *Nonprofits & Government: Collaboration & Conflict.* Washington, DC: Urban Institute Press.

Brewer, Cassady V. 2015. "Social Enterprise Entity Comparison Chart." May 17. http://ssrn.com/abstract=2304892.

Brody, Evelyn. 2012. "Sunshine and Shadows on Charity Governance: Public Disclosure As A Regulatory Tool." *Florida Tax Review* 12: 183–232.

California Office of the Attorney General. 2006. "Report on the Office of the Attorney General's Investigation of the J. Paul Getty Trust." *California Office of the Attorney General*, October 2. https://oag.ca.gov/system/files/attachments/press_releases/06-085_0a.pdf?

Carlson, Bob. 2013. "Protection and Regulation of Nonprofits and Charitable Assets." In *State Attorneys General Powers and Responsibilities*. Emily Myers, ed. (pp. 203–230). Washington, DC: National Association of Attorneys General.

Cause IQ. "About." *Cause IQ*. Accessed March 4, 2016. https://www.causeiq.com/about/.

Charity Navigator. "Charity Navigator—Your Guide to Intelligent Giving." *Charity Navigator*. Accessed March 14, 2016. http://www.charitynavigator.org.

Columbia Law School. "2013 Charities Regulation Policy Conference, The Future of State Charities Regulation and Enforcement." *Columbia Law School*. Accessed January 28, 2016. http://web.law.columbia.edu/attorneys-general/policy-areas/charities-law-project/conferences/2013-charities-regulation-policy-conference-future-state-charities-regulation-and-enforcement.

Community Foundations National Standards Board. 2016. "About Us." *Community Foundations National Standards Board*. Accessed March 4, 2016. http://cfstandards.org/about-us.

Connecticut Office of the Attorney General. 2015. "State Officials: State Receivership of Amistad Schooner Ends with Dissolution of Amistad America, Inc." Connecticut Office of the Attorney General, November 23, 2015. http://www.ct.gov/ag/cwp/view.asp?Q=573990&A=2341.

Cooper Jr., Robert E. 2015. "Why Taking Legal Action Against Charity Fraud Is So Hard." *Chronicle of Philanthropy*, July 23. https://philanthropy.com/article/Opinion-Why-Taking-Legal/231853.

Dale, Harvey P., Victoria Bjorklund, Jennifer Reynoso, and Jillian P. Diamant. 2014. "Evolution, Not Revolution: A Legislative History of the New York Prudent Management of Institutional Funds Act." *New York University Journal of Legislation and Public Policy* 17 (September): 377.

Delaney, Tim. 2014. "Express Lane to More Trouble for the IRS?" *The Hill*, June 2. http://thehill.com/blogs/congress-blog/economy-budget/207640-express-lane-to-more-trouble-for-the-irs.

Duncan, Justin. 2015. "In the fight for open nonprofit data, everything changed in one month." *Data Transparency Coalition*, July 2. http://www.datacoalition.org/in-the-fight-for-open-nonprofit-data-everything-changed-in-one-month/.

Federal Trade Commission. 2015. "Press Release: FTC, All 50 States and D.C. Charge Four Cancer Charities With Bilking Over $187 Million from Consumers." *Federal Trade Commission*, May 19. https://www.ftc.gov/news-events/press-releases/2015/05/ftc-all-50-states-dc-charge-four-cancer-charities-bilking-over.

Ferraro, Patrick. 2008. "Unveiled: The IRS Introduces the Redesigned Form 990." *Guidestar*, January 2008. https://www.guidestar.org/Articles.aspx?path=/rxa/news/articles/2008/unveiled-the-irs-introduces-the-redesigned-form-990.aspx.

Fishman, James J. 2010. "Stealth Preemption: The IRS's Nonprofit Corporate Governance Initiative." *Virginia Tax Review* 29: 545–591.

———. 2013. "Strange Silence: Attorneys General Reaction to the Internal Revenue Service's Corporate Governance Initiative." *Columbia University Academic Commons.* http://dx.doi.org/10.7916/D8K35RMD.

Fremont-Smith, Marion R. 2004. *Governing Nonprofit Organizations: Federal and State Law and Regulation.* Cambridge, MA: Harvard University Press.

———. 2007. "The Search for Greater Accountability of Nonprofit Organizations: Recent Legal Developments and Proposals for Change." *Fordham Law Review* 76: 609.

FTC, 50 States, and D.C. v. Cancer Fund of America, Inc., et al., No. CV-15-00884-PHX-NVW (D. Ariz. filed May 18, 2015), https://www.ftc.gov/system/files/documents/cases/150519cancerfundcmpt.pdf.

Gardenswartz, Alissa Hecht, President of the National Association of State Charity Officials. 2014. *Letter to the Office of Information and Regulatory Affairs regarding Proposed Internal Revenue Service Form 1023-EZ, OMB Number 1545-0056.* April 30.

Gary, Susan N. 2012. "A Model Act to Protect Charitable Assets will Benefit Charities." *Taxation of Exempts*, (January/February): 26.

Goff, Elizabeth. 2007. "Phone Forum—Draft Redesign Form 990." *Internal Revenue Service.* Last modified July 18–19, 2007. https://www.irs.gov/pub/irs-tege/990redesignphoneforumscript7_2007.pdf.

Guidestar. "About Us." *Guidestar.* Accessed March 4, 2016. http://learn.guidestar.org/about-us/.

Halper, Zach. 2013. "N.Y. Overhauls Nonprofit Laws, Regs." *NonProfit Times*, June 25. http://www.thenonprofittimes.com/news-articles/n-y-overhauls-nonprofit-laws-regs/.

Herman, Tom. 2001. "Tax Report." *Wall Street Journal*, August 1. http://www.wsj.com/articles/SB996610510926418 54.

Independent Sector. "Principles for Good Governance and Ethical Practice: A Guide for Charities and Foundations." *Independent Sector.* Last modified 2015. https://www.independentsector.org/principles.

———. 2016a. "Hybrid Position Statement." *Independent Sector.* Accessed January 28, 2016. https://www.independentsector.org/hybrid_position.

———. 2016b. "Panel on the Nonprofit Sector." *Independent Sector.* Accessed February 29, 2016. https://www.independentsector.org/panel.

Internal Revenue Service. 2007a. IR-2007-117. "IRS Releases Discussion Draft of Redesigned Form 990 for Tax Exempt Organizations." *Internal Revenue Service.* Last modified June 14, 2007. https://www.irs.gov/uac/IRS-Releases-Discussion-Draft-of-Redesigned-Form-990-for-Tax-Exempt-Organizations.

———. 2007b. IR-2007-204. "IRS Releases Final 2008 Form 990 for Tax Exempt Organizations, Adjusts Filing Threshold to Provide Transition Relief." *Internal Revenue Service.* Last modified December 20, 2007. https://www.irs.gov/uac/IRS-Releases-Final-2008-Form-990-for-Tax-Exempt-Organizations,-Adjusts-Filing-Threshold-to-Provide-Transition-Relief.

———. 2007c. "Overview of Form 990 Redesign For Tax Year 2008." *Internal Revenue Service.* Last modified December 20, 2007. https://www.irs.gov/pub/irs-tege/overview_form_990_redesign.pdf.

———. 2007d. "Form 990 Redesign for Tax Year 2008 Background Paper." *Internal Revenue Service*. Last modified December 20, 2007. https://www.irs.gov/pub/irs-tege/background_paper_form_990_redesign.pdf.

———. 2011. "Form 990 Redesign for Tax Year 2008 (Filed in 2009) Frequently Asked Questions." *Internal Revenue Service*. Last modified August 22, 2011. https://www.irs.gov/pub/irs-tege/990r_faqs.pdf.

———. 2015a. "Charter: Advisory Committee on Tax Exempt and Government Entities." *Internal Revenue Service*. Accessed May 11, 2015. https://www.irs.gov/pub/irs-tege/Advisory%20Committee%20on%20Tax%20Exempt%20and%20Government%20Entities%20(ACT)%20Renewal%20Charter.pdf.

———. 2015b. "Reports of the Advisory Committee on Tax Exempt and Government Entities (ACT)" *Internal Revenue Service*. Last modified October 7, 2015. https://www.irs.gov/Government-Entities/Reports-of-the-Advisory-Committee-on-Tax-Exempt-and-Government-Entities-(ACT).

———. 2016a. IR-2016-01. "National Taxpayer Advocate Delivers Annual Report to Congress; Focuses on IRS's Future Plans for Taxpayer Service." January 6, 2016.

———. 2016b. "Advisory Committee on Tax Exempt and Government Entities (ACT)" *Internal Revenue Service*. Last modified January 19, 2016. https://www.irs.gov/Government-Entities/Advisory-Committee-on-Tax-Exempt-and-Government-Entities-(ACT).

———. 2016c. "IRS Makes Changes to Its Advisory Committee on Tax Exempt and Government Entities (ACT)" *Internal Revenue Service*. Last modified January 19, 2016. https://www.irs.gov/Government-Entities/IRS-Makes-Changes-to-Its-Advisory-Committee-on-Tax-Exempt-and-Government-Entities-ACT.

Jones, Hugh R. 2013. "The Importance of Transparency in the Governmental Regulation of the Nonprofit Sector: Room for Improvement?" *Columbia University Academic Commons*. http://dx.doi.org/10.7916/D86H4FG7.

———. Supervising Deputy Attorney General, Tax & Charities Division, Hawaii Office of the Attorney General. 2015. Email message to author Cindy M. Lott. September 1.

Kadzik, Peter, Assistant Attorney Gen. for Legislative Affairs. 2015. Letter to Bob Goodlatte, Chairman, and John Conyers, Jr., Ranking Member, Comm. on the Judiciary, U.S. House of Representatives, October 23. http://static.politico.com/5e/cc/575deb8447a1ae21270d7481a108/justice-department-letter-declining-to-charge-lois-lerner.pdf.

Kingsley, Elizabeth J. 2012. "A New D.C. Nonprofit Corporation Act." *Taxation of Exempts* (January/February): 16–25.

Lott, Cindy M., Elizabeth Boris, Karin Kunstler Goldman, Belinda Johns, and Maura Ferrell. Forthcoming 2016. "State Regulation and Enforcement in the Charitable Sector." Columbia Law School's Charities Regulation and Oversight Project and the Urban Institute's Center on Nonprofits and Philanthropy.

Maryland Code Annotated, Business Regulation §§ 6.5-101–6.5-105.

McKeever, Brice S. 2015. "The Nonprofit Sector in Brief 2015: Public Charities, Giving, and Volunteering." *The Urban Institute*, October http://www.urban.org/sites/default/files/alfresco/publication-pdfs/2000497-The-Nonprofit-Sector-in-Brief-2015-Public-Charities-Giving-and-Volunteering.pdf.

Missouri Office of the Attorney General. 2015. "Press Release: AG Koster sues four sham cancer charities for defrauding donors of more than $187 million." *Missouri Office of the Attorney General*, May 19. https://ago.mo.gov/home/news-archives/2015-news-archives/ag-koster-sues-four-sham-cancer-charities-for-defrauding-donors-of-more-than-187-million.

Modisett, Jeffrey A., and Cindy M. Lott. 2000. "Cyberlaw and E-Commerce: A State Attorney General's Perspective." *Northwestern University Law Review* (1999–2000) 94: 643.

Multi-State Filer Project. "The Uniform Registration Statement." *Multi-State Filer Project*. Accessed March 1, 2016. http://multistatefiling.org.

Multi-state Registration & Filing Portal, Inc. "About." Multi-state Registration & Filing Portal, Inc. Accessed March 3, 2016. http://mrfpinc.org/about/.

Myers, Emily. 2013. "Common Law Powers." In *State Attorneys General Powers and Responsibilities*. Emily Myers, ed. (pp. 27–44). Washington, DC: National Association of Attorneys General.

National Association of Attorneys General. 2011. *Letter to the Honorable Max Baucus, Chairman, Comm. on Finance, United States Senate and the Honorable Orrin Hatch, Ranking Member, Committee on Finance, U.S. Senate.* October 28.

National Association of State Charity Officials. 2001. "The Charleston Principles: Guidelines on Charitable Solicitations Using the Internet." *NASCO*. Last modified March 14, 2001. http://www.nasconet.org/wp-content/uploads/2011/05/Charleston-Principles-Final.pdf.

———. 2016a. "History." *NASCO*. Accessed January 10, 2016. http://www.nasconet.org/about/history/.

———. 2016b. "Single Portal." *NASCO*. Accessed March 1, 2016. http://www.nasconet.org/category/single-portal/.

National Center for Charitable Statistics. "About NCCS." *Urban Institute*. Accessed March 3, 2016. http://nccs.urban.org/about/index.cfm.

National Council of Nonprofits. 2016a. "Commercial Co-Ventures and Cause Related Marketing." *National Council of Nonprofits*. Accessed March 5, 2016. https://www.councilofnonprofits.org/tools-resources/commercial-co-ventures-and-cause-related-marketing.

———. 2016b. "Principles and Practices." *National Council of Nonprofits*. Accessed March 5, 2016. https://www.councilofnonprofits.org/tools-resources/principles-and-practices.

National Council on Foundations. 2016. "National Standards for U.S. Community Foundations." *National Council on Foundations*. Accessed March 4, 2016. http://www.cof.org/public-policy/community-foundation-standards.

New York Office of the Attorney General. 2013a. Press Release: "A. G. Schneiderman Obtains Court Decision Shutting Down Major Charitable Fundraiser For Defrauding The Public." *New York Office of the Attorney General*, May 3. http://ag.ny.gov/press-release/ag-schneiderman-obtains-court-decision-shutting-down-major-charitable-fundraiser.

———. 2013b. "A. G. Schneiderman's Nonprofit Revitalization Act Signed Into Law." *New York Office of the Attorney General*, December 19. http://www.ag.ny.gov/press-release/ag-schneidermans-nonprofit-revitalization-act-signed-law.

———. "CharitiesNYS.com: Access, Reform, Accountability." *CharitiesNYS.* Accessed March 1, 2016. http://www.charitiesnys.com/home.jsp.

N.Y. State Senate. 2016. *A8072.* Accessed February 29, 2016. http://www.nysenate.gov/legislation/bills/2013/A8072.

Noveck, Beth Simone and Daniel L. Goroff. 2013. "Information for Impact: Liberating Nonprofit Sector Data." *The Aspen Institute*, September 26. http://www.aspeninstitute.org/sites/default/files/content/docs/pubs/Information_for_Impact_Report_FINAL_REPORT_9-26-13.pdf.

Office of Consumer Protection, Montana Department of Justice. 2012. "Montana Attorney General's Investigative Report of Greg Mortenson and Central Asia Institute." *Montana Department of Justice.* https://dojmt.gov/wp-content/uploads/2012_0405_FINAL-REPORT-FOR-DISTRIBUTION.pdf.

Owens, Marcus S. 2008. "Charities and Governance: Is the IRS Subject to Challenge?" http://www.caplindrysdale.com/files/Publication/C3941121-3CE4-412A-8ED0-0C170665ED50/Presentation/PublicationAttachment/BF33A906-9A00-44B4-847D-106B4E3A8863/Governance%20article.pdf.

Pension Protection Act of 2006, Pub. L. No. 109-280 (August 17, 2006).

Perry, Suzanne. 2015. "IRS Plans to Begin Releasing Electronic Nonprofit Tax Forms Next Year." *Chronicle of Philanthropy*, June 30.

Public.Resource.org v. United States Internal Revenue Serv., 78 F. Supp. 3d 1262 (N.D. Cal. 2015), appeal dismissed (June 24, 2015).

Revenue Act of Oct. 3, 1913, ch. 16, 38 Stat. 114 (1913).

Ripperda, Tamera L., Director, Exempt Organizations, Internal Revenue Service. 2015. Remarks at the Urban Institute's Emerging Issues in Philanthropy Seminar: Data Collection, Sharing, and Transparency in the Tax Exempt Sector: at the Intersection of Regulators, Technology and Sector Stakeholders, December 1.

Sheehan, James, Chief, Charities Bureau, New York State Office of the Attorney General. 2015. Statement on Charities Bureau's Business Process Analysis, December 16. http://static1.squarespace.com/static/514df9aae4b0123f55d14129/t/5672d016df40f3f d5f51bc61/1450364950229/Charities+Bureau+CSG+Announcement+-121615-F.pdf.

Standards for Excellence Institute. 2016. "The Standards for Excellence: History & Overview." *Standards for Excellence Institute.* Accessed Mar. 4, 2016. http://standardsforexcellence.org/home-2/about-the-institute/.

State v. Cody, 34 N.E.3d 189 (Ohio Ct. App. 2015).

Tampa Bay Times, "Navy Veterans Investigation." *Tampa Bay Times.* Accessed March 13, 2016. http://www.tampabay.com/topics/specials/navyveterans.page.

Tyler, John, Evan Absher, Kathleen Garman, and Anthony Luppino. 2015. "Producing Better Mileage: Advancing the Design and Usefulness of Hybrid Vehicles for Social Business Ventures." *Quinnipiac Law Review* 33: 235.

Uniform Law Commission. 2016a. "About the ULC." *Uniform Law Commission.* Accessed February 29, 2016. http://www.uniformlaws.org/Narrative.aspx?title=About%20the%20ULC.

———. 2016b. "Legislative Fact Sheet–Prudent Management of Institutional Funds Act." *Uniform Law Commission.* Accessed March 3, 2016. http://www.uniformlaws.org/LegislativeFactSheet.aspx?title=Prudent%20Management%20of%20Institutional%20Funds%20Act.

———. 2016c. "Legislative Fact Sheet–Trust Code." *Uniform Law Commission*. Accessed March 3, 2016. http://www.uniformlaws.org/LegislativeFactSheet.aspx?title=Trust%20Code.

———. 2016d. "Legislative Fact Sheet - Prudent Investor Act." *Uniform Law Commission*. Accessed March 3, 2016. http://www.uniformlaws.org/LegislativeFactSheet.aspx?title=Prudent%20Investor%20Act.

———. 2016e. "Protection of Charitable Assets Act, Model." *Uniform Law Commission*. Accessed March 3, 2016. http://www.uniformlaws.org/Act.aspx?title=Protection%20of%20Charitable%20Assets%20Act,%20Model.

Urban Institute. "About the Center on Nonprofits and Philanthropy." *Urban Institute*. Accessed January 28, 2016. http://www.urban.org/policy-centers/center-nonprofits-and-philanthropy/understanding-how-nonprofits-work-and-why-they-matter.

U.S. Government Accountability Office. 2014. *Report to the Ranking Member, Comm. on Homeland Security and Gov. Affairs, U.S. Senate; Tax Exempt Organizations: Better Compliance Indicators and Data, and More Collaboration with State Regulators Would Strengthen Oversight of Charitable Organizations*, GAO-15-164. Washington, DC, 2014.

———. 2015. IRS 2016 Budget: IRS is Scaling Back Activities and Using Budget Flexibilities to Absorb Funding Cuts, GAO-15-624. Washington, DC.

Wyland, Michael. 2014. "Is the 1023-EZ a Step Backward for Regulators and Nonprofits?" *Nonprofit Quarterly*, June 4.

Zeberkiewicz, John Mark and Blake Rohrbacher. 2011. "New Day for Nonstock Corporations: The 2010 Amendments to Delaware's General Corporation Law." *The Business Lawyer* 66: 271–313.

Chapter 6

Nonprofits and Advocacy

Roger Colinvaux

INTRODUCTION

Advocacy by nonprofit organizations is an explosive topic. Nonprofit advocacy involves fundamental speech protected by the First Amendment of the United States Constitution. Many nonprofit organizations have powerful institutional voices and want to defend or change public policy by lobbying for or against legislation or by engaging in electoral activity. A small neighborhood organization like a parent-teacher association or a community center inevitably will feel the tug of politics. Grassroots organizations often form explicitly to advocate for social change. Charitable organizations might believe that advocacy goes hand in hand with mission, whether the charity is a faith-based organization, an educational organization that informs the public about environmental issues, or a private foundation trying to cure a disease or eradicate poverty. Labor unions and trade associations have advocacy at their core. Individuals often want to fund advocacy activity through nonprofit organizations and remain anonymous. At first blush, nonprofits and advocacy seem to be a natural and comfortable fit.

Although the desire to organize, advocate, and take policy positions may reflect an inherent human trait, nonprofit advocacy requires some regulations by the government. The public interest in preventing corruption or the appearance of corruption in political and lobbying activity means that there are federal laws on campaign finance (overseen by the Federal Election Commission [FEC]), disclosure requirements relating to advocacy activities and donors, and rules about ethical behavior. In addition to federal law, a potpourri of rules also applies at the state and local levels. Further, the fact of organized advocacy means that interaction with the tax law and the Internal Revenue Service (IRS) is inevitable. Nonprofit advocacy is thus both a fundamental and a regulated activity.

This creates tension. There is no better example of the tension and the explosiveness of nonprofit advocacy than the scandal involving the formation of nonprofit groups affiliated with the emergent "Tea Party" after the Supreme Court's decision in *Citizens United v. Federal Election Commission* (Treasury Inspector General 2013). The IRS, which is tasked with enforcing the tax laws affecting nonprofits, had no choice but to assess the true nature of the "Tea Party" and other groups seeking tax exempt status. But the IRS's inability to make quick decisions, and its use of political labels to identify cases, spawned a scandal that has led to years of hostile hearings on Capitol Hill, a criminal investigation (that ended without charges), a climate of mistrust and suspicion of the IRS, and reduced funding for this essential government agency (*Hearing Before the Comm. on Oversight* 2013). All because when it comes to nonprofit advocacy, the tension between free speech and government regulation can be combustible.

Over many years, the laws on nonprofit advocacy have become complex and increasingly difficult for a nonexpert to access. The many and changing sources of law, the variety of groups that engage in advocacy, and misinformation from the media and other sources combine to make it hard to gain a general understanding of how advocacy activity is regulated.

This chapter provides an overview of the ways in which government, particularly the federal government, affects the ability of nonprofit organizations to advocate. As an initial matter, there are several categories of advocacy: lobbying, electoral or campaign activity, issue advocacy, nonpartisan advocacy, and other advocacy activity. Lobbying and campaign activity are the most regulated. The other categories may escape regulation (as advocacy). Nonprofit organizations must be able to distinguish the type of advocacy activity in order to know which rules apply and carefully monitor advocacy activities to be sure one category of activity has not changed over time into another.

The chapter focuses on federal tax law, in large part because tax law is at the root of how advocacy organizations are classified, and how advocacy is defined and limited. The chapter begins by outlining constitutional considerations relating to nonprofit advocacy under both campaign finance and tax law and describes the different types of nonprofit organizations that advocate. The chapter then provides an overview of the general rules and rationales that apply, first in the lobbying context, and then in the political activity context. Finally, the chapter discusses the main issues affecting nonprofits and government when it comes to advocacy activity.

CONSTITUTIONAL CONSIDERATIONS AND ORGANIZATION TYPES

At the outset, it is essential to frame a discussion of advocacy in the context of government power to regulate. The two main sources of federal regulation are campaign finance law and tax law.

Regulatory Framework under Campaign Finance Law

For campaign finance law, the Federal Election Campaign Act (FECA or Act) of 1971, as amended in 1974, established the basic regulatory structure. In the landmark decision *Buckley v. Valeo,* the Supreme Court affirmed the compelling government interest in preventing corruption or the appearance of corruption in campaign finance, thus providing the basis for government regulation.[1] On the other side, the Court equated spending money with speech, thus recognizing that the First Amendment protected spending as a form of expression. The Court affirmed limits on political contributions, struck down expenditure limits on individuals, and upheld the constitutionality of disclosure rules as appropriate to help ensure transparency, but only to the extent that the speech being regulated was for express advocacy. Limits on political expenditures from the general treasury funds of corporations and labor unions predated FECA and survived.

After *Buckley*, a key distinction, or loophole, emerged. Express advocacy as laid down in *Buckley* was very narrow, requiring express and active words like "vote for" Candidate Smith. Speech with the same general intent and effect as express advocacy could escape regulation under the act if express words of advocacy, so-called "magic words," were avoided. As a result, a distinction between express advocacy triggered by magic words (regulated speech) and issue advocacy (unregulated speech) became a key part of the legal landscape.

Thus, political parties, campaign committees, and other types of overtly political organizations fell within the ambit of the act. But organizations with issue advocacy at their core were outside the act. Accordingly, groups with a purpose of influencing elections could, with careful planning, escape regulation by the FEC. The main result, which developed over many years, was that sham issue advertisements that clearly were campaign related by any standard other than that of Buckley's magic words test, dominated the airwaves, and escaped regulation.

Congress eventually responded, in two key ways. One was through the Bipartisan Campaign Reform Act of 2002 (BCRA). BCRA, among other things, regulated "electioneering communications," a technical term for sham issue advertisements, barring them in some cases, and imposing disclosure rules. Electioneering communications generally were defined as broadcast communications that occur close to a federal election and refer to a clearly identified federal candidate. Express language, as in *Buckley*, was not required. The Supreme Court upheld BCRA's electioneering communication provisions in *McConnell v. FEC*, noting that the magic words test of *Buckley v. Valeo* was "functionally meaningless" and that such communications were the "equivalent of express advocacy." The Court also upheld BCRA's disclosure provisions.

The other congressional response (which happened earlier in 2000) was to attack the sham issue ad disclosure loophole. Political groups that were able to fall outside the political committee definition (and so escape FEC regulation) generally were organized under one section of the tax code, section 527.[2] These groups became notorious in the run-up to the year 2000 presidential election, running harsh issue ads attacking candidates but without any disclosure of contributors. Congress decided that 527 groups, which by definition were organized for a political purpose, should be subject to FECA-style disclosure rules. But instead of amending the campaign finance law, Congress amended the tax code. The result was to split jurisdiction over campaign-related speech between the FEC, which enforced the disclosure rules for political committees, and the IRS, which enforced the disclosure rules for other political groups.

The legal landscape shifted again with the Supreme Court's decision in *Citizens United v. Federal Election Commission*. In *Citizens United*, the Court overruled prior precedent (including aspects of the *McConnell* decision) and held that the long-standing limits on independent expenditures by corporations and labor unions from their general treasury funds were unconstitutional under the First Amendment. As a result, an entire category of campaign advocacy previously barred was unleashed. Corporations of (almost) all stripes (the exception being charitable organizations, for tax law reasons) suddenly were able to spend their funds directly and advocate expressly for or against candidates. The Court did not disavow the government interest in preventing corruption, but reasoned that independent expenditures, by definition, did not pose a threat. On the other hand, if expenditures are coordinated with a campaign or candidate, then the expenditure is not independent and limits apply.

Notably, the Court again upheld disclosure provisions as constitutional, but in the wake of *Citizens United*, a significant gap in the disclosure regime became evident. Corporations or labor unions that are not organized under section 527 of the tax code, but pursuant to *Citizen United*, are allowed to make independent expenditures, are not required to file publicly available disclosures about contributors to either the FEC or the IRS.

In summary, under campaign finance law, the federal government may regulate political speech to protect against corruption or the appearance of corruption. Disclosure provisions and contribution limits consistently have been held constitutional. Expenditures by campaigns and parties are not limited, nor are independent expenditures, but an expenditure that is coordinated with a campaign or party is considered a contribution and so subject to contribution limits.

Basis for Regulation under the Tax Law and Nonprofit Taxonomy

Campaign finance law is but one main source of regulation of advocacy for nonprofits; tax law is the other. In general, Congress has considerable authority when it comes to tax benefits. As stated by the Supreme Court, "[b]oth tax exemptions and tax deductibility are a form of subsidy that is administered through the tax system" (Regan 1983). Denying a deduction relating to speech merely means that taxpayers "are simply being required to pay for [constitutionally protected] activities entirely out of their own pockets" (Cammarano 1959). Accordingly, as a general matter, judicial review of tax law advocacy limitations is more deferential than in the campaign finance context. As discussed below, judicial review may also be more simplistic, in that the labels "deduction" and "exemption" can lead courts to presume that a subsidy exists when it may not.

As noted above, in the year 2000 Congress used tax law to impose FECA disclosure rules on 527 organizations. At the time, this seemed a prudent approach. Restrictions that might present constitutional problems if imposed directly (e.g., under campaign finance rules) might survive when imposed as part of overall tax scheme or tax subsidy. Thus, Congress may have been relying on tax law jurisprudence to impose disclosure obligations it thought might fail as a matter of campaign finance law but succeed as a matter of tax law (Aprill 2011). Indeed, the tax law disclosure rules were upheld largely on a condition of a subsidy theory by a federal appellate court (Mobile Republican Assembly 2003).

Nevertheless, notwithstanding a generally deferential posture, in one important concurring opinion, Supreme Court Justice Blackmun expressed reservations about tax law limits on fundamental speech. Justice Blackmun voted that tax law lobbying restrictions on charitable organizations were constitutional, but only because a charity can pursue the same type of speech through a related entity (Regan 1983). Thus, for one justice at least, the presence of an alternate channel for speech was critical. The constitutional need for an alternate channel has never been clear, but nonetheless has had considerable influence on the law (Aprill 2011; Galston 2007).

Apart from constitutional considerations, tax law is a natural starting point to understand government regulation of advocacy outside of the somewhat limited context of campaign finance. The entry point is the tax classification system. The tax code uses the generic term "exempt organization" to describe more than thirty organization types. For nonprofit organizations that engage in advocacy, the multiplicity can be narrowed to three principal categories, each of which has distinct rules.

Section 501(c)(3) organizations may be the best known. Often referred to generically as "charitable" organizations, the category is much broader, including educational organizations (schools, colleges, think tanks, research institutions), hospitals, religious organizations (including churches), museums, scientific groups, private foundations, community foundations, US-based international aid organizations, animal welfare groups, as well as the traditional charity such as a human services organization. The charitable moniker comes from the requirement that 501(c)(3) organizations serve a public purpose and from the many tax benefits associated with the status, including eligibility to receive tax deductible contributions (i.e., the "charitable" deduction).

The next category involves three subsections of the tax code: sections 501(c)(4), 501(c)(5), and 501(c)(6), which collectively may be referred to as non-charitable nonprofits.[3] Section 501(c)(4) covers "social welfare" organizations, an amorphous term that historically has been used as a catch-all category to cover nonprofits that in some sense serve the community or public interest, but do not qualify as charitable either because the community served is too narrow (a neighborhood association) or, less frequently (but more notoriously), because the group engages in advocacy activities that disqualify it from charitable status. Section 501(c)(5) covers labor unions, other labor organizations, and nonprofit agricultural organizations. Section 501(c)(6) generally describes trade associations, like a chamber of commerce or industry group.

The final category is the political organization, which, as already mentioned, falls under section 527 of the tax code. The political organization is formed with the primary purpose of political activity. It includes political parties, political action committees [PACs], and independent political groups (sometimes referred to as super PACs). Unlike charitable organizations or non-charitable nonprofits, nonprofit status is not required, though a for-profit political organization currently is more of theoretical interest than real (Tobin 2007).

The three categories—charities, non-charitable nonprofits, and political organizations—are subject to different rules relating to advocacy activities. Importantly, although the categories are distinct, organizations may and commonly do establish networks. These networks embody the alternate channels for advocacy referred to in Justice Blackmun's concurring opinion in the Regan decision. Thus, a 501(c)(3) organization can have an affiliated 501(c)(4) organization, which may also have a related political organization.

Nonprofit advocacy then must be understood both by knowing the rules that apply to each tax category and by keeping in mind that advocacy may be conducted through networks of nonprofit organizations.

LOBBYING

Lobbying in its most general sense involves a communication that is intended to influence public officials on a matter of law. Two main sources of federal law regulate lobbying activity: the Lobbying Disclosure Act and the tax law. Each takes a different approach to defining lobbying, and to regulation.

Lobbying Disclosure Act

In general, as the name suggests, the Lobbying Disclosure Act is about transparency. If nonprofits become involved in regular lobbying activity above a certain dollar amount, the nonprofit must disclose the activity.

The Lobbying Disclosure Act regulates "lobbying contacts." A lobbying contact includes an oral or written communication with certain executive or legislative branch officials on behalf of a client or employer regarding legislation, regulations, government programs, policy or positions, executive orders, federal contracts, or the nomination or confirmation of anyone to federal office (LDA 1602(8)(A)). The list of government officials is broad, including every member and employee of Congress, every White House employee, and senior officials and employees of the executive branch. Certain communications are exempt from the definition, including congressional testimony and inquiries about the status of a government proceeding (LDA 1602(8)(B)).

Compliance with the Lobbying Disclosure Act is straightforward. If a nonprofit employs a lobbyist who regularly engages in lobbying contacts (there are fairly precise thresholds), then the nonprofit may have to register, and the lobbyist must file semiannual reports. Many nonprofits will qualify for an exception from filing if the organization's total lobbying expenses are less than specified thresholds (adjusted for inflation). The registration and reports are made to both the House of Representatives and the Senate. Violations of the act can result in civil or criminal penalties.

Nonprofit Lobbying and Tax Law

Regulation of nonprofit lobbying activity by the tax law is intricate and requires careful attention. Not concerned primarily with disclosure (though lobbying activity may have to be disclosed on annual tax filings), tax law directly limits the amount of lobbying that is allowed, depending on whether the nonprofit is a 501(c)(3) or a non-charitable nonprofit. What constitutes lobbying for tax law purposes, however, generally is much narrower than the common understanding of lobbying (including that of the Lobbying Disclosure Act), meaning that many advocacy activities are not affected by the lobbying limitations.

501(c)(3) organizations. *Rationale and background.* Tax law directly limits the lobbying activity of section 501(c)(3) organizations. The general rule is that a section 501(c)(3) organization may not lobby as a substantial part of its activities (the "no substantial part" test), or, put affirmatively, only insubstantial lobbying activity is allowed.

The principle that lobbying activity generally is not consistent with charitable status is longstanding, dating at least to a 1919 Treasury regulation, which declared that: "associations formed to disseminate controversial or partisan propaganda are not educational within the meaning of the statute" (T.D. 2831). The leading explanation of lobbying limits appeared later in a 1930 court decision (Slee 1930). There, Judge Learned Hand articulated what became known as the neutrality rationale, namely that the government should not through tax subsidies favor one type of political speech over another, but should remain neutral.[4]

In 1934, Congress followed the Slee decision with an explicit rule in the Internal Revenue Code to limit lobbying. Although the legislative history is sparse and does not provide a clear rationale, the policy of not subsidizing lobbying has become the main, if imperfect, explanation for the lobbying limits. Congress (in subsequent enactments), courts, and scholars all cite the desire for government to remain neutral (Galston 1993). As the Supreme Court said when upholding the lobbying rules against a First Amendment challenge: "Congress has merely refused to pay for the lobbying out of public moneys," and "Congress chose not to subsidize lobbying as extensively as it chose to subsidize other activities that nonprofit organizations undertake to promote the public welfare" (Regan 1983). As a result, the tax baseline is that lobbying activity should be paid for with after-tax dollars.[5]

At the same time, policymakers have recognized that lobbying by some 501(c)(3) organizations can be an important voice in public policy debates. Many charitable nonprofits seek to inform the public on issues of the day as a part of their mission, conduct independent research, analyze the effects of legislation and proposed legislation, and do so in the general public interest. Congress recognized that the uncertainty of the "no substantial part test" combined with the severity of the sanction for violations (loss of tax exempt status) meant that 501(c)(3) organizations may be overly reluctant to engage in lobbying. Accordingly, in 1976 Congress passed what became known as the "expenditure test" for lobbying, which was intended to provide more certainty and a sanction short of loss of tax exemption for excess lobbying (I.R.C. §§ 501(h), 4911).

As a result, there are two alternative tax regimes that regulate lobbying—one governed by the "no substantial part" test articulated in section 501(c)(3) and, the other, "the expenditure test," an elective regime that measures lobbying based on expenditures and detailed regulatory definitions. Further, private foundations are not allowed to lobby at all, meaning that there are three different approaches to lobbying activity by 501(c)(3) organizations.

Violation of the lobbying limitations may result in excise taxes, loss of tax exempt status or both. Thus, 501(c)(3) organizations that intend to lobby need to understand how much lobbying is permitted consistent with their tax status and the tax law definition of lobbying.

No substantial part test. The no substantial part test is the default rule. Whether lobbying is substantial is based on the facts and circumstances, and thus the test is uncertain in application. Relevant factors include the percentage of an organization's budget devoted to lobbying, volunteer time spent on lobbying, the publicity of lobbying activities, and the regularity of lobbying. Both the courts and the IRS have made clear that a strict numerical test "obscures the complexity of balancing the organization's activities in relation to its objectives and circumstances" and that "substantiality does not lend itself to ready numerical boundaries" (Christian Echoes, Gen. Couns. Mem. 36148). That said, if the organization's lobbying budget does not exceed 5 percent of total expenditures (excluding fundraising and certain other expenses), there is a general sense that the lobbying is not likely to attract scrutiny (Seasongood, Gen. Couns. Mem. 36148). Caution nonetheless is advisable. The IRS denies that there is any safe harbor, and has revoked exemption based on lobbying expenses that were as low as 2 percent of total expenses.

Lobbying under the no substantial part test is sparsely defined in regulations as attempting to influence legislation. This includes contacting, or urging "the public to contact, members of a legislative body for the purpose of proposing, supporting, or opposing legislation" or "advocat[ing] the adoption or rejection of legislation" (Treas. Reg. § 1.501(c)(3)(ii)). Legislation includes federal, state, local, referenda, constitutional amendments, and similar.

Expenditure test. Organizations in search of more certainty may elect to be subject to the expenditure test. The expenditure test sets dollar limits on the amount of lobbying permitted each year in relation to the amount the organization spends on exempt purposes (a technical concept). As exempt purpose expenses increase, the permitted amount of lobbying increases, but must constitute a smaller overall percentage of total expenses.

Lobbying is divided into two categories: direct and grassroots. Grassroots lobbying is subject to a separate limitation. The most any organization may spend on lobbying in a year is $1 million, only $250,000 of which may be for grassroots lobbying. Churches may not elect the expenditure test.

The following table shows the permitted amounts.

Exempt Purpose Expenses	Total Lobbying Limit	Grassroots Lobbying Limit
Less than $500,000	20% (up to $100,000)	5% (up to $25,000)
$500,000 to < $1 million	$100,000 + 15% of excess above $500,000	$25,000 + 3.75% of excess above $500,000
$1 million to < $1.5 million	$175,000 + 10% of excess above $1 million	$43,750 + 2.5% of excess above $1 million
$1.5 million to < $17 million	$225,000 + 5% of excess above $1.5 million	$56,250 + 1.25% of excess above $1.5 million
Above $17 million	$1 million	$250,000

For organizations that elect the expenditure test, lobbying is defined in detail. Importantly, the lobbying definition is a narrow one, which means that many forms of advocacy activity are *not* considered lobbying and so are not limited.

The main ingredient to the lobbying definition under the expenditure test is a communication that is intended to influence legislation (which includes referenda and ballot initiatives). Lobbying is limited to legislative activity (federal, state, local, and foreign); thus, communications with executive branch officials are *not* lobbying. Lobbying includes communications to legislators and staff that refer to and reflect a view on specific legislation and, if the communication is to the general public, then it also includes a call to take action on the legislation. The "call to action" requirement is akin to a magic words test (i.e., the communication must be fairly specific about contacting public officials). This means that many communications about legislation with the general public can avoid the lobbying definition by eschewing a call to action. Mass media advertisements, however, will be deemed lobbying with or without a call to action depending on the timing of the ad (relative to the vote on the legislation) and the importance of the legislation. Communications to a nonprofit's members are privileged relative to communications to the general public. Member communications may identify the position of particular legislators who will vote on the legislation without constituting lobbying.

As important as the lobbying definition are specific exceptions to lobbying, that is, activities *not* subject to the tax law lobbying limits. Nonpartisan analysis, study, or research is not lobbying, even if the research discusses legislation and takes a position. Research is nonpartisan if it presents a "sufficiently full and fair exposition of the pertinent facts to enable the public or an individual to form an independent opinion or conclusion." The research may not contain a call to action and must not be distributed just to those on one side of the issue. Relatedly, broad policy discussions in public fora or in communications with legislators—that is, pure issue advocacy—are not lobbying, so long as the merits of any legislation are not discussed and there is no call to action. Thus, nonprofits may engage in policy debates for "a clean environment," "low taxes," and so on.

Two, more limited, exceptions to lobbying apply. So-called "self-defense" lobbying is allowed, meaning that 501(c)(3) organizations may lobby directly (not via the grass roots) on legislation that could affect the organization's existence, powers, or tax benefits. Thus, if Congress proposes reductions to the charitable deduction, charities may without limit lobby members of Congress on the legislation. In addition, section 501(c)(3) organizations may provide technical assistance to the government, so long as the request for assistance is in writing by the appropriate public official (e.g., a committee and subcommittee chair). This exception to lobbying favors organizations with similar views to the majority party, allowing such organizations, by invitation, an opportunity to discuss its views fully.

Private foundations. Private foundations are not allowed to lobby. In 1969, Congress enacted a wide array of reforms directed at preventing abuses at private foundations, including a lobbying ban. Foundations face a stricter regime than public charities for both political and doctrinal reasons. Foundations were viewed as sources of wealth and power that rivaled government. Although some lobbying by public charities might be in the public interest, private foundations often represent the private interests of the founder or the founder's family. A main concern therefore was that lobbying activity by a foundation is apt to be selfish—representing personal preferences and not the public interest—thus the ban. Some challenge this supposition, however, and argue that over time foundations may be more likely than public charities to foster independent policy work in large part because the foundation does not have to cater to a donor base.

Although a ban on private foundation lobbying sounds severe, in fact, foundations remain able to engage in a wide range of advocacy activity. The ban applies only to lobbying as defined in the expenditure test, which as discussed above, is very narrow. Thus, foundations generally may lobby the executive branch, place mass media advertisements (without a call to action), and engage in any of the activities that are specified as exceptions to lobbying: nonpartisan research, issue advocacy, self-defense lobbying, and technical assistance to lawmakers. Further, the law permits foundations to make general-purpose grants to public charities that engage in lobbying, so long as the grant is not earmarked for a lobbying activity. Foundations may even fund specific projects by public charities that involve lobbying up to the non-lobbying cost of the project. For example, if a public charity pursues a project on the benefits of pre-K education with a total cost of $250,000 and a lobbying cost of $50,000, the foundation may fund the project up to $200,000.

Non-charitable nonprofits. In contrast to charitable nonprofits, non-charitable nonprofits may engage in unlimited lobbying activity, so long as the activity is related to the nonprofit purpose of the organization. Thus, as a general matter, non-charitable nonprofits do not have to be concerned either with the tax law definition of lobbying or with the amount of their lobbying activity, unless the activity is undertaken for profit or is not mission related.

A subset of non-charitable nonprofits, however, may have filing and tax obligations if they lobby. If the nonprofit is a 501(c)(4), 501(c)(5), or 501(c)(6) organization that gets its revenue from member dues, then the organization may have either to inform its members not to deduct some or all of the dues payment to the nonprofit as a business expense, or the organization must itself pay a tax. This rule (known as the "proxy tax") enforces the tax policy that lobbying expenses are not deductible. The rule does not apply to labor unions, but does generally apply to other 501(c)(5) organizations, social welfare organizations, and trade associations, with exceptions.

For example, assume that a nonprofit trade association charges members $10,000 a year. The main activities of the association are to lobby on legislation that benefits the industry of its members. Each payment of $10,000 is deductible by the member as a business expense. If the deduction is not disallowed or otherwise recaptured, the effect is to allow a federal income tax deduction for lobbying. Thus, the law requires that either the nonprofit inform its members that the portion of the dues allocable to lobbying are not deductible or the nonprofit must pay back the deduction to the government (through a tax).

Political organizations. Political organizations face no prohibition on lobbying activity. As discussed below, however, to the extent political organizations engage in activity that is not political (which would include most types of lobbying), the limited tax exemption afforded political organizations is lost. Thus, as a practical matter, political organizations do not engage in lobbying. Some activities, however, are political for purposes of section 527 *and* lobbying for purposes of section 501(c)(3). The main example is action to affect a confirmation process, for example, a judicial nominee or executive branch official, who must be confirmed by a legislative body.

POLITICAL ACTIVITY

Political activity by nonprofits is laden with controversy. Part II already discussed federal election law. Layered on top is federal tax law, which has separate rules on political activity for charitable organizations, non-charitable nonprofits, and political organizations.

At the outset, it is important to note that the term "political activity" as used here is generic and not technical. In general, the term refers to advocacy activity that is connected to the electoral process and to nominations for public office, for example, for judicial or executive branch appointments (as well as to nominations for offices in a 527 organization). Political *campaign* activity is a subset of political activity and generally is limited to campaigns and does not include nominations. Political campaign activity here is used more in connection with charitable and non-charitable nonprofits; political activity is used more in connection with political organizations (527s). The meaning of the term depends upon the context.

Section 501(c)(3) Organizations

By statute, section 501(c)(3) organizations are not allowed to engage in *any* political campaign activity (they may not "participate in, or intervene in . . . any political campaign"). An organization that violates the prohibition faces loss of tax exempt status as a 501(c)(3) organization, excise taxes on its political expenditures, and is not permitted to reorganize as a 501(c)(4) organization. In general, the same rules apply whether the 501(c)(3) is a public charity or a private foundation, except that private foundations face a distinct set of excise taxes for engaging in political activity.

The prohibition on political campaign activity became part of the statutory law in 1954, famously driven by then-Senator Lyndon Baines Johnson, who countered a charity's electoral attacks in his reelection campaign for the US Senate with legislation. The personal nature of the legislation, and the absence of any helpful legislative history, has led to uncertainty about the prohibition's rationale.

The main explanations for the prohibition are the desire to maintain integrity in charitable organizations, the risk of political capture of the charitable sector, and the neutrality rationale (i.e., there should be no subsidy for political activity). The overarching policy concern is that charitable organizations, subsidized with public money, should remain nonpartisan. In addition, even though the prohibition was not codified until 1954 and the legislation passed on a fast track, limits on the political activities of charities had historical precedent in the law of charitable trusts (Chisom 1990) and had long been of concern to lawmakers (Murphy 2003; Colinvaux 2012). Thus, although the original income tax statute did not contain express limits on campaign activity, the extent to which campaign activity (or for that matter lobbying) was consistent with charitable status was never clear. In other words, the circumstances surrounding enactment of the prohibition and the absence of legislative history does not necessarily indicate a hasty policy.

Given the ban on political campaign activity by section 501(c)(3) organizations, defining the banned activity clearly is important. Political campaign activity, however, is determined based on the facts and circumstances—there is no positive definition or bright line test. That said, some activities without question are political and barred. These might be thought of as "direct" political campaign activity and would include endorsement of candidates for public office or any other form of express advocacy, contributions to political campaigns or political parties, and opposition to candidates (e.g., "don't vote for Candidate Smith") (Branch Ministries). Even here, however, there is room for ambiguity. The terms "candidate," "public office," and "campaign" are defined in regulations and leave room for interpretation. It is not always clear, for example, when a person becomes a "candidate" (upon the formation of an exploratory committee—yes; when others begin promoting a person as a candidate—maybe) (Kindell and Reilly 2001).

Other advocacy activities are harder to assess. Depending on the facts and circumstances, an advocacy activity might be allowed, or might constitute an indirect form of political campaign activity and be barred. Thus, charitable nonprofits must carefully consider many advocacy activities on a case-by-case basis. A general principle is that educational activities related to elections are allowed; partisan activities are not. For example, voter education activities, such as voter registration efforts, get-out-the-vote drives, and the sponsoring of candidate forums, are all permitted, so long as the activities are conducted in a nonpartisan manner (Rev. Rul. 2007–2011). Thus, in general, a get-out-the-vote drive must not favor one candidate or party over another; a candidate debate should not show bias (e.g., through questioning procedures or format) (Rev. Rul. 78–248, 74–574, 86–95).

Relatedly, the prohibition on campaign activity does not reach speech about issues—that is, pure issue advocacy—nor does the prohibition bar speech by persons acting in their individual capacity. In either case, however, close attention must be paid to the facts and circumstances, as what may seem like issue advocacy may turn out to be campaign intervention, potentially creating a trap for the unwary. Key factors include whether statements made refer to candidates or voting the timing of statements in relation to an upcoming election, and whether issues discussed are ones that distinguish candidates (Rev. Rul. 2007–2011).

The prohibition on campaign activity does not prevent a 501(c)(3) organization from establishing a related 501(c)(4) organization that engages in campaign activity. The 501(c)(4) may conduct the campaign activity directly, or indirectly through a related 527 organization (Branch Ministries). If the 501(c)(3) organization makes grants to the 501(c)(4) organization, however, the 501(c)(3) organization must earmark the grant for a charitable purpose of the 501(c)(4) organization. As a general matter, 501(c)(3) organizations should not make grants to a 527 organization, but not in all cases, as some activities, for example, advocating for or against a judicial nominee, are not campaign activity for 501(c)(3) purposes, but are political activity for 527 purposes.

Non-Charitable Nonprofits

Non-charitable nonprofits face a different regime. Legally, it is hard to generalize with complete confidence among all non-charitable nonprofits because some of the authority is soft (i.e., based on administrative rulings), but it is fairly certain that the same rules apply across the main categories of 501(c)(4), 501(c)(5), and 501(c)(6) organizations (I.R.S. Gen. Couns. Mem. 34, 233). Of these three groups, only section 501(c)(4) organizations have specific regulations on the topic, which then provide the basic analytical approach for all three categories.

The important decree of the 501(c)(4) regulations is that political activity does not further social welfare. "The promotion of social welfare does not include direct or indirect participation or intervention in political campaigns on behalf of or in opposition to any candidate for public office" (Treas. Reg. 1.501(c)(4)–1(a)(2)(ii)). IRS rules also provide, however, that 501(c)(4) organizations must "primarily" be engaged in activities that further exempt purposes. As a result, activities that do not promote social welfare, including political campaign activity, are permitted. The critical question is how much. In informal guidance, the IRS has indicated that up to 49 percent of an organization's activities (setting aside measurement issues) could be nonsocial welfare activities.

In the wake of *Citizens United*, however, as 501(c)(4) organizations have engaged in more campaign activity, this legal standard has come under intense scrutiny. As discussed in part V of the chapter, this is a key issue facing non-charitable nonprofits.

The rationale for the regulation providing that political campaign activity is inconsistent with social welfare is unknown (Kingsley and Pomeranz 2004). One explanation is that campaign activity serves the private ends of a candidate or party and so does not have a sufficient "social welfare" benefit. The IRS applied this rationale in the context of 501(c)(5) and 501(c)(6) organizations, concluding that support of a candidate "necessarily involves the organization in the total political attitudes and positions of the candidate" (I.R.S. Gen. Couns. Mem. 34,233). Another explanation reflects section 501(c)(4)'s historical role as a less restrictive version of 501(c)(3). Because the promotion of "social welfare" is a charitable purpose under the 501(c)(3) regulations, the Treasury Department might have reasoned that if campaign activity is inconsistent with charitable purposes, it is also inconsistent with social welfare purposes, but not prohibited outright (Colinvaux 2014).

As a complicating factor, non-charitable nonprofits that engage in political activity (in the broad sense) are subject to a tax. The tax is based on the lesser of the organization's political expenditures or its investment income. (The tax is further explained below in discussing political organizations.) Political activity for this purpose is defined consistent with section 527, rather than section 501(c)(3), making for additional complexity.

Importantly, non-charitable exempts are not required publicly to disclose donors. Non-charitable exempts may choose to conduct political activity through a separate segregated fund; however, any such fund would be treated as a section 527 organization and thus subject to disclosure rules.

Political Organizations (527s)

Political organizations round out the regulatory scheme. There is no tax law limit on their political activity. The main limit faced by political organizations is that any nonpolitical activity is tax disadvantaged, meaning that political activity is the main, if not only, activity conducted by political organizations. In contrast to non-charitable nonprofits, donors to political organizations must be publicly disclosed.

The definition of political activity is broad. It includes political campaign activity and also encompasses activity "to influence the selection, nomination, election, or appointment of any individual to a public office, office in a political organization, or the election of Presidential or Vice-Presidential electors." By thus including efforts to influence executive appointments and judicial nominations, political activity covers more than just political campaign activity. As noted, lobbying is not a 527 activity, and the IRS lists several factors that help distinguish the two (Rev. Rul. 2004–2006).

In general, political organizations represent one specialized slice of the nonprofit sector and so may seem to be of tangential interest. But their influence on the law is significant, in large part because the taxation of political organizations establishes a baseline for the appropriate tax treatment of political activity for other organizations and the necessary contours of the IRS's regulatory role. In contrast to charitable and non-charitable nonprofits, where limits to political activity require a rationale, the absence of limits on political organizations leads to the question of why political organizations are "exempt" organizations at all. That is, if the neutrality rationale requires the government to step aside and not subsidize political activity, then arguably there *should* be tax-based limits on the activity of political organizations.

The neutrality rationale, however, has little force as applied to political organizations. The "neutral" tax baseline discussed above, that political (and lobbying) activity should be funded with after-tax dollars, is consistent with the tax exemption for political organizations. This is because the political organization generally represents a pooling of contributions for political purposes. When an individual makes a contribution to a political organization, the contribution comes from after-tax dollars. The contribution income has already been taxed—the political organization merely pools the contributions and spends it on behalf of donors, often quickly (Polsky 2005; Halperin 2006). As Congress confirmed when codifying the tax treatment of political organizations (in broad agreement with the prevailing treatment by the IRS): "Political activity (including the financing of political activity) as such is not a trade or business which is appropriately subject to tax" (S. Rep. No. 93–1357). Almost by definition, political contributions are not income.

Tax exemption for contribution income (and no deduction for political expenses) then follows as a matter of course. However, to the extent contributions accumulate and generate investment income, there should be, and is, taxation. Thus, it is a misnomer fully to embrace the exempt organization label for political organizations. Political organizations are subject to tax on investment income and income from nonpolitical activity (unlike charitable and non-charitable nonprofits). Nevertheless, the idea that tax exemption for political organizations reflects a government subsidy often is touted as a reason to "reign in" or regulate political groups, explains the imposition of disclosure rules on 527s as a constitutional condition of a subsidy, and has been embraced by the courts (Mobile Republican Assembly 2003; Aprill 2011).

Relatedly, the tax on political organization investment income explains why political activity triggers a tax for non-charitable (and for that matter, charitable) nonprofits. Congress sought to equalize the tax treatment of political activity across the exemption categories and close a potential loophole. The basic premise is that if a non-charitable nonprofit accepts political contribution income and accumulates the income, there should be a tax, just as would apply to a political organization.

GOVERNMENT ENTANGLEMENTS: ISSUES RELATING TO ADVOCACY REGULATION

The First Amendment to the US Constitution provides that "Congress shall make no law . . . abridging the freedom of speech . . . ; or the right of the people peaceably to assemble, and to petition the Government for a redress of grievances." With clear, direct language, the Constitution thus establishes a powerful baseline: free speech and the right to lobby the government. It is no surprise then that government limitations on the lobbying and political activity of nonprofit organizations provoke controversy and consternation.

The threshold issue is government power and the constitutionality of advocacy limits. As part II of this chapter outlined, Congress has the power to impose limits on advocacy to prevent corruption or the appearance of corruption, or as part of an overall tax scheme or subsidy. Political contribution limits, disclosure rules, and limitations on charitable nonprofit lobbying, all have been held constitutional by the Supreme Court. Nevertheless, because of the First Amendment, there will *always* be a burden on advocacy limits. Nonprofit organizations represent people coming together for a collective cause, and as people learn, misunderstand, or reject the law, the people, often through nonprofit organizations, continually will subject the law to challenge and scrutiny.

The *Citizens United* decision shifted the legal landscape and creates new vulnerability to the tax law limits on political activity. If campaign finance law may not limit independent expenditures, on what basis may tax law limit the same speech without running afoul of the First Amendment? Most commentators agree that the constitutional conditions analysis of the Regan case remains viable, at least with respect to 501(c)(3) organizations, where the subsidy argument is stronger (Aprill 2011; Colinvaux 2012; Mayer 2011). But for non-charitable nonprofits, limits on political campaign activity might not survive a First Amendment challenge, especially considering that the current tax treatment of political campaign activity by non-charitable nonprofits is generally consistent with a neutral tax baseline.

Setting aside constitutional questions, the main issue in the regulation of advocacy overwhelmingly is disclosure of donor information. Federal law is inconsistent in requiring disclosure relating to political activity. Political organizations disclose donors but non-charitable nonprofits do not. This inconsistency drives behavior, creates political tension between the IRS and Congress, and leads to many negative ripple effects throughout the regulatory system.

When a group forms with political aims, but wants to keep donors anonymous, one option is to form as a 501(c)(4) social welfare organization. A legal organization need be not much more than a name (e.g., "Citizens for Peace"), a bank account, and officers to manage and spend money. No physical office or activities, apart from the raising and spending of money, is necessary. For new groups, the IRS has to make a judgment,[6] based on statements of intent by the group's founders and an often-limited track record, as to whether the group properly is a 501(c)(4) organization or is in reality a political organization. Without strong support for this regulatory function from both political parties in Congress, any categorical judgment by the IRS exposes the agency to scrutiny and voluble criticism.

Further, the law the IRS uses to make judgments in this area is weak. Unless the legal standards are changed,[7] the IRS must make a series of very difficult assessments, even when a group has an extensive track record. Is a group's activity political campaign activity? Or is the activity lobbying, issue advocacy, nonpartisan activity, educational activity, or something else? Groups intent on evading the political activity characterization can plan the activity to be close to but not clearly political activity, opening the door to ambiguity. In addition, because political activity is based on the facts and circumstances, in theory the IRS must make a separate assessment with respect to each act or expenditure, which allows any determined group to exploit uncertainties in the law and question the IRS's decision repeatedly.

Moreover, even if there is agreement that an activity is political, political activity is a permitted activity. The issue then becomes whether the political activity in the aggregate has crowded out social welfare activity as the primary activity of the organization. The legal standard for "primary," however, is another grey area, requiring more judgment by the agency and application of unclear standards. Notably, these weaknesses in the law had long existed, but were not especially significant until after the Citizens United decision, which, by removing the campaign finance law limits on independent expenditures, made non-charitable nonprofits attractive vehicles for campaign activity.

A further complicating factor is that, purely as a matter of collecting the right amount of federal income tax, whether an organization is classified as a 501(c)(4) or a 527 organization is of slight consequence. With one exception, the tax treatment of the two organization types with respect to political activity essentially is the same.[8] As a result, there is little revenue at stake in properly assigning an exemption category to a group. Normally, the absence of revenue concerns would allow the IRS to take a lax enforcement approach. With respect to political activity, however, because there is a disclosure consequence to tax classification, the IRS cannot ignore the issues, and the flaws to the system are magnified.

This leads to an erosion of the rule of law. On the one hand, groups are emboldened to challenge the IRS. Some groups plainly are not concerned about IRS enforcement, spending well over 50 percent of all expenses (in some cases, near 100 percent) on what would appear to be political activity. Other groups might exploit IRS weakness and disguise political activity through grants to other non-charitable nonprofits that engage in political activity. Moving money from organization to organization makes enforcement much more difficult by requiring that the IRS follow the (fungible) money. Still other groups might risk perjury through incorrect or false statements on the annual information return, leading to erosion of the integrity of the reporting regime.

Not only does the current legal framework foster disregard for the law, the rule of law also is damaged by the IRS's apparent inability to take effective enforcement action. As anonymous or "dark money" washes through the nonprofit world, voices opposed to undisclosed political spending blame the IRS for not enforcing the tax exemption laws. This criticism, however, feeds a misperception that political activity is tax favored by exemption and that the IRS's administrative impotence enables tax cheats. But any IRS failure properly to characterize nonprofit groups supports a disclosure shelter, not a tax shelter. The root of the problem is not vague exemption standards and uncertain political activity definitions but inconsistent disclosure rules and Congress' charge to the IRS to enforce the inconsistency.

In short, for nonprofits that advocate, whether politically or not, the fact of inconsistent federal law on disclosure of political activity means that issues of anonymous political speech, weak and hard to enforce exemption standards, questions about defining political activity, disrespect for the rule of law, and damage to the reputation of the IRS will be a core part of the legal landscape in which all nonprofits operate.

Charitable nonprofits face a distinct set of issues relating to advocacy. Most fundamentally are questions relating to the wisdom of current policy limits. There is a considerable scholarly literature on the pros and cons of the prohibition on political campaign activity. The main argument in support of the prohibition is that it protects the charitable sector from becoming a magnet for electoral speech. If charities were free to engage in campaign activity, the independent voice of the charity might be eroded and identified with a particular candidate or party (Colinvaux 2012; Galle 2013; Tobin 2007).

Under this view, the prospect of charitable PACs, or charities for hire to the highest bidder, is alarming and a highly plausible outcome, given that charitable contributions are deductible. If campaign activity restrictions were lifted, the 501(c)(3) organization would be a very attractive vehicle for direct campaign speech, or as a conduit through which political contributions would be made and then passed on to a related network of non-charitable organizations, as already occurs in the non-charitable nonprofit context. Even if many charities would refrain from campaign activity, the taint of politics within a vocal part of the sector likely would damage the reputation of the sector as a whole.

On the other side, the prohibition is criticized for a variety of reasons. The prohibition is viewed as a paternalistic restraint on fundamental speech; as vague, which means it chills both prohibited and permitted speech; as fencing out of the public square important (nonprofit) voices; as prone to abuse through uneven or intentionally political enforcement; and as requiring some organizations to compromise mission, especially those that are faith based (Buckles 2007). It has become almost a ritual in recent years to dare the IRS to enforce the law, as some faith-based organizations conduct "Pulpit Freedom Sunday"—intentionally coming close to or crossing the line in search of publicity and a court challenge to the constitutionality of the rules. In session after session of Congress, bills are introduced that would allow churches to engage in political campaign activity, an issue that inevitably gets more attention in presidential election years.

With respect to the lobbying limits, a main concern is that the lobbying regime does not work as Congress intended. When Congress enacted the expenditure test, and Treasury promulgated a narrow definition of lobbying, one expectation was that 501(c)(3) organizations would prefer the certainty and expansiveness of this regime to the uncertainty of the default "no substantial part" test. In fact, however, very few charities elect the expenditure test. Large organizations find the overall cap on expenditures ($1 million) too low, and the sublimit on grassroots lobbying a barrier to effective speech. Small organizations may not know of or understand the expenditure test, and confuse lobbying activity, which is allowed, with political campaign activity, which is not.

Compliance with the advocacy limits presents additional issues. Given the facts and circumstances standard for assessing campaign activity, and the unclear lines of the "no substantial part" test for lobbying, charitable nonprofits that want to comply with the law, but also to engage in permitted advocacy to the full extent of the law, operate in a state of caution and concern. This is made more dramatic because the potential sanction—revocation of 501(c)(3) status—is severe.

Some suggest that the IRS could alleviate the compliance burden with more guidance, providing brighter lines and clear definitions of, for example, political campaign activity (Colvin 2010). Indeed, the IRS attempted to write brighter definitional lines through proposed regulations for 501(c)(4) organizations. As the widespread condemnation of that regulation project showed, any effort to draw (serious) bright lines will be controversial, will generate winners and losers, and will also introduce new gray areas around the lines.

The same issues—unclear boundaries and a harsh sanction—also raise considerable enforcement challenges. The IRS is reluctant strictly to enforce the law. In recent years, the IRS undertook enforcement efforts (known as the Political Activities Compliance Initiative) under which many organizations were contacted and violations of the prohibition were discovered (e.g., campaign contributions) but tax exempt status was not revoked. The initiative was thus more in the nature of an educational effort by the IRS than a robust attempt to enforce the prohibition. In addition, inquiries into mooted campaign activities by a prominent church (the All Saints Church), and a large nonprofit (the NAACP) resulted in a media frenzy and a chastened IRS. As a result, and especially in light of events outside the charitable sphere (the alleged political targeting of "Tea Party" groups in 2013), enforcement not only is difficult, but inevitably exposes the agency to intense criticism.

At bottom, the issues for charities are intractable. As long as there is a charitable deduction, there will be problems of policy, compliance, and enforcement. Unless and until there is a seminal shift in policy that would allow deductible contributions to be used for political activity or for substantial lobbying, charitable nonprofits (and government) will be obliged to continue to decipher partisanship and lobbying from issue advocacy and education. Here, the IRS has an important and legitimate role to play in maintaining congressionally imposed advocacy limits.

A final issue relates to the tax exemption system as a whole. Increasingly, many nonprofit advocacy organizations should be viewed as conglomerates—networks of related exempt entities that maintain formal legal barriers and legally distinct identities. The educational or charitable arm is a 501(c)(3), and the lobbying and political arms are one or more non-charitable exempts or political organizations. These structures make sense from a legal perspective—allowing groups to maximize tax benefits and minimize disclosure burdens. From a regulatory perspective, however, monitoring money flows and maintaining formal barriers is very difficult. Perhaps most important, from the perspective of the general public, not attuned to legal niceties, networked groups likely do not appear as distinct entities but as one organization with a common message, delivered in different packages. In other words, networked groups raise the question whether advocacy limits are in name only.

CONCLUSION

Advocacy by nonprofit organizations is fundamental to our civil society and protected by the Constitution. Regulation of advocacy by government, however, is necessary as a shield against corruption and as part of a system of tax classifications among nonprofit organizations. For nonprofits generally, the scope of unregulated advocacy is broad, generally including nonpartisan activity, educational activity, and issue advocacy, but distinguishing these types of advocacy from political and lobbying activity is difficult.

Within the tax system, the long-standing public policy is to fund lobbying and political activity with after-tax dollars. This explains advocacy limits on charitable organizations, which are imposed as a part of an overall tax scheme or subsidy. IRS enforcement, or failure to enforce, the policy consistently leads to controversy—whether by organizations flouting the rules or because the uncertainty of the boundaries makes compliance difficult. Many of these problems, however, are part and parcel of the policy, which is not to say that the IRS could not improve its enforcement efforts, but merely to recognize the fact that the issues are and will remain difficult.

Unlike for charitable nonprofits, advocacy limits on non-charitable nonprofits are harder to justify under a subsidy theory. This has become more important in recent years because the *Citizens United* decision and inconsistent federal rules on disclosure have exposed weaknesses in the tax rules that apply to non-charitable nonprofits. Groups are able to exploit legal uncertainties and adopt tax classifications based on whether donors must be disclosed. This has led to a series of regulatory and compliance problems that are undermining the rule of law, problems that generally could be fixed by removing the inconsistent disclosure rules.

NOTES

1. Other government interests have been identified over the years, such as equalizing voices in the political process, but without support in the Court's decisions.

2. As discussed below, political committees under FECA are also 527 organizations but render disclosure to the FEC not the IRS.

3. Veterans organizations, organized under section 501(c)(19), are another, discrete, category. Unlike other non-charitable nonprofits, contributions to veterans organizations are deductible as charitable contributions but the advocacy limits of section 501(c)(3) do not apply.

4. Judge Hand opined: "Political agitation as such is outside the statute, however innocent the aim.... Controversies of that sort must be conducted without public subvention; the Treasury stands aside from them."

5. Section 501(c)(3) organizations in particular raise the neutrality rationale because they not only are exempt from federal income tax, but contributions to them also are deductible as charitable contributions (unlike non-charitable nonprofits), among other tax benefits.

6. The judgment should occur either when the group files an annual information return (Form 990) or if the group applies for 501(c)(4) status.

7. The IRS issued proposed regulations to change some of the standards in the area, imposing bright lines that would deem certain activity (e.g., voter registration drives, advertisements made within a certain proximity to an election) as political campaign activity. The regulations were widely criticized. Congress intervened by forbidding the IRS from taking further steps to develop the law in the area through fiscal year 2016.

8. The exception, potentially significant in some cases, is that donors of appreciated property (like stock) must pay tax on the appreciation if the property is given to a political organization but not if the property is given to a non-charitable nonprofit. Depending on how a group is financed, this creates an additional incentive not to use section 527. As of 2015, contributions to either group are exempt from federal gift tax.

SOURCE LIST

Bipartisan Campaign Reform Act, Pub. L. No. 107-155.
Federal Election Campaign Act, 2 U.S.C. 431 et. seq.
Lobbying Disclosure Act, 2 U.S.C. 1601 et. seq.
S. REP. NO. 93-1357, at 7502 (1974), *reprinted in* 1974 U.S.C.C.A.N. 7478.
T.D. 2831, 21 Treas. Dec. Int. Rev. 170, 285 (1919).
Treas. Reg. 1.501(c)(4)-1(a)(2)(ii).
Treas. Reg. § 56.4911-2.
Prop. Treas. Reg. § 1.501(c)(4)-1, 78 Fed. Reg. 71,535 (November 29, 2013).
I.R.S. Gen. Couns. Mem. 34,233 (December 30, 1969).
I.R.S. Gen. Couns. Mem. 36148.
I.R.S. Gen. Couns. Mem. 39,694 (February 22, 1988).
Buckley v. Valeo, 424 U.S. 1 (1976).
Cammarano v. United States, 358 U.S. 498 (1959).
Citizens United v. Federal Election Commission, 558 U.S. 310 (2010).
McConnell v. Federal Election Commission, 540 U.S. 93 (2003).
Regan v. Taxation with Representation of Wash., 461 U.S. 540 (1983).
Association of the Bar of New York v. Commissioner, 858 F.2d 876 (2d Cir. 1988).
Branch Ministries v. Rossotti, 211 F.3d 137 (D.C. Cir. 2000).
Christian Echoes Nat'l Ministry v. United States, 470 F.2d 849 (1972).
Mobile Republican Assembly v. United States, 353 F.3d 1357 (11th Cir. 2003).
Seasongood v. Comm'r, 227 F.2d 907 (6th Cir. 1955).
Slee v. Commissioner, 42 F.2d 184 (2d Cir. 1930).
Rev. Rul. 67-368, 1967-2 C.B. 194.
Rev. Rul. 74-574, 1974-2 C.B. 1670.
Rev. Rul. 78-248, 1978-1 C.B. 154.
Rev. Rul. 80-282, 1980-2 C.B. 178.
Rev. Rul. 81-95, 1981-1 C.B. 332.
Rev. Rul. 86-95, 1986-2 C.B. 73.
Rev. Rul. 2004-6, 2004-1 C.B. 328.
Rev. Rul. 2007-41, 2007-1 C.B. 1421.
I.R.S. Tax Guide for Churches and Religious Organizations, Pub. No. 1828 (August, 2015).
Political Activity Compliance Initiative (2008 Election), http://www.irs.gov/pub/irst-ege/FY2011_Workplan_Political_Activities_Project_Excerpt.pdf.
Treasury Inspector Gen. for Tax Admin., 2013-10-053, Inappropriate Criteria Were Used to Identify Tax-Exempt Applications for Review.
The IRS: Targeting Americans for Their Political Beliefs: Hearing Before the Comm. on Oversight and Gov't Reform, 113th Cong. (2013).
Ellen Aprill, *Regulating the Political Speech of Noncharitable Exempt Organizations After Citizens United*, 10 Election L.J. 363 (2011).
Johnny Rex Buckles, *Not Even a Peep? The Regulation of Political Campaign Activities by Charities Through Federal Tax Law*, 75 U. Cin. L. Rev. 1071 (2007).

Laura Brown Chisolm, *Politics and Charity: A Proposal for Peaceful Coexistence*, 58 Geo. Wash. L. Rev. 308 (1990).

Roger Colinvaux, *The Political Speech of Charities in the Face of Citizens United: A Defense of Prohibition*, 62 Case W. Res. L. Rev. 685 (2012).

Roger Colinvaux, *Political Activity Limits and Tax Exemption: A Gordian's Knot*, 34 Va. Tax Rev. 1 (2014).

Gregory L. Colvin, *Political Tax Law After Citizens United: A Time for Reform*, 66 Exempt Org. Tax Rev. 71 (2010).

Brian Galle, *Charities in Politics: A Reappraisal*, 54 Wm. & Mary L. Rev. 1561 (2013).

Miriam Galston, *Lobbying and the Public Interest: Rethinking the Internal Revenue Code's Treatment of Legislative Activities*, 71 Tex. L. Rev. 1269 (1993).

Miriam Galston, *Campaign Speech and Contextual Analysis*, 6 First Amend. L. Rev. 100 (2007).

Miriam Galston, *When Statutory Regimes Collide: Will* Citizens United *and* Wisconsin Right to Life *Make Federal Tax Regulation of Campaign Activity Unconstitutional?* 13 U. Pa. J. Const. L. 867 (2011).

Daniel Halperin, *Income Taxation of Mutual Nonprofits*, 59 Tax L. Rev. 133 (2006).

Judith Kindell and John Francis Reilly, *Election Year Issues, in* Exempt Organizations Continuing Professional Education Technical Instruction Program for Fiscal Year 2002 335 (2001).

Elizabeth Kingsley and John Pomeranz, *A Crash at the Crossroads: Tax and Campaign Finance Laws Collide in Regulation of Political Activities of Tax-Exempt Organizations*, 31 Wm. Mitchell L. Rev. 55 (2004).

Lloyd Hitoshi Mayer, *Grasping Smoke: Enforcing the Ban on Political Activity by Charities*, 6 First Amend. L. Rev. 1 (2007).

Lloyd Hitoshi Mayer, *Politics at the Pulpit: Tax Benefits, Substantial Burdens, and Institutional Free Exercise*, 89 B.U. L. Rev. 1137 (2009).

Lloyd Hitoshi Mayer, *Charities and Lobbying: Institutional Rights in the Wake of Citizens United* 10 Election L.J. 407 (2011).

Lindsey McPherson, *EO Training Materials Suggest 51 Percent Threshold for Social Welfare Activity*, 2014 Tax Notes Today 13-15 (January 21, 2014).

Ann M. Murphy, *Campaign Signs and the Collection Plate-Never the Twain Shall Meet?*, 1 Pittsburgh Tax Rev. 35 (2003).

Gregg D. Polsky & Guy-Uriel E. Charles, *Regulating Section 527 Organizations*, 73 Geo. Wash. L. Rev. 1000 (2005).

Donald B. Tobin, *Political Advocacy and Taxable Entities: Are They the Next "Loophole"?* 6 First Amend. L. Rev. 41 (2007).

Donald B. Tobin, *Political Campaigning by Churches and Charities: Hazardous for 501(c)(3)s, Dangerous for Democracy*, 95 Geo. L.J. 1313 (2007).

Chapter 7

No Taxation, No Representation

How Government Is Organized— or Not—to Address Nonprofit Issues

Alan J. Abramson

The nonprofit sector is an important part of society, with nonprofit organizations delivering a large portion of the health, education, and social services in this country; accounting for a substantial amount of advocacy activity; providing much of the art and recreation in the United States; and employing roughly 10 percent of the country's workforce.

It is therefore puzzling that the nonprofit sector, as a sector, has very limited representation within government. At a time when many major interests have significant representation within government—at the federal level, the business sector has advocates in the Commerce Department, labor has a voice through the Labor Department, farmers have the Agriculture Department—it is curious and problematic that there is not even a modest-sized office in the federal government that represents the nonprofit sector as a whole.

To be sure, different nonprofit subfields have allies within government (e.g., nonprofit health organizations, including hospitals and nursing homes, have a voice within the US Department of Health and Human Services; the concerns of private universities are important to the US Department of Education; arts organizations are aided by the National Endowment for the Arts). Moreover, government entities like the federal Internal Revenue Service (IRS) and state attorney generals regulate and monitor the nonprofit sector. However, there are few offices within government charged with strengthening the overall nonprofit sector to better serve our society.

To improve understanding of this puzzling gap, this chapter will describe how the government is currently organized to relate to the nonprofit sector; explore why the sector has minimal representation within government; identify problems that grow out of the current arrangements; and discuss options for reforming government so that it is better organized to work with the nonprofit sector. The chapter will focus mainly on the federal government, although there will be some discussion of current regulatory and representational activities at the state and local levels as well. Moreover, the chapter's major concerns are sector-wide rather than subsector issues, and 501(c)(3) charities and foundations rather than other kinds of nonprofits.

CURRENT ARRANGEMENTS

Governments at all levels are now set up largely to regulate and monitor the overall nonprofit sector but not to represent the sector's interests in a positive way. While individual nonprofit subsectors, such as health, education, and human services, are represented and have allies in different government agencies, the sector as a whole has only modest representation within government.

Regulatory Offices

Chapter 5, by Lott and Fremont-Smith in this volume, provides a detailed overview of government regulation of nonprofits. As they describe, the IRS and state charity regulators have "interlocking" jurisdiction over nonprofits. At the federal level, the IRS, which is located in the Treasury Department, is the main agency that administers laws and regulations affecting nonprofit organizations. As Lott and Fremont-Smith observe, "In the one hundred plus years since the Revenue Act of 1913, an act that afforded certain organizations exemption from the federal income tax, the IRS has had an outsized regulatory footprint in the collective mind of the sector." The IRS is the chief determinant of the tax exempt status of an organization through its review of Form 1023, and the main collector of information on the ongoing operation of nonprofits through Form 990.

State charity officials are "front line" regulators and enforcers of nonprofits. As Fremont-Smith (2004, p. 377) has written, "Charities are the creatures of the states, and the laws governing their establishment, their right to continuous existence, their freedom to operate, any limitations on the nature of their holdings, and the conditions for their dissolution have been and continue to be determined at the state level." According to data collected by the National Association of State Charity Officials (2016), a great majority of states handle regulation of charitable organizations in the Office of the Attorney General. States also oversee nonprofits' fundraising activities.

Support, Partnership, and Other Representational Offices

While nonprofit regulatory offices are well established at the federal and state levels, very few governments have significant offices to represent or provide support to the overall nonprofit sector. At the federal level, the Corporation for National and Community Service seeks to strengthen national service and volunteerism in the United States, and the corporation has counterpart service commissions in state governments (Corporation for National and Community Service 2016). The federal Small Business Administration provides some assistance to nonprofits—including, for example, disaster loans—but nonprofits are not the main focus of the agency's work.

At the federal level, a variety of agencies collect data on nonprofits, including the IRS which draws data from nonprofit Form 990 information returns and other sources; the Census Bureau which collects information periodically on organizational location, revenues, payroll expenses, employment, and other characteristics; and the Bureau of Labor Statistics which recently began publishing data on nonprofit employment (US Department of Labor 2015). USAspending.gov, which is operated by the Bureau of the Fiscal Service in the Department of Treasury, tracks federal funding generally, including payments to nonprofits.

Several recent presidents have established units within the Executive Office of the President that address, at least in part, nonprofit issues. Thus, President Reagan created a President's Task Force on Private Sector Initiatives; George W. Bush formed the Office of Faith-based and Community Initiatives; and Barack Obama launched the Office of Social Innovation and Civic Participation as well as an Office of Faith-based and Neighborhood Partnerships. (Another recent president, George H. W. Bush, established an independent, nonprofit Points of Light Foundation outside government.)

George W. Bush's White House Office on Faith-based Initiatives spawned similar offices in many of the executive branch cabinet departments, including the Departments of Health and Human Services, Labor, Housing and Urban Development, and elsewhere. Under President Obama these departmental offices are called Centers for Faith-based and Neighborhood Partnerships, reflecting the name of Obama's related White House Office.

More than supporting nonprofit organizations, some of these White House offices and other units in the executive departments have been mainly concerned with facilitating partnerships between the federal government and nonprofit organizations, including foundations. Ferris and Williams (2014) examined twenty-one government partnership offices that engage with foundations and businesses, including units on International and Philanthropic Innovation in the Department of Housing and Urban Development, Strategic Partnerships in the Department of Education, and Youth Partnerships and Service in the Department of the Interior. They found that these offices serve as matchmakers, demystifying other sectors for government officials, convening and facilitating stakeholders from multiple sectors, and leveraging the assets of multiple sectors for particular projects (Ferris and Williams 2012, 2014).

Another analysis suggests that these federal offices work mostly to serve their governmental masters rather than their outside nonprofit and foundation partners. One official in an agency liaison office explained that a major responsibility was to alert foundations to areas where government needed support. The official admitted that this strategy provoked some pushback from foundation staff who disliked being told what to do (Abramson, Soskis, and Toepler 2012, p. 6).

Very few states or cities have created cabinet-level positions to provide representation for the nonprofit sector, with California, Connecticut, Michigan, New York, and Newark, New Jersey standing out as some of the exceptional states or cities that have. Michigan's nonpartisan Office of Foundation Liaison (OFL) was created in 2003 and was the first state cabinet-level position for the foundation or nonprofit sector (Council of Michigan Foundations 2016). The mission of the office is "to develop strategic partnerships between philanthropy and the executive branch of State government in order to create better outcomes for all Michigan citizens within a commonly defined set of agendas." The OFL was initiated and is funded by members of the Council of Michigan Foundations.

In 2008, Governor Arnold Schwarzenegger in California established the position of secretary of service and volunteering. This cabinet-level official is designed to encourage volunteerism in California and to improve coordination of volunteer efforts between the state's departments and agencies (CA.GOV 2008). In 2011, Governor Dan Malloy of Connecticut created a cabinet-level position of "Nonprofit Liaison" and proposed a Community Nonprofit Services cabinet to advocate for nonprofit social service providers and to provide their input on how the state should deal with budget deficits. A separate group, a Commission on Nonprofit Health and Human Service, was asked to report on ways to improve state and nonprofit relations (Perry 2011). Other states have attempted to improve government-nonprofit relations by creating permanent and ad hoc task forces, most frequently to work on contracting issues.

WHY REPRESENTATIONAL OFFICES HAVE NOT BEEN ESTABLISHED

As described above, while some government units are focused on supporting the sector as a whole, they tend to be modest in size and scope and much less consequential than regulatory offices like the IRS and state attorney generals. Why is this the case?

Scholars who study the organization of government find that "politics" is an important determining factor in the formation and structure of government offices. As Stanford University political scientist Terry Moe puts it, "Structural choices have important consequences for the content and direction of policy, and political actors know it. When they make choices about structure, they are implicitly making choices about policy. And precisely because this is so, issues of structure are inevitably caught up in the larger political struggle" (Moe 1989, p. 268). In particular, as Moe (1989, p. 269) goes on to note, "Structural politics is interest group politics. . . . If one seeks to understand why structural choices turn out as they do, then, it does not make sense to start with politicians. The more fundamental questions have to do with how interest groups decide what kinds of structures they want politicians to provide."

Examining the interest group politics around broad nonprofit sector-wide issues suggests that there are few government offices representing the overall nonprofit sector because sector leaders themselves have been divided on whether or not they want such an office. Moreover, sector leaders have only modest influence with policymakers so that even if they advocated for a nonprofit office, it is not certain they would get one.

Sector Ambivalence

Many sector leaders favor a government office on the nonprofit sector that would provide increased legitimacy for the sector and a greater voice within government for nonprofit interests. However, at the same time, others register significant concerns, especially regarding the potential for increased government interference with sector independence. Casey (2011, p. 7) suggests a variety of reasons for the lack of closer ties between government and nonprofits in the United States. The first factor he cites is, "The dominant political and cultural norms continue to be the independence of private endeavors and 'small government.' The nonprofit sector is regarded as a paragon of private and voluntary initiatives, and there is a strong vein of distrust about attempts to strengthen ties to government."

Sector ambivalence about a government office goes back in history. Two important nonprofit commissions, the Peterson Commission, which issued its recommendations in 1970, and the Filer Commission, which reported in 1975, both included proposals for quasi-public entities to advance the nonprofit sector (Brilliant 2000). With regard to the Filer Commission, Brilliant (2000, p. 130) indicates:

> Of all the commission recommendations, among those most worked over was the proposal for an ongoing "independent" commission for the nonprofit sector. . . . The major problem was the nature of auspices: some commissioners were convinced that, like the Charity Commission for England and Wales, a future commission had to have a degree of public authority, through approval of the President and Congress; others were equally adamant that such a commission had to be established under private auspices, in addition to being funded totally from the private sector.

As Brilliant (2000, p. 160) reports, those against the creation of a government office were driven largely by fear of excessive government regulation and oversight.

Ultimately, the Filer Commission's recommendation for a "quasi"—and not completely—public commission failed for several reasons (Brilliant 2000). As indicated, the proposal received only lukewarm support—or even opposition—from many nonprofit leaders concerned about government encroachment on nonprofit independence. Moreover, the administration of President Jimmy Carter, which took office in January 1977, was not very supportive of a new public-private commission on the nonprofit sector, feeling that there were already too many commission-type entities in and around government and because its priorities lay in other areas, such as urban affairs.

Also important was the July 1978 death in a car crash of John D. Rockefeller III, one of the most influential proponents of a government office. Finally, the failure of a quasi-government entity was sealed by the increasingly determined efforts of nonprofit leaders to form a unified, private advocacy body for the nonprofit sector. This endeavor ultimately led, in 1980, to the creation of Independent Sector, which is still today a major, national umbrella and advocacy group for the nonprofit sector.

Sector ambivalence about a new nonprofit office in government also helped to defeat a more recent proposal to restructure the federal government's relationship with the nonprofit sector by Representative Betty McCollum, a Democrat from Minnesota. In June 2010, Congresswoman McCollum introduced a Nonprofit Sector and Community Solutions Act (HR 5533) to strengthen the ability of nonprofits to address public challenges (Congress. gov 2016). In particular, the bill would have:

- Established the US Council on Nonprofit Organizations and Community Solutions with sixteen members appointed by the president and Congress to study how the federal government can work more effectively with nonprofits to achieve better outcomes;
- Created an Interagency Working Group on Nonprofit Organizations and the Federal Government made up of the heads of executive branch departments;
- Directed the Secretary of Commerce to collect and analyze nonprofit data from all agencies with relevant data; and
- Established a nonprofit research fund within the National Science Foundation.

The bill had few backers and died for a variety of reasons at the end of the 111th Congress in December 2010. Some thought the bill would create government entities that might crimp nonprofit independence, with a special concern for foundations and churches (Perry 2010). The change from

Democratic to Republican control of the House of Representatives also hurt the chances of a bill that had been introduced by a Democratic member. But what also seemed to happen was that at least some sector leaders opposed pushing legislation that might invite hostile amendments which could hurt nonprofits or foundations.

Sector Weakness

While doubts about the wisdom of having a government office on the nonprofit sector helped defeat some efforts to create this kind of entity, the sector's overall weakness in policymaking has also likely contributed to the failure to establish a more supportive governmental infrastructure for the sector.

As discussed in Abramson (2016), there are a variety of reasons why the nonprofit sector has been a relatively weak advocate for broad sector interests:

- Free riders—Individual nonprofits can "free ride" on efforts to strengthen the overall nonprofit sector because they enjoy the benefits of successful advocacy initiatives whether or not they help pay for them. Because of the ability to free ride, there is an underinvestment by nonprofits in advocacy organizations like Independent Sector and therefore, perhaps, a suboptimal level of advocacy activity.
- Subsector orientation of many nonprofits—Nonprofits also underinvest in sector-wide advocacy and therefore weaken themselves in policymaking on sector issues because they identify more with their subsector and other subsector organizations (e.g., youth services agencies, museums, hospitals) than with the nonprofit sector as a whole. It is difficult for the very diverse and fragmented nonprofit sector to come together to advocate on sector-wide issues (see also Casey 2011).
- Lack of nonprofit appreciation and funder support for advocacy, including sector advocacy—Most nonprofits and foundations are focused much more on providing services than on advocating for causes, including sector-wide interests.
- Limits on nonprofit lobbying and electoral activity—501(c)(3) charities, the major group of nonprofits, are limited in the extent to which they can lobby, and they and foundations are also completely prohibited from engaging in partisan political activity. Moreover, nonprofit stakeholders do not form an identifiable voting bloc. The upshot is that elected officials have little incentive to pay attention to nonprofits or to defer to their interests in establishing a government office or other matters.
- Lack of visibility of nonprofit sector to policymakers—While most policymakers undoubtedly recognize some well-known nonprofits, like the

Red Cross, Salvation Army, and United Way, many do not have a deep understanding of the sector and so may fail to support efforts to strengthen it by establishing a government office. The tax committees in the House (Ways and Means) and Senate (Finance) have jurisdiction over nonprofit tax issues, but no other congressional committees are engaged in watching out for other kinds of sector interests.
- Absence of a compelling vision for the overall nonprofit sector—Sector advocates are also weakened by the lack of a compelling rationale for the nonprofit sector. With for-profit institutions having entered many nonprofit program areas, Americans wonder whether there is anything distinctive about nonprofit organizations and what justifies their special treatment. Overall, there is not a clear understanding of the "value added" of the sector that elicits strong support for the sector among government officials.

Other Explanations

Rather than looking to government for support on sector issues, nonprofits seem more absorbed in their relationship to philanthropy even though government provides two to three times as much funding to nonprofits as philanthropy. Nonprofits' independence from government is a myth, at least as far as funding is concerned. Yet, many nonprofit leaders seem beholden to this myth in opposing a government office and in focusing more energy on the sector's relationship to philanthropy (Casey 2011).

John Casey (2011), who has studied government-nonprofit relations in the United States and around the world, also observes that the federalism structure in the United States, which separates federal, state, and local governments, complicates efforts to create a nonprofit office in government. In the context of federalism, it is hard to know which level of government should be the focus of efforts to create a nonprofit office. Should there be 50 state nonprofit offices or one federal entity?

Finally, there is an argument that it is improper for an industry to have a presence in government and that government should be more of a neutral umpire. This conception of government is hostile to efforts to establish an office within government that would represent the nonprofit sector (Hall 1992, p. 78).

ASSESSING CURRENT ORGANIZATIONAL ARRANGEMENTS

With this background, we turn to consider in more detail how well government is now organized to regulate and represent the nonprofit sector.

Regulation

The preceding pages suggest that with regard to sector-wide issues government regulation overshadows government support. However, it seems that even regulation of the sector by the IRS and state charity officials is not very robust. Marcus Owens, former director of the IRS's Exempt Organizations Division which oversees nonprofits, finds that the IRS is actually a rather weak monitor of nonprofit activity. Along these lines, Owens (2013, p. 6) recently observed that while the number of nonprofit organizations more than doubled in a roughly forty-year period, the number of IRS examinations of nonprofit tax returns is approximately one-third of what it was. Owens goes on to identify a variety of reasons for the IRS's limited oversight of charities:

- Inadequate funding of IRS's nonprofit work by Congress and the president;
- Civil service constraints that limit IRS staff pay and make it impossible for the IRS to be competitive in hiring and retaining high-quality personnel;
- An institutional culture within IRS that prioritizes the agency's tax-collecting role vis-à-vis businesses and individuals rather than oversight of nonprofits, which for the most part do not owe taxes; and
- Tax exemption–based oversight that ties IRS monitoring of nonprofits to their annual filing of Form 990 returns even when more timely oversight triggered by a particular event might be called for.

At the state level, oversight of nonprofits is also under-resourced. As Lott and Fremont-Smith report (chapter 5 in this volume), "Almost 40 percent of state attorney generals' offices dedicated less than one (or the equivalent of one) full-time employee to charities regulation for the entire state." While there was some good news that the number of state charity regulators has remained relatively stable in recent years, Lott and Fremont-Smith find that "the unfortunate reality is that as the nonprofit sector grew in numbers, dollars, and stature, regulatory and enforcement resources did not keep pace."

Representation

If government regulation and oversight of nonprofits are modest in intensity, then government efforts to strengthen the overall sector are even weaker. There are few entities within government that stand up for the nonprofit sector and help to inform policymakers about nonprofits, call attention to nonprofit sector capacities and needs, and help address problems in government's relationship with nonprofits. The absence of offices and staff within government that understand nonprofits and speak up for their interests contributes to government misunderstanding the sector, ignoring it, and treating it poorly, as described in the examples that follow.

One important case of government misunderstanding the nonprofit sector dates back to the early years of the Reagan presidency. Ronald Reagan took office in January 1981 determined to make significant cuts in domestic federal spending but also arguing that increased philanthropy would help to offset these cuts and fill the gap left by reduced federal funding. In fact, Reagan sought a broader shift of government functions to the private sector. As he put it, "With the same energy that Franklin Roosevelt sought government solutions to problems, we will seek private solutions. The challenge before us is to find ways once again to unleash the independent spirit of the people and their communities. . . . Voluntarism is an essential part of our plan to give the government back to the people" (Salamon 1984, p. 261).

Unfortunately, this strategy of replacing public with private action failed to recognize just how important funding partnerships between government and nonprofits had become by the early 1980s, and the impossibility of philanthropy making up for sizable government budget cuts, especially in the short term (Salamon and Abramson 1982; Salamon 1984). Without officials within government knowledgeable about the nonprofit sector and able to speak up for its interests, the administration proceeded in ignorance.

While official presidential budget documents include a variety of special analyses about the implications of budget proposals for state and local governments, research and development, information technology, and other concerns, there is no special analysis focused on budget impacts on nonprofits. Of course, even if the Reagan administration had this kind of analysis and understood the faulty assumptions that were being made about the capacity of philanthropy to offset federal spending cuts, it may have gone ahead with the budget reductions anyway. However, at the least, with deeper understanding of the issues, the administration's justification, and perhaps the substance of its actions, would have had to change. Unfortunately, still today there are few government offices with deep understanding about nonprofit and philanthropic activities.

In addition and related to its lack of understanding of the nonprofit sector, government also too often ignores the potential for the nonprofit sector as a sector to help address difficult social problems and overlooks damage that may be being done to nonprofits' capacity to serve society. As noted earlier, the federal government gathers a large amount of data about the nonprofit sector, but the data is collected by and analyzed in different agencies, including the IRS, other offices within the Treasury Department, the Bureau of Labor Statistics, and the Census Bureau, among others. While some government agencies, such as the Government Accountability Office and the Congressional Research Service, have occasionally produced reports that put together data from different government offices (see, e.g., US Government Accountability Office 2007; Sherlock and Gravelle 2009), overall there seems to be little effort by government offices to integrate different data sources to know how the nonprofit sector is doing and whether and where there may be untapped capacity in or significant problems with this important sector of the economy.

For example, as noted at the start, the nonprofit sector employs about 10 percent of the workforce, and many of the dollars going into nonprofits fund salaries. In times of high unemployment, government would get good return on its investment by funneling funding to nonprofits to increase employment. However, in the early stages of the recent Great Recession, as key policymakers tried to figure out how to put the unemployed back to work, it seems that there was little thought given to the nonprofit sector as an important employer.

Moreover, while government paid great attention to the financial problems of business during the Great Recession, it seemed largely to ignore the challenges that nonprofits were facing, even with many of these problems caused by government's slowness in paying nonprofits what they were owed in contracts. During this time, nonprofit leaders urged Congress to consider a nonprofit bridge loan program to help organizations cope with the financial stress of the recession and the failure of government agencies to pay their contracting bills on time. The idea was touted as a way to help nonprofits bounce back with minimal risk to the government. Proposals recommended that the federal government enlist community banks and financial institutions in offering low-interest loans to nonprofits, or create a program similar to the Auto Supplier Support Program in which nonprofits would be able to use money owed to them by government as collateral for short-term loans (Aviv and Nicoll 2009). Independent Sector specifically advocated for a $15 billion bridge loan fund to help charities that fell behind on payments as a result of states' failure to uphold contract agreements. The organization also requested a nonprofit stimulus fund to distribute government and private money to innovative nonprofit groups (Perry 2009b).

Other suggestions from nonprofit leaders included expanding existing national service programs, creating a Community Services Protection Fund to help charities meet basic needs, and setting aside 10 percent of the stimulus dollars for nonprofit groups (Perry 2009a). In the end, while significant portions of the $800 billion stimulus bill, the American Recovery and Reinvestment Act, funded nonprofits to deliver services, there was little special support for the sector as a whole. Unlike some businesses, clearly nonprofits were not seen as "too big to fail."

More generally with regard to government's contracting with nonprofits, the National Council of Nonprofits and the Urban Institute have teamed up on two studies that demonstrate the significant problems with contracting in many states. The studies, based on nationwide surveys of thousands of nonprofits in 2009 and 2012, found important problems with government's late payments to nonprofits, government imposing complex reporting requirements on nonprofits, and government changing contract terms in the middle of the contract period (Boris et al. 2010; Pettijohn et al. 2013). The National Council of Nonprofits and its state nonprofit association partners used the research reports to press state and local governments to address problems, and a variety of task forces were formed in different states. However, the lack of government offices responsible for nonprofit issues means that such problems will likely persist.

The debate over health care reform evidences the same lack of—or only belated—concern for the needs of nonprofit organizations. The 2010 Patient Protection and Affordable Care Act raised significant concerns for nonprofits as employers and care providers. The act included new requirements for businesses to provide health insurance for employees. This drew alarm from the nonprofit community, especially with regard to the act's effect on health care costs for small and mid-sized charities. At the time of the bill's passage, nonprofits reportedly spent over 4.6 percent of their expenditures on health care and insurance coverage (Wilhelm 2009). This represents a major cost for cash-strapped charities, particularly in an economic downturn. Nonprofits were reportedly "left out" of the conversation regarding health care reform, despite the fact that charitable organizations are important employers (Strom 2009).

Proposals in the House of Representatives failed to address whether small-business tax credits would be extended to nonprofit organizations. Although proposals from the Senate provided credits to charities with fewer than twenty-five full-time employees, these credits applied mostly to very small organizations and left out the significant group of nonprofits with twenty-five to fifty. In 2010, Independent Sector issued a statement urging lawmakers to adopt more flexible standards allowing nonprofits to seek more cost-effective options in the interim period between the bill's passage in 2010 and the increase in available options in 2014 (Aviv 2010). Other ideas included a proposal to allow groups of charities to pool their resources to pay for insurance coverage (Wilhelm 2009).

These concerns were successfully voiced and at least some were taken into account in the final regulations. As of 2015, nonprofits with fewer than fifty employees are considered "small employers" and as such allowed to purchase health insurance through state plans designed to make it easier for small employers to find affordable options (National Council of Nonprofits 2016). Getting Congress to extend the subsidies was considered a "major victory" for the nonprofit sector, though concerns have now shifted to properly informing nonprofits of their rights and resources as employers (Cohen 2013).

Another important win for the nonprofit sector, led by the National Council of Nonprofits and its allies, was convincing the Office of Management and Budget to issue new Uniform Guidance requiring federal, state, and local governments to pay nonprofits at least 10 percent of their direct costs to cover nonprofits' indirect—or overhead and administrative—expenses when the work is funded in whole or in part by federal funds (Delaney 2015).

However, overall, government does not seem well structured to attend to nonprofit concerns. In addition to nonprofit interests being largely overlooked, at least initially, in the Recovery Act and health care reform efforts, their concerns were also not taken fully into account in the development of the Anti-Terrorist Financing Guidelines. While the Treasury Department made some accommodation to the concerns of nonprofit and foundation leaders in drafting the guidelines, overall, according to former IRS official Marcus Owens, "The standards developed were, based on public comments, of questionable legal import and were difficult, as well as costly, to implement even by the most well-intentioned tax exempt organization" (Owens 2013, p. 15). Similarly, Owens (2013, pp. 12–13) suggests that the development of provisions in the Pension Protection Act of 2006 relating to supporting organizations, which are nonprofits that have supporting relationships to other nonprofits, also illustrates the negative consequences of government not taking sufficient account of the hardships that new regulations may impose on legitimate nonprofits, in this case hospitals and universities.

OPTIONS FOR REFORM

What can be done to improve government regulation of nonprofits and increase government understanding of and support for these important institutions?

Regulation

To enhance government regulation and oversight of nonprofits, former IRS official Marcus Owens (2013, p. 2) favors establishing a strong regulatory body with minority representation from the nonprofit sector and significant government representation. Owens (2013, pp. 12, 15) argues:

> Charities need some institutional voice that can accurately and credibly inform Congress about the consequences of its proposed rules—or better yet, design rules that will not have those negative effects, making legislation unnecessary.... Greater sector representation *within* the body responsible for regulating charities would give charities the chance to influence guidance priorities

to ensure that due attention is also given to formulating rules identifying areas of permissible conduct.... Furthermore, a properly structured regulatory body with representatives from both the IRS and the sector would provide a much more fluid mechanism for ensuring that charities' legitimate needs are adequately taken into account in the development of regulations and other authoritative guidance.

Drawing on models from the financial sector, Owens' solution is a quasi-governmental Charity Oversight Board to address the ineffectiveness of the current regulatory regime. He argues convincingly that this partly public, partly private, body would be better funded and more vigorous than the IRS.

Another reform option described by Boris and Lott (2016) would parcel out regulatory responsibility over nonprofits beyond the IRS to other federal agencies that are already engaged in other, relevant regulatory activity. For example, the Federal Trade Commission, which monitors business activity with the goal of protecting consumers and promoting competition, might gain new authority over the businesslike activities of nonprofits, which seem to be on the rise.

Representation

However, while these recommendations for new oversight mechanisms address concerns about the weakness of current regulation of nonprofits, the proposals do relatively little to speak to the need for an entity within government that provides more positive support for nonprofits.

In many ways, what the nonprofit sector is missing is an agency like the Small Business Administration (SBA) that helps the small business community. SBA was created in 1932 to assist new and existing small businesses in America. The SBA's four programmatic functions include business financing, entrepreneurial development, federal procurement assistance, and advocacy for small business (US Small Business Administration 2016). The SBA does not directly invest in or make loans to small businesses. Rather, the administration coordinates programs that connect small business owners to government and private resources and is designed to act as the "voice" for small businesses within government.

In fact, the creation of an "SBA for the nonprofit sector" is the recommendation of Shirley Sagawa, who has served as a senior staff member in the White House, Congress, and the Corporation for National and Community Service (see also Sherlock and Gravelle 2009, pp. 53–54). As Sagawa (2008, pp. 37–38) points out, "The Internal Revenue Service focuses on tax compliance, and the Corporation for National and Community Service supports volunteer programs. No agency, however, counts nonprofit health or capacity as central to its mission.... What is needed, specifically, is an SBA for nonprofits—a government agency that can provide both funding and guidance to the nonprofit sector."

In creating a new government office, an important consideration is where to put it, at the federal, state, or local level and, then, where at each level. For example, at the federal level, a nonprofit office could be placed in the Executive Office of the President, executive branch departments, independent agencies, Congress, or elsewhere (Lewis and Selin 2012). Of course, establishing a new independent office for the nonprofit sector—like the SBA or the National Endowments for the Arts or Humanities—is an option, as is placing an office in an existing agency, such as the Corporation for National and Community Service, the Department of Commerce, or the Department of Housing and Urban Development.

What is needed, especially at the start, is not a massive new federal bureaucracy. Rather, a government office on the nonprofit sector might be a modest-sized entity with the capacity to develop information and research on the nonprofit sector, including integrating nonprofit data collected by other offices, with the brief to create and implement strategies for addressing important nonprofit issues, such as problems with the government-nonprofit contracting relationship, and with the permission to be an advocate for nonprofits especially within government where such a voice is missing.

Besides the question of where to locate an office on the nonprofit sector, another critical issue is how to establish this kind of office. Many nonprofit and foundation leaders are reluctant to support any new legislation about nonprofits and philanthropy for fear it would become a magnet for unwanted provisions. As noted above, these fears seemed to contribute to the failure of Representative McCollum's bill in 2010 when some sector leaders turned against her proposal.

In this context, it may make sense to work toward the establishment of a nonprofit office incrementally through more limited, presidential action. As described earlier, a succession of White House offices has addressed nonprofit issues, and the Obama White House contains an Office of Faith-based and Neighborhood Partnerships that convenes the similar centers that have been created in the executive branch departments. It would also make sense to establish a White House Office that coordinates the foundation liaisons in the different executive departments.

Of course, the downside of these White House offices is that they tend to come and go with changes in administrations, and there is not the kind of institutional capacity and memory that would usefully be gained from a more permanent home. However, establishing a permanent office would likely take congressional action, which would increase nervousness within the sector.

Again, according to Terry Moe who was cited earlier, interest groups are key movers in establishing new governmental structures. So, it is likely that a new government office in the nonprofit sector will be established only if nonprofit and foundation leaders actively advocate for it. Whether this kind of backing for a nonprofit office exists is uncertain.

CONCLUSION

Today a variety of regulatory and representational agencies within government at all levels focus on nonprofit and philanthropic issues. Among these, the IRS, with its regulatory and oversight functions, looms large; but few government agencies—and none at the federal level—are devoted to representing and strengthening the nonprofit sector as a whole.

As Terry Moe (1989) has argued, the structure of government largely reflects interest group politics. The current governmental arrangements regarding nonprofits thus have a lot to do with the ambivalence of nonprofit leaders about creating a government office on the nonprofit sector. Their fear seems to be that such an office will inevitably open the door to potentially undesirable regulation of the nonprofit sector.

With the IRS and state charity officials under-resourced, the nonprofit sector has been only loosely regulated. However, without a stronger, positive voice in government, the nonprofit sector is also misunderstood and ignored by government. In recent years, for example, broad sector strengths and needs were largely overlooked in the Recovery Act and health care reform, and government contracting with nonprofits is rife with problems.

Numerous options exist for reforming the way government relates to the nonprofit sector. Based on the analysis in this chapter, strengthening oversight of nonprofits and, perhaps even more importantly, giving nonprofits a greater voice within government seem like sensible goals. One approach at the federal level would be to leave oversight responsibility with the IRS and better resource it and to, at the same time, establish a new SBA-like agency, along the lines suggested by Shirley Sagawa (2008), that could work to strengthen the nonprofit sector and be a voice within government for broad sector interests, much as the SBA supports and advocates for small business. Owens and Boris and Lott offer other reform ideas aimed more at restructuring just the regulatory responsibilities.

The practical drawback of many approaches is the need for legislative action to establish one or more new agencies and the concern that legislating could turn out badly for the nonprofit sector if hostile amendments are attached to an otherwise desirable bill. One way around this conundrum is to start with a presidentially created entity within the White House Office, although it is also desirable to go beyond the temporary presidential offices that have come and gone in recent decades. Ultimately, however, only if nonprofit and foundation leaders are convinced of the benefits of a new government office is one likely to be created.

ACKNOWLEDGMENT

The author gratefully acknowledges the helpful research assistance of Shelley Bradley and the thoughtful comments on draft versions of this paper by several reviewers.

REFERENCES

Abramson, Alan J. 2016. "Making Public Policy toward the Nonprofit Sector in the U.S.: How and Why Broad, 'Sector' Interests Are Advanced—or Not—in Federal Policymaking." *Nonprofit Policy Forum.* Published online May 11, 2016. http://www.degruyter.com printahead/j/npf.

Abramson, Alan, Benjamin Soskis, and Stefan Toepler. 2012. "Public-Philanthropic Partnerships: Trends, Innovations, and Challenges." Arlington, VA: Council on Foundations. http://www.cof.org/sites/default/files/documents/files/Final%20GMU-Report%20on%20PPPs.pdf.

Aviv, Diana. 2010. "Comments on Interim Final Rules for Group Health Plans and Insurance Coverage Relating to Status as a Grandfathered Health Plan under the Patient Protection and Affordable Care Act." August 13, 2010. Washington, DC: Independent Sector. https://www.independentsector.org/uploads/Policy_PDFs/CommentsonInterimRulesforGrandfatheredHealthPlans081610.pdf.

Aviv, Diana and Neil Nicoll. 2009. "Let's Start a Loan Fund to Keep Social-Services Groups in Business." *Chronicle of Philanthropy.* October 15, 2009. https://philanthropy.com/article/Lets-Start-a-Loan-Fund-to/173235.

Boris, Elizabeth T., Erwin de Leon, Katie L. Roeger, and Milena Nikolova. 2010. "National Study of Nonprofit-Government Contracting: State Profiles." Washington, DC: Urban Institute. http://www.urban.org/sites/default/files/alfresco/publication-pdfs/412227-National-Study-of-Nonprofit-Government-Contracting-State-Profiles.PDF.

Boris, Elizabeth T., and Cindy M. Lott. 2016. "The United States' Regulatory Framework: Opportunities and Challenges, Current and Future." In M. McGregor-Lowndes and R. Wyatt (Eds.), *Regulating Charities: The Inside Story.* New York, NY: Routledge.

Brilliant, Eleanor L. 2000. *Private Charity and Public Inquiry: A History of the Filer and Peterson Commissions.* Bloomington and Indianapolis, IN: Indiana University Press.

CA.GOV. 2008. "Governor Schwarzenegger Announces First-in-the-Nation Cabinet Position for Service and Volunteering." https://www.gov.ca.gov/news.php?id=8865.

Casey, John. 2011. "A New Era of Collaborative Government-Nonprofit Relations in the U.S.?" *Nonprofit Policy Forum* 2(1), Article 3.

Cohen, Rick. 2013. "Are Nonprofit Employers Prepared for Health Care Reform Rules?" *Nonprofit Quarterly*. January 25, 2013. https://nonprofitquarterly.org/2013/01/25/are-nonprofit-employers-prepared-for-health-care-reform-rules/.

Congress.gov. 2016. "H.R. 5533—Nonprofit Sector and Community Solutions Act of 2010." https://www.congress.gov/bill/111th-congress/house-bill/5533/text.

Corporation for National and Community Service. 2016. "State Service Commissions." http://www.nationalservice.gov/about/contact-us/state-service-commissions.

Council of Michigan Foundations. 2016. "Office of Foundation Liaison." https://www.michiganfoundations.org/ofl.

Delaney, Tim. 2015. "Nonprofits Win Key Victory in Overhead Battles With Government." *Chronicle of Philanthropy,* January 13, 2015. https://philanthropy.com/article/Opinion-Nonprofits-Win-Key/151979.

Ferris, James M., and Nicholas P. O. Williams. 2012. "Philanthropy and Government Working Together: The Role of Offices of Strategic Partnerships in Public Problem Solving." Discussion Paper. Los Angeles, CA: University of Southern California, Center on Philanthropy and Public Policy. http://www.isgimpact.com/wp-content/uploads/2013/03/PhilGovtWorkingTgthr.pdf.

Ferris, James M., and Nicholas P. O. Williams. 2014. "Catalyzing Collaboration: The Developing Infrastructure for Federal Public Private Partnerships." Discussion Paper. Los Angeles: University of Southern California, Center on Philanthropy and Public Policy. http://cppp.usc.edu/wp-content/uploads/2014/10/Oct-2014-CPPP-Report-Catalyzing-Collaboration-The-Developing-Infrastructure-for-Federal-Public-Private-Partnerships.pdf.

Fremont-Smith, Marion R. 2004. *Governing Nonprofit Organizations: Federal and State Law and Regulation*. Cambridge, MA: Belknap Press of Harvard University Press.

Hall, Peter Dobkin. 1992. *Inventing the Nonprofit Sector and Other Essays on Philanthropy, Voluntarism, and Nonprofit Organizations*. Baltimore: The Johns Hopkins University Press.

Lewis, David E., and Jennifer L. Selin. 2012. *Sourcebook of United States Executive Agencies*. Administrative Conference of the United States. https://www.acus.gov/sites/default/files/documents/Sourcebook%202012%20FINAL_May%202013.pdf.

Moe, Terry. 1989. "The Politics of Bureaucratic Structure." In *Can the Government Govern?* John E. Chubb and Paul E. Peterson, eds. Washington, DC: Brookings Institution Press.

National Association of State Charity Officials. 2016. "Resources: State-Specific Resources." http://www.nasconet.org/resources/.

National Council of Nonprofits. 2016. "Frequently Asked Questions by Nonprofits about the Affordable Care Act." https://www.councilofnonprofits.org/tools-resources/frequently-asked-questions-nonprofits-about-the-affordable-care-act#matter.

Owens, Marcus S. 2013. "Charity Oversight: An Alternative Approach." http://web.law.columbia.edu/sites/default/files/microsites/attorneys-general/Marcus%20Owens%203.18.pdf.

Perry, Suzanne. 2009a. "A Plea for Nonprofit Priorities: Coalitions Urge the President-elect to Create a Stimulus Plan to Promote Jobs and Aid Charities." *Chronicle of Philanthropy.* January 15, 2009. https://philanthropy.com/article/A-Plea-for-Nonprofit/174533.

Perry, Suzanne. 2009b. "Looking for Relief: Nonprofit Groups Hope to Benefit from Economic-Stimulus Program." *Chronicle of Philanthropy.* January 29, 2009. https://philanthropy.com/article/Looking-for-Relief/175483.

Perry, Suzanne. 2010. "Bill to Improve Government Support for Charities Faces a Tough Climb." *Chronicle of Philanthropy.* December 7, 2010. https://philanthropy.com/article/Bill-to-Improve-Government/159365.

Perry, Suzanne. 2011. "Connecticut's New Governor Creates Cabinet Position for Nonprofits." *Chronicle of Philanthropy.* January 6, 2011. https://philanthropy.com/article/Connecticuts-New-Governor/195327.

Pettijohn, Sarah L., Elizabeth T. Boris, and Maura R. Farrell. 2013. "National Study of Nonprofit-Government Contracts and Grants 2013: State Profiles." Washington, DC: Urban Institute. http://www.urban.org/sites/default/files/alfresco/publication-pdfs/412949%20-%20National-Study-of-Nonprofit-Government-Contracts-and-Grants-State-Profiles.pdf.

Sagawa, Shirley. 2008. "An SBA for Non-Profits." *Democracy: A Journal of Ideas.* Spring 2008, no. 8. http://democracyjournal.org/magazine/8/an-sba-for-non-profits/.

Salamon, Lester M. 1984. "Nonprofit Organizations: The Lost Opportunity." In *The Reagan Record: An Assessment of America's Changing Domestic Priorities.* John L. Palmer and Isabel V. Sawhill, eds. Washington, DC: Urban Institute Press.

Salamon, Lester M., and Alan J. Abramson. 1982. "The Nonprofit Sector." In *The Reagan Experiment: An Examination of Economic and Social Policies under the Reagan Administration.* John L. Palmer and Isabel V. Sawhill, eds. Washington, DC: Urban Institute Press.

Molly E. Sherlock and Jane G. Gravelle. 2009. "An Overview of the Nonprofit and Charitable Sector." Washington, DC: Congressional Research Service. https://www.fas.org/sgp/crs/misc/R40919.pdf.

Strom, Stephanie. 2009. "Nonprofit Groups Upset at Exclusion from Health Bills." *New York Times*, September 13, 2009. http://www.nytimes.com/2009/09/14/health/policy/14nonprofit.html?_r=0.

U.S. Department of Labor, Bureau of Labor Statistics. 2015. "Business Employment Dynamics: Research Data on the Nonprofit Sector." http://www.bls.gov/bdm/nonprofits/nonprofits.htm.

U.S. Government Accountability Office. 2007. "Increasing Numbers and Key Role in Delivering Federal Services." Report GAO-07-1084T. Washington, DC: Government Accountability Office. http://www.gao.gov/products/GAO-07-1084T.

U.S. Small Business Administration. 2016. "About the SBA." https://www.sba.gov/about-sba/what-we-do.

Wilhelm, Ian. 2009. "Lawmakers Asked to Weigh Overhaul's Impact on Charities." *Chronicle of Philanthropy*, August 20, 2009. https://philanthropy.com/article/Lawmakers-Asked-to-Weigh/174145.

Chapter 8

Philanthropy

Shaping and Being Shaped by Public Policy

Lewis Faulk and Jasmine McGinnis Johnson

INTRODUCTION

This chapter focuses on organized philanthropy, which we define broadly as giving that is formally coordinated among individuals or conducted through an institutional form. We review the various forms of organized philanthropy, highlighting the differences among them from policy and donor perspectives. Relevant implications and emerging perspectives concerning nonprofits and public policy are discussed, including current regulatory challenges and the ways in which these philanthropic forms may be used to influence public policy.

Historically, organized philanthropy has taken place through institutions that have been established either for purposes other than philanthropic giving (such as religious institutions, civic associations, hospitals, and universities) or for the specific purpose of accumulating and then distributing assets for charitable purposes (such as community funds and private foundations). This is no different today. But the mix of philanthropic forms has grown. As Hammack and Anheier (2013, x) explain, endowed foundations were not common in America until after the US Constitution established protections for private property and freedom to act and support particular causes according to one's own beliefs. After the Constitution was ratified, endowed and institutionalized charitable activity proliferated. While the number, net worth, and roles of private foundations grew over the last 220 years, other legal forms of organized philanthropy now offer compelling alternatives from both donor and policy perspectives. Just as public policies affecting foundations were introduced, challenged, and developed over the last two centuries, policies regarding more recently introduced philanthropic forms, such as donor-advised funds (DAFs), are currently evolving. Because of their size and influence, many of the regulatory concerns focus on foundations and DAFs—those larger and newer forms of institutions around which the term "philanthropy" is often applied.

FORMS OF PHILANTHROPY IN THE UNITED STATES

For a philanthropist, there are many options for giving financial assets. In addition to direct gifts to nonprofits, a broad spectrum of legal institutions, conduits, and actions exist for individuals to transfer financial wealth to charitable entities. In the United States, endowed philanthropic foundations traditionally have provided donors and their families with a way to leave an enduring legacy. In recent years, the charitable sector has witnessed new ways of encouraging philanthropy (e.g., The Giving Pledge, whereby wealthy individuals and families commit to donate the majority of their resources to philanthropy), renewed attention to the creation of limited life foundations, in which philanthropic assets are distributed during the donors' lifetimes (Boris, De Vita, and Gaddy 2015), and new institutional forms including DAFs.

In general, many trade-offs exist as to how formal and institutionalized philanthropic giving will be and the extent to which the donor maintains control over the ultimate use of the charitable gifts. Tax benefits, in turn, are sometimes, though not always, limited according to the amount of donor control. As such, organized philanthropy ranges along a spectrum from less formal and less restricted forms to the more institutionalized and regulated forms. Less institutionalized forms include corporate-giving programs, giving circles, and pass-through giving through religious congregations, membership associations, clubs, or other groups. Under those modes, donors typically retain full control over their assets until they transfer them to charities, at which point they receive a charitable tax deduction for those gifts, and control switches to the formal charities.

Another form of philanthropy that is slightly more structured allows a certain level of donor control over the use of assets after being donated to the charity, while still granting tax exemption to the charity, charitable deductions to the donors, and the legal protections of a corporate form. These include DAFs, endowed gifts to hospitals, universities, or other public charities, and donations to public charity foundations, such as community foundations, discussed below.

At the most independently structured, but also the most heavily regulated extreme, donors may establish or fund private foundations. Here, we refer mainly to nonoperating foundations, which are generally endowed with assets from a single donor or family, and distribute grants to other charities, as opposed to operating foundations that tend to carry out their own charitable purposes more directly. Though private foundations are charities, they have fewer tax benefits and receive greater scrutiny than other forms of endowed giving. Among private foundations, many family foundations maintain a voting majority of family members on the foundation's governing board, while nonfamily-controlled independent foundations have a majority of nonrelated board members who direct the foundation. While "family" and "independent" are not legal distinctions, they are useful categories for distinguishing generally among types of foundations.

INSTITUTIONALIZED FORMS OF ORGANIZED PHILANTHROPY

Corporate-Giving Programs

Corporate-giving programs allow for-profit corporations to coordinate and direct employee contributions (which may be matched by the corporation) or funnel corporate gifts from company profits or inventory directly to nonprofit organizations. Because these gifts come directly from the corporation instead of being accumulated, endowed, or passed through a separately incorporated tax exempt company-sponsored charity, they are not subject to the regulations or disclosure requirements that apply to corporate foundations. This allows companies to engage in sustained or ad hoc corporate social responsibility (CSR) activities without establishing, maintaining, and supporting a separate board of directors, organizing documents, staff, and infrastructure required of a company foundation. However, the programs still require corporate resources, typically the company's paid staff, board members, or employee volunteers who add these responsibilities to their other job duties.

US corporations may deduct up to 10 percent of their taxable income for donations made to domestic charitable organizations or to company-sponsored foundations. Once corporate philanthropy reaches a certain level, there are advantages to establishing a separately incorporated company-sponsored foundation, including the ability to accumulate funds to distribute over time while receiving immediate tax benefits for the company. Corporate foundations are institutionally separate 501(c)(3) tax exempt organizations. However, because corporate foundations are aligned with their parent companies, strict self-dealing rules limit the expenditures made by the foundation to or on behalf of the corporation's officers, directors, and staff (Silk 2004).

In 2013, there were 1,753 corporate-giving programs listed under Foundation Center's Foundation Directory, compared to 2,577 corporate-sponsored foundations. Corporate foundations represented 3 percent of all US grantmakers in 2013 and held 3 percent of all foundation assets. However, corporate foundations made 10 percent of all charitable grants in that year, totaling over $5.3 billion (Foundation Center 2016). Corporate foundations often have small endowments, but they may receive yearly or periodic resources from the sponsoring corporation that they distribute as grants. Because reporting and disclosure of direct giving programs are voluntary, available data probably vastly under-represent direct giving activity from US corporations, which may range from little league sponsorship or ad hoc philanthropic donations to formal requests for applications and grantmaking cycles. In addition to an income tax deduction for their corporate giving, corporations may also deduct additional charitable activities as business expenses when the company or its employees receive a benefit, such as when the company receives advertising through sponsorships or when the corporation provides direct charitable assistance to its employees during floods or other natural disasters (Silk 2004).

Giving Circles

Similar to the way in which corporate-giving programs allow companies to funnel donations toward preferred charitable activities, giving circles allow collective groups of otherwise disconnected individuals to combine and make gifts to common causes. As Eikenberry (2006) describes, these groups often operate through informal networks of like-minded donors who organize and coordinate their giving through horizontally structured, democratic processes. These groups may be very informal or they may be formally incorporated. They may also operate as a program of a public charity, such as a women's giving circle that is coordinated through a local community foundation. Because many are informal groups, they are not subject to public disclosure and reporting, as is the case with almost all other forms of individual giving, and the exact number of giving circles is unknown. Individuals participate in giving circles for a variety of reasons, including to gain social benefits and education on community issues while continuing to enjoy personal income tax deductions for their gifts.

Pass-Through Giving through Religious Congregations, Membership Associations, Civic Clubs, Youth Groups, Scouting, Sports, Schools, or Other Groups

Other less formal avenues for donors include pass-through gifts that are solicited and coordinated by groups that are primarily engaged in other activities. These include monetary or in-kind gifts made to nonprofits through religious congregations, member associations, civic, youth, scouting, recreation groups, schools, or other clubs. From an empirical perspective, it is unknown exactly how much of the $350 billion in private philanthropy each year is encouraged, coordinated, managed, and distributed through voluntary organizations, associations, clubs, or other groups. In large part, these groups were not established for the specific purposes of collecting and distributing donations. Rather, these coordinated philanthropic activities take place as one of many activities undertaken by the group, often addressing a specific need or organized at specific times of the year. These philanthropic activities are not formalized or regulated beyond a particular state's Charitable Solicitation Act or similar legislation that regulates general charitable fundraising. These activities therefore rely on trust established between the group and donors that their donated goods or money will be passed to charitable entities or used for broader charitable purposes. Donors generally would be entitled to individual tax deductions on their gifts through these groups, but the donations are typically small or token, including gifts of canned goods or other donations that combined may still be substantial.

On the public end of this spectrum are pass-through funds that are organized, coordinated, or managed by government entities. These funds may benefit nonprofit organizations, such as the Combined Federal Campaign that coordinates and encourages federal workplace giving. Other funds may support or supplement the work of government, such as the UN Foundation that funnels private giving to UN funds, programs, and agencies. Other funds that fit within this category of organized philanthropy include various state and local government-coordinated funds that attract private funds to help individuals in need, organizations that are established to improve or protect public assets such as public parks and libraries, and foundations that collect donations to support public universities. In general, these entities blur the boundaries between government action and private philanthropy, expanding the impact that private contributions can make toward government work and vice versa. Because these activities are closely associated with government, their programs and funding are generally publicly disclosed in an effort to maintain transparency, and they are subject to demands for greater public accountability than pass-through funding that is organized and coordinated by nongovernmental groups.

FORMS OF INSTITUTIONALIZED PRIVATE PHILANTHROPY THAT PROVIDE VARYING LEVELS OF DONOR CONTROL

Establishing or funding private foundations provides donors with a form of legacy philanthropy which can last beyond donors' or their heirs' lifetimes.

From a tax perspective, direct donations to 501(c)(3) public charities garner more favorable benefits than donations that pass through private foundations. Both are tax-deductible gifts, but donations to public charities allow donors to deduct up to 50 percent of their taxable income in the year of the donation as opposed to a 30 percent cap on taxable income for donations to private foundations. The logic behind this distinction is that direct gifts to charities are more efficient from a public benefits perspective than pass-through funding that occurs through private foundation intermediaries. Donations to private foundations allow donors control over the final charitable use of those funds. Additionally, private foundations may accumulate assets that they distribute on an incremental basis into perpetuity, reducing the immediate public benefits of a donation to a foundation in a particular year. Given the administrative costs of maintaining foundation assets and making grants, private foundation spending may also benefit private individuals through salaries and other remuneration for performing work for the foundation, which may include individuals related to the foundation's donors. Therefore, gifts to and spending by private foundations are subjected to greater formal oversight, which involves ongoing costs from both foundation and government perspectives.

There are alternatives to donating to or through a private foundation that still provide donors with influence over the final use of those gifts, including DAFs, endowment gifts to hospitals, universities, and other public charities, and donations to community foundations. These alternatives provide donors with the same tax benefits as donating directly to public charities; they provide long-term, legacy benefits, and in general they are less costly compared to starting and managing a private foundation.

Donor-Advised Funds

DAFs are philanthropic funds that are held and managed by 501(c)(3) public charities. Traditionally, DAFs were held by community foundations, but now they may be started and managed by other public charities such as universities or hospitals or by 501(c)(3) charitable funds founded by for-profit corporations. These funds allow donors to transfer charitable assets to a DAF and advise the organization managing the fund on the final charitable use of those assets. Because DAFs are held by public charities, donors receive the full tax benefits of donating to a public charity in the year they contribute to the DAF, and they may add to those funds over time, even though the final distribution of those funds to other public charities may be made in later years. In this way, DAFs provide an alternative to both establishing a private foundation and donating to endowments that may fund a single organization. From an efficiency perspective, DAFs pool assets from many donors which are then managed and distributed by a single organization over time. For donors, it can be more efficient, too. For instance, donors who make their giving through a DAF and itemize their tax deductions can simplify their tax returns by only needing to claim and keep records of donations to the DAF while still directing those funds to several organizations.

Since the early 1990s, for-profit banks and investment institutions, such as Fidelity, Schwab, Bank of America, Vanguard, and others, increasingly established and grew charitable DAF arms of their businesses as a way to attract and serve clients (Lenkowsky 2012). Within 20 years, DAFs were predominantly held within such national entities, and by 2015 total donations made through the largest of these, the Fidelity Charitable Gift Fund, surpassed gifts from all other grantmakers in the United States other than the Bill and Melinda Gates Foundation (Steele and Steuerle 2015). Across the country, grants made by DAFs held by community foundations and national funds grew to over $12.49 billion in 2014, representing 27 percent growth from the year before and continuing a general trend of rapid growth in the number of funds and assets held, donations to, and average account size (National Philanthropic Trust 2015). Grants by 48 national institutions maintaining DAFs that were tracked by the National Philanthropic Trust grew by 28 percent from 2013 to $5.47 billion in 2014, which was more than the amount of grants made by DAFs of over 600 community foundations, which grew 41 percent from 2013 to $4.18 billion in 2014 (National Philanthropic Trust 2015).

From a tax policy perspective, donations made to DAFs are treated the same as donations to other 501(c)(3) public charities. In contrast to private foundations, DAFs are not required to publicly disclose their donors, they do not pay excise taxes on their investment income, and they are not subject to publicly mandated annual payout requirements. This allows donors to establish multigenerational philanthropy without the burdens, administrative oversight, or disclosure requirements of a private foundation (Steele and Steuerle 2015). Donors may choose to name a DAF and establish a lasting legacy, or they may choose to keep their DAF grants completely anonymous. Along with these benefits, distributions of grants from DAFs receive less oversight than grants from private foundations. Organizations that maintain DAFs must report aggregate statistics on the DAFs they manage on schedule D of their annual Form 990, including the number of DAF accounts and aggregate values of all DAF contributions and grants for the year, while private foundations must report the value, recipient, and purpose of each grant made.

From a regulatory oversight perspective, organizations that maintain DAFs must report grants they make to other organizations on their Forms 990, but grants to organizations may be aggregated across DAFs they manage and may remain unattributed to individual donors' funds. Donors to DAFs or private foundations that fund DAFs therefore have the potential to mask the flow of their donations through DAFs. This can potentially include flows of money that ultimately go to 501(c)(4) organizations, 527 organizations, or other legal forms under specific circumstances, consistent with the general regulation of 501(c)(3) public charities. The trade-off is that the organization that sponsors DAFs may determine the payout policies specific to its funds, including how long funds may be held before they are distributed or what types of organizations may be funded. Legally, the ultimate use of the funds is determined by the sponsoring organization that manages the DAFs, although, in practice, living donors to DAFs retain general advisory discretion as long as the donations fit within the sponsoring organization's DAF guidelines.

Endowment Gifts to Hospitals, Universities, or Other Public Charities

Another form of legacy donations is a gift of permanently restricted assets that may be used by the recipient organization for charitable purposes defined by the donor. Such gifts may include gifts of property, such as art collections, or they may include financial gifts that establish or contribute to endowed funds. Similar to DAFs and other donations to public charities, these donations come with favorable tax benefits compared to gifts to noncharitable organizations or private foundations. They also allow donors the option of placing permanent restrictions on the gifts, which may be updated over time based on the donor's discretion or a court order.

In contrast to general donations that legally transfer the control over donated assets to charitable organizations, permanently restricted donations allow donors to exert lasting control over the use of those gifts. For organizations receiving these gifts, this can raise complex issues related to honoring donor intent over other potential uses of restricted, or endowed, assets especially as charitable institutions that receive gifts may change their priorities and preferences over time. Legally, donors or their heirs may sue organizations for not following original donor intent, which may lead to costly court battles or settlements, such as the Princeton University–Robertson family settlement in which Princeton paid $40 million in legal fees and distributed $50 million to a foundation controlled by the Robertson heirs because the family believed Princeton had mostly ignored donor intent (Hoffman 2009; Lewin 2008).

Donations to Public Charity Grantmakers and Community Foundations

Similarly, donations made to grantmakers that file with the IRS as public charities come with the same tax benefits as donations made directly to the final charitable recipient organization. The distinction between public and private foundations is discussed more fully below. Public grantmakers include organizations that are funded by multiple donors or through other public funding mechanisms. These include prominent organizations such as the United Way, Susan G. Komen, and the Clinton Foundation. Because these organizations satisfy the tests for public charity status, they are afforded favorable tax benefits and tax deductibility for their donors. For example, community foundations are a class of organizations that fit under the profile of public grantmakers. Community foundations are typically funded by many individuals in a given community, and donors receive the full tax benefits of donating to a public charity with their gifts to these grantmakers. These donations may be directed toward specific funds or programs, but the foundation retains ultimate control over the use of those funds after the donor has made a gift.

Legal Distinction between Public and Private Foundations

In order to receive *public charity* status, a 501(c)(3) organization operating for charitable purposes must pass a public support test in which it demonstrates that it receives substantial support from the general public or government. If an organization cannot demonstrate public support but otherwise meets the criteria for 501(c)(3) status, it is generally classified as a *private foundation*, which is subject to greater scrutiny and regulations than *public charities*. It is important to note that the distinction between public charities and private foundations is not based on whether an organization makes grants to other organizations but rather on their sources of revenue. In general, for grantmaking entities this leads to two legal forms of organizations that are generally referred to as foundations: public and private. Each is distinguished by the source of its funds and comes with specific reporting requirements. Both are 501(c)(3) tax exempt nonprofit organizations, benefit from tax-deductible contributions, are managed by their own trustees and directors, and make grants primarily to other nonprofit organizations. In terms of funding, private grantmaking foundations generally have a principal fund or endowment received from a single or limited number of sources that could either be an individual, a family, or a company. Public foundations (also known as grantmaking public charities) are required to receive funding from numerous sources and must continue to seek money from diverse sources in order to maintain public charity status.

From a regulatory perspective, private foundations have greater restrictions and fewer tax benefits than public foundations, which are public charities. Importantly, private foundations are limited in their ability to engage in advocacy through lobbying or funding of lobbying activities. Private foundations may not take the 501(h) election (expenditure test), which allows public charities to lobby under clearer definitions and allowances for activities that influence public policy. In contrast to public charities, private foundations are also subject to excise taxes if they directly or indirectly fund other organizations' lobbying activities. In addition, private foundations are subject to a 2 percent tax on net investment income that can be reduced to 1 percent if the private foundation maintains or increases its rate of qualifying distributions out of its net worth for charitable purposes. In practice, this may prevent foundations from increasing charitable grants in any given year because they would be penalized with a higher tax in future years once their giving returned to normal (Dietz et al. 2015; Steuerle and Sullivan 1995). Private foundations are subject to additional excise taxes for failing to take certain required actions, including maintaining prudent investments. Furthermore, private foundations are required to make annual distributions equal to 5 percent of the aggregate fair market value of all investment assets of the organization. Finally, federal income tax deductions that donors receive for contributions to a private foundation are more limited than deductions for gifts to public charities, as discussed previously in the chapter.

Public charity grantmakers receive differential treatment by the IRS because it is assumed that the variety of donors that public foundations rely on will compel them to direct funds toward collective community problems, and a variety of donors will provide greater informal oversight mechanisms of the organization's activities. There is a range of organizations legally classified as public foundations. They include community foundations, Jewish Federated Funds, women's funds, United Way agencies, funding intermediaries, and other funds serving specific population groups and fields, such as health funding foundations set up with proceeds from health care conversions.

Community foundations and United Way agencies are the largest group of public foundations. Graddy and Morgan (2006) conceptualize a prominent public purpose of community foundations as serving as community leaders, serving as conveners and catalysts in localities, bringing diverse segments of the community together in addition to raising and distributing funds to address local public concerns. They find three potential roles for community foundations: donor focused (primarily focused on raising funds), matchmakers (fulfilling an intermediary role between funders and grantees), and community leaders (serving as conveners for various issue areas). Scholars note that United Way agencies also pursue similar goals (Barman 2007; Grønbjerg, Martell, and Paarlberg 2000). Although the pursuit of public outcomes seems obvious for this set of foundations, growing competition for donors and the rise of interest in DAFs within community foundations can raise tensions between the need for attracting donors and serving the community. Consequently, it can be difficult for public foundations to fulfill community leadership role while also being donor focused (Graddy and Morgan 2006).

Types of Foundations

Beyond the legal distinctions between public and private foundations discussed above, grantmaking foundations are commonly categorized by type of grantmaker, including family foundations, independent foundations, corporate foundations, community foundations, and operating foundations.

The Foundation Center reported over 87,000 private and public foundations in the United States in 2013 that controlled $798 billion in assets and awarded over $55 billion in grants annually. Institutional giving by independent and corporate foundations makes up approximately one-fifth of total donations to US nonprofits each year (Giving USA 2013). The vast majority (91 percent) of foundations in the United States are independent foundations, of which approximately 53 percent are family foundations.[1] Five percent of foundations in the United States are operating foundations, 3 percent are corporate, and approximately 1 percent are community foundations (Foundation Center 2016).

Among the most common foundation types, family and independent foundations make up the largest proportion of private foundations and control the greatest proportion of assets. Both family and independent foundations are private foundations, but they are often distinguished by the governance structures of the foundations' board and staff. Family foundations tend to have a board of directors that is composed primarily of family members related to the original donor who established the foundation. Independent foundations are often older, or more professionally staffed and have less family involvement (Gersick and Stone 2004).

Of the more than 87,000 US foundations in 2013, independent and family foundations made up close to 80,000 and distributed over $37 billion in charitable grants (Foundation Center 2016). Of these, family foundations represented more than 42,000 foundations and made $24 billion in grants. Despite the recession, foundation giving has grown. For instance, "between 2002 and 2013, the number of family foundations grew by 44%—increasing roughly from 29,400 to 42,300 . . . total giving by family foundations almost doubled—from $12.4 billion to $23.9 billion" (Boris, De Vita, and Gaddy 2015, x). While family foundations represent a significant portion of total grantmakers, a recent survey indicated that they were very concerned about attracting the next generation of relatives to participate in the foundation's activities. As a result, we may see more variability in the composition of board membership of family foundations in the future, including less family control, but it is unclear whether this will lead to greater demographic diversity (Boris, De Vita, and Gaddy 2015). Understanding the governance structures of foundations is especially important since most foundations are small and have few or no staff (Boris et al. 2006).

As a distinct category, operating foundations are different from other types of foundations in that they primarily fund their own direct charitable programs. This makes operating foundations hybrids between public charities and private foundations. Legally, they may receive many of the same benefits as public charities and have fewer restrictions than other private foundations if they meet specific tests regarding the receipt of general public support and direct most of their expenses toward their own programs (Hopkins 2005). There were approximately 4,100 operating foundations in 2013. Operating foundations made around $7.5 billion in grants in 2013, which roughly compares to the total grants made by community foundations and corporate foundations in that year (Foundation Center 2016).

Of the $55 billion given annually, 22 percent of foundation grant dollars are given to health and education, while 16 percent is given to human services (Foundation Center 2016). A growing body of research on the determinants of grantmaking by foundations suggests that similar to individual giving, foundations prefer to give grants to nonprofits that are larger, more stable, and have a proven track record, such as having received grants in the past (Ashley and Faulk 2014; Faulk, McGinnis Johnson, and Lecy 2016; Faulk, Willems, McGinnis Johnson, and Stewart 2015; McGinnis Johnson 2013; McGinnis and Ashley 2011). Studies have compared the characteristics of grant award winners by foundations of different types and do not find significant differences (Ashley and Faulk 2010; McGinnis and Ashley 2011).

THE BENEFITS AND TRADE-OFFS OF PRIVATE FOUNDATIONS

In general, 501(c)(3) private foundations provide philanthropists with a legal vehicle to pursue philanthropic goals into perpetuity while receiving immediate individual tax benefits and long-term tax exemptions for activities the foundation pursues. Exploring whether or not private foundations pursue entirely public outcomes however has been a question of considerable debate in the sector and dates back to the earliest days of the establishment of private foundations and throughout their regulatory history. In the late nineteenth and early twentieth centuries, private foundations' wealth and influence on community development and the public sphere at times rivaled that of established, but small, governments. This included the direct development of institutions and communities. Perhaps as importantly, foundations also used their wealth to fund research and analysis of public problems, solutions, and policies (Prewitt 2006). Some foundations exerted influence in other ways as well, including the funding of social movement activities, such as during the US civil rights movement.

By the 1950s, the growth of wealth in private foundations and their public influence led to greater public scrutiny and eventual oversight. The potential abuse of private foundations as tax shelters and the relative lack of regulations led to concerns that mounted in the 1950s and 1960s and culminated with the introduction of greater regulation of private foundations in the Tax Reform Act (TRA) of 1969 (Frumkin 1999; Hall 2006; Stewart and Faulk 2014; Simon 1995; Troyer 2000). Scholars Karl and Katz (1987, p. 60) noted that "the privacy of foundations is an accident of history" when Rockefeller lost the battle to receive a congressional charter for his foundation. However, foundation discretion was limited by regulations included in the TRA of 1969, which served to distinguish private foundations from public charities in terms of their specific tax benefits and oversight.

The TRA of 1969 established several regulations of private foundations, including a mandatory foundation grant payout policy, which required private foundations to spend a minimum of 6 percent of the value of their assets each year on charitable purposes (Mehrling 1999). However, this led to a depreciation of foundation assets, so IRS rules were revised in 1981 to reduce the minimum payout to 5 percent (Mehrling 1999). Along with a variable excise tax rule to encourage higher future payouts, this regulatory policy was designed to allow foundations to maintain the real value of their funds over time (based on an estimated 5 percent long-term real return on investments) while ensuring a stable philanthropic output. Although this policy was also intended to dampen the rate of accumulation of wealth and power in private foundations, a proliferation of foundations and increased donations over the subsequent decades caused foundation wealth to increase threefold since these policies were established.

THE ROLES OF ORGANIZED PHILANTHROPY IN PUBLIC POLICY AND RELATIONSHIPS WITH GOVERNMENT

As discussed above, current formal public policies restrict the ability of private foundations to engage directly in lobbying or fund lobbying activities performed by other organizations. This should not be taken to suggest that private foundations do not perform or have not played important roles in public policy change, social movements, community problem solving, infrastructure and capacity development, and evolving public perceptions on important social issues over time. Indeed, there are examples of prominent foundations from early modern foundations such as the Carnegie Corporation, Russell Sage, Rockefeller, Ford, and the Twentieth Century Fund to more recently introduced foundations such as Gates that have directly engaged in policy issues through funding work to address social needs, influencing political and social perceptions of public and social problems, researching policy issues and solutions, funding organizations involved in social movements, and developing coalitions and partnerships in local, regional, national, and international contexts to support collective action to solve public problems (Hall 2006). As Mosley and Galaskiewicz (2010, 194) discuss, "Despite restrictions on formal lobbying, foundations play important public policy roles by convening critical stakeholders, building coalitions, funding and disseminating important research, and building capacity for advocacy in other nonprofit organizations."

From theoretical perspectives on nonprofit relationships with government, by Dennis Young and John Casey in chapter 1 of this volume, foundations undoubtedly engage in complementary, supplementary, and adversarial relationships with government. The general character of these relationships has arguably changed over time as early foundations provided funding and capacity support for supplementary activities that filled gaps in public services, and developed key philanthropic, educational, and scientific infrastructure organizations at a time when private wealth rivaled government capacity. Throughout the twentieth century, foundations had to adapt to changing roles of government, greater government social welfare funding, and US economic growth (Smith 2010). Especially with the introduction of greater government oversight and regulation of foundation activity, foundations played increasingly adversarial roles—not only by engaging in adversarial functions they had performed already, such as policy research and funding social movements, but increasingly in efforts to define their roles in society, defend their legitimacy, and reduce the burdens of government regulation (Smith 2010).

The introduction of new philanthropic forms and the rise of DAFs, impact investing, and prominent public charity grantmakers have provided opportunities as well as threats to traditional private foundations (Smith 2010). While the relative scale of their assets is marginal compared to twenty-first-century government budgets, the introduction of diverse policy tools combined with foundations' private character and prominent position within nonprofit fields of practice position them to engage in greater complementary relationships with government through public-private partnerships, collaborative infrastructure development, and convening activities that bridge sectors to address pressing public problems on a scale that government could not accomplish alone, such as the US Department of Education's Promise Neighborhoods initiative or foundations' role in Detroit's recovery from bankruptcy filing. As Kerlin and Reid (2010) discuss, the use of complex organizational combinations also allows private foundations to play specific roles within their legal limits to fund, coordinate, and develop organizational capacities, research, and network infrastructure while engaging other organizational forms in lobbying and election activities to accomplish broader policy goals (also see chapter 6 by Roger Colinvaux in this volume). Overall, this changing legal, governmental, and institutional landscape has led to a more complex set of relationships between organized philanthropy and government. Below, we discuss specific trends that are worthy of additional consideration within this context.

EMERGING PHILANTHROPIC TRENDS AND POLICY ISSUES

Giving Pledges and Hybridity

While the forms of organized philanthropy discussed above have many tax advantages which incentivize the use of those forms and potentially the combination of them in complex ways, philanthropists are not required to use them. Especially considering the restrictions, such as mandatory disclosure and oversight that accompany tax exempt forms of philanthropic vehicles, individuals instead may choose to hold and accumulate their wealth privately in noncharitable trusts and noncharitable institutions, or as privately held assets and investments, which they distribute over time for charitable purposes. An example of this model is Facebook founder and CEO Mark Zuckerberg and his wife Dr. Priscilla Chan's pledge to give 99 percent of their wealth during their lifetime to charitable causes through the Chan Zuckerberg Initiative, a limited liability company they established to manage and distribute that wealth (Goel and Wingfield 2015), which Cordes, Steuerle, Dietz, and Broadus discuss more fully in chapter 9 of this volume. By choosing to maintain these assets in a noncharitable form, Zuckerberg and Chan retain ultimate control over how to distribute them. They may decide to donate directly to charities, form private foundations, donate to government entities, donate to political activities, fund advocacy initiatives, donate to social enterprises, or invest in for-profit initiatives that have social goals. Or they may decide to pursue some or all of these through a hybrid approach. Alternatively, they may also hold the wealth indefinitely, pause their giving, or pay out all of the wealth overnight without needing to comply with formal policies regarding mandatory payouts, adhere to giving policies of DAFs, or gain approval from a board of directors, which they do not need with the choice of organizational form they established. From a policy perspective, while each of these forms may be appropriately regulated in isolation, the combined use of various legal philanthropic forms and potentially veiled transfers of assets between them introduces regulatory complexities that may have yet to be fully appreciated.

The Surge of Donor-Advised Funds—
New Grantmakers in an Old Form

As discussed above, grantmaking dollars from traditional foundations have continued to increase in recent years. However, the fastest philanthropic growth has occurred in public charity grantmakers, and specifically within DAFs, especially those that are maintained under a for-profit umbrella. Assets held by national DAFs grew by 30 percent between 2013 and 2014 to over $24 billion, double the rate of growth for DAFs maintained by US community foundations, which amounted to $22 billion in that year (Steele and Steuerle 2015).

Even though much of the growth in DAFs has taken place under for-profit conglomerates, DAFs largely emerged out of nonprofit community foundations, which may serve as competitors to for-profit-related DAFs. Unlike Schwab and Fidelity, community foundations are located within donors' communities, have long histories of effectiveness at the local level, and are known for strong local leadership (Graddy and Morgan 2006). The more efficient ones are uniquely positioned to advise donors on pressing needs and promising local organizations. It is unclear if DAFs maintained by organizations that are national in scope and community foundation DAFs compete with or complement each other. As Madoff (2014) discusses, while DAF growth has outpaced the general economy in recent years, overall individual giving (which includes DAF activity) has changed very little over time, hovering around 2 percent of GDP. This suggests that the increase in DAF funding may be crowding out instead of adding on top of other forms of philanthropy. Instead, as discussed above, given the benefits of DAFs for donors, channeling gifts through DAFs may just be a smart way for donors who are already making gifts throughout the year to organize their giving.

It is likely that the rise in national DAFs represent both an opportunity and a threat to community foundations. While national DAFs are poised to continue to grow their share of the market, for-profit marketing of these funds has raised awareness of this philanthropic vehicle and perhaps has created new potential clients for community foundations. In the midst of the surge in funds at national DAFs, community foundations feel competitive pressure to improve donor-targeted services to appeal to, acquire, and retain donors. At the same time, community foundations have strategically pursued community leadership activities in part to maintain a comparative advantage as local philanthropic experts relative to national for-profit firms in the DAF market (Bernholz, Fulton, and Kasper 2005). This has not led to community foundations reducing the use of DAFs in their overall activities; however, community foundations report using it as a civic engagement tool by both providing leadership and involvement opportunities for their donors as well as engaging younger donors in local philanthropy (Boris and Dietz 2014).

Community foundation DAFs have grown alongside national DAFs, but as discussed above, national organizations' market share has surpassed that held by local community organizations. The implications of this trend for local organizations that seek those donations are not clear. On the one hand, philanthropists who coordinate their giving through national DAFs may already be knowledgeable of their local nonprofit community and direct their DAF funds to those recipients. On the other hand, new donors attracted into national DAFs rather than DAFs held by their local or regional community foundation may not benefit from the same level of matchmaking between their philanthropic interests and their local community's needs and organizations. The implications for the distribution of local philanthropic resources and the capacity for local communities to respond to changing public needs could be informed by future empirical research into these questions.

From a policy perspective, the recent growth in DAFs and the relative lack of regulations of them compared to private foundations have led to questions of whether DAFs should receive greater oversight and regulation. Of course, the parallel argument is whether some of the regulations on foundations are inefficient. The concerns stem first from endowments and donor control: whether donors should receive immediate tax deductibility when they retain a certain level of control over the funds; and there are potential costs to the tax base and society if assets in DAFs are hoarded instead of distributed in a timely manner (Hopkins 2005; Steele and Steuerle 2015). Recent changes to the IRS Form 990 have increased oversight and accountability of DAFs, but remaining policy questions include whether mandatory payout rates or excise taxes similar to those that apply to private foundations should be introduced and, if introduced, whether such regulations would reduce the efficiency that these vehicles provide. As Steele and Steuerle (2015) discuss, observed payout rates from DAFs appear to be much greater than those of private foundations, which would suggest that imposing a specific payout rate may not be warranted and may disrupt activities such as building up DAFs for some large community investment, or establishing a legacy of giving in a family. Additionally, sector self-oversight and private resolution of these issues may be sufficient. For instance, new tools such as DAFdirect, introduced by Fidelity, Schwab, and the Kansas City Community Foundation, allow nonprofits a greater role in introducing themselves to donors whose funds are held in DAFs (Schaefer 2015). Regardless of these initiatives, DAFs will likely continue to receive increased scrutiny and regulation over the coming years.

Continued Growth in Private Foundations and Related Policy Issues

While Congress has revisited the 5 percent payout rule and excise tax rules in recent decades, the rules have remained largely unchanged since the implementation of the TRA of 1969. Over time, arguments over these regulations have developed with two major claims emerging. One side argues that the 5 percent payout rule allows for sustained fund levels over time, given historical rates of return for investments, and should not be increased or changed. The other side argues that having a 5 percent minimum payout really acts as a 5 percent maximum, limiting the amount of charity that foundations actually provide (e.g., see Deep and Frumkin 2001). As a result, foundation payouts that hover at 5 percent lead to total grant distributions that rise and fall procyclically with the economy, in effect reducing total payouts when they are most needed during poor economic circumstances (Dietz et al. 2015). These and other studies (e.g., see Toepler 2004) have suggested countercyclical variable payout rates to build foundation funds in good economic times and disperse them more rapidly in poor economic cycles. Studies from this viewpoint argue that the payout minimum should be increased or changed to allow lower payouts in good economic times (to allow for accumulation of funds) and to require higher payouts in poor economic times (to provide greater charitable impact when foundation funding is more necessary). However, as Irvin (2007) suggests, these more complex policy recommendations, apart from being untested, require more complex reporting and costlier oversight, which may cause such policies to be less efficient in the long run, even if they are more effective in the short run. A minority position within the argument for higher payouts argues that regimenting foundation behavior through any payout policy is not necessary and has the unintended consequences of suppressing the overall giving levels of foundations.

More practical approaches that have been introduced but not yet passed include reducing the variable excise tax on investment income to a flat rate between 1 and 2 percent. These proposals were included in the TRA of 2014, America Gives More Act of 2015, and President Obama's annual budget proposals. Those in favor of these changes argue that reducing the tax to a flat rate will reduce the regulatory complexity and inefficiency of a dual rate system and reduce disincentives for foundations to increase their charitable grant payouts in any given year. Relatedly, other proposals include changing the carry-forward rule to allow foundations to apply increases in a given year's payout to future years' payouts, which are again argued to incentivize increased grant payouts in response to greater societal needs (Dietz et al. 2015).

Impact Investing—New Rules, Increased Use of Program-Related Investments, Funding Social Enterprises

Program-related investments (PRIs) or mission-related investments (MRIs) are tools that foundations use to make low-interest loans to nonprofit, hybrid, or for-profit organizations that create social impact in line with foundations' mission and objectives. When organizations pay back these loans, foundations then use those resources to create new PRIs/MRIs or grantmaking. Additionally, PRIs can be applied to their 5 percent distribution rate. However, fewer than a third of foundations in recent studies use PRIs and most that do are large organizations (Boris et al. 2015), which may be due to the capacity needed in developing these tools. Additionally, there are very few nonprofits that have the capacity to accept a PRI and perform in ways that illicit a return on a foundation's investment (Osili et al. 2013). Although many scholars and practitioners suggest PRIs could have a significant impact in the philanthropic marketplace, and may even incentivize nonprofits to begin more entrepreneurial revenue-generating practices, we lack evidence of whether this is widespread in practice. Prominent examples of foundations that use PRIs include Heron Foundation, the Bill and Melinda Gates Foundation, and Rockefeller Foundation. With the introduction of pay-for-success social impact investment policy tools, such as Social Impact Bonds, which allow investors to receive a profitable return for funding successful social initiatives, foundations could be well positioned to expand the use of PRIs for funding Social Impact Bond initiatives.

ADDITIONAL ISSUES RELATED TO FOUNDATION MANAGEMENT AND SECTOR SELF-OVERSIGHT

In addition to the emerging forms and methods of institutional philanthropy described above, there are several issues for practice that intersect directly with foundations' own professional standards of practice, which at times overlap with the policy environment. Some of these issues have been around for decades, while others have received new or renewed interest, including efforts to democratize philanthropy, the introduction of more socially efficient payout policies, pressure for foundation transparency, congressional concerns over effectiveness, and the use of affiliated government foundations. We discuss several of these concerns below.

Foundation Transparency

Many concerns have been raised about the public versus private nature of foundations and their grantmaking dollars. These concerns have been raised about the role of foundations in policy debates, such as the Gates Foundation's role in setting the agenda for education (Reckhow 2012) and about whether or not foundation dollars are public dollars, and if they are, why aren't foundation operations and processes more transparent (Tyler 2013). These arguments have largely been normative as the majority of foundations in the United States are private foundations and as such are private institutions that do not legally have accountability to stakeholders other than requirements to pursue their organization's charitable mission in a financially responsible way (Brody and Tyler 2009). Additionally, many of these concerns center around the fact that foundations are often involved in the policy process, service delivery, and implementation despite the fact that they are unelected individuals who do not have any incentives to be accountable to the broader public, but make decisions that affect the broader public (Eisenberg 1999).

However, this has not prevented the growth in organizations both internal and external to the philanthropic ecosystem that provide information to the public to increase the transparency of foundation structures. Most of these organizations ask foundations to self-report more information to the public. Examples include glasspockets.org (of the Foundation Center) and GuideStar (collecting demographic information). However, there are also examples of foundations being monitored by organizations that then release that information to the public. One example, is the National Committee for Responsive Philanthropy (NCRP) Philamplify campaign where staff members of NCRP interview stakeholders and produce reports of what type of impact the foundation has, delving more into foundations' processes and structures than most organizations voluntarily disclose.

Foundation and Grantee Diversity

Similar to calls for greater foundation transparency, many argue that a greater diversity of stakeholders should be involved in grantmaking decisions. These concerns are largely driven by the lack of diversity on philanthropic boards in terms of race/ethnicity and/or gender diversity (Lindeman 1988; Burbridge et al. 2002; Enright and Bourns 2010). The assumption underlying increased stakeholder involvement in philanthropic boards is that traditional boards do not make decisions that are similar to or representative of decisions that community members would make. An example of these claims can be seen in the arguments surrounding California Assembly Bill 624. Proponents of the bill argued that because individuals serving as philanthropic board members are not representative of the public, they do not make decisions that the "public" would agree with or make themselves (González-Rivera 2009). In 2002, a national study of 600 grantmakers found that "white men represent 56 to 72 percent of board members . . . [and] white women represent 17 to 33 percent of all board members" (Burbridge et al. 2002, 12). This same study found that 10 percent of foundation board members were people of color, while only 33 percent were women (Burbridge et al. 2002). Similar statistics are found in a 2006 study by Ostrower and Stone who indicate that although women make up about 43 percent of *nonprofit* board members, they constitute only 34 percent of foundation board members. Finally, a 2009 study of the forty-six largest foundations in the country found that 28 percent had no board members of color (González-Rivera 2009). In 2009, researchers found that grants from the *ten* foundations with the most minority foundation board members made up half of all grants to minority-led nonprofit organizations, which lends some support to existing assumptions that there is some connection between the governance of a philanthropic organization and the effectiveness and equity of its grantmaking decisions (González-Rivera 2009).

Unfortunately, most of these studies stop at the collection of statistics on the racial/ethnic and gender diversity of boards because it is difficult to collect qualitative or quantitative data on how the lack of board diversity impacts grantmaking, as there are no legal requirements for reporting any demographic information related to foundation boards or their grantees. In fact, the D5 Coalition (a five-year coalition to advance conversations, data and information sharing on diversity, equity and inclusion in philanthropy) found that many times when these studies are done, it is difficult to determine which grantees are minority serving and which are not. The lack of robust data in this arena, lack of legal regulations to report demographic information, and controversy over whether or not diversity matters in philanthropy may explain why legislation proposed in California in 2007—Assembly Bill 624, which would have required California's largest foundations to report the demographic information on their boards—did not pass. Alternatively, in Florida, Senate Bill 998 did pass in 2010, which legislated that foundations would never have to report or share the demographic information of their boards.

As the number and type of foundations continue to grow in the United States, questions remain as to what role philanthropy should play in policy debates and local solutions to community problems. Although data available on the Forms 990-PFs provide some insight into foundations' grantmaking, there are many unknown components, aside from case studies on the realities of foundations' structures, processes, and decision-making strategies. Since these debates have occurred since the advent of the modern foundation in the early 1900s, it is likely these discussions will continue. It is less clear whether this discourse will lead to significant future legislative or policy changes that affect the philanthropic sector—and how those changes may affect relationships between organized philanthropy and government moving forward.

NOTE

1. It should be noted that because family and independent foundations are not legal categories, researchers often have to find schema for identifying family foundations, such as percentage of board members that share the last name of the original donor. This means that numbers are not precise and there is some random error in these estimations.

REFERENCES

Ashley, Shena, and Lewis Faulk. (2014). "Financial Analysis for Measuring and Comparing Risk in Grantmaking Portfolios." *The Foundation Review,* 6(3), article 8. DOI: 10.9707/1944-5660.1212.

Ashley, Shena, and Lewis Faulk. (2010). "Nonprofit Competition in the Grants Marketplace." *Nonprofit Management and Leadership,* 21(1), 43–57.

Barman, Emily. (2007). "With Strings Attached: Nonprofits and the Adoption of Donor Choice." *Nonprofit and Voluntary Sector Quarterly,* 37(1), 39–56.

Bernholz, Lucy, Katherine Fulton, and Gabriel Kasper. (2005). On the Brink of New Promise: The Future of U.S. Community Foundations. Blueprint Research & Design, Inc. and Monitor Company Group, LLP.

Boris, Elizabeth, and Nathan Dietz. (2014). "Community Foundations and Donor-Advised Funds." Washington, DC: Urban Institute. http://www.cof.org/sites/default/files/documents/files/Urban-Survey-Summary.pdf.

Boris, Elizabeth, Carol J. De Vita, and Marcus Gaddy. (2015). "National Center for Family Philanthropy's 2015 Trend Study." Retrieved January 2015 https://www.ncfp.org/resource/trends-research/.

Boris, Elizabeth, Loren Renz, Asmita Barve, Mark A. Hager, and George Hobor. (2006). "Foundation Expenses & Compensation: How Operating Characteristics Influence Spending." Retrieved January 2016. http://foundationcenter.org/gainknowledge/research/pdf/fdn_exp_comp.pdf.

Brody, Evelyn and John Tyler. (2009). How Public is Private Philanthropy? *Washington, DC* Philanthropy Roundtable. Retrieved January 2016. http://www.philanthropyroundtable.org/file_uploads/Public_Private_Monograph_high_res_Final.pdf.

Burbridge, L., W. Diaz, T. Odendahl, and A. Shaw. (2002). The Meaning and Impact of Board and Staff Diversity in the Philanthropic Field. Retrieved January 2016.

Deep, A., and P. Frumkin. (2001). "The Foundation Payout Puzzle." Hauser Center for Nonprofit Organizations Working Paper No. 9. Available at SSRN: http://ssrn.com/abstract=301826.

Dietz, N., B. McKeever, E. Steele, and C. E. Steuerle. (2015). *Foundation Grantmaking over the Economic Cycle*. Urban Institute, Washington, DC.

Eikenberry, A. M. (2006). Giving Circles: Growing Grassroots Philanthropy. *Nonprofit and Voluntary Sector Quarterly*, 35(3), 517–532.

Eisenberg, P. (1999). "The 'New Philanthropy' Isn't New—or Better." *The Chronicle of Philanthropy*. January 28, 1999.

Enright, Kathleen P., and Courtney Bourns. (2010). "The Case for Stakeholder Engagement." *Stanford Social Innovation Review*.

Faulk, Lewis, Jasmine McGinnis Johnson, and Jesse Lecy. (2016). "Competitive Advantage in Nonprofit Grant Markets: Implications of Network Embeddedness." *International Public Management Journal*. Published online January 25, 2016. DOI: 10.1080/10967494.2016.1141811.

Faulk, Lewis, Jurgen Willems, Jasmine McGinnis Johnson, and Amanda J. Stewart. (2015). "Network Connections and Competitively Awarded Funding: The Impacts of Board Network Structures and Status Interlocks on Nonprofit Organizations' Foundation Grant Acquisition." *Public Management Review*. Published online December 8, 2015. DOI: 10.1080/14719037.2015.1112421.

Foundation Center. (2016). *Foundation Stats*. Retrieved January 2016. http://data.foundationcenter.org/#/foundations/all/nationwide/total/list/2013.

Frumkin, Peter. (1999). "Private Foundations as Public Institutions: Regulation, Professionalization, and the Redefinition of Organized Philanthropy." In *Philanthropic Foundations: New Scholarship, New Possibilities*. Ellen Condliffe Lagemann, ed. (pp. 69–98). Bloomington: Indiana University Press.

Gersick, Kelin E., and Deanne Stone. (2004). *Generations of Giving: Leadership and Continuity in Family Foundations*. Lexington Books.

Giving USA. (2013). *Giving USA 2013: The Annual Report on Philanthropy for the Year 2012*. Giving USA Foundation and The Center on Philanthropy at Indiana University.

Goel, Vindu and Nick Wingfield. (2015). "Mark Zuckerberg Vows to Donate 99% of His Facebook Shares for Charity." *The New York Times*, December 1, 2015. http://www.nytimes.com/2015/12/02/technology/mark-zuckerberg-facebook-charity.html?_r=0

González-Rivera, C. (2009). "Diversity on Foundation Boards of Directors." Greenlining Institute. http://greenlining. org/resources/pdfs/foundationboarddiversityreport 2009. pdf.

Graddy, Elizabeth A., and Donald L. Morgan. (2006). "Community Foundations, Organizational Strategy, and Public Policy." *Nonprofit and Voluntary Sector Quarterly* 35(4), 605–630.

Grønbjerg, Kirsten A., Laura Martell, and Laurie Paarlberg. (2000). "Philanthropic Funding of Human Services: Solving Ambiguity through the Two-Stage Competitive Process." *Nonprofit and Voluntary Sector Quarterly* 29, suppl 1, 9–40.

Hall, P. D. (2006). "A Historical Overview of Philanthropy, Voluntary Associations, and Nonprofit Organizations in the United States, 1600–2000." In W. W. Powell and R. Steinberg (Eds.) *The Nonprofit Sector: A Research Handbook, Second Edition*, 32–65. New Haven: Yale University Press.

Hammack, D. C., and Anheier, H. K. (2013). *A Versatile American Institution: The Changing Ideals and Realities of Philanthropic Foundations.* Brookings Institution Press.

Hoffman, M. (2009). "The Unraveling of Donor Intent: Lawsuits and Lessons." Partnership for Philanthropic Planning. http://www.pgdc.com/pgdc/unraveling-donor-intent-lawsuits-and-lessons.

Hopkins, B. R. (2005). *Nonprofit Law Made Easy.* John Wiley & Sons.

Irvin, R. A. (2007). "Endowments: Stable Largesse or Distortion of the Polity?" *Public Administration Review*, 67(3), 445–457.

Karl, Barry D., and Stanley N. Katz. "Foundations and Ruling Class Elites." *Daedalus* (1987): 1–40.

Kerlin, J. A., and Reid, E. J. (2010). "The Financing and Programming of Advocacy in Complex Nonprofit Structures." *Nonprofit and Voluntary Sector Quarterly*, 39(5), 802–824.

Lenkowsky, L. (2012). "Foundations and Corporate Philanthropy." In Lester Salamon (Ed.), *The State of Nonprofit America.* Washington, DC: Brookings Institution Press.

Lewin, T. (2008). "Princeton Settles Money Battle Over Gift." *The New York Times*, December 10, 2008. http://www.nytimes.com/2008/12/11/education/11princeton.html.

Lindeman, E. (1988). *Wealth & Culture: A Study of One Hundred Foundations and Community Trusts and Their Operations During the Decade 1921–1930.* New Brunswick, NJ. Transaction Publishers.

Madoff, R. (2014). "5 Myths About Payout Rules for Donor-Advised Funds." *The Chronicle of Philanthropy*, Jan. 13, 2014.

McGinnis, Jasmine, and Shena Ashley. "The Family Difference? Exploring the Congruence in Grant Distribution Patterns between Family and Independent Foundations." *The Foundation Review* 3, no. 4 (2011): 74–81.

McGinnis Johnson, Jasmine. (2013). "Necessary But Not Sufficient: The Impact of Community Input on Grantee Selection." *Administration & Society*, 48(1): 73–103.

Mehrling, P., 1999. *Spending Policies for Foundations: The Case for Increased Grants Payout.* National Network of Grantmakers.

Mosley, J. E., and Galaskiewicz, J. (2010). "The Role of Foundations in Shaping Social Welfare Policy and Services: The Case of Welfare Reform." In H. K. Anheier and D. C. Hammack (Eds.), *American Foundations: Roles and Contributions* (pp. 182–204). Brookings Institution Press.

National Philanthropic Trust. (2015). *2015 Donor Advised Fund Report.* http://www.nptrust.org/daf-report/downloads.html.

Osili, Una, Reema Bhakta, Amy Thayer, Amir Hayat, Adriene Davis Kalugyer, Cynthia Hyatte, Heng (Ellie) Qu, and Patterson, Zachary (2013). *Leveraging the Power of Foundations: An Analysis of Program-Related Investing.* Lilly Family School of Philanthropy.

Ostrander, S. A. (2007). "The Growth of Donor Control: Revisiting the Social Relations of Philanthropy." *Nonprofit and Voluntary Sector Quarterly*, 36(2), 356–372.

Ostrower, F., and Stone, M. M. (2006). "Governance: Research Trends, Gaps, and Future Prospects." *The Nonprofit Sector: A Research Handbook, Second Edition*, 612–628.

Prewitt, Kenneth. (2006). "Foundations." In *The Non-Profit Sector: A Research Handbook*. Walter W. Powell and Richard Steinberg, eds. (pp. 355–377). New Haven, CT: Yale University Press.

Reckhow, Sarah. (2012). *Follow the Money: How Foundation Dollars Change Public School Politics*. Oxford University Press, USA.

Schaefer, Patricia. (2015). "Donor-Advised Funds Growing Ever Faster: How Should Nonprofits Access the Wealth?" *Nonprofit Quarterly*, November 19, 2015.

Silk, T. (2004). Corporate Philanthropy and Law in the United States: A Practical Guide to Tax Choices and an Introduction to Compliance with Anti-Terrorism Laws. *International Journal of Not-for-Profit Law*, 6(3).

Simon, John. (1995). "The Regulation of American Foundations: Looking Backward at the Tax Reform Act of 1969." *Voluntas*, 6(3): 243–254.

Smith, S. R. (2010). "Foundations and Public Policy." In *American Foundations: Roles and Contributions*. H. K. Anheier and D. C. Hammack, eds. (pp. 371–387). Brookings Institution Press.

Steele, E., and Steuerle, C. E. (2015). *Discerning the True Policy Debate over Donor-Advised Funds*. Urban Institute. Tax Policy and Charities Initiative.

Steuerle, C. Eugene and Martin A. Sullivan. (1995). "Toward More Simple and Effective Giving: Reforming the Tax Rules for Charitable Contributions and Charitable Organizations." *American Journal of Tax Policy* 12(2): 399–447.

Stewart, Amanda J., and Lewis Faulk. (2014). "Administrative Growth and Grant Payouts in Nonprofit Foundations: Fulfilling the Public Good amid Professionalization?" *Public Administration Review*, 74(5): 630–639. DOI: 10.1111/puar.12231.

Toepler, S. (2004). "Ending Payout as We Know It: A Conceptual and Comparative Perspective on the Payout Requirement for Foundations." *Nonprofit and voluntary sector quarterly*, 33(4), 729–738.

Troyer, Thomas A. (2000). "The 1969 Private Foundation Law: Historical Perspective on Its Origins and Underpinnings." *Exempt Organization Tax Review* 27: 52–65.

Tyler, John. Transparency in Philanthropy: An Analysis of Accountability, Fallacy and Volunteerism. Washington, DC Philanthropy Roundtable. (2013). Retrieved January 2015. http://www.philanthropyroundtable.org/file_uploads/Transparency_in_Philanthropy.pdf.

Chapter 9

New Ways of Creating Social Value

Hybrids and Impact Investing

Joseph Cordes, Nathan Dietz, C. Eugene Steuerle, and Erica Broadus

INTRODUCTION

Economists and lawyers note that what differentiates nonprofit from for-profit organizations is the presence of a legal "non-distribution constraint": nonprofit managers and employees cannot directly appropriate any profit or surplus garnered by an organization that has the legal status of a nonprofit. Over time, however, the dividing line between traditional nonprofits and for-profit enterprises has become less clear-cut as the range of entities involved in creating social value has grown to include charities that rely heavily on donations (e.g., United Way), nonprofits that earn (untaxable) income (e.g., Goodwill Industries), for-profit businesses or their leaders who establish charities (e.g., Fidelity Charitable), and commercial entities that set aside money to serve social purposes (e.g., Google).

Recently, there were new entrants into the ranks of social enterprises that further defy easy definition because they combine attributes of both nonprofits and for-profits in a single entity. Such hybrids cross legal boundaries between charities and for-profit enterprises to allow investors and social entrepreneurs to pursue the social change they desire, yet avoid some of the constraints on behavior imposed on either nonprofit or for-profit organizations.

The CEO and cofounder of Facebook, Mark Zuckerberg, and his wife, Priscilla Chan, provide one example. Following the birth of their first child, Zuckerberg and Chan pledged to donate 99 percent of the couple's Facebook shares to charitable causes during their lifetimes. Naturally, this announcement made headlines; as of January 2016, the couple's wealth is estimated at $35.7 billion. But in addition to the pledge's enormity, the couple's philanthropic vehicle of choice caused a stir. Rather than giving directly to a nonprofit or establishing a foundation, they formed the Chan Zuckerberg

Initiative, a for-profit limited liability company. Though the Chan Zuckerberg Initiative was established mainly for the purpose of engaging in charitable-like activities, it can engage in activities not permissible for, or more difficult for, charities such as making private investments, raising private equity, hiring lobbyists, donating to political campaigns, and participating in political debates.

Several factors have contributed to the growing interest in creating hybrid legal forms. These include greater emphasis on using performance-based metrics such as social return on investment (SROI) to gage the impact of nonprofit organizations, and the creation of venues for program-related investments (PRIs) by philanthropic foundations, as well as renewed, if at times controversial, calls for greater social responsibility in the for-profit sector. Also, for very wealthy donors, whose income is largely in the form of unrealized capital gains, there is little incentive to limit their gifts to traditional charities because their contributions may be well in excess of deductions allowed against realized income (Steuerle 2016). The focus of this chapter is on the growing convergence between the goods and services provided by both nonprofit and for-profit enterprises.

In the analysis below, we take up the following questions: (1) What is the range of possible hybrid forms that strategically combine social purpose with for-profit activities? (2) How does the emergence of these forms impact the space occupied by more traditional social enterprises? (3) What are the public policy implications of the emergence of what some have termed the fourth sector? We then provide a brief outline of the common legal structures that have been adopted by states to date and a summary of the problems facing those who try to create such structures while accommodating both their charitable and profit-making purposes.

COMMON "ALTERNATIVE" ORGANIZATIONAL STRUCTURES

Table 9.1 below is a useful starting point for examining reasons for the emergence of hybrid organizational structures among social enterprises. Table 9.1 shows a continuum of possible legal structures ranging from purely donative nonprofit organizations to for-profit organizations without charitable purposes. The nonprofit end of the continuum comprises organizations that have 501(c)(3) legal status, which exempts all (or most) income received by such organizations from taxation and allows them to receive tax-deductible private contributions. Entities at this end of the spectrum focus on mission-related activities such as providing services or serving clients and, in exchange for their tax-favored status, must accept a nondistribution constraint that prevents trustees, managers, or staff from directly appropriating the value created by such activities. (The non-distribution constraint is enforced easily when it comes to any surplus earned, since there are no shareholders. However, because excess compensation is hard to measure, managers and staff may still be able to draw down surplus funds.) Other distinguishing features of organizations at this end of the spectrum are accountability to multiple stakeholders—the general public as well as their beneficiaries and donors—and a primary reliance on contributions and grants, among their revenue sources.

The other end of the spectrum in table 9.1 is occupied by for-profit businesses. In contrast to pure nonprofit organizations, such enterprises see as their mission the generation of economic surplus (profit) to be distributed to owners and shareholders along with the maximization of shareholder value. For-profit entities obtain their income on sales of goods and services, rely on access to private capital markets to finance their operations, and are accountable in the marketplace to their shareholders and creditors.

In practice, however, the range of possible organizational forms is wider than indicated by these polar cases. Many nonprofit organizations, for example, rely as much or more on revenue from sales of goods and services as they do on contributions and grants (see chapters 2, 3, and 4, by Steuerle et al., Smith, and Brody and Cordes, respectively, in this volume). Nonprofit reliance on fees, charges, and returns on assets for much of their income is not new. What has changed, however, is that more nonprofits are making strategic decisions to combine business and charitable activities. Thus, although one still finds organizations conforming to the canonical ideal types of nonprofit and for-profit organization, respectively, one now can find many examples of enterprises combining important attributes of both nonprofit and for-profit organizations.

One example of such a combination is that of a nonprofit organization that owns one or more for-profit subsidiaries. Benetech, for example, is the umbrella name for two public charities (Beneficent Inc. and Beneficent Technologies) and a wholly owned for-profit engineering subsidiary, Bengineering. The umbrella company, a registered nonprofit, was created from the sale of Arkenstone, a nonprofit that specialized in the sale of products designed for the visually impaired. Benetech's business model is more ambitious: rather than producing and selling products, they develop new technologies, build markets for them, and sell them to for-profit companies that can produce them efficiently and sell them at affordable prices. Organizing as a nonprofit allows Benetech to focus on the design of socially valuable products that for-profit organizations might not pursue because of their limited profit potential. The organization funds its work by approaching large donors with detailed business plans that describe how the project will eventually become financially self-sustaining while providing significant social value. Meanwhile, the for-profit engineering component allows Benetech to pay market wages for the best-qualified technical expertise to carry out the development of the products.

Nonprofit organizations can also enter into less formal partnerships with for-profit companies to increase their capacity to promote charitable causes. The Susan G. Komen Foundation, founded in 1982 in memory of Susan Komen, is based on a promise by the founder to end breast cancer forever. Komen's iconic pink ribbon is well known in the cause-related-marketing arena and garners millions of dollars each year for the organization through corporate partnerships and programs. Some of the most prominent partnerships include "Cook for the Cure," through which Kitchen Aid has donated $10 million since 2001, and Bank of America's "Pink Ribbon Affinity" program, which has contributed $6 million since 2009. These partnerships have brought the foundation additional marketing resources that have raised Komen's profile, but have also increased scrutiny and criticism of its tactics. Komen has been criticized for its partnerships with Kentucky Fried Chicken (whose food is perceived as unhealthy) and the National Football League (following bad press related to player misconduct and the health risks of football). Komen can be viewed as a cautionary tale for nonprofit organizations whose high-powered marketing campaigns are similar to those used by large corporations. Critics have cited the foundation for "pink-washing": oversaturation of breast cancer–related promotions that encourage a culture of consumerism. Perhaps in response, Komen and New York Attorney General Eric T. Schneiderman established consumer guidelines and posted on the foundation's website, to give consumers a clearer understanding of what their donations support.

While the Susan G. Komen Foundation uses its corporate connections to support its cause-related marketing campaign, many other nonprofits use their business operations to fund their core mission with less publicity. Many nonprofits derive a substantial amount of their annual revenues from earned income—the sale of products or services—and direct the proceeds toward their charitable activities. For many people, Goodwill Industries is a business that operates a chain of stores that accept donations of used and surplus clothes and materials and sell them at a discount. However, Goodwill's mission is not to sell secondhand goods, but to "enhance the dignity and quality of life of individuals and families by strengthening communities, eliminating barriers to opportunity, and helping people in need reach their full potential through learning and the power of work." In 2014, Goodwill's job training programs helped over 318,000 people find jobs and helped 26.4 million people obtain the training and support they need to seek employment in industries such as banking, information technology, and health care (Goodwill 2016).

New Community Corporation (NCC) operates a number of for-profit businesses through a community development nonprofit based in Newark,

New Jersey. It helps "residents of inner cities improve the quality of their lives to reflect individual God-given dignity and personal achievement" (New Community Corporation 2015). As one of the largest and most comprehensive community development organizations in the United States, NCC provides access to housing, health care, education, job training, childcare, and economic development. NCC has owned and managed a wide variety of for-profit businesses in Newark's Central Ward, including Priory Restaurant; a Pathmark supermarket; Dunkin' Donuts; NCC Neighborhood Shopping Center; The World of Foods food court, which housed Pizza Hut, Nathan's, Taco Bell, and NCC's Southern Kitchen; the NCC Print & Copy Shop; and Fashion Institute, which produces garments, upholstery, and uniforms (Cordes and Steuerle 2009). Not only have these businesses provided revenue for NCC's community-based programs, but they have also benefited Central Ward residents by bringing valuable services and jobs into a depressed inner-city area.

In other cases, an entity that is legally organized as a for-profit business has enjoyed positive publicity after following through on commitments to devote a portion of its profits to charitable causes. To take one well-known example, Newman's Own, which the late actor Paul Newman started from his home, now sells over 200 products (mostly organic food products) to a global market. From the beginning, the company pledged to bestow 100 percent of all profits after taxes, and all licensing revenue, to the Newman's Own Foundation. As of January 2016, the foundation has given $450 million to beneficiaries such as the SeriousFun Children's Network, a global community of camps and programs founded by Paul Newman that empowers children with serious illnesses to believe in themselves and lead fuller lives, and Shining Hope for Communities, which provides free education for girls and a network of empowerment and poverty alleviation programs in Nairobi, Kenya (Newman's Own 2015).

The newest form of social enterprise occupies a place in the middle of the spectrum depicted in table 9.1, though tending more toward the for-profit end. Like other for-profit businesses, but unlike nonprofits, such enterprises eschew imposing the nondistribution constraint on themselves and thus have as a goal garnering a profit that can be distributed to owners, workers, and shareholders. However, unlike for-profit businesses, these enterprises care not only about the traditional profit and loss statement but also about the achievement of other, social objectives. For instance, such businesses might produce and sell goods and services for profit, but be willing to accept less than the maximum profit possible in order to offer their products and services to the poor at substantial discounts (Wexler 2009).

Panera Cares community cafés are one example. Panera Bread, a national chain of casual dining restaurants, launched its first nonprofit café through the Panera Bread Foundation in 2010. Panera's approach is "designed to help raise awareness about the very serious and pervasive problem of food insecurity (hunger) in the U.S." Patrons act on an honor system and pay what they can, from nothing at all to any amount above the suggested retail price. Residual funds cover operating costs and make up for those who cannot pay. Additionally, the cafés serve local communities by conducting job training programs and allowing patrons to volunteer for one hour to "pay" for their meals.

The middle region of table 9.1 is also the place where various types of partnerships between for-profit and nonprofit organizations can be found. For many nonprofit organizations, the challenge they face is how to work with for-profit organizations, or enter into revenue-producing ventures, without jeopardizing their tax exempt status. Many nonprofit entities consider creating so-called hybrid enterprises that involve formal partnerships with for-profit organizations. However, such arrangements present definite challenges for nonprofits. Robert Wexler, a lawyer who frequently provides legal advice to social enterprises, notes, "The two most complicated issues that typically arise in the hybrid model are (1) taking substantive and procedural steps to avoid any excess benefits, and (2) ensuring that the activities of the for-profit and the charity can be sufficiently separated so that the activities of the business are not attributed to the charity, thereby compromising its tax exempt status." Wexler gives the example of an entrepreneur who wants to form a nonprofit entity that "owns" a website that provides educational content, and also a for-profit enterprise that will "manage" the website—in particular, to attract advertising for the site and its products. The entrepreneur's major challenge in this case is to make sure that the two types of activities are different enough to justify the need to create two separate legal entities (Wexler 2009).

Recently, these mixed organization forms have grown in popularity and are hard to classify using a one-dimensional spectrum anchored by purely donative nonprofit and non-charitable for-profit organizations. One important factor creating a more porous border between nonprofit and profit-making organizations and activities is an economy-wide shift in consumer demand toward the kinds of goods and services that nonprofits provide, which leads profit-making organizations to compete more in these realms (Cordes et al. 2004; Tuckman 2004). Thus, the current economy produces more products of the sorts associated with organizational models B and H in table 9.1—products that could, but need not, qualify as charitable under the Internal Revenue Service (IRS) 501(c)(3) definition.

A striking example is health care, which used to make up 1/30th of the economy and now is more than 1/6th of it. Similarly, the production of knowledge or information is a rapidly growing sector of the economy that, though often associated with the nonprofit sector, can be sold for profit or not. Perhaps just as important, as information-related goods have become more valuable, nonprofits also find themselves possessing potentially valuable

Table 9.1 A Continuum of Organizational Forms

Organizational Form	Examples/Organizational Features
A. Pure nonprofit	Receipts primarily from contributions, not operations
B. Nonprofit whose core charitable activities are financed primarily by fees and charges	Nonprofit health care and education; also arts, social services
C. Nonprofit that operates businesses in areas related to its charitable mission	University bookstores; hospital laundries and catering services; job training programs
D. Nonprofits in partnership with for-profit business	Cause-related marketing, corporate sponsorships
E. Nonprofits with active stakes in for-profit businesses	Nonprofits with substantial shares in for-profit affiliates
F. Not-for-profit firms	Organizations legally organized as private businesses or corporations but distribute everything as wages
G. For-profit businesses contributing preannounced shares of profits to charity	Ben and Jerry's, Target Stores, Newman's Own
H. For-profits in direct competition with nonprofits	Hospitals, for-profit education providers
I. Pure for-profit business	No outputs defined as education, health, or other product that could also be defined as charitable

assets that are produced jointly with their primary mission-related activities. Exploiting the revenue potential of such assets may require creating hybrid forms or partnerships with for-profits as in organizational models D, E, and F.

As the inputs and outputs of production become more and more alike in both sectors, one should not be surprised to find more overlapping organizational structure through, for example, more subsidiaries (or related organizations) in one sector controlled by a member of the other sector, and more partnerships between nonprofits and for-profits producing related or complementary goods and services. At the individual level, workers in each sector would also be more apt to have easily transferable skills, permitting them to move back and forth between sectors not only at different points in their careers, but even daily on the job.

This "new economy" is also likely to be more conducive to creating a pool of potential entrepreneurs whose skills could be used to found either for-profit businesses or nonprofit organizations. Entrepreneurial skills are also more portable between the nonprofit and for-profit sectors. Table 9.2 below shows clearly that occupations with significant nonprofit penetration have grown more rapidly than other occupations between 2004 and 2014.

Indeed, some observers cite the growth in interest in such hybrid forms as an indication that a "fourth sector," composed of organizations that share

Table 9.2 Relative Growth of Industries with Potentially Charitable Output

Industry	2012 NAICS	Employment					Compound Annual Rate of Change (%)	
		Thousands of Jobs			Change			
		2004	2014	2024	2004–2014	2014–2024	2004–2014	2014–2024
Nonprofit-Related Sectors								
Computer systems design and related services	5415	1,149	1,778	2,187	629	409	4.5	2.1
Management, scientific, and technical consulting services	5416	763	1,244	1,574	481	329	5.0	2.4
Social assistance	624	2,374	3,367	3,698	993	331	3.6	0.9
Other information services	519	117	218	251	101	33	6.4	1.4
Museums, historical sites, and similar institutions	712	118	145	160	27	14	2.1	0.9
Education services: private	61	2,763	3,417	3,756	655	339	2.2	0.9
Ambulatory health care services	621	4,952	6,645	8,978	1,693	2,333	3.0	3.1
Performing arts, spectator sports, and related industries	711	368	448	468	80	20	2.0	0.4
Religious, grantmaking, civic, professional, and similar organizations	NA	2,908	2,964	3,032	57	67	0.2	0.2
Scientific research and development services	5417	550	635	674	85	39	1.4	0.6
Other professional, scientific, and technical services	5419	507	630	708	122	78	2.2	1.2
Software publishers	5112	236	313	393	77	81	2.9	2.3
Legal services	5411	1,163	1,120	1,129	−43	10	−0.4	0.1
Advertising, public relations, and related services	5418	429	476	486	47	11	1.0	0.2
Subtotal		18,396	23,399	27,494	5,003	4,094	2.4	1.6
Other Sectors		125,651	127,141	132,835	1,490	5,695	0.1	0.4
All Sectors		144,047	150,540	160,329	6,493	9,789	0.4	0.6

characteristics found separately in the nonprofit, for-profit, and public sectors, is emerging (Sabeti 2009). The "fourth sector" is sometimes described as an "evolutionary process" that not only stimulates the creation of organizations that pursue social purpose while engaging in business activities but also pushes existing organizations to "grow" in the same way. While the ultimate result of this evolutionary process may be a large, influential, and constantly growing new breed of organizations, most observers would agree that government has been challenged to design legal forms that meet the needs of enterprises that want to respond to these new forces.

HOW HAS GOVERNMENT BEEN INVOLVED, AND WHAT CHANGES HAS GOVERNMENT INVOLVEMENT PRODUCED?

Although a budding nonprofit or for-profit entrepreneur may wish to work in an environment in which he or she can draw from the best features of different organizational forms, structural or legal constraints prevent organizations from moving freely between one type of enterprise and another. For example, some nonprofit organizations have always derived the majority of their revenues from earned income and have adopted business practices that are more commonly found in the for-profit sector. The law, especially the nondistribution constraint, limits the way these organizations can spend their revenues and also imposes additional taxes for income unrelated to the organization's core business and for commercial business that does not fit into the fairly extensive definitions of what is considered charitable. Similarly, many for-profit organizations have sought ways to promote their social missions without neglecting responsibility to their shareholders. In some cases, "those who oversaw and managed such companies had to choose between benefitting owners and hurting those who provided labor or vice versa. What arguably qualified those enterprises as hybrids was that it was not always the owners who won!" (Tyler et al. 2015).

According to a 2007 poll conducted by the Social Enterprise Alliance, 71 percent of social entrepreneurs said that the biggest challenge they faced was finding the right legal structure (Bromberger 2008). The new legal forms that have emerged in recent years have been motivated, at least in part, by this dissatisfaction with the current alternatives. However, the number of available varieties of hybrid organizations suggests that policymakers have responded to this demand in different ways under different circumstances. In the U.S. alone, state governments have created several different models for organizations to choose from (see table 9.3). These models share many basic features, primarily because the basic forces that attract organizations to hybrid organizational forms are not new. One of the reasons an organization

Table 9.3 States with Hybrid Legal Forms, November 2015

	L3C	Benefit Corporation	Social Purpose Corporation	Potential Holder of Records
Alabama	No	No	No	N/A
Alaska	No	No	No	N/A
Arizona	No	Yes	No	Arizona Corporation Commission
Arkansas	No	Yes	No	Secretary of State
California	No	Yes	Yes	Secretary of State and/or Attorney General
Colorado	No	Yes	No	Secretary of State
Connecticut	No	Yes	No	Secretary of State
Delaware	No	Yes	No	Secretary of State
District of Columbia	No	Yes	No	Department of Consumer and Regulatory Affairs
Florida	No	Yes	Yes	Department of State Division of Corporations
Georgia	No	No	No	N/A
Hawaii	No	Yes	No	Department of Commerce and Consumer Affairs-Business Registration Division
Idaho	No	Yes	No	Secretary of State
Illinois	Yes	Yes	No	Secretary of State
Indiana	No	Yes	No	Secretary of State
Iowa	No	No	No	N/A
Kansas	No	No	No	N/A
Kentucky	No	No	No	N/A
Louisiana	Yes	Yes	No	Secretary of State
Maine	Yes	No	No	Secretary of State
Maryland	Yes	Yes	No	State Department of Assessments and Taxation
Massachusetts	No	Yes	No	Secretary of the Commonwealth
Michigan	Yes	No	No	Michigan Department of Licensing and Regulatory Affairs, Securities and Commercial Licensing Bureau
Minnesota	No	Yes	No	Secretary of State
Mississippi	No	No	No	N/A
Missouri	No	No	No	N/A
Montana	No	Yes	No	Secretary of State
Nebraska	No	Yes	No	Secretary of State
Nevada	No	Yes	No	Secretaty of State
New Hampshire	No	Yes	No	Secretary of State
New Jersey	No	Yes	No	State of New Jersey Division of Revenue and Enterprise Services-Business Records Service
New Mexico	No	No	No	N/A
New York	No	Yes	No	Department of State, Division of Corporations, State Records & UCC
North Carolina	Previously	No	No	Secretary of State
North Dakota	No	No	No	N/A
Ohio	No	No	No	N/A
Oklahoma	No	No	No	N/A
Oregon	No	Yes	No	Secretary of State
Pennsylvania	No	Yes	No	Department of State-Bureau of Corporations and Charitable Organizations
Rhode Island	Yes	Yes	No	Office of the Secretary of State-Division of Business Services
South Carolina	No	Yes	No	Secretary of State
South Dakota	No	No	No	N/A
Tennessee	No	Yes	No	Secretary of State
Texas	No	No	No	N/A
Utah	Yes	Yes	No	Utah Department of Commerce Division of Corporations and Commercial Code
Vermont	Yes	Yes	No	Secretary of State
Virginia	No	Yes	No	State Corporation Commission

	L3C	Benefit Corporation	Social Purpose Corporation	Potential Holder of Records
Washington	No	No	Yes	Secretary of State Corporations Division
West Virginia	No	Yes	No	Secretary of State
Wisconsin	No	No	No	N/A
Wyoming	Yes	No	No	Secretary of State

Note: Only includes states with past or present legislation on the books; introduced and pending legislation is not included.

might want to incorporate as a hybrid organization, rather than as a for-profit or tax exempt nonprofit organization, is to obtain the combined benefits associated with both of these "standard" organizational forms. More specifically, organizations will consider adopting a new legal form if they are convinced that the new "brand" will tell their stakeholders that they are interested in both profit-making and mission-oriented activities.

Organizations seeking to establish their commitment to social missions and responsible environmental practices can already seek several types of certifications. Some certifications are specific to particular types of industries. Fair Trade USA certifies agricultural producers who meet quality standards for workforce empowerment, economic development (especially in the places where the products are grown), social responsibility, and environmental stewardship (Fair Trade USA 2013), while LEED certification indicates that a building was recently built or renovated according to green principles or practices. However, the best-known certification system for "socially responsible businesses" is offered by B Lab, an entity that has encouraged thirty-one states (as of November 2015) to permit the formation of benefit corporations, a new legal form discussed below in more detail. While nonprofit organizations may seek one of these certifications so they can advertise their expertise in a particular substantive area, many of these certifications are aimed at for-profit organizations that are working against the presumption that they are not socially or environmentally responsible. Still, a growing number of organizations in both sectors have the incentive—and, in many cases, face pressure—to show that they can compete in the market for the goods and services they produce, while also conducting their business in a socially acceptable way.

Another reason that organizations might consider new hybrid legal forms is to attract revenue from sources that would be inaccessible for "pure" nonprofit or for-profit organizations. Nonprofit organizations that engage in commercial activities to generate revenues may need to pay tax on the proceeds, or may even lose their tax exempt status, if the activities are too far removed from their primary charitable purposes. Nonprofits are also unable to attract equity capital because they are unable to sell ownership stakes to investors. For-profit organizations, meanwhile, often feel constrained from pursuing social benefits because of the need to maximize profits for their shareholders (one reason that initiatives like Zuckerberg-Chan, noted above, often involve only a few individual "owners" who separate this activity from the corporations that might initially have generated much of their wealth). For-profits are also unable to allow donors to make tax exempt contributions to support their mission-oriented activities, even if they can provide the most efficient solution to social problems. As a recent article summarizes, "Hybrid entrepreneurs can claim the organizational benefits of only one of the multiple forms of value they create. Further complicating the choice is the reality that entrepreneurs cannot fully anticipate their future resource needs at the time legal registration choices are made, and thus risk being prematurely locked in to one sector or the other" (Battilana et al. 2012).

Finally, many organizations want more flexibility to focus on more than a single bottom line than nonprofit or for-profit organizations tend to have, even when they partner with other organizations. Nonprofit organizations cannot simply use the proceeds of their business activities for non-charitable purposes without jeopardizing their tax exempt status, so hybrid structures, in theory, promise to allow them at least some relief from this fiduciary responsibility. Conversely, for-profit organizations have somewhat more latitude to devote some of their profits to charitable causes, but may have trouble determining how much of their resources they can confidently devote to non-profitmaking activities.

Many for-profit organizations have devised specialized agreements that allow them to devote some of their resources to social purposes instead of holding them for distribution to their shareholders. For-profit organizations can divide owners into classes that have distinct responsibilities for the enterprise's profit-making and mission-oriented activities. In such cases, the division of responsibilities may be enforced by a contract signed by the owners, and decisions are made in some cases by supermajority votes to ensure that leadership supports all major policy choices (Tyler et al. 2015). Such agreements can help an organization pursue social benefits as long as all owners agree to abide by them, which is easier with fewer owners dedicated to a common set of goals. Still, some observers have noted that the law seems to protect the rights of shareholders if they stake specific claims to the organization's profits. Problems can also arise when the original owners decide to reduce their commitment to charitable causes, or when they are replaced by more profit-oriented leaders. As a recent paper concluded: "The collective weight of these uncertainties suggests that traditional for-profit entity forms—even if modified—will often not be the best vehicles for social enterprise, and, therefore, alternative forms are indeed in order" (Tyler et al. 2015).

In general, government legislation to create new organizational forms seems to be influenced by five major factors:

1. *Requiring that charitable contributions and income exempted from tax are devoted toward charitable activities*: One of the most complicated problems that governments face is how to ensure that organizations follow through on their implicit or stated promise that any tax benefit due to tax exemptions and charitable deductions will be devoted to activities that deliver social or charitable benefits. Tax exempt nonprofit organizations are constrained by a well-established regulatory structure, but the statutory language that allows hybrid organizations to form grants them much more flexibility in how they govern themselves. One major challenge for government is to create laws that prevent the organization's stakeholders from deciding to redistribute any subsidized revenues to its shareholders. In most cases, hybrid legislation (statutes that permit the creation of new legal forms) requires organizations to promise to engage in mission-oriented activities of some sort, but allows them considerable flexibility to decide how much emphasis they want to place on profit-making versus charitable activities.

2. *Enforcing the organization's commitment to charitable activities*: Requiring that charitable dollars go to charity is not enough. Other enforcement practices must also be developed. Almost all statutes require hybrid organizations to submit some type of public report that describes the efforts devoted to the pursuit of social or charitable benefits. This reporting requirement is viewed as necessary, given that the new organizational forms are not regulated as strictly as charities. These legal forms act as signals to the public that the organization has made a serious investment of resources into its charitable purpose and activities. Legislators face several common challenges when designing the reporting provisions. First, and most importantly, they need to develop standards that the public can use to assess the accuracy of the report's claims. Such standards help to distinguish the requirements from the expectations of corporate social responsibility, for which reporting has been described as "voluntary and malleable" (Esposito 2012). Second, the law must allow the government to enforce the reporting requirement to make sure that the reports submitted by hybrids meet quality standards. As several observers note, some standards are too vague to be enforceable: for instance, organizations can comply with some statutes simply by considering the interests of various groups of stakeholders, even if they take actions that are opposed to their interests (Tyler et al. 2015). Finally, the information reported by organizations needs to be available in a timely way to the interested public, and not simply reported to a government official for compliance purposes.

3. *Encouraging expanded investment in charitable causes*: Governments are also motivated to create hybrid organizational forms because they

are capable of attracting support outside of the normal sources of philanthropic funding. The motivation behind several prominent innovations is to encourage *impact investing*, a term that is used to refer to "an investment discipline that considers environmental, social and corporate governance criteria to generate long-term competitive financial returns and positive societal impact" (2010 US-SIF Report; quoted in Esposito 2013). For instance, the legal form known as the low-profit limited liability company (L3C; see below for more details) was designed, in part, to encourage PRIs by foundations, which are underused due to uncertainties about whether an investment will qualify as "program related." Several observers have argued that the need for social enterprises is driven at least in part by the "inevitable and irreversible" (Cohen 2014b) diminishment of government funding for social programs; see chapter 2, by Steuerle et al. in this volume, for charitable subsectors where funding was cut as well those where funding was increased. Regardless, the desire to increase the amount of private support for social and charitable causes has influenced the creation of new hybrid legal forms.

4. *Considering the interests of multiple stakeholder groups*: Although the specificity of the language can vary, hybrid statutes sometimes state that organizations can consider the interests of stakeholder populations, other than shareholders or investors, when making business decisions. Examples of stakeholder groups can include employees, customers (as beneficiaries of the organization's mission-related activities), the community where the organization is located, and the larger community that is affected by the organization's environmental practices. In most cases, the legislation does not specify how much attention the organization needs to pay to each type of stakeholder, or whether the needs of a particular group need to be considered at all.

5. *Encouraging innovation*: While government officials who craft hybrid legislation may not be purposely responding to this argument, supporters of hybrid legislation have argued that the new legal forms "democratize" the process of forming profit-seeking organizations that can devote resources to social or charitable purposes. The formation of a "traditional" for-profit organization that has a nonprofit organization as a subsidiary or partner, or the creation of articles of incorporation that specifically permit the organization to pursue charitable aims, often requires a great deal of costly legal work that is unaffordable to entrepreneurs who are not sufficiently capitalized. However, as some observers note, the process of forming a hybrid organization can also involve considerable work by lawyers, mainly because "templates" that can be used to guide their formation are not yet fully developed (Tyler et al. 2015).

NEW LEGAL ORGANIZATIONAL FORMS

In this section, we chronicle in a bit more detail the ways in which state governments in the United States have created several new types of hybrid organizations, partly in response to the demand from entrepreneurs and partly to satisfy public policy goals of legislators. Keep in mind that some observers, including those who advise the founders of new enterprises, feel that the safest and most prudent approach for an organization is the more traditional route of incorporating as a for-profit entity and, later, to consider partnering with other organizations, or even changing to another legal form. For one reason, whatever ease these new organizational forms may provide at the state level, they do nothing to change requirements of federal tax regulations.

Most observers also describe the available list of legal options as "nascent" or "preliminary," since the most prominent and prevalent legal forms (as of March 2016) share many common characteristics. The most common hybrid legal forms are the L3C, which is currently available in nine states as of November 2015; the benefit corporation, which has been adopted by thirty-one states; and two less common forms, flexible purpose corporations (FPCs) and social purpose corporations (SPCs). As of this writing, three states (Florida, California, and Washington) permit the formation of SPCs; in 2015, California retitled its statute and allowed all existing FPCs to continue operating as social purpose corporations. While dozens of articles have been written about these new hybrid organizational forms, this brief overview highlights the distinctive features of each variety, and discusses the impact that their introduction has had, or may have, on the ability of nonprofits to compete in the "marketplace" for charitable goods and services.

L3Cs

The L3C is an offshoot of the limited liability corporation, or LLC. LLCs may be formed in all fifty states as well as in the District of Columbia and are organized like corporations, but allow income to "flow through" the entity to the owners and investors for tax purposes. Most importantly, they can be formed for any lawful purpose, while a non-LLC corporation needs to be formed for a lawful business purpose (Wexler 2014). The states that allow L3Cs have amended their LLC statutes to permit the formation of entities that are specifically designed to receive PRIs from private foundations (Esposito 2012). To provide assurance that they will serve as "safe harbors" for PRIs, L3Cs are required by statute to ensure that the enterprise significantly furthers "charitable" purposes as defined by the Internal Revenue Code—not broadly social or public purposes—and that "but for" the connection to those purposes the entity would not have been created. Additionally, the production of income cannot be a significant purpose of an L3C (although they are allowed to undertake profit-making activities), and L3Cs are prohibited from engaging in political activities (Wexler 2014).

In principle, the existence of L3Cs should have stimulated the widespread use of PRIs by foundations. However, in practice, this has not occurred, partly because foundations have not responded to the appearance of L3Cs by awarding more PRIs. With only a few prominent exceptions, foundations have preferred to fulfill their "payout" requirements by awarding grants rather than PRIs, because PRIs require additional monitoring, specialized expertise in lending, and—at least in the eyes of many foundations—prior approval from the IRS for the investment (Cohen 2014a). Moreover, many of the founders of the first L3Cs were attracted to the legal form because they permitted access to new markets for their services, not because they made their enterprise more appealing to potential PRI investors. According to several of the first entrepreneurs to form L3Cs in Vermont, many of them chose the new legal form to obtain greater access to foreign markets like China, which was unwilling to do business with nonprofit organizations (Schmidt 2010).

The L3C has also been criticized for the way the legislation attempts to enforce the organization's commitment to its charitable purpose. The statutory language makes the requirements clear: for L3C organizations, "charitable purposes must dominate" and the purpose of maximizing profits for the owners cannot be "significant" (Tyler et al. 2015). However, L3Cs are not required to publish, or even to submit to regulators, specific information about their mission-oriented activities or their finances, as tax exempt nonprofits are required to do. As a result, the information available about an L3C's recent charitable activities—or even its intended purpose—is often "painfully thin," giving regulators little to work with if they choose to investigate the organization's commitment to its charitable purpose. However, the L3C statutes have also been criticized for provisions that would apparently strip an organization of its L3C designation, and convert it automatically to a regular LLC, if it fails to fulfill the charitable-purpose requirements. Because this reversion would permit the organization to retain its contributions while removing the incentive to use them for charitable goals, this provision has been called "self-defeating" and "illogical and unfortunate" (Tyler et al. 2015).

As a result of these perceived flaws and the failure of L3Cs to attract PRIs from foundations, L3C legislation has been criticized as being unnecessary and dangerously vague. The critics of the L3C form have pointed out that L3C statutes do not permit any ventures that cannot be achieved by LLCs, and that the safeguards that would prevent the owners from diverting charitable resources to private investors are inadequate. Some observers argue that L3Cs are only tangentially related to the nonprofit sector, given that L3Cs tend to be formed as for-profit organizations that want to engage in some social benefit activities. Others note that the L3C designation retains at least some power to signal to investors that "L3Cs are superior to nonprofits in their ability to function and generate a return on investment because [. . .] L3Cs are tuned into and responsive to the market" (Cohen 2014a). Perhaps as an indication that the criticisms of L3Cs have taken hold, their growth has slowed in recent years: North Carolina's repeal of its L3C statute in January 2014 has led some to wonder whether support for the concept is eroding.

Benefit Corporations

While the momentum in support of L3Cs seems to have stalled, interest in another legal form, the benefit corporation, has grown in the last few years. By far the most prevalent type of hybrid organization, benefit corporations, can be formed in 31 states, as of November 2015. Although the legislative language that enables the creation of benefit corporations varies by states, most states have patterned their legislation after one of two models: the Model Benefit Corporation Legislation (or "Model Act") and the "Delaware version," which is closely related to the Model Act.

The Model Act is a product of a for-profit organization called B Lab, which has been very successful in marketing the concept to state governments. B Lab also offers certification services to its customers, for-profit organizations that are allowed to license the designation of "certified B Corporations" if they include socially beneficial standards into their governing documents (Wexler 2009). Although many observers confuse the "B Corp" certification with the legal form known as a benefit corporation, the benefit corporation is a hybrid organization with several distinctive features.

The Model Act spells out requirements for purpose, accountability, and transparency that are found, in original or modified form, in the state statutes. Benefit corporations must form around the purpose of providing general social benefits and, if desired, specific social benefits. The requirements are not specific: general public benefits create a "material positive impact on society and the environment," while specific benefits can be chosen from a list of examples, some of which would count as charitable purposes under the IRS definitions. Benefit corporations have considerable latitude to choose the general and specific social benefits that fit their missions, but in most states their work toward the general social benefit needs to be assessed against a third-party standard. Benefit corporations must also consider the impacts of their business decisions on six specific stakeholder interests, ranging from specific groups (the organization's workforce and customers) to larger concerns (the local and global environment; the long-term interests and capacity of the organization). The legislation does not tell the organization how to prioritize these interests and prevents stakeholders from holding the organization liable for not considering their interests. Instead, shareholders are empowered to enforce this duty (Esposito 2012).

The most distinctive feature of benefit corporations is the mention of third-party standards by which the organization's mission-oriented activities must be assessed. In all states, benefit corporations must produce an Annual Benefit Report (ABR), which is assessed against an external standard (Wexler 2014). The ABR usually contains narrative statements about how the benefit corporation pursued both general and specific public benefits, what obstacles they encountered while creating these benefits, and how the organization would assess its social and environmental performance (Esposito 2012). The statutory language that describes the ABR requirement tends to include very specific language about how to ensure that the assessment standard is created by an unbiased third party, but does not require the ABR to be written or certified by a third party (Brakman Reiser 2013). While the lack of a verification process for the ABR and of standards to assess the results have been criticized by some observers, the ABR publication requirement enhances the transparency of the reporting process for benefit corporations.

In addition to the ABR, the benefit corporation also has a number of distinguishing features related to its governance process. In several states, the statutory language mandates the appointment of a benefit director, a board member whose primary responsibility is to create the ABR, and permits the appointment of a benefit officer, who is in charge of the process of creating general and specific public benefits. Many states also allow shareholders, directors, or others who are mentioned in the articles of incorporation to bring a benefit enforcement proceeding against the corporation when it has failed to provide sufficient general or specific public benefits. Like the ABR, these specific roles and processes add credibility to the benefit corporation's promise to devote a substantial amount of resources toward the creation of social benefits in addition to profits. However, questions remain about the limited capacity of state governments to provide oversight for charities in general (see chapter 5, by Lott and Fremont-Smith, this volume), let alone to enforce promises for social benefits and other specific governance requirements laid out in the Model Act and other statutes.

Flexible Purpose Corporations

The FPC was introduced in California in 2011. As of this writing, after California changed its law to convert all FPCs into SPCs (Chiodini 2014), which are discussed in detail below, the FPC legal form is not available in any US state. Like the benefit corporation, the FPC is designed to allow a corporation to take into account social purposes as well as profit making

(Wexler 2014). However, FPCs are required to only consider the specific social purposes that the corporation lists in its Articles of Incorporation (Brakman Reiser 2013), rather than benefits to the general public or to specific stakeholder groups (Wexler 2014). The unique characteristic of the FPC is found in its reporting requirements. In addition to publishing an ABR-style report that contains an end-of-year balance sheet, FPCs are required to publish periodic reports within forty-five days of a significant material expenditure related to the public benefits they promised to pursue. Like benefit corporations, these provisions are designed to boost confidence in the ability of FPCs to govern themselves, although critics noted that nothing interfered with the ability of the board of directors to determine the content of all required reports.

Social Purpose Corporations

Available in Washington state, Florida, and (since 2015) California, the SPC shares features with several other types of hybrid organizations, but offers investors more assurance of the organization's commitment to producing social benefits in addition to profits. SPCs must add language to their articles of incorporation that states that they are organized "in a manner intended to promote positive short-term or long-term effects of, or minimize adverse short-term or long-term effects of, the corporation's activities upon any or all of (1) the corporation's employees, suppliers, or customers; (2) the local, state, national, or world community; or (3) the environment" (Esposito 2012). The SPC can also list specific public benefits they intend to pursue; the reporting requirements for the organization's pursuit of social benefits are similar to those of the FPC, and the reports must be published on the organization's website.

However, the most distinctive feature of the SPC is the explicit warning, issued publicly to stakeholders in the organization's mission statement, that SPC leaders may decide to pursue social benefits instead of profits, even at the expense of shareholders (Tyler et al. 2015). While this language does not require SPC leaders to privilege social benefits over profits, it has been called "a notable development in social enterprise law," because it is explicitly designed to protect the interests of investors against the possibility of a "hostile takeover" by shareholders who want greater profits.

FUTURE DEVELOPMENTS

In the United States, the landscape of state hybrid legislation frequently changes (Brewer 2015c); entrepreneurs who are considering the creation of hybrid organizations face a wide variety of available alternatives. The states vary widely in terms of how much information is available about these organizations, since many states do not require hybrids to publish required reports, or any other information about their mission-oriented activities. This leaves the door open for organizations to claim the public benefits of a brand that is associated with socially responsible behavior while committing most, or all, of their resources to generating profits for shareholders. Some observers (Tyler et al. 2015) argue that this loophole can be filled by the creation of new legal forms that require the directors to make the social purpose primary and dominant, so that this purpose always takes precedence over profit maximization. While the landscape for hybrid organizations continues to change, some of the issues faced by hybrid organizations—as well as by nonprofit organizations that often compete with them in the market for resources and business opportunities—seem likely to persist.

Problems and pitfalls. The existing hybrid organizations face many of the challenges identified in an overview article published in 2012 in the Stanford Social Innovation Review (SSIR) (Battilana et al. 2012). Since the article's publication, new hybrid forms have become much more prevalent: for instance, twenty-two additional states have introduced legislation allowing benefit corporations to form. However, the appearance of new hybrid legal forms only adds to the regulatory issues, which include not simply compliance with the laws of the state of incorporation, but the laws of other states in which the charity may operate and of the federal government itself.

Legal structure. One of the main benefits that the new hybrid legal forms have over "traditional" partnerships, including subsidiary relationships between organizations from different sectors, is the impact of the "brand name" associated with the new form. In practice, many organizations that choose to organize themselves according to one of these new legal forms may enjoy the benefits associated with the new brand. However, the challenges these "new" hybrids encounter include the need to obtain services from providers that are unfamiliar with the specific needs of hybrid organizations, and the backlash against the claims made by some champions of these new legal forms.

In response to the claims that new hybrid forms represent the best of both worlds—for-profit efficiency combined with nonprofit nobility of purpose—several observers have risen to the defense of the traditional forms. After all, the traditional legal forms act as a powerful indicator of the organization's primary objective (McCambridge 2014), whereas an organization that claims to observe two bottom lines may not be productive or effective according to either one. One source of this suspicion is the fact that reporting requirements are not yet well developed enough to allow observers to evaluate the performance of hybrids. And how does one deal with organizations that change their legal forms or acquire certifications of their social purposes? One such example is Etsy, a publicly traded online shopping site with an Irish subsidiary. When their B Corp certification became publicly known, critics objected that Etsy was dodging Irish laws and attempting to paper over these concerns by securing B Corp certification. Still, some observers took a "let's wait and see" approach to this controversy, arguing that, as time passes, the actual performance of organizations like Etsy will settle some of these arguments (Brewer 2015a).

The unfamiliarity of these new legal forms means that organizations sometimes have problems finding the help they need to get started and to operate. Lawyers who want to offer advice to new hybrid organizations lack case law by which to offer sound advice to their clients (Tyler et al. 2015). The conscientious lawyer must search through the available precedents to learn about these new forms. Complicating the issue is the fact that the legislation governing these new forms varies across states, and some states do not allow the creation of any new hybrid forms. Lawyers must then familiarize themselves with the statutes and case law of other states to advise their clients (Tyler et al. 2015).

Financing. Another challenge facing new hybrid enterprises is that of raising capital to operate and grow. Some hybrids seek funding from for-profit-seeking investors for commercial activities, and turn to philanthropic sources and public subsidies for social activities (Battilana et al. 2012). The lack of a performance track record makes sales pitches to potential funders difficult. Hybrid organizations soliciting funding from both profit-seeking and traditional nonprofit financers face challenges in showing both that a market exists for their products or services and that they are capable of delivering substantial social benefits (Tyler et al. 2015). While certification can help, hybrids may feel the squeeze most acutely in fields such as education and health care, where they must compete against both nonprofit industry leaders in service provision and for-profit entities that offer higher returns to investors.

Customer-beneficiary distinctions. There is also an ethical issue that is unique to hybrids: the distinction between people who purchase their goods and services and the recipients of the social services they offer. For some hybrid organizations, the lack of a meaningful distinction is an important measure of their success: their objective is to sell their products or services at affordable prices to people who could not afford them at market prices (Battilana et al. 2012). Organizations that provide microfinancing, for instance, are some of the fastest-growing enterprises because the growth of the organization is directly tied to the success of their mission-oriented activities. Other hybrids, including highly successful enterprises like Hot Bread Kitchen or Greyston Bakery, have little overlap between their customers and their beneficiaries. However, even successful organizations in this category occasionally encounter the need to pursue success for both the profit-making and social services activities of an organization.

Organizational culture and talent development. Finally, hybrid organizations face staffing challenges. Experienced professionals often tend to have experience in either for-profit or nonprofit settings. Battilana et al. quote a Bolivian entrepreneur who sought to staff his microfinance enterprise by training his employees to perform both business-oriented and mission-oriented functions—or, in his words, by "converting social workers into bankers and bankers into social workers" (Battilana et al. 2012). The attempt led to confusion and resentment. The late Rick Cohen of the *Nonprofit Quarterly* expressed concern that the enthusiastic support of millennial entrepreneurs for profit-making, mission-driven enterprises appeared to be based on "belief and ideology" rather than experience, and that the reality of these hybrid enterprises might not live up to their ideals (Cohen 2014b).

Regulatory challenges. Lastly, regulators face their own challenges in dealing with hybrids. But investors and regulators must face up to scenarios in which the organization suddenly decides to devote fewer resources to mission-oriented activities. In 2012, Yvon Chouinard, the founder of Patagonia, a privately owned outdoor apparel company, registered as one of the first benefit corporations in California. Since 1986, Patagonia operated as a traditional business but donated 1 percent of sales or 10 percent of profits, whichever was greater, to environmental causes; it also implemented progressive and socially responsible workforce practices, such as no private offices at company headquarters and a cafeteria that serves mainly vegetarian meals (Patagonia 2016). Chouinard noted that the decision to reorganize as a benefit corporation would allow Patagonia to "stay mission-driven through succession, capital raises, and even changes in ownership, by institutionalizing the values, culture, processes, and high standards put in place by founding entrepreneurs" (King 2012). However, the protection offered by California to benefit corporations is not standard across states (Esposito 2012), and hybrid organizations everywhere are vulnerable to "hostile takeovers" in which shareholders transfer the organization's assets to a for-profit corporation. Some legal scholars have proposed remedies to the legislative language to increase protection against this possibility (Murray 2013), but the threat remains.

A related question, and one that has implications for nonprofit regulation, is where the regulatory authority for hybrid organizations should be located within state governments. Hybrid organizations are not obligated, as nonprofit charities are, to treat their assets as if they were held in a charitable trust. Only in Illinois are L3Cs regulated by the state attorney general through a state requirement that the assets be held in charitable trusts (Wexler 2013). Some observers argue that, unless the government is willing to require hybrids to devote their assets to charitable purpose, the attorney general's office need not serve as the regulatory agency. Moving the regulatory authority to another state agency would relieve the already-intense resource pressures on the attorneys' general offices, which are also responsible for regulating the nonprofit sector (Brakman Reiser 2013). Some argue that the problem is more fundamental: any state office would have a hard time regulating hybrid organizations, given that hybrids are required to submit little information that regulators can review. As one article notes: "None of the corporate hybrid statutes require that reports be filed with the government, or any type of oversight enterprise, nor is there a central repository for those reports. Even if such a requirement existed, the duty of care seems to have been refined to the point that, absent securities fraud, regulators have no ability to intercede in the corporate hybrids. What will they enforce? And based on what cause of action?" (Tyler et al. 2015).

Future trends and recent government activity. In the midst of the rush of recent activity, state and local governments and other stakeholders have tried to measure and solve problems faced by the growth of hybrid organizations. One of these projects, the Fourth Sector Mapping Initiative (FSMI), which is cosponsored by the Urban Institute and the Fourth Sector Network, is an attempt to identify and describe so-called "for-benefit" organizations around the world. The term "for-benefit" describes organizations that have the same general characteristics as hybrids—they engage in revenue-generating activities and also work to produce social benefits—even though they may be organized as "standard" for-profits or nonprofits. The FSMI intends to fill a need by collecting data about these organizations and their activities, in order to track their growth across traditional sectoral boundaries. The FSMI has engaged scholars, business leaders, policymakers, and many other stakeholders in its efforts to identify and describe the fourth sector and for-benefit organizations. The initiative's leaders convene these stakeholders at least once a year and organized events in January 2015 ("Mapping the Fourth Sector," held at George Washington University, Washington, DC) and June 2015 ("Growing the Impact Economy," held at the Presidio Trust, San Francisco, California).

While state governments have been busy enacting legislation to enable the creation of new hybrid legal forms, local governments have been developing new ways of engaging with hybrids, and federal lawmakers have attempted to clear up some of the issues that may restrict the growth of hybrids. In San Francisco, the city's board of supervisors in 2012 proposed a bill that would award preferential procurement treatment to benefit corporations, which had been authorized earlier by state government. However, the bill attracted strong opposition from the chief executive officer of California Nonprofits, who testified, "We're not against the existence of these corporations. We're against them getting nonprofit-like preferences, without nonprofit-like restrictions and oversight." In response, the director of policy at B Lab argued that corporations are "not competing in the marketplace with nonprofits [. . .] Social benefit corporations only help nonprofits in the long run" (Hrywna 2012).

At the national level, much of the activity regarding hybrids seems to have been motivated by a desire to encourage profit-seeking investors to support organizations that pursue charitable activities. For instance, government officials have taken steps in recent years to clarify the regulations around impact investments, such as PRIs, by foundations. The Philanthropic Facilitation Act (Esposito 2012) was introduced in the Senate in November 2015, as well as in earlier Congresses, to amend the Internal Revenue Code to facilitate PRIs (S. 2313). Under the act, organizations could obtain prior approval letters from the IRS certifying them as suitable recipients of PRIs. Also in the fall of 2015, the IRS issued new guidance on mission-related investments (MRIs) by foundations for nonprofits and hybrid organizations (Internal Revenue Service 2015, Mission Investors Exchange 2015). While MRIs do not count toward a foundation's required annual payout, they are a way for foundations to earn returns while supporting charitable causes, and may provide a previously untapped source of support for hybrid activities and organizations.

CONCLUSION

The original lines between strictly nonprofit and for-profit enterprises have been blurring over the past two decades. An important driver of this process has been the decreasing separation of activities, industries, and occupations that formerly could be identified as nonprofit or profit-making. In the view of at least some budding social entrepreneurs, the established legal enterprise forms found in the traditional nonprofit and for-profit sectors have not been adequate to respond to this trend, leading to the creation of several new organizational forms.

The most recent development has been the emergence of organizations that expressly seek to combine attributes otherwise associated with either traditional nonprofit organizations or for-profit firms: hybrids which seek to harness an explicit profit-making strategy with the pursuit of social goals. While new hybrid forms—L3Cs, SPCs, benefit corporations, and their many variants—have not replaced "traditional" hybrid structures that bring two or more organizations together, they have stimulated the creation of many innovative enterprises.

Now that the momentum behind the creation of new legal hybrid structures seems to have slowed, governments and nonprofits have challenges ahead of them. They might engage in yet more creative ways to organize around the traditional separation of charity from business activities, remembering that owners of business can always devote returns to charity. Governments might also continue to adapt the statutes so that the new hybrid forms meet the needs of entrepreneurs, while crafting regulations that protect charitable dollars but do not unduly burden activity. In both cases, the goal is to uncover new sources of philanthropic funds, such as impact investing. Meanwhile, nonprofits and hybrids must determine how to treat the public fairly when claiming the charitable "halo" that nonprofits wear, while at the same time being open to ways to bring greater efficiency to charitable activities. Whether a "fourth sector" that is distinct from the nonprofit, government and for-profit sectors emerges, we believe that the increasing integration of activities across business and charitable sectors will continue apace as health care and information become still larger parts of the total economy. The developments present both challenge and opportunities to nonprofits, business, and government alike.

REFERENCES

Batey, Doug. 2011. "Rhode Island Becomes the Newest State to Authorize Low-Profit LLCs: What's Going on Here?" *LLC Law Monitor*. Stoel Rives LLP.

Batey, Doug. 2013. "North Carolina Becomes the First State to Drop L3Cs." *LLC Law Monitor*. Stoel Rives LLP. http://www.llclawmonitor.com/2013/07/articles/low-profit-llcs/north-carolina-becomes-the-first-state-to-drop-l3cs/.

Battilana, Julie, Matthew Lee, John Walker, and Cheryl Dorsey. 2012. "In search of the hybrid ideal." *Stanford Social Innovation Review* 10, no. 3: 50–55.

Brakman Reiser, Dana. 2013. "Regulating Social Enterprise." Presented at the 2013 Columbia Law School Charities Regulation and Oversight Project Policy Conference on "The Future of State Charities Regulation."

Brewer, Cass. 2014. "Hybrid Business Entities in 2014." New York: SocentLaw. http://socentlaw.com/2014/01/hybrid-business-entities-in-2014/.

Brewer, Cass. 2015a. "'Dodging' Taxes and B Corp Status." New York: Socent Law. http://socentlaw.com/2015/09/dodging-taxes-and-b-corp-status/.

Brewer, Cass. 2015b. "States with Hybrid Forms as of November 2015." New York: Socent Law.

Brewer, Cass. 2015c. "Yet Another U.S. Hybrids Map with Hyperlinks: Rhode Island Should be Green." New York: Socent Law. http://socentlaw.com/2015/03/yet-another-u-s-hybrids-map-with-hyperlinks-rhode-island-should-be-green/.

Bromberger, Allen R. 2008. "Social enterprise: A lawyer's perspective." New York: Perlman+Perlman LLP. http://www.perlmanandperlman.com/publications/articles/2008/socialenterprise.pdf.

Chiodini, Steven R. 2014. "Goodbye Flexible Purpose Corporation, Hello Social Purpose Corporation." Washington, DC: LexMundi Pro Bono Foundation. http://www.lawforchange.org/NewsBot.asp?MODE=VIEW&ID=6384.

Cohen, Rick. 2014a. "Social Responsibility or Marketing Ploy? The Branding of L3Cs." *Nonprofit Quarterly*.

Cohen, Rick. 2014b. "Some Unanswered Questions about Benefit Corporations, L3Cs, and Social Enterprise More Generally." *Nonprofit Quarterly.*
Cordes, Joseph J., and C. Eugene, eds. 2009 *Nonprofits and Business.* Washington, DC: Urban Institute.
Esposito, Robert T. 2012. "Social Enterprise Revolution in Corporate law: A Primer on Emerging Corporate Entities in Europe and the United States and the Case for the Benefit Corporation, The." *Wm. & Mary Bus. L. Rev.* 4 (2012): 639.
Fair Trade USA. 2013. "Principles: Fair Trade Standards." Oakland, CA: Fair Trade USA. http://fairtradeusa.org/sites/all/files/wysiwyg/filemanager/standards/FTUSA_Standards_Principles.pdf.
Goodwill. 2016. "About Us." Rockville, MD: Goodwill Industries International, Inc. http://www.goodwill.org/about-us/.
Grant, Elizabeth M. 2013. "Hybrid Enterprises and the Application of State Charitable Regulatory Principles as a Guide Toward an Effective Regulatory Framework." Presented at the 2013 Columbia Law School Charities Regulation and Oversight Project Policy Conference on "The Future of State Charities Regulation".
Hrywna, Mark. 2012. "Benefit Corporation in California Meets Chill in San Francisco." *The NonProfit Times*, March 23.
Internal Revenue Service. 2015. "Investments Made for Charitable Purposes: Notice 2015–62." Washington, DC: Internal Revenue Service.
King, Bart. 2012. "Patagonia Is First to Register for 'Benefit Corporation' Status in California." *Sustainable Brands.* http://www.sustainablebrands.com/news_and_views/articles/patagonia-first-register-%E2%80%98benefit-corporation%E2%80%99-status-california.
Kleinberger, Daniel S. 2012. "ABA Business Law Section, on behalf of its committees on LLCs and Nonprofit Organizations, opposes legislation for low profit limited liability companies (L3Cs)." *William Mitchell Legal Studies Research Paper* 2012-05.
McCambridge, Ruth. 2014. "Hybrids, Hybridity, and Hype." *Nonprofit Quarterly.* https://nonprofitquarterly.org/2014/04/30/hybrids-hybridity-and-hype/.
Mission Investors Exchange. 2015. "IRS Issues Notice Clarifying Treatment of Mission-Related Investments by Private Foundations." Mission Investors Exchange. https://www.missioninvestors.org/news/irs-issues-notice-clarifying-treatment-of-mission-related-investments-by-private-foundations.
Murray, J. Haskell. 2013. "Defending Patagonia: Mergers & Acquisitions with Benefit Corporations." *Hastings Business Law Journal* 9, no. 485.
New Community Corporation. 2015. "Mission and Vision." Newark, NJ: New Community Corporation. http://www.newcommunity.org/about/mission-and-vision/.
Newman's Own. 2015. "Charity." Newman's Own. http://newmansown.com/charity/
Patagonia. 2016. "Patagonia's Mission Statement." Ventura, CA: Patagonia. http://www.patagonia.com/us/patagonia.go?assetid=2047.
S. 2313. 114th Congress (2015).
Sabeti, Heerad. 2009. "The emerging fourth sector." Washington, DC: *Aspen Institute.*
Schmidt, Elizabeth. 2010. "Vermont's social hybrid pioneers: early observation and questions to ponder." *Vermont Law Review* 35, no. 1 (2010): 163–209.

Social Investment Forum Foundation. 2010. Report On Socially Responsible Investing Trends In The United States. http://www.ussif.org/store_product.asp?prodid=10.

Steuerle, C. Eugene. 2016. "The Zuckerberg Charitable Pledge and Giving from One's Wealth." *The Government We Deserve.* http://blog.governmentwedeserve.org/2016/01/11/the-zuckerberg-charitable-pledge-and-giving-from-ones-wealth/.

Tyler, John E., Anthony J. Luppino, Evan Absher, and Kathleen Garman. 2015. "Producing Better Mileage: Advancing the Design and Usefulness of Hybrid Vehicles for Social Business Ventures." *Quinnipiac Law Review* 33, no. 2: 235–337.

Tyler, John. 2013. "State Attorney General Regulation Of Charitable Hybrid Forms: To Be Or Not To Be Charitable." Presented at the 2013 Columbia Law School Charities Regulation and Oversight Project Policy Conference on "The Future of State Charities Regulation."

Wexler, Robert A. 2009. "Effective social enterprise—a menu of legal structures." *The Exempt Organization Tax Review* 63, no. 6: 565–575.

Wexler, Robert A. 2013. "Attorney General Regulation of Hybrid Entities as Charitable Trusts." Presented at the 2013 Columbia Law School Charities Regulation and Oversight Project Policy Conference on "The Future of State Charities Regulation."

Wexler, Robert A. 2014. "For-Profit Social Enterprise Models: Understanding the Legal Landscape." Washington, DC: Independent Sector.

Chapter 10

Performance Measurement and Management

The Tangled Web of Nonprofit-Government Relationships

Saunji D. Fyffe, Teresa Derrick-Mills, and Mary K. Winkler

INTRODUCTION

Performance measurement and performance management are strategies to improve accountability, efficiency, and effectiveness of organizations. Throughout the United States, performance and accountability in nonprofit organizations, primarily 501(c)(3) charities, and governments at all levels are linked together through service delivery. According to a 2012 study by Pettijohn and Boris, local, state, and federal governments contracted with almost 56,000 nonprofit organizations for a broad range of services. The nonprofits receiving these contracts and grants ranged from revenues of less than $250,000 to revenues of more than $5 million. These complementary relationships, primarily in health and human services, weave together the performance of nonprofits and governments. In other words, governments are reliant in large part on the performance of nonprofits to accomplish the work that legislatures have authorized and funded. At the same time, nonprofits have other important roles in society such as elevating issues that are ignored or underrepresented in government (the adversarial role) or supplying services not provided by government (the supplementary role); these other roles are supported largely by philanthropists and foundations. And, nonprofits are independent organizations with constituents of their own. Thus, nonprofit accountability and performance are defined and driven by a tangled web of nonprofit-government and nonprofit-civil society relationships. We examine here the evolution of this tangled web, how this web interacts with organizational learning, and the accountability and performance tensions it creates for nonprofits.

HOW ARE PERFORMANCE MEASUREMENT AND PERFORMANCE MANAGEMENT DEFINED?

The terms "performance management," "continuous quality improvement," and "data-informed decision-making" describe the organizational processes and functions for using data to improve program performance (Derrick-Mills 2015). Performance management is the terminology common in public and nonprofit organizations, while continuous quality improvement is typically used in health care and data-informed decision-making is associated with the field of education (Derrick-Mills et al. 2014). Continuous quality improvement has its roots in the Plan-Do-Study-Act cycle which originated in the business world to quickly test innovation and put into place new strategies (Derrick-Mills et al. 2014). Performance measurement focuses on selecting the indicators and benchmarks that let managers and the public know if programs, strategies, systems, governments, and other organizations are accomplishing what they set out to do (Poister 2004). Thus, performance measurement is an important part of a performance management system. By itself, performance measurement serves as a tool for accountability (Wholey 2001; Hatry et al. 2005; Moynihan 2007), which is frequently required by funders.

Performance management, however, creates the possibility for organizational learning and improvement. Types of organizational improvement include improving service delivery (Wholey 2001; Hatry et al. 2005; Moynihan 2007), providing motivation (Wholey 2001; Hatry et al. 2005; Moynihan 2007), increasing capacity (Wholey 2001; Hatry et al. 2005; Moynihan 2007), supporting resource allocation (Wholey 2001; Hatry et al. 2005; Moynihan 2007), and identifying best practices (Hatry et al. 2005). At the systems level, it fosters learning that may promote systemic policy or regulatory change (Wholey 2001; Hatry et al. 2005). Metzenbaum (2003) emphasizes the importance of goal setting and performance management in government agencies. She indicates that goals can improve both democratic accountability and improve outcomes because goals clearly articulate agency priorities, serve as a motivating factor for individuals within agencies, and form the basis for internal and external collaborative efforts. Likewise, performance measurement helps agencies focus on strategies to meet their stated goals especially when annual progress must be reported, when comparisons over time or to similar agencies are included, and when standardized measures across programs allow for identification of factors contributing to stronger or weaker performance and outcomes.

In this chapter, we use the terms "performance measurement," "performance management," and "continuous improvement."

WHAT TYPES OF NONPROFIT ORGANIZATIONS ARE IN THE PERFORMANCE WEB?

Three types of nonprofit organizations are typically involved in the performance web: (1) nonprofits that have been contracted to perform government services, typically 501(c)(3) public charities; (2) nonprofit associations, intermediaries, or umbrella organizations that build nonprofit capacities or coordinate fundraising services, like the United Way; and (3) foundations of all kinds that distribute funds to and set expectations for their grantees—typically 501(c)(3) public charities. The focal point of this chapter is how 501(c)(3) public charities navigate the performance and accountability web created by the interplay among requirements levied from their various funders (government and foundations), the guidance and best practices suggested by the intermediary organizations, and the nonprofit's own mission, role in civil society, and commitment to serving its constituents.

STRUCTURE OF THE CHAPTER

Much of the performance and accountability web is based on a funder relationship where contracts or grants stipulate the terms of performance and the accountability requirements associated with them. The next section of this chapter focuses on understanding the performance measurement and management movements emerging simultaneously in the government, foundation and intermediary arenas that provide many strands of the web, some of which pull at each other. Following this, we discuss the tensions that nonprofits face in navigating the tangled web of performance measurement, management, and learning as we explore an evolving emphasis from accountability to learning.

PERFORMANCE MEASUREMENT AND MANAGEMENT MOVEMENTS

This section provides a brief overview of several key initiatives that have influenced nonprofits in their pursuit of measurement and evaluation activities. Included are federal, state, foundation, and intermediary efforts. Each of these movements influenced nonprofits because they provide complementary services for various levels of government, and are agents of government and foundations in terms of the services they provide and the attendant outcomes. Other motivations and drivers of performance measurement and assessment efforts emanate from several high-profile scandals in the nonprofit sector, including those involving the United Way and American Red Cross following 9/11—"crisis of accountability" (LeRoux and Wright 2010, p. 572).

Since the 1970s governments increasingly have been contracting with nonprofit organizations to deliver public services. Hence, the reporting of performance measures by nonprofit organizations has become more prevalent over time. In the 1980s, "increased attention was given to fiscal accountability and management effectiveness of programs" (Rossi and Freeman 1989, p. 35). For example, in the early 1980s, the Job Training Partnership Act (JTPA) was the first federal program to implement a performance standards system that established concrete performance measures as part of its contracting process (Barnow and Smith 2004). A decade later, performance measurement assumed greater importance due to legislative policies and a performance measurement movement coinciding with the business management emphasis in the public and nonprofit sectors (Newcomer 2004). Requirements for accountability are not unique to nonprofits that receive government contracts and grants. While the government's performance measurement movement was gaining momentum, foundations, intermediaries, and other private funders also were developing accountability and performance standards for their nonprofit grantees (Buhl 1996).

1990s

Efforts to improve government performance have been evident at both the state and federal levels since the 1990s, stemming from the "Reinventing Government movement" (a phrase coined by Osbourne and Gaebler (1992)) that began shifting focus away from accountability only to a focus on the outcomes of government (Callahan 2007).

The Government Performance and Results Act (GPRA) was enacted by Congress in 1993 as the result of congressional concern about waste, inefficiency, and an inadequate ability to demonstrate program performance. The federal agencies were required to begin implementation by having strategic planning processes and performance plans in place by the end of fiscal year 1997.

Frustrated with perceived lack of performance improvements generated by GPRA, the Bush administration adopted the Program Assessment Rating Tool (PART) in 2002. Because GPRA was congressionally mandated, PART became an additional, rather than a replacement, performance management tool. This legislation compelled nonprofits that receive government money to establish performance metrics and processes to assess their own performance in order to secure financial resources (Cairns et al. 2005). Critics of GPRA and PART point to conflicting priorities across performance initiatives and failure to recognize that federal programs are largely implemented by third-party organizations, in many cases, nonprofits.

Simultaneously, state governments were also initiating performance measurement and management initiatives. According to The Government Performance Project (GPP), a multiyear research effort at the Pew Research Center (2000), states had mixed levels of success in creating performance measures that accurately represented their agency's goals. The states that used or created a centralized agency to assist with vertical integration tended to be the most successful in preventing the creation of conflicting cross-agency goals and ensuring that goals and measures matched. The GPP study indicated that in most states there was little evidence that data were being used to inform decisions, although information certainly was being reported out to increase transparency. The 2000 GPP report indicated that one challenge to success was that administrators receiving data had not been given the administrative discretion needed to act on information they acquired; in other words, if data indicated that a change in strategy were needed, they could not initiate that change. The 2000 GPP indicated that when administrators perceived a leadership priority for the use of the data, they tended to utilize it more in their decisions.

The United Way of America was one of the first private funders to require nonprofit providers to develop and systematically track and measure performance and program outcomes (Murray and Balfour 1999). As one of the largest private funders of nonprofit organizations, the United Way substantially increased its requirements for performance measurement in the mid-1990s, and provided guidance for its members in "Measuring Program Outcomes: A Practical Approach" (United Way of America 1996).

In this same period, a growing number of private funders began implementing similar requirements and even invested in providing tools and resources to support nonprofit efforts and capacity to measure their performance. Foundations, including the Ford Foundation, Kaiser Family Foundation, W. K. Kellogg Foundation, Lily Endowment, and the Rockefeller Foundation, developed materials pertaining to performance measurement and evaluation (Alie and Seita 1997). In 1998, the Edna McConnell Clark Foundation decided to hold itself accountable for measurable results in its grantmaking. It contracted from five programs to a single new one and from several hundred grantees to seventeen; grants increased from an average of $75,000 to approximately $2 million. The foundation broke new ground in working with grantees to improve their capacities to deliver effective services, to help them implement performance management systems, and to use new metrics tied to outcomes of intended beneficiaries (Hunter 2006a, 2006b; Hunter and Koopmans 2006). Also, the Hewlett Foundation funded a series of working groups convened by the Urban Institute that resulted in the *Series on Outcomes Management for Nonprofits* (Lampkin and Hatry 2003) and a set of logic models with recommended outcomes and indicators for 14 program areas (http://www.urban.org/policy-centers/cross-center-initiatives/performance-management-measurement/projects/nonprofit-organizations/projects-focused-nonprofit-organizations/outcome-indicators-project). These are still among the most downloaded publications on the Urban Institute website (Boris and Winkler 2013).

Gradually, new voices promoting effectiveness gained strength as an increasing number of foundations were showing interest in performance measurement. Umbrella and membership associations, such as the Grantmakers Evaluation Network, a group of 300 foundation members, and Grantmakers for Effective Organizations (GEO), a community of over 500 grantmakers, debated and endorsed performance measurement as a critical part of grantmaking (Buhl 1996). For instance, in 1997, GEO convened a group of grantmakers with a goal of helping foundations employ strategies that lead to successful grantees. Other examples include the *Harvard Business Review* article, "Virtuous Capital: What Foundations Can Learn from Venture Capitalists" (Letts, Ryan, and Grossman 1997), which challenged foundations to take a venture-capital approach to philanthropy and recommended investing in the capacity of nonprofits to do their work effectively; and Porter and Kramer (1999), who asked whether foundations were creating sufficient value to offset the cost to society of their favored tax status.

2000s

In 2002, the American Competitiveness and Corporate Accountability Act (Sarbanes-Oxley Act) mandated that publicly traded companies set standardized governance, financial and auditing practices (Carman 2005). Even though the legislation was directed at the for-profit sector, state attorney generals and nonprofit leaders pushed for similar guidance and requirements in the nonprofit sector (BoardSource and Independent Sector 2003; Carman 2005). Additionally, in 2004, the US Senate Finance Committee urged the Independent Sector to form the panel on the Nonprofit Sector to improve the oversight and governance of charitable and nonprofit organizations to ensure a high standard of ethics and accountability. These congressional actions came in response to a "crisis of accountability" (Fitzgibbon 1997; LeRoux and Wright 2010) emerging from the Enron and WorldCom scandals in the for-profit arena and issues of questionable financial management in the United Way, Nature Conservancy, and American Red Cross (Fleishman 1999; Jeavons 1994).

In 2009, a new wave of federal performance management strategies began with the Obama Administration's Executive Agency launch of the High Priority Performance Goals and the congressional update of the Government Performance and Results Act, the GPRA Modernization Act of 2010. Both of these new federal strategies attempted to address some of the flaws in the previous federal attempts to foster use of performance data for improvements and to acknowledge the presence of third-party implementers (e.g., other levels of government, nonprofit and for-profit organizations) of government programs (Public Law 111-352 § 1115. Federal Government and agency performance plans, (b)(5)(C), January 4, 2011).

Similar to Obama's High Priority Goals, GPRA 2010 requires federal agencies to identify a few priorities among their annual goals. Each agency's goals must align with its strategic plan. The act requires quarterly (instead of annual) review of data to determine if progress is being made in accomplishing the goals and requires transparency of agency goals and results. The response to this performance improvement and demonstrated effectiveness imperative was broad. For example, in 2009, the federal government established the Social Innovation Fund, a $200 million public-private partnership designed to support results-oriented nonprofits (Brest 2010) in scaling up their evidence-based efforts (http://www.nationalservice.gov/programs/social-innovation-fund/our-model).

At the state level, Pew's Government Performance Project assessed state performance again in 2005 and 2008, but the categories were renamed and the criteria significantly refined. The "managing for results" assessment was renamed "information." The assessment criteria include five areas: strategic direction, budgeting for performance, managing for performance, program evaluation, and electronic government (Government Performance Project 2005). The 2005 GPP assessments indicated that more states were using their performance information to inform management decisions. In 2008, the GPP report noted improvements in how states were facilitating web-based transactions, an increase to four out of five states regularly conducting performance audits or evaluations, and an increase to forty-one states with either strategic plans or collections of agency plans (Government Performance Project 2008).

Meanwhile, foundations and intermediary organizations were shifting away from measuring outputs toward measuring outcomes. In performance measurement, outcomes are the results that guide future actions, ensure accountability, and demonstrate effectiveness (Benjamin and Misra 2006). In effect, funders started paying more attention to performance measurement as a management tool to improve performance. Thus, the adoption of outcome measurement frameworks and outcome-based funding grew.

In addition, some funders began using outcome measurement internally for their own programs (Benjamin and Misra 2006). Three nonprofits funded by foundations began to promote strategic philanthropy and assist foundations in defining, assessing, and improving their own effectiveness: The Center for Effective Philanthropy (CEP), the Foundation Strategy Group (now FSG), and the Bridgespan Group. The *Stanford Social Innovation Review,* organized in 2003 with foundation support, promoted these types of practices (Boris and Winkler 2013).

In light of the changing landscape, a change in private funders' approaches to accountability also was unfolding. As pressure to show results and demonstrate accountability increased, some private foundations began embracing a "donor-as-investor" view of themselves. This new trend reshaped philanthropic thinking among some funders to focus accountability efforts on "investing in a set of results or social outcomes" (Benjamin and Misra 2006, p. 152). As "investors," private foundations expect measurable social returns on their investments by holding nonprofits accountable for results and requiring evidence that their money has been well spent (Meehan, Kilmer, and O'Flanagan 2004). They therefore seek information on a nonprofit's prior performance and ancillary systems before making funding decisions.

Some foundations started making impact investments that, unlike grants, are intended to generate a financial and measureable social return. The Edna McConnell Clark Foundation (EMCF) was among the first foundations to take this approach using a growth capital aggregation investment model to scale programs that work. Under this model, funders and nonprofits come to agreement about objectives at the outset to minimize reporting burdens and establish performance milestones upon which payouts are contingent (http://www.emcf.org/capital-aggregation/, accessed 03/03/2016). And, in 2009 the Boston Foundation began giving larger grants with fewer restrictions to nonprofits that evince effectiveness (Ailworth 2009; Lynch-Cerullo and Cooney 2011). In 2012, the Council on Foundations convened a group of foundation leaders to discuss how best to equip foundations to define and employ impact investing programs.

Also on the rise were nonprofit investment funders, such as Venture Philanthropy Partners (VPP), the Roberts Enterprise Development Fund (REDF), and the Acumen Fund, that operate like venture capital funds. These nonprofits raise money from individuals, corporations, and foundations and "invest" it in "portfolios" aimed at addressing the root cause of a social problem. Most recently, EMCF announced Blue Meridian Partners, a collaborative effort to invest over $1 billion in high-performing nonprofits to improve the lives of disadvantaged youth. EMCF's "approach for identifying, investing in and holding nonprofits accountable for performance" is cited as the "engine" driving this investment strategy (http://www.emcf.org/capital-aggregation/blue-meridian-partners/, accessed 03/03/2016). In contrast to government and private foundations, these investment groups tend to ignore conventional performance metrics designed for compliance purposes, and favor the collection and use of social performance data that measure results and demonstrate impact.

Some of these foundations are trying to support the capacity of their nonprofit grantees to better measure their work and use their data to improve. The EMCF and VPP are particularly notable for their focus on building the capacity of their grantees to more effectively use data to monitor and manage performance and encouraging their peers to do the same. Both have made deep financial commitments and offered a wide array of technical assistance to cultivate high-performing nonprofits. In 2011, VPP published Mario Morino's monograph, *Leap of Reason: Managing to Outcomes in an Era of Scarcity*, with about 90,000 copies in circulation to date. About a year and a half later, the Leap of Reason Ambassadors Community was founded. This community now includes over one hundred practitioners, experts, and sector leaders committed to increasing the expectation and adoption of high performance in the nonprofit sector. Through their day-to-day professional interactions and various dissemination strategies, members of this community are striving to "inspire, motivate, and support nonprofit and public sector leaders (and their stakeholders) to build great organizations for greater societal impact" (http://leapofreason.org/performance-imperative/leap-ambassadors-community/).

Even though a few foundations have led some of the efforts as discussed above, the bulk of foundations at the beginning of the twenty-first century were slow to implement recommended performance measurement and management practices internally or in their grantmaking (Boris and Winkler 2013). A national survey conducted by Francie Ostrower in collaboration with GEO in 2003 found that although many foundation executives (CEOs) believed that they needed to improve their effectiveness and knew what those practices entailed, most did not implement them (Ostrower 2004). Yet, a later study by Benjamin and Misra (2006) showed that funders were making incremental changes in their practices including making structural changes (using outcome measurement internally for their own programs), procedural changes (incorporating regular evaluations into grantmaking and requiring nonprofits to report on measurable outcomes), and resource changes (investing more heavily in building the capacity of their nonprofit grantees).

NAVIGATING THE TANGLED WEB OF PERFORMANCE MEASUREMENT, MANAGEMENT, AND LEARNING: BALANCING EXTERNAL AND INTERNAL ACCOUNTABILITY

The complex, and sometimes contradictory, tangled web of nonprofit-government and nonprofit-civil society relationships, can create tensions that make it difficult for nonprofits to effectively engage in data-driven practices to improve operations and impact. The tangled web in which nonprofits operate includes having multiple and competing accountability pressures and mandates from government and other funders, the communities they serve, various stakeholders, as well as internally from their own organizational mission. Operating in an environment that rewards success and penalizes failure undermines the likelihood that nonprofits will acknowledge weaknesses and examine failures even when such efforts could lead to learning that may produce better outcomes and improved effectiveness (Behn 2003; Edwards 2002; Ebrahim 2005; Christensen and Ebrahim 2006; Smillie and Hailey 2001). On the one hand, nonprofit funders generate ongoing pressure for accountability and outcomes—efforts to be more accountable at the federal level and through strategic philanthropy, putting pressure on the nonprofits delivering the services to report on measures useful to their funders, but sometimes less useful internally to the nonprofit. As a result, nonprofit organizations have become accustomed to the monitoring and reporting of outputs and short-term outcomes information that may be of limited use in informing decisions about mission improvement, thwarting their ability to move beyond a culture of compliance to a culture of continuous improvement. On the other hand, nonprofits need to become efficient and effective in their own right and responsive to their constituent communities. Therefore, for nonprofits to evolve into learning organizations requires finding a balance between external and internal accountability in order to facilitate critical reflection and internal (or organizational) learning (Behn 2003; Christensen and Ebrahim 2006; Marsick and Watkins 2003). These tensions are described in more detail below.

AN EVOLVING EMPHASIS FROM ACCOUNTABILITY TO LEARNING

The movements in the federal, state, foundations, and intermediary organizations demonstrate a gradual shift from a focus purely on accountability to a focus on learning. As nonprofits increase their capacity to collect and report on data, they facilitate the learning of the entities that fund them about how the portfolio of activities is performing. At the same time, some of the funders and the nonprofits themselves are attempting to transform the nonprofit service delivery agencies into learning organizations. Tools and frameworks such as the balanced scorecard for nonprofits (Kaplan 2001), the public value scorecard (Moore 2003), and Sowa, Selden, and Sandfort's (2004) multidimensional, integrated modes of nonprofit organizational effectiveness (MIMNOE) have been introduced to help nonprofits assess their effectiveness. Similarly, PerformWell (www.performwell.org), a collaborative effort of the Urban Institute, Child Trends, and Social Solutions Global was launched as a free, online resource to help nonprofits identify performance measures and assessment tools and obtain practitioner-friendly advice about a variety of performance management topics through its webinar series.

Instruments and outlets have also emerged for nonprofits to showcase their performance as they define it. In 2011, the BBB Wise Giving Alliance, GuideStar USA, and Independent Sector launched "Charting Impact," a common tool organized around a series of five questions, to help nonprofits document their organizational impact. In 2015, the Leap of Reason Ambassador Community released the "Performance Imperative: A Framework for Social Sector Excellence," which lays out a common definition of and seven organizational disciplines for achieving high performance. This framework can be used by a variety of stakeholders for diverse purposes. For example, nonprofit boards can use it to assess mission effectiveness; funders can use it to spur new thinking about ways to support high performance among their grantees; executives can use it in strategic planning and professional development efforts; and professors might use it to augment courses on performance measurement and management. (http://leapofreason.org/performance-imperative/about-pi/). In 2016, GuideStar launched a fourth tier to the GuideStar Exchange, which offers the opportunity for nonprofits to report program data; organizations that provide these data receive a "platinum" designation from GuideStar.

Despite many nonprofits recognizing the benefits of becoming a learning organization, numerous organizations, especially small nonprofits, find it difficult to achieve. For example, in 2010, the Bridgespan Group surveyed nonprofits about how they learn and translate the knowledge gained into practice. The survey results indicate that even though nonprofit leaders attach importance to capturing and sharing knowledge across their programs and fields, they confront obstacles that lessen their ability to convert and use data to inform continuous improvement and better manage their programs and operations (Milway and Saxton 2011). Securing the necessary resources, creating a culture of learning, and balancing top-down and bottom-up pressures are three issues facing nonprofits, that are attempting to make the shift.

SECURING THE NECESSARY RESOURCES

Developing a performance management system that facilitates organizational learning requires significant commitment and resources (e.g., time, money, training, and technology). Studies show that some nonprofits with large budgets are more likely to invest in management structures that support learning than those with small budgets (Zimmermann and Stevens 2006). An Urban Institute study (Farrell, Fyffe, and Valero 2015) examined the nonprofit-government relationship at the local level and found a reliance on small nonprofits to address complex social issues. Although small nonprofits are usually better positioned to identify and address specific issues or target populations more efficiently than their government partners, they also tend to have fewer resources and lower capacity. In this same study, nonprofits reported feeling pressured to choose between investing resources in program quality or building staff capacity.

Although many types of resources are important, three core resources are frequently associated with high-capacity nonprofit performance in the literature: human resources, financial resources, and infrastructure (Bozeman and Bretschneider 1986; Derrick-Mills et al. 2014; Frederickson and London 2000; Hall et al. 2003; Jaskyte 2004; Kamal 2006; Misener and Doherty 2009).

Human resources refer to the collective competencies, knowledge, attitudes, motivation, and behaviors of individuals in the organization. How well an organization analyzes and uses data for continuous improvement will depend on its staff capacities. The literature emphasizes the importance of skills of inquiry, integration, and analysis, as well as the ability to translate what has been learned into effective and appropriate actions (Derrick-Mills et al. 2014). The staff need to understand how the data systems work. However, the public management literature highlights the lack of staff training on how to translate data into action as a barrier to data use (Hatry et al. 2005; Poister 2004; Wholey 2001). Moreover, the nonprofit literature notes similar barriers; an Idealware (2012) survey indicates that 60 percent of responding nonprofits find it challenging to translate their program data into usable information for decision-making.

Financial resources refer to an organization's ability to allocate the proper amount of funds to fulfill its mission and support operations. Although funders are increasingly asking nonprofits to become more data driven, they have not provided the financial resources to do so. Carman (2009) found that the majority of nonprofit organizations use some internal funds to support these activities, while one quarter assigns no funds. In another study, 70 percent of nonprofits report that at least half of their funders ask for impact or program metrics in reports (Nonprofit Finance Fund 2014).

Infrastructure refers to the day-to-day operational systems and physical assets that contribute to the organization's capacity to systematically collect, assess, and use performance data. In particular, having sufficient data systems and physical assets (e.g., suitable equipment and technology) facilitates a nonprofit's capacity to learn from its experiences, make better strategic decisions, set realistic programmatic and organizational goals, and assess performance on an ongoing basis.

Operational resources can affect nonprofit and government relationships. Government funding typically provides little to no funds to cover administrative expenses (i.e., those expenditures incurred by a nonprofit organization to support its stated mission or purpose that are associated with the organization's overall functions and management). The government's tendency to pare down administrative expenses to the bare minimum can place significant constraints on nonprofit operations, which has serious implications for a nonprofit's organizational capacity and ultimately its ability to deliver programs and services to clients (de Leon, Pettijohn, and DeVita 2012; Fyffe 2015). According to Tierney and Steele, "Without the necessary investments in overhead, the organization underperforms. It can't meet expectations, it becomes difficult to retain high-quality talent . . . it might be hampered in attracting new funding and in ultimately serving the people it aims to serve" (2011, 7).

Nonprofits and foundations express similar concerns. Although the challenges can be a bit more nuanced as nonprofits and funders do not always share the same perspectives when it comes to the type or amount of support needed and the extent to which it is provided. For example, a recent analysis from the Center on Effective Philanthropy concludes that foundation CEOs are "significantly more likely to report providing funding support for nonprofit assessment efforts than nonprofit CEOs are to report receiving it." In fact, 75 percent of foundation CEOs indicated that they "supported nonprofit efforts to collect data about performance," contrasted with 71 percent of nonprofit CEOs who said they "do not receive any support for assessment efforts" (Buteau, Chaffin, and Gopal 2014). Similarly, the *2014 State of the Nonprofit Sector Survey* reports that 71 percent of nonprofits say funders "never or rarely cover the costs associated with impact measurement" (Nonprofit Finance Fund 2014).

Because of the general lack of operational resources, especially for small nonprofits, developing and implementing performance management learning systems often takes a lower priority to established traditional performance measurement mechanisms that may be familiar and mandated by funders. However, given the interdependency of nonprofits, foundations, and government for producing results, more support (financial and nonfinancial) is needed to help nonprofits effectively engage in performance management.

SHIFTING TO A CULTURE OF LEARNING

Organizational culture refers to how things are done at an organization as well as prevailing attitudes, patterns of accepted and expected behavior, and the habits that become part of the organization's principles and philosophy

(Drennan 1992; Khademian 2002; Schein 2010). Organizational culture is pervasive across an organization and is considered an "important means for organizations to integrate internal processes and adapt to external conditions" (Kim 2014, p. 399; Tusi et al. 2006). An organization's culture can also explain why certain organizational behaviors and practices do or do not occur (Trice and Beyer 1993).

Research shows that an organizational culture that values learning can be a key facilitator of data use for continuous quality improvement (Derrick-Mills et al. 2014). Learning is a key factor in the push for continuous improvement. Hence, organizations that form a culture of learning have staff who not only are interested in learning, but apply what they have learned to help improve their organizational, program, or individual performance and also share this knowledge with others.

Nonprofits, like other types of organizations, confront certain barriers to creating a culture of learning. For instance, traditional accountability mechanisms have inundated the nonprofit sector with a way of thinking that often does not facilitate developing a culture of continuous improvement. Because nonprofit organizations have been using data for external reporting and not necessarily for internal improvement, to engage in performance management and become a data-driven, learning organization the entire culture of the organization may need to change (Hendricks, Plantz, and Pritchard 2008; Hoefer 2000; Morino 2011; Wholey 2001).

The literature suggests that before developing a process for performance management and learning, an organization's senior leadership and its board must agree to manage the organization efficiently and with ongoing attention to quality and effectiveness of its work (Hunter 2009). Therefore, changing a nonprofit organization's culture lies largely in the hands of its leaders, including the board. A nonprofit's leadership must be willing to adjust, and in some cases abandon, conventional ways of managing to incorporate an approach that opposes the use of data solely for reporting to funders and instead fosters an environment where data are seen as a tool for ongoing learning. Such an approach will create an organizational culture open to receiving and using the knowledge that data can unmask and where data collection and use is integrated into everyday activities. To move beyond a culture of compliance to a culture of continuous improvement nonprofits will need leaders to help transform attitudes and actions that support data for compliance and accountability purposes.

Another barrier faced by nonprofits is their environments. Organizations are embedded in and strongly influenced by their environments, which comprise other organizations that exert various forces of an economic, political, or social nature and provide key resources that sustain the organizations (Daft 2001; Derrick-Mills et al. 2014). Nonprofits rely heavily on external funding sources, and many rely exclusively on government funding (Froelich 1999;

Smith 1996; Pettijohn and Boris 2013). As a result of these relationships, nonprofits may adapt their internal structures, objectives, strategies, and operations to align with those of their government funders. It is one thing for nonprofits to move toward a culture of learning, but unless their government funders recognize that "organizational learning is foundational for a broader view of accountability and crucial for focusing organization attention on mission" (Ebrahim 2005, p. 56), there will be tension between nonprofit and government accountability and performance management systems.

Some studies show that government is gradually changing how it approaches relationships with the nonprofit organizations it funds by becoming less compliance driven and concentrating more on building nonprofit knowledge and capacity. An Urban Institute study on nonprofit-government contracts and grants (Fyffe 2015) showed that state government agencies were intentionally approaching their nonprofit partners with less rigid, authoritative postures and instead were using a more collaborative style and conducting much-needed training and technical assistance to provide nonprofits with tools and resources to strengthen their knowledge and capacity. Additionally, the Office of Planning, Research and Evaluation (OPRE) contracted with the Urban Institute in 2012 to conduct the *Head Start Leadership, Excellence, and Data Systems* (LEADS) project to assess and document promising practices in Head Start programs around data use for continuous quality improvement and to produce a resource guide to help Head Start programs move beyond a culture of compliance to a culture of continuous improvement (Derrick-Mills et al. 2015).

BALANCING TOP-DOWN AND BOTTOM-UP PRESSURES

An organizational culture that values learning attempts to involve both its staff and stakeholders, typically clients, in making sense of the data and determining where to focus improvement efforts (Derrick-Mills et al. 2014). Researchers such as Benjamin (2008) and Smith (2010) have pointed out the conflicts that nonprofits experience between funder expectations for particular performance outcomes and the desire to engage citizens and beneficiaries of services in determining which outcomes are most meaningful to them. Traditionally, top-down referred to the ideas of the nonprofit leaders themselves and was characterized as philanthropic paternalism or parentalism (Steinberg 2006) when the clients or beneficiaries of services were not consulted about what they wanted to achieve. The recent movements to include clients or beneficiaries of services in the construction of programs are designed to counter that paternalism (Twersky et al. 2013; Fund for Shared Insight http://www.fundforsharedinsight.org/#improvement).

Some funders and initiatives have been moving beyond performance measurement to more advanced evaluative methods in an effort to promote the use of evidence in developing and delivering services. For example, Head Start, a federally funded initiative to prepare children birth to age of five years to perform better in school and in life, has begun to incorporate more and more of an evidence base into its performance standards and expectations. As taxpayers and citizens, we would expect nothing less to assure high-quality programming for our youngest citizens. These expectations begin to form the measures for success and may crowd out the constituent viewpoint on particular strategies and successes. Another Head Start requirement, however, is to consider the constituent voice in structuring the program; this is because the program originated with a two-generation focus to empower parents while helping their children. The organizations delivering the services, primarily nonprofit organizations, must struggle to find the right balance in the professional evidence and their constituent-expressed needs.

FINAL REFLECTIONS

It has become increasingly clear that while performance measurement is an important tool of accountability, it does not necessarily involve the continuous use of data to make informed management decisions. Performance measurement is a precursor to performance management, and when both are connected, they lead to organizational learning that can help nonprofits achieve better outcomes for program participants and the communities they serve. Across the sector nonprofits are conceptualizing and responding to institutional accountability pressures in different ways and for different reasons. Some nonprofit organizations have figured out how to navigate the tangled web of performance measurement, management, and learning, while others have not. For them a culture of learning is largely nonexistent, with the use of data for compliance and accountability purposes only. Nonprofits that focus solely on traditional accountability mechanisms tend to do so because of funder and stakeholder demands, as well as the continued limited capacity to effectively engage in performance measurement, management and learning. Those that deliver services complementary to government are particularly susceptible to these challenges because government is reliant on their performance and reporting for contract compliance purposes.

The focus on accountability is not going away anytime soon. In fact, demands for evidence-based strategies and approaches for demonstrated impact are becoming more prevalent. At the same time, economic and budgetary pressures are creating greater competition for increasingly limited resources to support service delivery. As a result, the pressure on nonprofits to prove that their programs and services are having an impact means increased emphasis on organizational systems that do more than collect, analyze, and report data. Current and future accountability eras will require nonprofits to develop internal accountability mechanisms comprised of self-correcting processes that enable them to examine failures and weaknesses on a regular basis with the aim of adjusting activities as needed and making programmatic and operational improvements. The health of civil society depends on the ability of nonprofits to act in supplementary and adversarial roles which may be put at risk as nonprofits attempt to meet the requirements of complementary service delivery. In the future, the web of requirements is likely to become more tangled, and the challenges of balancing internal and external pressures more persistent. Like a spider's web, this web is resilient, and the nonprofits inhabiting it must be equally so.

REFERENCES

Ailworth, E. "Stressing Results, Charity Retools Grant-Giving." *Boston Globe*, September 16, 2009, A-1, A-7.

Alie, R. E., and J. R. Seita. 1997. "Who's Using Evaluation and How: New Study Gives Insight." *Nonprofit World* 15, no. 5 (September): 40–49.

Barnow, Burt S., and Jeffrey A. Smith. 2004. "Performance Management in U.S. Job Training Programs." In *Job Training Policy in the United States*, edited by Christopher J. O'Leary, Robert A. Straits, and Stephen A. Wander, 21–55. Kalamazoo, MI: W. E. Upjohn Institute for Employment Research.

Behn, Robert D. 2003. "Why Measure Performance? Different Purposes Require Different Measures." *Public Administration Review* 63, no. 5: 586–606.

Benjamin, L. M. 2008. "Account Space: How Accountability Requirements Shape Nonprofit Practice." *Nonprofit and Voluntary Sector Quarterly* 37, no. 2: 201–223.

Benjamin, L. M., and K. Misra. 2006. "Doing Good Work: Implications of Performance Accountability for Practice in the Nonprofit Sector." *International Journal of Rural Management* 2: 147–162.

Board Source & Independent Sector. 2003. "The Sarbanes-Oxley Act and Implications for Nonprofit Organizations." March 11, 2016. http://www.independentsector.org/uploads/Accountability_Documents/sarbanes_oxley_implications.pdf.

Boris, Elizabeth T., and Mary K. Winkler. 2013. "The Emergence of Performance Measurement as a Complement to Evaluation among U.S. Foundations." In *Performance Management and Evaluation*, edited by Steffen Bohni Nielsen, David E. K. Hunter and Paul R. Brandon. San Francisco: Jossey-Bass.

Bozeman, Barry and Stuart I. Bretschneider. 1986. "Public Management Information Systems: Theory and Prescription." *Public Administration Review* 46, special issue: 475–487.

Brest, P. 2010, Spring. "The Power of Theories of Change." *Stanford Social Innovation Review*.

Buhl, Lance C. 1996. "The Evaluation Paradox." *Foundation News and Commentary* 37, no. 1: 34–37.

Buteau, Ellie, Mark Chaffin, and Ramya Gopal. 2014. "Transparency, Performance Assessment, and Awareness of Nonprofits' Challenges: Are Foundations and Nonprofits Seeing Eye to Eye?" *The Foundation Review* 6, no. 2: 67–80.

Cairns, Ben, Margaret Harris, Romayne Hutchison, and Mike Tricker. 2005. "Improving Performance? The Adoption and Implementation of Quality Systems in U.K. Nonprofits." *Nonprofit Management and Leadership* 16, no. 2: 135–151.

Callahan, Kathe. 2007. *Elements of Effective Governance: Measurement, Accountability and Participation*. Boca Raton, FL: Auerbach Publication.

Carman, J. G. 2009. "Nonprofits, Funders and Evaluation: Accountability in Action." *The American Review of Public Administration* 39, no. 4: 374–390.

———. 2005. "Program Evaluation Use and Practice in Nonprofit Organizations: A Theory-Based Study of Nonprofit Organizations in New York State." A doctoral dissertation, SUNY Albany.

Christensen, R., and A. Ebrahim. 2006. "How Does Accountability Affect Mission? The Case of a Nonprofit Serving Immigrants and Refugees." *Nonprofit Management & Leadership* 17, no. 2: 195–209.

Daft, R. L. 2001. *Organization Theory and Design,* 7th ed. Florence, KY: South-Western College Publishing.

de Leon, Erwin, Sarah L. Pettijohn, and Carol J. De Vita. 2012. "Community Services Block Grant Administrative Expenses." Washington, DC.

Derrick-Mills, Teresa. 2015. "Understanding Data Use for Continuous Quality Improvement in Head Start: Preliminary Findings." Washington, DC: Office of Planning, Research and Evaluation, Administration for Children and Families U.S. Department of Health and Human Services.

Derrick-Mills, Teresa, Heather Sandstrom, Sarah Pettijohn, Saunji D. Fyffe, and Jeremy Koulish. 2014. "Data Use for Continuous Quality Improvement: What the Head Start Field Can Learn from Other Disciplines, a Literature Review and Conceptual Framework." Washington, DC: Office of Planning, Research and Evaluation, Administration for Children and Families. U.S. Department of Health and Human Services.

Drennan, D. 1992. *Transforming Company Culture*. London: McGraw-Hill.

Ebrahim, A. 2005. "Accountability Myopia: Losing Sight of Organizational Learning." *Nonprofit and Voluntary Sector Quarterly* 34, no. 1: 56–87.

Edwards, M. 2002. "Organizational Learning in Non-Governmental Organizations: What Have We Learned?" In *The Earthscan Reader on NGO Management,* edited by M. Edwards and A. Fowler, 331–346. London: Earthscan.

Farrell, Maura, Saunji D. Fyffe, and Jesus Valero. 2015. "Government-Nonprofit Contracts and Grants: A Case Study of Prince George's County, Maryland." Washington, DC: The Urban Institute.

Fitzgibbon, Michael. 1997. "Accountability Misplaced: Private Social Welfare Agencies and the Public in Cleveland." *Nonprofit and Voluntary Sector Quarterly* 26, no. 1: 27–40.

Fleishman, Joel L. 1999. "Public Trust in Not-for-Profit Organizations and the Need for Regulatory Reform." In *Philanthropy and the Nonprofit Sector in a Changing*

America, edited by Charles Clotfelter and Thomas Ehrlich. Bloomington, IN: Indiana University Press.

Frederickson, P., and R. London. 2000. "Disconnect in the Hollow State: The Pivotal Role of Organizational Capacity in Community-Based Development." *Public Administration Review* 60, no. 3: 230–239.

Froelich, K. A. 1999. "Diversification of Revenue Strategies: Evolving Resource Dependence in Nonprofit Organizations." *Nonprofit and Voluntary Sector Quarterly* 28, no. 3: 246–268.

Fyffe, Saunji D. 2015. "Nonprofit-Government Contracts and Grants: The State Agency Perspective." Washington, DC: The Urban Institute.

Government Performance and Results Modernization Act of 2010. Public Law 111-352 § 1115. Federal Government and Agency Performance Plans, (b)(5)(C), January 4, 2011.

Government Performance Project. 2005. "Grading the States 2005: A look inside." Washington, DC. Retrieved from http://www.pewtrusts.org/uploadedFiles/www.pewtrustsorg/Reports/Government_Performance/GPP_Report_2005.pdf.

———. 2008. "Measuring Performance: The State Management Report Card for 2008." Washington, DC. Retrieved from http://www.pewcenteronthestates.org/uploadedFiles/Grading-the-States-2008.pdf.

Hall, M. H., A. Andrukow, C. Barr, K. Brock, M. de Wit, D. Embuldeniya, and E. Al. 2003. *The Capacity to Serve: A Qualitative Study of the Challenges Facing Canada's Nonprofit and Voluntary Organizations*. Toronto, ON: Canadian Centre for Philanthropy.

Hatry, H. P., E. Morely, S. B. Rossman, and J. S. Wholey. 2005. "How Federal Programs Use Outcome Information: Opportunities for Federal Managers." In *IBM Center for the Business of Government, Managing for Results 2005*, edited by J. M. Kamensky and A. Morales, 197–274. Lanham, MD: Rowman & Littlefield Publishers, Inc.

Hendricks, M., M. Plantz, and K. J. Pritchard. 2008. "Measuring Outcomes of United Way-Funded Programs: Expectations and Reality." In *Nonprofits and Evaluation: New Directions for Program Evaluation*, edited by J. G. Carman and K. A. Fredericks, 13–35. San Francisco: Jossey-Bass.

Hoefer, R. 2000. "Accountability in Action? Program Evaluation in Nonprofit Human Service Agencies.". *Nonprofit Management and Leadership* 11, no. 2: 167–177.

Hunter, David E. K. 2006a. "Daniel and the Rhinoceros." *Evaluation and Program Planning* 29: 180–185.

———. 2006b. "Using a Theory of Change Approach to Build Organizational Strength, Capacity and Sustainability with Not-for-Profit Organizations in the Human Services Sector." *Evaluation and Program Planning* 29: 193–200.

———. 2009. *Yes We Can! Performance Management in Nonprofit Human Services*. Baltimore, MD: Social Solutions Inc.

Hunter, David E. K., and M. Koopmans. 2006. "Calculating Program Capacity Using the Concept of Active Service Slot." *Evaluation and Program Planning* 29: 186–192.

Idealware. 2012. "The State of Nonprofit Data." Portland, OR: The Nonprofit Technology Network.

Jaskyte, K. 2004. "Transformational Leadership, Organizational Culture, and Innovativeness in Nonprofit Organizations." *Nonprofit Management and Leadership* 15, no. 2: 153–168.

Jeavons, Thomas. 1994. "Ethics in Non-Profit Management: Creating a Culture of Integrity." In *The Jossey-Bass Handbook of Non-Profit Leadership and Management*, edited by Robert D. Herman and Associates. San Francisco: Jossey-Bass.

Kamal, M. M. 2006. "It Innovation Adoption in the Government Sector: Identifying the Critical Success Factors." *Journal of Enterprise Information Management* 19, no. 2: 199–222.

Kaplan, Robert S. 2001. "Strategic Performance Measurement and Management in Nonprofit Organizations." *Nonprofit Management & Leadership* 11, no. 3: 353–369.

Khademian, Anne M. 2002. *Working with Culture: The Way the Job Gets Done in Public Programs*. Washington, DC: CQ Press.

Kim, Hougyun. 2014. "Transformational Leadership, Organizational Clan Culture, Organizational Affective Commitment, and Organizational Citizenship Behavior: A case of South Korea's public sector." *Public Organization Review* 14, no. 3: 397–417.

Lampkin, L., and H. P. Hatry. 2003. "Key Steps in Outcome Management." In *Urban Institute Series on Outcomes Management for Nonprofits*. Washington, DC.

LeRoux, K., and N. S. Wright. 2010. "Does Performance Measurement Improve Strategic Decision Making? Findings from a National Survey of Nonprofit Social Service Agencies." *Nonprofit and Voluntary Sector Quarterly* 39: 571–587.

Letts, Christine W., William Ryan, and Allen Grossman. 1997. "Virtuous Capital: What Foundations Can Learn from Venture Capitalists." *Harvard Business Review* March–April: 36–44.

Lynch-Cerullo, Kristen and Kate Cooney. 2011. "Moving from Outputs to Outcomes: A Review of the Evolution of Performance Measurement in the Human Service Nonprofit Sector." *Administration in Social Work* 35: 364–388.

Marsick, Victoria J., and Karen E. Watkins. 2003. "Demonstrating the Value of an Organization's Learning Culture: The Dimensions of the Learning Organization Questionnaire." *Advances in Developing Human Resources* 5, no. 2: 132–151.

Meehan, William, Derek Kilmer, and Maisie O'Flanagan. 2004. "Investing in Society." *Stanford Social Innovation Review* Spring: 34–35.

Metzenbaum, S. 2003. "Strategies for Using State Information: Measuring and Improving Program Performance." Washington, DC.

Milway, Katie Smith and Amy Saxton. 2011, Summer. "The Challenge of Organizational Learning." *Stanford Social Innovation Review*: 44–49.

Misener, K., and A. Doherty. 2009. "A Case Study of Organizational Capacity in Nonprofit Community Sport." *Journal of Sport Management* 23: 457–482.

Moore, M. H. 2003. "The 'Public Value Scorecard': A Rejoinder and an Alternative to 'Strategic Performance Measurement and Management in Non-Profit Organizations' by Robert Kaplan." Boston: Hauser Center for Nonprofit Organizations, Harvard University.

Morino, M. 2011. *Leap of Reason: Managing to Outcomes in an Era of Scarcity.* Washington, DC: Venture Philanthropy Partners.

Moynihan, D. P. 2007. "The Reality of Results: Managing for Results in State and Local Government." In *In Pursuit of Performance: Management Systems in State and Local Government*, edited by P. Ingraham, 151–177. Baltimore, MD: The Johns Hopkins University Press.

Newcomer, K. E. 2004. "How Might We Strengthen Evaluation Capacity to Manage Evaluation Contracts." *American Journal of Evaluation* 25, no. 2: 209–218.

Nonprofit Finance Fund. 2014. State of the Nonprofit Sector Survey Results. Retrieved from http://nonprofitfinancefund.org/files/docs/2014/2014survey_natl_summary.pdf.

Office of Management and Budget. 2011. "President's Budget for Fiscal Year 2011. Performance and Management in the Analytical Perspectives Supplement," edited by Office of Management and Budget.

Osbourne, David and Ted Gaebler. 1992. *Reinventing Government: How the Entrepreneurial Spirit Is Transforming the Public Sector.* Reading, MA: Addison-Wesley Publishing Company.

Ostrower, F. 2004. "Attitudes and Practices Concerning Effective Philanthropy: Survey Report." Washington, DC.

Pettijohn, Sarah L., and Elizabeth T. Boris. 2013. "Federal Government Contracts and Grants for Nonprofits." Washington, DC.

"Philanthropy Open for Improvement." Fund for Shared Insight, accessed March 14, 2016, http://www.fundforsharedinsight.org/#improvement.

Poister, T. H. 2004. "Performance Monitoring." In *Handbook of Practical Program Evaluation*, edited by J. S. Wholey, H. Hatry and K. E. Newcomer, 98–125. San Francisco: John Wiley & Sons.

Porter, M. E., and M. R. Kramer. 1999. "Philanthropy's New Agenda: Creating Value." *Harvard Business Review*, November–December.

Rossi, Peter H., and Howard E. Freeman. 1989. *Evaluation: A Systematic Approach*, 4th ed. Newbury Park, CA: Sage Publications.

Schein, E. H. 2010. *Organizational Culture and Leadership*, 4th ed. San Francisco: Jossey-Bass.

Smillie, I., and J. Hailey. 2001. *Managing for Change: Leadership, Strategy and Management in Asian NGOs.* London: Earthscan.

Smith, S. R. 1996. "New Directions in Nonprofit Funding." *Philanthropic Fundraising* 12: 5–28.

———. 2010. "Nonprofits and Public Administration: Reconciling Performance Management and Citizen Engagement." *The American Review of Public Administration* 40, no. 2: 129–152.

Sowa, J. E., S. C. Selden, and J. R. Sandfort. 2004. "No Longer Unmeasurable? A Multidimensional Integrated Model of Nonprofit Organizational Effectiveness." *Nonprofit and Voluntary Sector Quarterly* 33, no. 4: 711–728.

Steinberg, R. 2006. "Economic Theories of Nonprofit Organizations." In *The Nonprofit Sector: A Research Handbook*, edited by Powell and Steinberg. New Haven, CT: Yale University Press, 117–139.

"The Leap Ambassadors Community." Leap of Reason, accessed March 14, 2016, http://leapofreason.org/performance-imperative/leap-ambassadors-community/.

"The Performance Imperative Campaign." Leap of Reason, accessed March 14, 2016, http://leapofreason.org/performance-imperative/about-pi/.

Tierney, Thomas J., and Richard Steele. 2011. "The Donor-Grantee Trap: How Ineffective Collaboration Undermines Philanthropic Results for Society and What Can Be Done About It." Boston, MA.

Trice, H. M., and J. M. Beyer. 1993. *The Culture of Work Organizations*. Upper Saddle River, NJ: Prentice Hall.

Tusi, A. S., H. Wang, and K. R. Xin. 2006. "Organizational Culture in China: An Analysis of Culture Dimensions and Culture Types." *Management and Organization Review* 2: 345–376.

Twersky, F., P. Buchanan, and V. Threlfall. 2013. "Listening to Those Who Matter Most, the Beneficiaries." *Stanford Journal of Social Innovation Review,* Spring: 40–45.

United Way of America. 1996. "Measuring program outcomes: A practical approach." Alexandria, VA.

U.S. Government Accountability Office. "Performance budgeting: PART focuses attention on program performance, but more can be done to engage Congress. GAO 06-28. Report to the Chairman, Sub-committee on Government Efficiency and Financial Management, Committee on Government Reform, House of Representatives." United States Accounting Office, October 2005.

Wholey, J. 2001. "Managing for Results: Roles for Evaluators in a New Management Era." *American Journal of Evaluation* 22, no. 3: 343–347.

Zimmermann, J., and B. Stevens. 2006. "The Use of Performance Measurement in South Carolina Nonprofits." *Nonprofit Management & Leadership* 16, no. 3: 315–327.

Chapter 11

International Trends in Government-Nonprofit Relations

Constancy, Change, and Contradictions

Susan D. Phillips and Mark Blumberg

INTRODUCTION

The "associational revolution" that Salamon (1994) described in the early 1990s has continued on a global scale well into the twenty-first century (Casey 2016a; Hudson Institute 2015). The worldwide expansion of numbers of nonprofits over the past decade suggests that we are living in an era in which "civil society's time has come" (World Economic Forum 2013). Nonprofits are not only delivering a wide and expanding range of services, but serving as vehicles for the expression of cultural identities and sources of social innovation and taking activist roles in social and policy change.[1] While growth of this sector is a global phenomenon, the patterns of government-nonprofit relationships vary considerably across locales. In some countries, governments have been adaptive in responding to an evolving nonprofit sector and proactive in creating an enabling environment for its work, but in other places the story is one of policy drift in the absence of political incentives and pressure from the sector for constructive reform. In a substantial number of countries, governments have intentionally closed the space in which civil society organizations (CSOs) operate, particularly limiting their ability to advocate, and in more extreme cases are exercising outright repression of them (Rutzen 2015; Carothers and Brechenmacher 2014). The conditions that led to this divergence in government-nonprofit relationships are changing quite rapidly under the pressures of several trends: changing demographics; heightened public expectations of transparency and demonstration of impacts; diversification and hybridization of this sector; and the globalization of philanthropy and nonprofit activities, making once mainly domestic phenomena transnational in scope. Can we expect these emerging trends to produce new models of government-nonprofit relationships and greater convergence of public policies for the nonprofit sector across countries?

This chapter assesses the implications of these trends on approaches to public policy and regulation for the third and emerging "fourth" sector (Sabeti 2009) across a wide range of countries. We focus on developments in four aspects of public policy governing nonprofits: registration, oversight, and promotion of transparency; tax incentives; regulation of political and business activities; and "meta-policy"—the ideational policy framework that articulates a vision for the relationship between the state and nonprofit sector and gives rise to governmental machinery and programs to implement this vision (Phillips and Smith 2014). To be manageable within a single chapter, the analysis is necessarily high level, identifying key patterns and major recent developments, rather than offering a systematic and comprehensive country-by-country assessment.

THE STATE OF THE NONPROFIT SECTOR: AN INTERNATIONAL OVERVIEW

Comparative research has established that, internationally, the nonprofit sector is larger and more significant than is often perceived (Salamon 1999). According to the Johns Hopkins Comparative Nonprofit Sector Project (JHCNSP), if the operating expenditures of nonprofits across the 40 countries it studied were aggregated, it would rank as the world's seventh largest economy, only slightly smaller than France (Salamon et al. 2010). In terms of employment, the nonprofit sector constitutes, on average, 7.4 percent of the workforce (including the contributions of volunteers for 13 countries for which reliable data are available), placing it ahead of other major industries such as transportation and finance (Salamon et al. 2013). Globally, this sector has been growing, in both number of organizations and economic contributions to gross domestic product (GDP), with an annual growth rate from the late 1990s to the mid-2000s estimated to be 5.8 percent, compared to 5.2 percent for the economies as a whole (Salamon et al. 2013). These economic measures, however, do not capture the contributions of the nonprofit sector to the social, cultural, and democratic life of citizens through both service delivery and expressive activities (Frumkin 2002; Salamon et al. 2003). In general, service functions dominate expressive ones (with little difference between developed and developing countries): 63 percent of the sector's paid and volunteer personnel is dedicated primarily to services and 32 percent to expressive activities, as measured across thirty-two countries (Salamon et al. 2003). The range of services provided is diverse, although education (23 percent of the workforce), social services (19 percent), and health

(14 percent) dominate; among expressive functions, 19 percent of nonprofit personnel are engaged in cultural activities, 7 percent in professional, and 4 percent in civic and advocacy roles (Salamon et al. 2003).

The revenues for the sector come from three main sources: the sale of goods and services (which, on average, account for 50 percent of income), governments (36 percent), and philanthropy (14 percent) (Salamon et al. 2013). An international trend is the growing reliance on fees due to the marketization of services, even in social democratic countries (Bode 2011), the shrinking availability of government grants, and the growing preference for social entrepreneurship as business models. As Salamon and colleagues (2010) note, governments remain critical of the financial sustainability of the sector, and nowhere are nonprofits supported primarily by philanthropy. The significance of donations varies greatly across subsectors, however, and may be more important for the "typical" mid-sized nonprofit than averages suggest (Lasby 2011).

While aggregate figures are impressive, there are significant variations in the size, composition, and revenue sources of the nonprofit sector across regions. For countries with national satellite account data, the economic contributions as a percentage of GDP range from 8 percent in Canada to 0.8 percent in Thailand (Casey 2016a). Although the United States has the largest number of nonprofits, the relative size of its sector, compared to the economically active population, is actually smaller than in many European countries (Salamon et al. 2010). The countries with the largest nonprofit sector, constituting more than 10 percent of paid employment, are the Netherlands, Canada, Belgium, Israel, the United Kingdom, and Ireland (the United States constitutes 9.2 percent); those in which the nonprofit sector is less than 1 percent include Slovakia, Pakistan, Poland, and Romania (Salamon et al. 2010). The common perception that a large welfare state crowds out nonprofits and philanthropy is, in fact, not supported as the Scandinavian countries have both large welfare states and nonprofit sectors. One explanation is that in Scandinavian countries a large number of nonprofits are engaged in sports and expressive activities, including advocacy, rather than the provision of quasi-public services. Further, in testing the "social origins" (Salamon and Anheier 1998) hypothesis that charitable giving is highest in liberal democracies, Einoff (2015) finds the opposite—that people are more likely to give in countries with larger public sectors. Across developed countries, however, philanthropy has become increasingly concentrated with fewer numbers of people carrying the bulk of giving and volunteering. The overall percentage that households donate has remained unchanged for decades (Cowly et al. 2011), and overall giving levels have remained stable only as a result of larger gifts by high net worth (HNW) individuals.

Transition and developing countries tend to have the least developed nonprofit sectors, although, as Casey notes (2016a; see Themudo 2013), the relationship between economic development and size of the sector is "not necessarily linear," given that economic stability, as opposed to mere size, and a philanthropic culture are important factors. Although comparative research emphasizes consistent regional variations, for instance, a Nordic, industrialized Asian or African model (Salamon et al. 2003), significant intra-regional differences are evident, and at critical junctures governments have taken quite different routes to supporting (or restricting) the growth of nonprofits. China and Vietnam, for example, have fostered substantial nonprofit sectors while keeping them under state control (Wang et al. 2015). By comparison, when South Korea, with virtually no domestic giving or organized civil society under the period of dictatorship, began its path of rapid growth in the mid-1980s, the government adopted a corporatist, collaborative approach that promoted a very vibrant nonprofit sector (Einolf 2015; Kang et al. 2015). Similarly, the nonprofit sectors in Eastern Europe and EurAsia are evolving in quite different ways. With a population of only 1.3 million, Estonia supports more than 30,000 CSOs and ranks highest on the USAID (2014) CSO Sustainability Index, in large part due to its supportive legal environment and sector infrastructure. Belarus and Turkmenistan, in contrast, have, respectively, only 2,600 and 106 registered CSOs, and they operate in a legal environment that is highly restrictive with very limited access to funding and little space for advocacy (USAID 2014). On top of these differences, the military conflict and humanitarian crisis in Ukraine following Russia's annexation of Crimea in 2014 had a "spillover effect" on the region with some following Russia to exert tighter controls over civil society and others consolidating a commitment to "democratic values," accentuating two very different trajectories of government-nonprofit relations in the region (USAID 2014).

Comparative analysis must acknowledge that measurement methods may not consistently capture civil society activity across societies. Use of a uniform definition of "nonprofit" and consideration of engagement only through these formal organizations, as done in the JHCNSP, may overlook a large portion of more informal activity that is not captured by notions of philanthropy, volunteerism, or nonprofit. An example is the South African philosophy and practice of *ubuntu*, which has pan-African versions and equivalents in indigenous philanthropy elsewhere. Based on "principles of reciprocity and co-operation grounded in unwritten, but widely understood, behaviours of giving" (Mottiar and Ngcoya 2016), *ubuntu* has its own formalized traditions and structures, but in many studies these would not be counted as part of the nonprofit sector. In the context of Latin America, Oxhorn (2011; see also Butcher and Tagtachian 2016) argues that Western analytical conceptions of civil society, nongovernmental organizations (NGOs), and nonprofits are inadequate for understanding the more collectivist components of its social structures and cultures. In addition, the blunt division between service and expressive activities may miss important dynamics of this sector. Comparing Mexico and Brazil, Lavelle and Bueno (2011) observe that a "modernization" and "functional diversification" of this sector in recent years has introduced new organizations, including new kinds of social movements, coordinating bodies and church-inspired issue-oriented "pastorals," that are working alongside more traditional neighborhood associations and service nonprofits. Collectively, they are enhancing the capacity for influencing public policy, but do not fit into tidy definitional categories or functions.

In sum, the nonprofit sector is large, diverse in its functions—including service delivery and expressive and advocacy activities—and growing in most countries. Similar cultural frames (Casey 2016a) and welfare regimes (Salamon and Anheier 1998) have generated regional similarities in nonprofit sectors, albeit with significant country-specific variations. While deeply embedded cultural factors and historical patterns of government-nonprofit relationships tend to carve path-dependent channels that produce mainly incremental change, quite rapid disruption also occurs, for instance through the effects of natural disasters on giving, as occurred in China and Japan in recent years, and through uprisings and widespread dissent, as happened with the "colored revolutions" in the Balkans in the early 2000s and the "Arab Spring" beginning in 2010 (Civicus 2014). In addition to these sudden disruptions, government-nonprofit relationships are also being influenced—in gradual but more predictable ways—by changes in demographics and the geographies of wealth, heightened expectations of transparency, diversification of the sector, and transnationalism.

Changing Demographics

Engagement in philanthropy and nonprofits is being reshaped by two demographics: women and Millennials (those born between 1980 and 2000). A growing number of women are able to make substantial gifts in their own right (TD and Investor Economics 2015; US Trust and Lilly Family School 2014), and their patterns for engagement are different from their male counterparts, including being more internationally oriented (Mensch and Paxton 2016; Micklewright and Schnepf 2009). Women are leading new forms of collective philanthropy, such as giving circles, through which they seek to transform communities or address causes "from the bottom up" (Eikenberry 2016) and have assumed highly effective roles—as leaders not just clients—in microfinance and financial inclusion across many developing countries (Cosgrove 2010). The Millennial generation is the largest, most diverse cohort in history, currently representing almost a third of the global population, and by 2025 it will constitute about 75 percent of the global workforce (Deloitte 2014). As digital natives, they are highly networked, less religious than their parents, and entrepreneurial; they value authenticity, want to "solve real problems" with systemic solutions (Johnson Center 2013), and volunteer at higher rates than their parents or the Boomer generation, preferring to support causes in various ways rather being loyal to specific organizations (Achieve 2014; Nielsen 2014).

Religious affiliation and attendance at faith services has been a strong predictor of giving and volunteering, and religion is still the primary destination of philanthropy in many countries. However, religious attachment (particularly among Christians) is declining rapidly in many European and North and South American countries, and the composition of religions among once quite homogenous populations is changing due to immigration. In France, for example, only 16 percent of the population participates regularly in religious practice, and its nonprofit sector is more secular than in the United States (Gauthier et al. 2015). Similarly, in Ireland, the number of people defining themselves as having no religion in 2011 grew by 44 percent from five years earlier, and the fastest-growing religions are (Eastern) Orthodox, Hinduism, and Islam (Irish Census 2016). Globally, Islam is significant for its growth (Hackett et al. 2015); in addition, its culturally embedded but largely informal charitable practices are increasingly relying on the formal tools of philanthropy (Wagner 2016), and a wide range of associated new nonprofits, including community foundations, are being registered and assuming active roles in community development (Herrold 2015; Kuttab et al. 2015).

Changing Expectations of Transparency and Impact

Public trust is the currency of the nonprofit sector. A variety of surveys indicate that public trust in nonprofits remains high compared to other sectors, but there is evidence of a decline in recent years. In its 2015 survey, the Edelman Trust Barometer (2015) reported an average decrease in public trust from 66 to 63 percent from the previous year, declining in nineteen of twenty-seven countries surveyed. As indicated by sharp drops in the United Kingdom, Brazil, and China, public trust is sensitive to instances of wrongdoing that receive extensive media coverage (Dobbs 2015). Even when trust has remained more or less constant, two messages are clear from these surveys. First, the public is concerned about waste and wants to know more about where the money goes; second, people increasingly want evidence of impact, which is that nonprofit programs are effective in achieving results (Wixley and Noble 2014; Muttart 2013). The interest in impact is particularly strong among women and Millennials who tend to conduct considerable due diligence on the organizations they are considering supporting,

HNW entrepreneurs interested in social innovation and systems change, and the investors exploring the burgeoning new asset class of impact investments through which they anticipate both financial and social returns. These expectations of transparency increase the need for both a credible state regulator and more effective self-regulation.[2]

In an era of big data and "the network effect of the internet" (Bria 2015), transparency no longer means just access to standardized information such as nonprofit Internal Revenue Service (IRS) information returns, but entails coproducing meaningful information that is used to mobilize public good. A rapidly expanding movement of digital social innovation is working with governments and nonprofits to open up and cocreate data, produce more meaningful data, and increase their capacity to use this information more effectively (see Bria 2015; www.poweredbydata.org).

Diversification of the Sector

Hybridity—the embodiment of more than one institutional logic in an organization (Skelcher and Smith 2014)—has long characterized the nonprofit sector, as evidenced by charity shops, community economic development corporations, cooperatives, and quasi-public institutions such as universities and museums. Hybridity has become more extensive and more complex in recent years as nonprofits and charities pursue new revenue sources, private investors seek both financial and social returns on impact investments, foundations look to put their endowments to work through program-related investments (PRIs), and for-profits value a triple bottom line. In some cases, business and social purposes are intertwined in a single organization, often called "social enterprises"; in others, new ownership chains and relationships are created when nonprofits own for-profit entities, create affiliated foundations, or participate in joint ventures (Sebati 2009; Smith 2011). Although the rhetoric of hybridization has outpaced practice, the public policy challenge is that historically, at least in common law countries, regulation has been organized to cover three discrete categories: (1) charities and foundations; (2) other nonprofits that meet a non-distribution constraint but are absent charitable purposes; and (3) for-profits. The development of a mixed "fourth" sector raises questions of whether new legal forms are needed, what should be regulated and how? The Zuckerberg-Chan "gift" put a spotlight on these legal forms because they, like many wealthy young entrepreneurs, prefer using vehicles over which they retain control; in this case, putting the $45 billion in Facebook shares the couple will ultimately contribute into a limited liability company rather than a philanthropic vehicle (Levine 2015).

Transnationalism

Like hybridity, cross-border philanthropy and nonprofit activity are not new: for instance, more money flows as remittances through diasporas than as official government aid (Schmid and Nissim 2016). International influences and funding have been instrumental in building civil society in many countries as diverse as Israel, South Korea, and Lebanon (see Wiepking and Handy 2015). International-scale NGO federations such as World Vision and Oxfam have been engaged in humanitarian assistance and development for sixty years, with the seven largest having a combined income of over $7 billion, and still growing (Boabab 2015). The global reach of philanthropy and nonprofit action has assumed a new scale, however, with new implications for public policy.

The geographies of wealth are undergoing significant change due to the spread of the hyper-wealthy and the rise of the middle class in the Global South. Described as akin to a "billionaire social movement" (Smith 2014), more than 142 of the world's richest people, including 25 from outside the United States, have signed on to the Giving Pledge initiated by Bill Gates and Warren Buffet, committing to give away a total of $708 billion of their personal wealth. These philanthropists tend to be hands-on and purport to seek the "best innovations and the most effective institutions wherever they find them" (CAF 2014) while potentially maintaining cultural affinities with their countries of origin. The Bill and Melinda Gates Foundation was the "tipping point" of such internationalization as it operates in over 100 countries and has become the largest funder of global health programs other than the US and UK governments, spending more than the World Health Organisation (McGregor-Lowndes 2016).[3] Although at first this American brand of strategic philanthropy did not export well due to differing cultural perspectives and legal regimes restrictive of nonprofits, the interest is growing, particularly in Asia, where it may be an impetus for policy change that is more enabling of nonprofits. The geographic redistribution of wealth is occurring not only at the very high end, but through a growing middle class in the Global South. Despite intractable poverty in many countries, the portion of the world's middle class residing in the Global South is predicted to constitute 80 percent by 2030 (UNDP 2013). When combined with the changing roles of women and Millennials, the geographic rearrangement of wealth can be expected to reshape intra-regional and cross-border patterns of philanthropy in major ways that break the traditions of remittances and international relief that move mainly "from West to East and from North to South" (CAF 2013), as well as altering preferences for the kinds of causes and organizations supported.

On the darker side of transnationalism are money laundering and financing of terrorist organizations which may, albeit acknowledged as rarely, involve nonprofits as complicit in raising and transferring funds illegally or as victims in having legitimate funding diverted or their interconnections and work exploited, particularly in conflict zones (van der Does de Willebois 2010). The Financial Action Task Force (FATF) and other intergovernmental entities which have been established to coordinate efforts against illegal transborder flows have been vocal in stressing the need for better information and transparency about nonprofits, more effective self-regulation that encourages good governance, and stronger state controls and the designation of risky nonprofits (FATF 2014; van der Does de Willebois 2010). A fundamental tension is that the existing policy regimes were built on assumptions that philanthropy and the work of nonprofits are strictly domestic affairs, and they are now grappling with the challenge of how to support, or control, cross-border monetary flows and nonprofit activities.

Our argument is that collectively these factors are transforming, in both quiet and bold ways, the policy approaches and instruments for nonprofit policy.

THE NONPROFIT POLICY TOOLKIT

Public policy for the nonprofit sector takes many forms, although four primary rationales form a common core for purposes of comparative analysis: promoting transparency and providing oversight to prevent abuse and maintain public trust; providing exemptions from taxation and tax incentives to encourage giving; regulating political and business activities to ensure spending primarily on charitable and "public benefit" purposes; and creating an overall ethos and framework by which to manage relationships between governments and nonprofits.[4] The four goals with their associated policy instruments and issues of implementation are presented in table 11.1. This should be thought of as a *conceptual* toolkit, implemented in different ways, with some tools not used at all, in different countries.

ART OF THE STATE-NONPROFIT RELATIONS: INTERNATIONAL TRENDS

In this section, we examine contemporary patterns and recent developments for each of the four aspects of government-nonprofit relationships.

Transparency and Oversight

A virtually universal trend in recent years has been toward increased accountability and regulation of nonprofits, but this movement has taken two

Table 11.1 Policy Goals and Instruments

Policy Goal	Primary Policy Instruments	Issues of Implementation
Promote transparency, good practices and trust; provide government oversight for accountability; prevent abuse	• Basic human and civil rights • Forms to establish legal identities • Registration with government regulator • Annual reporting on finances and activities (and public benefit) • Self-regulation	• Auspices of the regulator: in the tax agency, independent commission or line department • Information to be reported: usefulness and accuracy; administrative burden of reporting • Coverage: whether organizations other than those with charitable purposes require registration and oversight; availability of alternative corporate and legal forms
Provide tax exemption on income that is nonprofit; create incentives for charitable giving; build a broad culture of philanthropy; protect the integrity of the tax system	• Determination of eligible organizations, through legislation, common law, or tax code • Exemptions on income, property, and value-added taxes • Tax incentives for charitable giving • Regulations on cross-border giving; antiterrorism regulations • Education and moral suasion to promote giving and volunteering	• Eligibility: does eligibility for tax exempt status fit the contemporary nature of the sector and policy goals; does it enable or repress nonprofits? • Harmonization: whether eligibility for tax exemptions and ability to offer tax incentives and registration are automatic or different • Size and basis of tax incentives: what can be donated (including tax relief on social investments); whether a tax deduction or credit • Distribution of donations: whether differential incentives should be given to different causes, or donor choice should determine distribution • Strings attached: appropriate restrictions on nonprofit activities related to tax exemption • Domestic vs. international: extent to which cross-border giving (with tax receipts) and foreign funding are allowed
Ensure charities and tax exempt organizations spend primarily on charitable purposes; maintain fair treatment relative to business; restrict political activities	• Regulation of political and business activities, fundraising, and administrative costs • Corporate entities for social enterprises and social purpose businesses	• Degree of restrictiveness: whether restrictions are appropriate or intended to contain or repress, regardless of tax exemption • Enabling and regulating social enterprise: provision of different corporate forms and regulations for the "fourth" sector
Establish a guiding framework ("meta-policy") with which to provide political leadership and manage relationships with nonprofits and public expectations	• Political philosophy and policy frameworks or "compacts" • Government machinery for relationship management • Partnerships and engagement of the sector in policy and co-production of services • Financing sector infrastructure and capacity and supporting the ability to innovate • Regulations and support for transnational work and organizations	• Independence of sector: respecting autonomy • Scope and relevance: managing a government and sector-wide framework when each is diverse and changing; stance toward international and transnational operations • Monitoring and compliance for both government and the sector

markedly different paths based on disparate motivations: one is to enhance transparency and trust in nonprofits and the other to retain state control over their creation and operations. Aligned with the first track, a number of common law jurisdictions—notably Australia, New Zealand, Ireland, Scotland, and Northern Ireland—have established new regulators[5] with mandatory registration and reporting systems for "charities." Across Europe, sixty-five government initiatives designed to increase transparency and accountability have been undertaken in recent years, motivated by a recognition of the social, economic, and policy importance of this sector and the need to reinforce public confidence and safeguard nonprofits from abuse related to terrorist financing and other illegal activity (ECNL 2009).[6] Many of Europe's civil law countries (e.g., Bulgaria, Hungary, Italy, Netherlands, and Poland) have enacted a new status of "public benefit organization" that unifies accountability requirements across different legal forms and are accompanied by new national registries or requirements that make existing information on nonprofits more publicly accessible (ECNL 2009; Bullian and Toftisova 2005).[7]

In addition to providing greater transparency of finances, two new dimensions are being added to accountability: reporting on public benefit and on internal governance. England has not only legislated a statutory definition of charity, which includes a public benefit requirement, but with 2011 revisions to its legislation, now requires that charities demonstrate in their annual reports how they are meeting a public benefit test. So far, compliance has been uneven, with greater take-up by large charities that recognize the public benefit requirement "as a potential opportunity to develop and maintain confidence in the 'charity brand'" (IVAR and Sheffield Hallam 2012). Wider compliance by organizations with more limited capacity will depend to a large extent on effective review and guidance by the Charity Commission. Given the heightened public interest in impact, England may serve as a model for other countries that are attempting to enhance public benefit and trust in this sector (Blumberg 2016). In addition, the established regulators, notably in the United States, England, and Canada, are increasingly seeing good governance as a key means to regulatory compliance, and are requiring more information on governance and fundraising practices (House of Commons 2016; McGregor-Lowndes 2016; Phillips 2013). How far government regulators will go with intensive monitoring of nonprofit governance is an open question because such oversight would be enormously resource intensive and, like reporting on results, would require the regulator to provide education and guidance regarding good practice rather than simply relying on standard setting, auditing, and sanctions.

State regulation seems to be moving away from this kind of "responsive" regulation based on education first, however, with state regulators more narrowly focused on preventing abuse, and the enhancement of good practices left to self-regulation. In part, this narrowing of regulatory focus has occurred as a reaction to significant cases of abuse, for instance, the use of charities as tax shelters in Canada where over $6.3 billion CDN was claimed by donors on these fraudulent schemes (CRA 2015), and the public outcry and exposure of questionable practices (e.g., selling of donor lists and lack of protection of privacy) that followed the 2015 suicide of the ninty-two-year-old "poppy lady" in England, who was said to be "hounded to death" by charities (Birkwood 2015). This has led to the replacement of the sector-led voluntary system of fundraising regulation by a more independent model, backed up by the Charity Commission that is expected to more publicly "name and shame" charities in violation of fundraising standards (House of Commons 2016). A number of other countries (Finland, Austria, Bulgaria, and Ireland) have similarly introduced more stringent regulations on fundraising with strengthened reporting requirements (ECNL 2009).

No matter the scope of its mandate, the credibility of the regulator is key to effective oversight: that of several of the well-established "model" regulators has recently been seriously challenged, albeit in different ways. Cuts of almost one-half to the budget of England's Charity Commission greatly undermined its work (Morgan 2015), leading to a parliamentary review declaring it "not fit for purpose" (Public Accounts Committee 2014) and recommending it to refocus on catching abuses rather than providing guidance. Only a year after the creation of Australia's not-for-profit commission, the Abbott government slashed its budget and announced it would be dismantled, although a change in government has reversed this plan. In the United States, questions of neutrality of IRS officials damaged the agency's credibility, with subsequent cuts in personnel further weakening its performance (Casey 2016b; Hicks 2014).[8] Similarly, in Canada, the allocation by the former Conservative government of major new funding directed to political activity audits resulted in the tax agency being perceived politicized; recognizing the damage of such perceptions, the new Liberal government has asserted its desire to protect "the independence of the Charity Directorate's oversight role for charities" (Blumberg 2016). With a larger, more diverse sector and public expectations of enhanced transparency, nonprofit regulators cannot be allowed to simply limp along, and thus an important task in the government-nonprofit relationship is to (re)define and support their responsibilities and restore their legitimacy.

In many other countries, governments are on a different trajectory where the intended destination is not a well-functioning, pluralistic nonprofit sector, but a more contained and controlled one. Since 2012, more than 100 laws have been proposed or enacted in a wide range of countries to restrict the registration, activities, or funding of nonprofits (Rutzen 2015; see also Breen 2015; Carothers and Brechenmacher 2014; Civicus 2014). With the perception that

CSOs provoke opposition to the government (see Ibrahim 2015 on Egypt; Wood 2016 on Kenya), such restrictions are achieved in a variety of ways, including burdensome registration and reporting requirements, tight restrictions on activities, limits or bans on foreign funding, overzealous application of counterterrorism and money-laundering rules, and limits on freedom of assembly and the media (Civicus 2014; Rutzen 2015). The majority of recently legislated constraints on nonprofits are in the former Soviet countries and sub-Saharan Africa (Civicus 2014), where, in addition to more general restrictions, targeted measures (in Russia, Uganda, and Nigeria) have been taken to silence LGBT activists. For instance, Russia requires nonprofits that receive funds from foreign sources to register as "foreign agents" if they intend to conduct political activities, and this has been used to impede election monitoring, LGBT and human rights organizations, and anticorruption initiatives (Hudson Institute 2015; INCL 2016). Although such restrictions are more common in developing and transition countries (see figure 11.1), the Hudson Institute (2015) in its comparison of sixty-four countries observes that the freedom for philanthropy and nonprofits "is largely influenced by deliberate choices made by policymakers, choices that are not necessarily dependent upon a country's level of development."

Controls on foreign funding have become one of the most common means of diminishing the capacity of nonprofits to engage in advocacy. As Breen

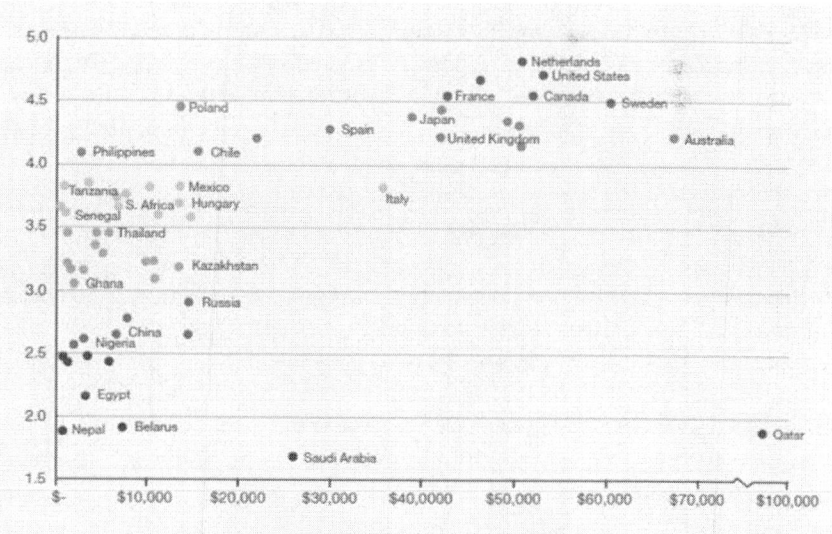

Figure 11.1 Vertical scale: 1 = an environment that restricts and impedes nonprofits; 5 = an environment that supports them. *Source*: The Hudson Institute, Index of Philanthropic Freedom, 2015.

(2016) notes, the breadth of such restrictions shows that nonprofits are being viewed as "troublesome adversaries more than as supportive allies." A 2011 CIVICUS survey of thirty-three countries reports that 87 percent identified constraints on foreign funding as hindering their work, and since 2013 there has been a spate of copycat legislation, mainly by (semi-)authoritarian regimes (Kai 2013; Carothers and Brechenmacher 2014). However, resistance to foreign funding is also being felt in Israel where proposed legislation would require nonprofits to receive a majority funding from foreign governments to be "foreign agents" and declare foreign funding on all official documents a measure most likely to stigmatize groups on the political left that are involved with human rights work (Gancman 2016). The emerging industrialized countries[9] are characterized by an ambivalence toward nonprofits involving an interest in legitimizing them "but only if they can control them carefully" (Spero 2014). For instance, India has recently strengthened restrictions on foreign funding (and political activities), which have been emulated by other governments in the region (Sidel 2016). The direction that China takes (which ranks 133 of 135 countries on the World Giving Index and has low levels of trust for nonprofits, but where philanthropy is growing very quickly) will be particularly consequential. China has significantly strengthened the environment for charitable organizations providing social services, including drafting new charity legislation that would provide a registration system and more coherence to its fragmented system of separate regulations for social organizations, foundations, and "private non-enterprise units" (Sidel 2016; China Development Brief 2016). At the same time, tighter government controls over foreign nonprofits are proposed, requiring them to have government sponsors and giving wide latitude to police to oversee their funding and activities, a measure that is widely criticized internationally and is currently being reconsidered (*Straits Times* 2016).

Tax Incentives

Exemptions for nonprofits from income, property, value-added and inheritance taxes, as well tax incentives to donors for charitable gifts have become "almost universal policy across market economies," albeit with different rationales, means, and conditions attached (Carmichael 2016; CAF 2006). In recent years, many countries have increased the scope of these tax privileges (CAF 2006; Dehne et al. 2008), both as a means to create a broadly based culture of philanthropy and to substitute private capital for reduced public spending. Following the 2008 recession, for example, Spain significantly increased the amount of the tax benefit as the government looked to private giving to replace some of the public funding that was cutback as part of its austerity measures (Hudson Institute 2015). The effects of tax incentives on individual giving is debated: evidence suggests that they tend to "nudge" but are not the determining factor in promoting philanthropy (Layton 2015), although there is no definitive comparative research (CAF 2006). On one hand, only about a third of tax filers claim the benefit (Government of Canada 2014); on the other hand, tax incentives may be of greater significance to HNW donors making substantial gifts which, given that philanthropy has become more reliant on such donors, need to be encouraged. Three issues are currently affecting the application of tax incentives.

The first issue is which organizations should qualify to be tax exempt and whether the determination of such status automatically awards the privilege of being able to issue tax-deductible receipts to donors. In recent years, a number of countries have reviewed the basis for registration and tax privileges, for instance, Japan and Turkey revised the terms of this status for associations, and India has allowed protection of the environment and yoga to qualify. In Canada, which is the only common law country without a statutory definition of charity, the new Liberal government has directed the tax agency to "modernize the rules governing charity" including a new legislative framework (Prime Minister of Canada 2015). In order to incentivize social finance and social enterprise, the United Kingdom has introduced the first tax relief for social investment (loans and other investments rather than gifts), the effects of which are still unfolding (Cabinet Office UK 2015). As societies become increasingly secular, can they adopt the approach of Australia, which recognizes religion as charitable but not automatically able to issue tax receipts for donations?

Second, a hint of a new debate—the clash of tax incentives with concerns over inequality—is emerging, with the United States serving as the proverbial canary. Tax incentives, particularly if they are deductions rather than credits, disproportionately benefit the wealthy making large donations (Reich 2005; Layton 2015). Under the logic of creating greater equity across tax brackets, the Obama administration has seven times proposed a cap on the charitable deduction for the highest tax bracket (which would affect individuals with incomes over $200,000). This proposal has met vigorous opposition among organized philanthropy predicting it would reduce giving by $9.4 billion in one year (Brooks 2013); due to the stalemate in Congress, it has not passed. Whether this debate is an example of American exceptionalism or likely to be felt elsewhere is an open question. When the idea of reducing the tax incentives was floated in the United Kingdom and Mexico, opposition led to its quick dispatch, and Canada has moved in the opposite direction of significantly increasing for income earners its already very generous tax credits.

The third issue reflects the increasing cross-border flows of philanthropic capital and nonprofit activity, and is playing out as restrictions on inflows of foreign funding noted earlier and as attempts to facilitate transnationalism. How tax systems, even in more facilitating countries, accommodate transborder giving varies greatly, as illustrated by Australia and the United Kingdom (McGregor-Lowndes 2016): Australia has adopted a restrictive (and opaque) policy, while the United Kingdom has extended tax relief for donations to organizations outside the country, with controls on illegal activities (McGregor-Lowndes 2016). The prime example of how limitations on cross-border flows are serious impediments to philanthropy is Europe, and the attempt—unfortunately failed—to create a common European Foundation Statute illustrates the challenges of trying to harmonize diverse domestic systems (Breen 2016; Hartnell and Milner 2015). The approximately 110,000 foundations in Europe annually disperse more than €153 billion, which outstrips their counterparts in the United States, with 67 percent engaged in international activities (Breen 2016). Yet, a myriad of obstacles impair their ability to fund organizations in other parts of Europe. Supported by the European Court, which ruled against tax discrimination based on whether the recipient organization is domestic or located in another member state, a common legal form was negotiated over a number of years that would have enabled foundations to operate and fund uniformly across the European Union (EU). As Breen (2016) observes, the European Foundation Statute ultimately failed when it encountered the "delicacies of host-country ownership" over their domestic regimes. Peak associations such as England's National Council of Voluntary Organisations (NCVO) (2014) continue to call for a more open Europe through simplification of the "byzantine" regulations on foundations and nonprofits, but to date there are no intimations of a second attempt at harmonization.

In sum, tax incentives have been one of the most stable components of public policy for nonprofits, but they have been rooted in an assumption that philanthropy is domestic, and that absent regulatory competition, countries will not "outbid" each other to attract contributions and nonprofits from other places. Like business capital, however, philanthropy capital is increasingly footloose, and countries now need to determine whether they will embrace and facilitate this, recognizing it might produce outflows as well as inflows of giving, and manage it against oversight of transnational money laundering and financing of terrorist activities.

Political and Business Activities

The strings attached to tax exempt status generally include limitations on political and business activities, the former often reinforced by concerns over criticism of government and the latter by preventing unfair advantage relative to business. Among countries that accept nonprofits as part of democratic life, there is substantial variation—and growing divergence—in how political and business activities are treated (Carmichael 2016).

The ability to advocate (in nonpartisan ways) is seen as a criterion for the independence of the nonprofit sector in (Panel on the Independence of the Voluntary Sector 2015), but there is a very lively debate over how unconstrained this should be, especially relative to the common law doctrine of political purposes which makes nonprofits that have politically oriented missions ineligible to be considered "charitable" (Parachin 2015). In both common and civil law countries, the interpretations of eligibility and limits on advocacy vary widely, even among the relatively homogenous OECD countries (Bloodgood 2010), and recent court cases have widened the gap of legal interpretations.[10] Sweden and Norway are among the most permissive as political purposes are considered an aspect of public benefit and are eligible for registration (Carmichael 2016). Rules on advocacy have been slow to be updated in most countries, except those seeking tight restrictions, and thus tend to reflect the period in which they were created (Bloodgood 2010). The real limits on advocacy may not be regulatory, however. Although there is considerable talk in democratic countries of a "chill" on advocacy because regulation unduly circumscribes it, evidence indicates that charities are undertaking only a fraction of the amount of political activities that they can legally do under current rules (Blumberg 2013; Bass et al. 2014), likely due to lack of expertise or interest in investing in advocacy, a desire to focus on services or concern over stakeholder backlash.

Most regulatory regimes are still marked by the historical legacy of separate systems governing charities and public benefit organizations, other nonprofits, and for-profits. Yet, business activities already account for 50 percent of the revenues of nonprofit sectors; and, with growing interest in social enterprise, they are being pursued even more actively with more creative ways of blending the commercial with social good. When business activities are undertaken by nonprofits recognized as charitable or public benefit, they may be regulated under three distinctive models. In only a very few cases are they prohibited from carrying on business activities, although this is the case in Turkey where nonprofits need to establish a separate legal entity which is treated for tax purposes like any other for-profit (ECNL 2015). At the other extreme is a permissive model, allowing nonprofits to undertake economic activities without limitation, as long as it is not the primary purpose of the organization and does not distribute the profits, which applies in France, Germany, and other countries of Western Europe. The revenues may be taxed as in the United States, fully tax exempt as in France, or exempt as long as they their destination is the charitable purpose. The third model permits business activity only if it is "related" and "incidental" to the organization's charitable purposes, as in India, Canada, and most of Eastern Europe.

Current regulatory approaches thus provide very differing degrees of flexibility when social entrepreneurs try to meld business and social good into one organizational form. The trend across Europe and Asia is to allow more scope for economic activities (Sidel and Moore, ND), although approaches vary considerably. A means of facilitating social enterprise in England and several US states, now being emulated elsewhere, has been to create new hybrid corporate forms, Community Interest Companies (CICs) in the United Kingdom and low-profit limited liability companies (L3Cs) in the United States, to legitimate dual purposes and allow greater flexibility in raising capital, pursuing activities, and using revenues and assets (Manwaring and Valentine 2011). To date, only England has established a regulatory authority, albeit a light-touch one, for these new vehicles, and whether regulation is needed at all for this emerging hybrid fourth sector is debated. In spite of the hype about social enterprise, the use of CICs and L3Cs is still very limited (Pearse and Hopkins 2014). What seems to be occurring instead, although almost invisibly, are more complicated chains of ownership: charities and nonprofits owning for-profits, or being controlled by for-profits. While such linked ownership chains may ultimately be more adaptable than hybrid corporate forms in accommodating public benefit, business, and political activities, they are also more opaque, raising new challenges for accountability and transparency.

Meta-Policies

Meta-policy reflects an overarching philosophy—explicit or implicit—about the appropriate roles of the state and the nonprofit sector (and the market), which gives rise to specific policies, programs, and governmental machinery, and guides reform. This may take the form of a publicly articulated policy, ideally designed to enable nonprofits and establish a constructive relationship with them. In the 1990s and early 2000s, several governments adopted such public philosophies, notably the "Third Way" of New Labour in the United Kingdom (followed for a brief period by the Coalition government's "Big Society"), Ireland's Social Partnership, and China's notion of "small government, big society" that was part of administrative reform in the 1990s (Brødsgaard and Strand 1998; Healy and Donnelly-Cox 2016). A popular policy instrument was the "compact," a negotiated framework agreement setting out the expectations and terms of engagement between government and the sector. These began in the United Kingdom and were transferred widely, including to Estonia, France, Spain, Sweden, Canada, and several Australian states (Casey et al. 2010; Reuter et al. 2012; Bullian and Toftisova 2005). As governments changed and priorities shifted to addressing austerity measures, however, most of these enabling frameworks quietly faded away:

even the heralded Big Society is rarely mentioned in England. In recent years, a few nonprofit sectors have been successful in obtaining new strategies for collaboration, for example in Brazil where in 2015, after ten years of advocacy, the legislature approved a New Regulatory Framework for CSOs that includes measures to incentivize nonprofits and create a more favorable tax environment (Instituto C&A 2015). In general, however, coherent, publicly articulated meta-policies are strikingly absent.

Most meta-policies for this sector are not so explicit, nor do they arise from a base of mutual agreement. For many governments, particularly those favoring a smaller state or dealing with tight financial constraints, the policy is a quiet one of privatized services in which "charity" is supported by private philanthropy and social investment. Tax incentives for charitable giving are sizable; social investment is embraced; regulations restrict advocacy; the main role of the regulator is to prevent abuse and waste; umbrella and peak associations are intentionally weakened; and discussions in the public sphere about government-nonprofit relationships are lacking. Canada under a Conservative government from 2006 to 2015 and Australia under its neoliberal governments (Lyons and Dalton 2011; Ronalds 2015) are prime examples.

Arguably, the United States fits neither an enabling or charity model well. While several high-level, cross-sector task forces have been established to examine the relationship and recommend reforms (Casey 2016b), governments matter less to the "collective organizational psyche of U.S. nonprofits" than they do elsewhere (Casey 2011).

A third model is one in which government is openly adversarial to nonprofits (Young 1998), restricting their activity in a variety of ways and isolating the sector from international funding and influences, as discussed above (Rutzen 2015; Civicus 2014; Carothers and Brechenmacher 2014). Several large economies, notably China and possibly India (Sidel 2016; China Development Brief 2016), seem to be drifting from more restrictive models toward more supportive policies for nonprofits and more openness to internationalization. Where they land over the next few years will have important implications for other countries.

Finally, depending on how the current enchantment with social investment unfolds, particularly pay-for-success contracting (also called social impact bonds), a model of privatized charity may be reinforced, only with greater access to private capital, or a new approach germinated. The central issue of social investment is no longer the ability to attract capital but to build sufficient capacity on the demand side, including removing regulatory barriers. The policy agenda laid out by Social Investing Steering Group established in 2015 as a follow-up to the G8 Task Force (involving thirteen countries and the EU) includes not only regulatory and tax incentives for impact investment and relaxing barriers that limit nonprofits from generating revenues

Table 11.2 Models of Government-Nonprofit Relationships

Model	Basis	Features
Enabling	Relationship based	Well-articulated, mutually supported policy for the government-nonprofit relationship and divisions of labor across sectors; capable public and nonprofit sectors; extensive collaboration; enabling regulation and credible regulator; transparency; tax incentives support a broad culture of philanthropy; respect for independence of the nonprofit sector and advocacy; adaptable to evolving needs of the relationship
Charity	Tax-incentivized provision of services	Sizeable tax incentives to encourage private giving; interest in social investment; nonprofit services substitute for public services; limits on advocacy; main role of state regulation is to prevent abuse; few policy debates about the role of nonprofits
Restrictive	State control	Legislative and regulatory restrictions on formation, registration and activities of nonprofits; intolerance for advocacy; limits on foreign funding and influence; lack of transparency; no investment in capacity building; may be outright repression and conflict
Drifting and transition	Mixed elements; lack of political incentives for change	Ambivalence between developing a pluralistic nonprofit sector and controlling it; still an emphasis on service roles of nonprofits; mixed signals regarding legitimacy of advocacy and internationalization

through business, but building the capacity of nonprofits to participate in social and impact investments. While social investment has not yet lived up to the claims made for it—and will not in itself produce a more constructive government-nonprofit relationship—the Task Force's recognition of the need to build sector infrastructure and capacity building is an important development (see table 11.2).

CONCLUSION

Has civil society's time come in terms of building more constructive relationships with governments? Patterns of government-nonprofit relationships show considerable consistency across regions and over time, but they also demonstrate marked differences, even among subsectors within specific countries, depending on the policy goals and strategies pursued by both governments and nonprofits. How advocacy groups are treated may be very different from social service organizations, and in many places, environmental and LGBT organizations are singled out for even tighter controls. Surprisingly few countries have an overarching philosophy or meta-policy to guide development of this relationship that is visibly and coherently directed toward enabling a vibrant, pluralist nonprofit sector that contributes to policy making and citizenship, as well as service provision. Indeed, the troubling development of recent years has been the shrinking spaces for civil society and cross-border philanthropy, which have been declared priority concerns by the UN, EU, the Obama administration, and a variety of other governments and international organizations (Rutzen 2015).

Even in places that see a positive role for this sector, a variety of contradictions are pulling the government-nonprofit relationship in opposing directions. Philanthropy's increased reliance on HNW donors favors expanded tax incentives, which is countered by concerns over inequality, the policy influence of wealth, and the cost in tax expenditures. While tax privileges have been granted only to eligible categories of charitable or registered organizations, the entrepreneurial super rich and Millennials tend to be "sector agnostic" (Smith 2015), caring little if the organization they support is officially charitable, a hybrid social enterprise, or a social purpose business. The interest in accommodating the hybridization arising from new ways of blending economic activities and social must grapple with unforeseen issues of accountability and transparency. Although acknowledging the autonomy of the sector, regulators are increasingly interested in oversight of nonprofit governance and fundraising. Countries feel a sense of ownership over their domestic regulatory regimes; at the same time, increased cross-border philanthropy and nonprofit activity are creating pressures to liberalize and harmonize their approaches. The convention of a sharp divide between charity and political activity and current attempts to restrict nonprofit advocacy do not sit well with the Millennial generation's activism.

How these tensions will be worked out in different places is what will make analysis of government-nonprofit relationships so fascinating in coming years. The one outcome that is quite certain is that greater transparency will be the norm, and more meaningful data will be co-created and put to work for public benefit through digital social innovation. And, such transparency may create the political incentives for positive reform of government-nonprofit relations that are currently lacking.

NOTES

1. In many contexts, the term "civil society organization (CSO)" is preferred over that of "nonprofit" because it emphasizes that the primary function may be engagement in citizenship and civic life rather than service delivery, and that many are not as highly institutionalized as they are in the United States and other developed countries.

2. Although charity regulators are not the most high profile institutions, public confidence in them matters, as demonstrated by an Australian survey which found that public confidence in charities increased significantly among those who were aware of and understood the role of the newly created not-for-profit commission (ACNC 2015).

3. The pledge of $3 billion by Jack Ma, one of China's richest people, to aid causes related to health care and environmental protection could have a significant influence on how nonprofits and governments address these issues (*Economist* 2014; Soskis 2014).

4. Direct government financing, through grants and contracts is of course also important, providing operational support and purchasing public services from nonprofits and indirectly regulating their activities. Such financing is difficult to assess without a deep dive into government data, a task beyond the scope of this chapter.

5. Following the model of the Charity Commission of England and Wales (created in 1853), all were established as independent commissions, although New Zealand's commission has been moved into a line department. The US and Canada have long-standing regulators, both housed in the tax agency.

6. In most countries, sector self-regulation goes hand-in-hand with state regulation, and ranges from voluntary codes of standards to a rigorous (albeit voluntary) certification system recently established by the sector in Canada. Although participation in and effectiveness of self-regulation varies considerably, it is an important component of the evolving co-regulatory relationship with governments, but also beyond the scope of this chapter.

7. In common law countries, the legal concept of charity, defined by centuries of case law, focuses on purposes and activities; if they meet eligibility criteria of purposes and activities, organizations are registered and receive associated tax benefits. In most cases (e.g., UK and Canada), registered charities automatically qualify for tax exemptions and receipting privileges, whereas in Australia, registered charities need to apply separately to the tax office to become eligible as Designated Gift Recipients. This means that while religion is considered charitable and exempt from income tax, unless a religious charity can demonstrate it provides some other public benefit it will not be able to issue tax receipts for donations. In civil law countries, the legal form determines the treatment of nonprofits, and "registration" refers to acquiring this legal form. There is often much greater variety of legal forms within civil law countries, and many recent reforms have aimed at greater harmonization of treatment among them. While a number of common law countries (except the US and Canada) have created independent charity commissions, the tendency for civil law countries is to house primary regulatory functions in the tax agency.

8. The claim that in reviewing applications for 501(c)(4) status, IRS officials targeted for greater scrutiny organizations associated with conservative causes, including the Tea Party movement, led to an investigation which faulted the IRS for its "scant" oversight (see GAO 2014).

9. These fast growing industrializing countries are often referred to as the "BRICS"—Brazil, Russia, India, China, and South Africa—although their booming economic conditions have changed significantly since the term was first coined in 2001.

10. The Australian High Court determined that advocacy related to a charitable purpose can itself be considered charitable, while a New Zealand court decided in favour of Greenpeace being considered a charity as political purposes can be charitable, and in 2014 a UK tribunal went even further to reason that human rights based advocacy can be "immune to the rules restricting political advocacy" (Parachin 2015).

REFERENCES

Achieve. (2014). *2014 Millennial Impact Report: Millennial Usability Testing.* Indianapolis, IN: Achieve Inc.

ACNC—Australian Charities and Not-for-Profits Commission. (2013). *Public Trust and Confidence in Australian Charities.* Sydney: ACNC.

Australian Government. (2014). *Australian Charities Report 2014.* Sydney: Australian Government.

Baobab. (2015). *ICSO Global Financial Trends.* Retrieved from http://www.baobab.org.uk/wp-content/uploads/2015/07/ICSOGlobalFinancialTrends2015.pdf.

Bass, Gary D., Abramson, Alan J., and Dewey, E. (2014). Effective Advocacy: Lessons for Nonprofit Leaders from Research and Practice. In R. J. Pekkanen, S. R. Smith, and Y. Tsujinaka (Eds.), *Nonprofits and Advocacy: Engaging Community and Government in an Era of Retrenchment* (pp. 254–294). Baltimore, MD: Johns Hopkins University Press.

Birkwood, S. (2015). "Fundraising Standards Board to Investigate Death of Poppy Seller Olive Cooke, Says Chief Executive Alistair McLean." *Third Sector*, May 18. Retrieved from http://www.thirdsector.co.uk/fundraising-standards-board-investigate-death-poppy-seller-olive-cooke-says-chief-executive-alistair-mclean/fundraising/article/1347535.

Bloodgood, E. (2010). "Institutional Environment and the Organization of Advocacy NGOs in the OECD." In A. Prakash and M. K. Gugerty (Eds.), *Advocacy Organizations and Collective Action.* Cambridge UK: Cambridge University Press.

Bloodgood, E., Tremblay-Boire, J., and Prakash, A. (2013). "National Styles of NGO Regulation." *Nonprofit and Voluntary Sector Quarterly*, 43(4), 716–736.

Blumberg, M. (2013). "Initial T3010 Descriptions of Political Activities by Canadian Charities." Retrieved from http://www.globalphilanthropy.ca/images/uploads/Initial_T3010_Descriptions_of_Political_Activities_by_Canadian_Charities.pdf.

Blumberg, M. (2016). *Increasing the Productivity of the Charity and Non-profit Sector through Greater Transparency and Accountability Submission to the House of Commons Standing Committee on Finance.* Toronto, ON: Blumberg Segal LLP. Retrieved from http://www.globalphilanthropy.ca/images/uploads/Submission_to_Finance_Committee_by_Mark_Blumberg_of_Blumberg_Segal_LLP_January_2016_docx.pdf.

Bode, In. (2011). "Creeping Marketization and Post-corporatist Governance: The Transformation of State-Nonprofit Relations in Continental Europe." In S. D. Phillips and S. R. Smith (Eds.), *Governance and Regulation in the Third Sector: International Perspective* (pp. 115–141). London: Routledge.

Breen, O. (2015). "Allies or Adversaries? Foundation Responses to Government Policing of Cross-Border Charity." *International Journal of Not-for-Profit Law*, 7(1), 45–71.

Bria, F. (2015). *Growing a Digital Innovation System for Europe*. Brussels: Digital Social Innovation. Retrieved from https://issuu.com/digitalsocialinnovation/docs/dsireport-forwebsite-print.

Brødsgaard, K. E., and Strand, D. (1998). *Reconstructing Twentieth Century China: State Control, Civil Society, and National Identity*. Oxford: Oxford University Press.

Brooks, A. C. (2013). "The Great Recession, Tax Policy, and the Future of Charity in America." Washington, DC: American Enterprise Institute.

Bullain, N., and Toftisova, R. (2005). "A Comparative Analysis of European Policies and Practices of NGO-Government Cooperation." *International Journal of Not-for-Profit Law*, 7(4), 64–112.

Butcher, J., and de Tagtachian, B. B. (2015). "Latin America and the Caribbean Revisited: Pathways for Research." *Voluntas*, 27(1), 1–18.

Cabinet Office UK Government. (2015). *Social Investment Tax Relief*. London: UK Government. Retrieved from https://www.gov.uk/government/publications/social-investment-tax-relief-factsheet/social-investment-tax-relief.

CAF. (2006). "International Comparisons of Charitable Giving." *Charities Aid Foundation Briefing Paper* (November), London: CAF.

CAF. (2013). *Future World Giving: Unlocking the Potential of Global Philanthropy*. London: CAF.

CAF. (2014). *Philanthropy: A Gift or Investment? How Young, Socially-Conscious Investors are Balancing Approaches to Philanthropy*. London: CAF.

Carmichael, C. (2016). "The Fiscal Treatment of Philanthropy from a Comparative Perspective." In T. Jung, S. D. Phillips and J. Harrow (Eds.), *The Routledge Companion to Philanthropy* (pp. 244–259). London: Routledge.

Carothers, Thomas and Brechenmacer, S. (2014). *Closing Spaces: Democracy and Human Rights Support under Fire*. Washington, DC: Carnegie Endowment for International Peace.

Casey, J. (2011). "A New Era of Collaborative Government-Nonprofit Relations in the U.S.?" *Nonprofit Policy Forum*, 1(1).

Casey, J. (2016a). *The Nonprofit World: Civil Society and the Rise of the Nonprofit Sector*. Boulder and London: Kumarian Press.

Casey, J. (2016b). "Tsars, Task Forces and Standards: The New 'IRS?'" *Nonprofit Policy Forum*, 7(1), 29–37.

Casey, J., Bronwen, D., Melville, R., and Onyx, J. (2010). "Strengthening Government-Nonprofit Relations: International Experiences with Compacts." *Voluntary Sector Review*, 1(1), 56–76.

China Development Brief. (February 23, 2016). "An Interview with Mark Sidel: Engaging with Chinese Philanthropy from a Global Perspective." Retrieved from http://chinadevelopmentbrief.cn/articles/an-interview-with-mark-sidel-engaging-with-chinese-philanthropy-from-a-global-perspective/.

CIVICUS. (2013). *State of Civil Society 2013: Creating an Enabling Environment*. Johannesburg: Civicus.

Civicus. (2014). *State of Civil Society Report: Reimaging Global Governance.* Johannesburg: Civicus.

Cosgrove, S. (2010). *Leadership From the Margins Women and Civil Society Organizations in Argentina, Chile, and El Salvador.* New Brunswick, NJ: Rutgers University Press.

Cowly, E., McKenzie, T., Pharoah, C., and Smith, S. (2011). *The New State of Donation: Three Decades of Household Giving to Charity 1978–2008.* Centre for Charitable Giving and Philanthropy, London: Cass Business School.

CRA—Canada Revenue Agency. (2015). "The Canada Revenue Agency Revokes the Registration of the Canadian Friends of Pearl Children." Ottawa, ON: CRA. http://news.gc.ca/web/article-en.do?nid=1002989.

Dehne, A., Friedrich, P., Nam, C. W., and Parsche, R. (2008). "Taxation of Nonprofit Associations in an International Comparison." *Nonprofit and Voluntary Sector Quarterly, 37*(4), 709–729.

Deloitte. (2014). *Big Demands and High Expectations: The Deloitte Millennial Study.* London: Deloitte Touche Tohmatsu Limited.

Dobbs, J. (2015). *Trust and Confidence in Charities An Overview of the Existing Evidence.* London: NCVO.

Economist. (2014). "China's Carnegie." *The Economist*, May 3. http://www.economist.com/news/leaders/21601510-jack-mas-establishment-new-charitable-foundation-offers-his-country-important.

Edelman. (2015). *Edelman Trust Barometer 2015.* Retrieved from www.edelman.com.

Eikenberry, A. (2016). "Could Giving Circles Rebuild Philanthropy from the Bottom Up?" *Nonprofit Quarterly,* February 4. Retrieved from https://nonprofitquarterly.org/2016/02/04/could-giving-circles-rebuild-philanthropy-from-the-bottom-up/.

Einolf, C. J. (2015). "The Social Origins of the Nonprofit Sector and Charitable Giving." In P. Wiepking and F. Handy (Eds.), *Palgrave Handbook of Global Philanthropy* (pp. 509–529). Basingstoke, UK: Palgrave Macmillan.

ECNL—European Center for Not-for-Profit Law. (2009). *Study on Recent Public and Self-Regulatory Initiatives Improving Transparency and Accountability of Non-Profit Organisations in the European Union.* Budapest: ECNL.

ECNL—European Center for Not-for-Profit Law. (2015). *Legal Regulation of Economic Activities of Civil Society Organizations.* Budapest: ECNL.

Financial Action Task Force—FATF (2014). *Risk of Terrorist Abuse in Non-Profit Organisations,* Paris: FATF.

Frumkin, P. (2002). *On Being Nonprofit: A Conceptual and Policy Primer.* Cambridge, MA: Harvard University Press.

Gancman, L. (December 27, 2015). "Cabinet Moves to Force NGOs to Declare Foreign Government Funding." *Times of Israel.* Jerusalem. Retrieved from http://www.timesofisrael.com/cabinet-moves-to-force-ngos-to-declare-foreign-government-funding/.

GAO—United States Government Accountability Office. (2014). *Tax Exempt Organizations: Better Compliance Indicators and Data, and More Collaboration with State Regulators would Strengthen Oversight of Charitable Organizations.* Washington, DC: GAO. http://www.gao.gov/assets/670/667595.pdf.

Gautier, A., Pache, A-C., and Mossel, V. (2015). "Giving in France: A Philanthropic Renewal after Decades of Distrust." In P. Wiepking and F. Handy (Eds.),

The Palgrave Handbook of Global Philanthropy (pp. 137–154). Basingstoke, UK: Palgrave Macmillan.

Global Social Impact Investment Steering Group. (2015). *Social Impact Investment*. Retrieved from http://www.socialimpactinvestment.org/index.php.

Government of Canada, Department of Finance. (2014) *Tax Expenditures and Evaluations*. Ottawa: Department of Finance.

Hackett, C., Cooperman, A., and Ritchey, K. (2015). *The Future of World Religions: Population Growth Projections, 2010–2050*. Philadelphia: Pew Research Center.

Hartnell, C., and Milner, A. (2015). "Rejection of European Foundation Statute a 'Missed Opportunity.'" *Alliance Magazine*, *20*(1), 8–9.

Healy, J., and Donnelly-Cox, G. (2016). "The Evolving State Relationship: Implications of 'Big Societies' and Shrinking States." In T. Jung, S. D. Phillips, and J. Harrow (Eds.), *The Routledge Companion to Philanthropy* (pp. 200–212). London: Routledge.

Herrold, C. (2015). "Giving in Egypt: Evolving Charitable Traditions in a Changing Political Economy." In P. Wiepking and F. Handy (Eds.), *Palgrave Handbook of Global Philanthropy* (pp. 307–315). London: Palgrave Macmillan.

Hicks, J. (2014). "Senate Panel Hits Auditor but Clears IRS of Bias in Targeting Scandal." *Washington Post,* September 5. Retrieved from https://www.washingtonpost.com/news/federal-eye/wp/2014/09/05/senate-panel-clears-irs-of-bias-in-targeting-scandal-but-hits-auditor/.

House of Commons Public Administration Select Committee—UK. (2016). *The 2015 Charity Fundraising Controversy: Lessons for Trustees, the Charity Commission, and Regulators*. London: PAC.

Hudson Institute. (2015). *The Index of Philanthropic Freedom 2015*. Washington, DC: Hudson Institute.

Ibrahim, B. (2015). "States, Public Space, and Cross-border Philanthropy: Observations from the Arab Transitions." *International Journal of Not-for-Profit Law*, *17*(1), 72–85.

Instituto C&A. (2015). "Regulatory Framework Rules are Approved with Changes." Retrieved from http://www.institutocea.org.br/noticias/Detalhe-noticia.aspx?id=2849.

International Center for Not-for-Profit Law. (2016). *NGO Law Monitor: Russia*. Retrieved from http://www.icnl.org/research/monitor/russia.html#reports.

Irish Census 2011. (2016). *Faith Survey*. Dublin: Government of Ireland. Retrieved from http://faithsurvey.co.uk/irish-census.html.

IVAR and Sheffield Hallam University. (2012). *The Impact of the Public Benefit Requirement in the Charities Act 2006: Perceptions, Knowledge and Experience*. London: Charity Commission.

Johnson Center on Philanthropy. (2013). *#Nextgen Donors, Respecting Legacy, Revolutionizing Philanthropy*. Grand Rapids, MI: Johnson Center on Philanthropy at Grand Valley State University.

Kai, M. (2013). *Report of the Special Rapporteur on the Rights to Freedom of Peaceful Assembly and of Association,*. New York: UN. Retrieved from http://www.ohchr.org/Documents/HRBodies/HRCouncil/RegularSession/Session23/A.HRC.23.39_EN.pdf.

Kang, C., Auh, Yoonkyung, E., and Hur,Y. (2015). "Giving in South Korea: A Nation of Givers for the Population under Public Assistance." In P. Wiepking and F. Handy (Eds.), *Palgrave Handbook of Global Philanthropy* (pp. 426–454). Basingstoke, UK: Palgrave Macmillan.

Kuttab, A., Matic, N., and ElMikawy, N. (2015). "Arab Philanthropy: From Social Giving to Social Change." *Alliance Magazine, 20*(3), 22–24.

Lasby, D. (2011). "What T3010 Data tell Us about Charity Financing." *The Philanthropist, 24*(2), 155–160.

Lavalle, A. G., and Bueno, N. S. (2011). "Waves of Change Within Civil Society in Latin America Mexico City and São Paulo." *Politics & Society, 39*(3), 415–450.

Layton, M. D. (2015). "The Influence of Fiscal Incentives on Philanthropy across Nations." In P. Wiepking and F. Handy (Eds.), *Palgrave Handbook of Global Philanthropy* (pp. 540–557). Basingstoke, UK: Palgrave Macmillan.

Levine, M. (2015). "Chan Zuckerberg LLC: No Tax Breaks + No Accountability = What Exactly?" *Nonprofit Quarterly*, December 7. Retrieved from http://nonprofitquarterly.org/2015/12/07/chan-zuckerberg-llc-are-no-tax-breaks-plus-no-accountability-good-for-the-public/.

Lyons, Mark and Dalton, B. (2011). "Australia: A Continuing Love Affair with New Public Management." In S. D. Phillips and S. R. Smith (Eds.), *Governance and Regulation in the Third Sector: International Perspective* (pp. 238–259). London: Routledge.

Manwaring, Susan and Valentine, A. (2011). *Social Enterprise in Canada: Structural Options*. Toronto, ON: MaRS.

McGregor-Lowndes, M., Tarr, J-A., and Silver, N. (2016). "The Fisc and the Frontier: Approaches to Cross-border Charity in Australia and the UK." *The Philanthropist*, May.

Mesch, D., and Pactor, A. (2016). "Women and Philanthropy." In T. Jung, S. D. Phillips, and J. Harrow (Eds.), *The Routledge Companion to Philanthropy* (pp. 88–101). London: Routledge.

Micklewright, J., and Schnepf, S. V. (2009). "Who Gives Charitable Donations for Overseas Development?" *Journal of Social Policy, 38*, 317–341.

Morgan, G. (2015). "The End of Charity?" Valedictory Lecture. Sheffield: Sheffield Hallam University. Retrieved from https://www.shu.ac.uk/_assets/pdf/the-end-of-charity-morgan.pdf.

Mottiar, S., and Ngcoya, M. (2016). "Indigenous Philanthropy: Challenging Western Preconceptions." In T. Jung, S. D. Phillips, and J. Harrow (Eds.), *The Routledge Companion to Philanthropy*. London: Routledge.

Muttart Foundation. (2013). *Talking about Charities 2013*. Edmonton, AB: Muttart Foundation.

NCVO—National Council of Voluntary Organisations. (2014). "Towards a More Open Europe." London. Retrieved from https://www.ncvo.org.uk/images/documents/policy_and_research/europe/eu-manifesto-2014-towards-a-more-open-europe.pdf.

Nielsen. (2014). *Millennials–Breaking the Myths*. New York: Nielsen.

Noble, J., and Wixley, S. (2014). "Matter of Trust: What The Public Thinks of Charities and How it Affects Trust." London: NPC. Retrieved from http://www.thinknpc.org/publications/matter-of-trust/.

Oxhorn, P. (2011). *Sustaining Civil Society Economic Change, Democracy, and the Social Construction of Citizenship in Latin America*. University Park, PA: Penn State University Press.

Panel on the Independence of the Voluntary Sector. (2015). *An Independent Mission: The Voluntary Sector in 2015*. London: Baring Foundation. Retrieved from http://www.independencepanel.org.uk/wp-content/uploads/2015/02/Independence-Panel-Report_An-Independent-Mission-PR.pdf.

Parachin, A. (2015). "Charitable Foundations and Advocacy; Reimagining the Doctrine of Political Purposes." Montreal: Montreal Research Laboratory on Canadian Philanthropy.

Pearse, J. A., and Hopkins, J. P. (2014). "Regulation of L3Cs for Social Enterprise: A Prerequisite to Increased Utilization." *Nebraska Law Review*, 92(2), 259–288.

Phillips, S. D. (2013). "Shining Light on Charities or Looking in the Wrong Place? Regulation-by-Transparency in Canada." *Voluntas*, 24(3), 881–905.

Phillips, S. D., and Smith, S. R. (2014). "A Dawn of Convergence?: Third Sector Policy Regimes in the 'Anglo-Saxon' Cluster." *Public Management Review*, 16(8), 1141–1163.

Phillips, S. D., and Smith, S. R. (Eds.). (2011). *Governance and Regulation in the Third Sector: International Perspectives*. London: Routledge.

Prime Minister of Canada. (2015). "Mandate Letter to the Minister of National Revenue." Ottawa. Retrieved from http://pm.gc.ca/eng/minister-national-revenue-mandate-letter.

Public Accounts Committee, House of Commons, UK. (2014). *The Charity Commission*. London: PAC. Retrieved from http://www.publications.parliament.uk/pa/cm201314/cmselect/cmpubacc/792/792.pdf.

Reich, R. (2005). "A Failure of Philanthropy: American Charity Shortchanges the Poor, and Public Policy is Partly to Blame." *Stanford Social Innovation Review*, Winter, 25–33.

Reuter, M., Wijkström, F., and von Essen, J. (2012). "Policy Tools or Mirrors of Politics. Government-Voluntary Sector Compacts in the Post-Welfare State Age." *Nonprofit Policy Forum*, 3(2).

Ronalds, P. (2015). "Australia: Federal Government and Nonprofit Relations in Australia." In J. Brothers (Ed.), *Rebalancing Public Partnership*. London and New York: Routledge.

Rutzen, D. (2015). "Aid Barriers and the Rise of Philanthropic Protectionism." *International Journal of Not-for-Profit Law*, 17(5), 5–44.

Sabeti, H. (2009). "The Emerging Fourth Sector: A New Sector of Organizations at the Intersection of the Public, Private and Social Sectors." Washington, DC: Aspen Institute. Retrieved from www.fourthsector.net.

Salamon, L. M. (1991). "Rise of the Nonprofit Sector: A Global Associational Revolution." *Foreign Affairs*, 73(4), 109–124.

Salamon, L. M. (2010). "Putting Civil Society Sector on the Economic Map." *Annals of Public and Cooperative Economics*, 81(2), 167–210.

Salamon, L. M., Sokolowski, S. W., Megan, A., and Tice, H. S. (2013). "The State of Global Civil Society and Volunteering: Latest Findings from the Implementation of the UN Nonprofit Handbook." *Working Papers of the John Hopkins Comparative Nonprofit Sector Project, 49*, 18.

Salamon, L. M., Sokolowski, S.-W., and List, R. (2003). *Global Civil Society. An Overview*. Baltimore, MD: Johns Hopkins University Press.

Salamon, L. M., and Anheier, H. K. (1998). "Social Origins of Civil Society: Explaining the Nonprofit Sector Cross-Nationally." *Voluntas, 9*(3), 213–248.

Schmid, H., and bar Nissim, H. S. (2016). "The Globalization of Philanthropy: Trends and Channels of Giving." In T. Jung, S. D. Phillips and J. Harrow (Eds.), *The Routledge Companion to Philanthropy* (pp. 162–177). London: Routledge.

Sidel, M. (2008). "Counter-terrorism and the Enabling Legal and Political Environment for Civil Society: A Comparative Analysis of 'War on Terror' States." *International Journal of Not-for-Profit Law, 10*(3), 50–78. Retrieved from http://www.icnl.org/research/journal/vol10iss3/vol10iss3.pdf.

Sidel, M. (2016). "Philanthropy in Asia: Evolving Public Policy." In T. Jung, S. D. Phillips, and J. Harrow (Eds.), *The Routledge Companion to Philanthropy* (260–272). London: Routledge.

Sidel, Mark and Moore, D. (n.d.). *The Law Affecting Civil Society in Asia: Developments and Challenges for Nonprofit and Civil Society Organizations: Report prepared by the International Center for Not-for-Profit Law (ICNL)*. Retrieved from https://media.law.wisc.edu/m/fjfgn/SidelMooreICNLAsiaLawAug2015.pdf.

Skelcher, C., and Smith, S. R. (2015). "Theorizing Hybridity: Institutional Logics, Complex Organizations, and Actor Identities: The Case of Nonprofits." *Public Administration, 93*(2), 433–448.

Smith, B. K. (2013). "Version 2.0: The Giving Pledge Globalizes. New York, NY: The Foundation Center." Retrieved from http://blog.glasspockets.org/2013/02/smith-20130221.html?_ga=1.21495932.674833088.1456840336.

Smith, R. (2008). "Nonprofits and Philanthropy: Scenario II—An Interview with Ralph Smith." *Nonprofit Quarterly, 15*(4). Retrieved from https://nonprofitquarterly.org/2008/12/21/nonprofits-and-philanthropy-scenario-ii-an-interview-with-ralph-smith/.

Smith, S. R. (2010). "Hybridization and Nonprofit Organizations: The Governance Challenge." *Policy and Society, 29*(3), 219–229.

Soskis, B. (2014). "How the Giving Pledge is Inspiring Foreigners to Give." *The Atlantic*, May 15. http://www.theatlantic.com/business/archive/2014/05/how-us-philanthropy-is-inspiring-foreigners-to-give/370889/.

Spero, J. E. (2014). *Charity and Philanthropy in Russia, China, India and Brazil*. New York: The Foundation Center.

TD Bank and Investor Economics. (2015). *Time, Treasure, Talent: Canadian Women and Philanthropy*. Toronto, ON: TD Bank.

The Straits Times. (2016). "China Defends NGO Law, Says Still Being Revised." *The Straits Times*, March 4. Retrieved from http://www.straitstimes.com/asia/east-asia/china-defends-foreign-ngo-law-says-still-being-revised.

Themudo, N. S. (2013). *Nonprofits in Crisis: Economic Development, Risk and the Philanthropic Kuznets Curve*. Bloomington, IN: Indiana University Press.

Transnational Giving Europe and European Foundation Centre. (2014). *Taxation of Cross-Border Philanthropy in Europe After Persche and Stauffer*. Brussels: European Foundation Centre.

UNDP—United Nations Development Programme. (2013). *The Rise of the South: Human Progress in Diverse World. Human Development Report*. New York: UNDP.

US Trust and Lilly Family School of Philanthropy. (2014). *The 2014 US Trust Study of High Net Worth Philanthropy*. Boston, MA, and Indianapolis, IN: US Trust and Lilly Family School of Philanthropy.

USAid. (2012). *The 2012 CSO Sustainability Index for Central and Eastern Europe and Eurasia*. Washington, DC: USAid.

Wagner, L. (2016). *Diversity and Philanthropy: Expanding the Circle of Giving*. Santa Barbara, CA: Praeger.

Wang, X., Liu, F., Nan,F., Xiaoping, Z., and Xiulan, Z. (2015). "Giving in China: An Emerging Nonprofit Sector Embedded within a Strong State." In P. Wiepking and F. Handy (Eds.), *Palgrave Handbook of Global Philanthropy* (pp. 354–368). Basingstoke, UK: Palgrave Macmillan.

Wiepkiing, P., and Handy, F. (Eds.). (2015). *The Palgrave Handbook of Global Philanthropy*. London: Palgrave Macmillan.

Willebois, E. V. D. D. De. (2010). *Nonprofit Organizations and the Combatting of Terrorism Financing: A Proportionate Response*. Washington, DC: World Bank Publications.

Wood, J. (2016). "Regulatory Waves and a Rising Tide: CSO Regulation and Self-Regulation." Unpublished paper. Ottawa, ON: Carleton University, School of Public Policy and Administration.

World Economic Forum. (2013). *The Future Role of Civil Society*. Geneva: World Economic Forum.

Young, D. R. (1999). "Complementary, Supplementary, or Adversarial? A Theoretical and Historical Examination of Nonprofit-Government Relations in the United States." In E. T. and S. Boris (Eds.), *Nonprofits and Government: Collaboration and Conflict* (pp. 31–70). Washington, DC: The Urban Institute Press.

Index

501(c)(3) charities:
corporate foundations, 239;
described, 196, 264–65;
for lobbying by nonprofits, 20;
modern venture philanthropy and, 53;
political activity by, 203–5;
private versus public, 245–47;
tax exemption for, 134;
tax law limiting lobbying by, 198–99.
See also charitable nonprofits
501(c)(4) (social welfare) organizations:
Citizens United decision and, 61;
controversy about partisan use of, 37;
for lobbying by nonprofits, 20;
non-advocacy functions of, 29n8;
political aims by, 208

ABR (Annual Benefit Report), 280
Abramson, Alan J., 71–101, 217–35
ACA. *See* Affordable Care Act
Addams, Jane, 57
adversarial government-nonprofit relationship:
advocacy and, 37, 46, 191;
conflicting interests and, 46–48;
described, 39;
First Amendment to the Constitution and, 60;
government failure theory and, 46;
government oversight and contract failure theory, 47;
government protection of majority interests, 47–48;
graph illustrating, 40;
history viewed through lens of, 58–63, 64, 65;
innovation and, 46;
overlap with other modes, 39–40, 48–49, 50;
overview, 45–48;
shifting social contract, 65;
women's movements, 61;
Advisory Committee on Tax-Exempt and Government Entities, 171–72
advocacy and lobbying, 191–215;
501(c)(3) charities for, 20;
501(c)(4) organization for, 20;
adversarial government-nonprofit relationship and, 37, 46, 191;
campaign finance law regulating, 193–95;
Citizens United decision and, 192, 194, 205;
to conserve or protect values, 21;
direct versus grassroots lobbying, 200;
expenditure test for lobbying, 198–201;
explosiveness of, 191–92;

First Amendment protections for,
  191, 192, 195, 196–97, 207–8;
international trends, 328–30,
  335n10;
issues relating to regulation, 207–12;
limits for CSOs, 313;
limits on, nonprofit representation in
  government and, 223;
lobbying regulation, 197–202;
"magic words" of express advocacy,
  193, 194, 200;
narrative of government-nonprofit
  relationship, 37;
by non-charitable nonprofits, 202;
no substantial part test for
  lobbying, 199;
not addressed by economic
  theories, 45–46;
opposition to, 21;
political activity, 202–7;
by political organizations, 202;
private foundations not allowed to
  lobby, 201–2;
profound social changes due to,
  20–21;
public education for, 20;
tax law regulating, 195–97;
types of regulations on, 191–92.
  See also political views of nonprofits
Affordable Care Act (ACA):
  contraception controversy, 23;
  increased health funding and, 103;
  nonprofits' concerns about health
    care costs, 228, 229;
  shift to MCOs and, 111
America Gives More Act of 2015, 254
American Bar Association, 177–78
American Law Institute (ALI), 178
American Recovery and Reinvestment
  Act, 227
Anheier, H. K., 237
Annual Benefit Report (ABR), 280
Anti-Terrorist Financing Guidelines, 229
appreciated property donations, 149–50,
  156n9, 213n7

arts and culture nonprofits:
  controversies over values and, 22, 23;
  examples, 5;
  government funding for, 106;
  grants for, 109;
  during the Great Depression, 54;
  growth in, 2003–2013, 5
Association of Nonprofit Professionals,
  179, 183–84n28

benefit corporations, 279–80
Benetech, 265–66
Benjamin, L. M., 305
Ben-Ner, Avner, 47
Bill and Melinda Gates Foundation, 320
Bipartisan Campaign Reform Act
  (BCRA), 193–94
B Labs certification, 273, 279
Blackmun, Justice, 195
Blumberg, Mark, 313–42
bonds:
  cap on tax-exempt borrowing, 147;
  social impact (SIBs), 110–11;
  tax exempt, 117–18, 140–41,
    155n4
Boris, Elizabeth T., 1–35, 230, 291
Breen, O., 325
Bremner, Robert H., 51, 53, 60
Brilliant, Eleanor L., 221–22
Broadus, Erica, 263–89
Brody, Evelyn, 133–61
Buckley v. Valeo, 193
Buffet, Warren, 320
Bush, George H. W., 56, 219
Bush, George W., 219
business activities of nonprofits:
  conversion to for-profit, 7;
  for-profit subsidiaries, 265–66;
  international trends, 328–30;
  mission funding through, 266–67;
  partnership with for-profit
    companies, 266, 268;
  strategic, 265;
  types of, 7.
  See also hybrid structures

Camp, Dave, 150
campaign finance law, 193–95
capital:
  federal financing and, 117–19;
  social, 18–19;
  sources for nonprofits, 2;
  tax treatment of capital income, 148–49
Carnegie, Andrew, 51, 52, 55
Carter, Jimmy, 222
Casey, John, 37–70, 221, 224, 250
Catholic Community Services of Western Washington (CCSWW), 113
Chan, Priscilla, 251, 263–64
Chan Zuckerberg Initiative, 263–64
charitable deductions:
  benefits to nonprofits, 155n4;
  cost of, 136;
  for donations of appreciated property, 149–50, 156n9;
  economic value of, 136–38;
  higher-income donors and, 145;
  subsidy view of, 116, 142–43;
  tax rate changes and, 148.
  See also tax incentives
charitable nonprofits, 71–101;
  during the Great Depression, 52;
  growth of small charities, 2003–2013, 10;
  impact of tax-exempt status on scope and range of, 144–45;
  inevitable inadequacy of meeting social needs, 73–76;
  potentially taxable income, by subsector, 2011, 140;
  public confidence and trust needed by, 4;
  tax law changes that would benefit, 154;
  types of, 4.
  See also 501(c)(3) charities
charity-monitoring organizations, 16
Charleston Principles, 166, 175
charter schools, funding and, 103, 108

Child Care and Dependent tax credit (CDCTC), 114
Citizens United decision, 61, 192, 194
civic activities of nonprofits, 19–20
civic clubs, pass-through gifts through, 240–41
civil society:
  approach to roles of nonprofits, 18;
  growth of nonprofits and, 313;
  interaction between government and nonprofits in, 3;
  nonprofit roles in, 3;
  public education by nonprofits, 19;
  public policy influence, 19–20
civil society organizations (CSOs), 313, 333n1
Clinton, Bill, 56
Cole, David, 21
Colinvaux, Roger, 17, 20, 191–215
collaboration, government-nonprofit, 6–7, 8
Columbia University, 54
Combined Federal Campaign, 54–55
common good, promotion of, 2
community foundations:
  DAFs and, 247, 252–53;
  donations to, 245;
  services of, 246
Community Foundations National Standards Board, 179, 183n27
community social service programs, 107–8
complementary government-nonprofit relationship:
  described, 39;
  "free riding" problem and solutions, 43, 223;
  graph illustrating, 40;
  history viewed through lens of, 53–58, 64–65;
  overlap with other modes, 39–40, 48–49, 50;
  overview, 43–45;
  reverse model of private financing and public provision, 45, 55;

situations skewed toward
government, 45;
supplementary lens compared to, 56;
tax revenue-based, 56–57;
transaction costs theory and, 44–45
continuous quality improvement, 292.
  See also performance management
contract failure theory, 47
"Cook for the Cure," 266
Cordes, Joseph J., 133–61, 263–89
corporate giving programs, 239–40, 267
corporate misconduct concerns, 62–63
Council on Foundations, 62
CSOs (civil society organizations), 313, 333n1
culture. See arts and culture nonprofits

Dartmouth College, 58–59
Derrick-Mills, Teresa, 291–312
Dietz, Nathan, 263–89
diversity:
  of foundation stakeholders, 256–58;
  of international nonprofits, 25–26;
  of the nonprofit sector, 95–97;
  regional variation among nonprofits, 11–13
donor-advised funds (DAFs), 238, 242–44, 252–54

economic impacts of nonprofits, 24–25
economic theory:
  advocacy role not addressed by, 45–46;
  contract failure, 47;
  government failure, 16, 17, 46;
  government-nonprofit modes and, 39;
  government oversight and, 47;
  market failure, 16, 17;
  nonprofit failure, 16, 17;
  roles of nonprofits and, 17;
  theory of public goods, 43, 45;
  transaction costs theory, 44–45.
  See also supplementary-complementary-adversarial model
Edna McConnell Clark Foundation (EMCF), 295–96, 297–98

education nonprofits:
  charter schools and increased funding, 103, 108;
  early universities, 54;
  examples, 5;
  growth in, 2003–2013, 5;
  growth in funding for, 108;
  programs taken over by other sectors, 6
Eikenberry, A. M., 240
employment:
  entry point provided by nonprofits, 25;
  government financing and staff costs, 122–24;
  in the nonprofit sector, 1977–2012, 77, 86–87;
  percent of labor force employed by nonprofits, 8, 77, 78, 77, 99n2;
  professionalization of staff, 122–24;
  staffing challenges for hybrid structures, 284.
  See also volunteering
endowment gifts, 244
Engines of Liberty, 21
estate tax, 148
ethnicity, volunteering and, 85
expenditure test for lobbying, 198–201
expenses of nonprofits:
  concentrated in largest organizations, 14, 15, 95–96;
  government financing and staff costs, 122–24;
  government spending compared to, 86–87;
  by region, 2013, 13;
  spending by sector, FY 1980 and FY 2015, 94.
  See also finances of nonprofits

family foundations, 247–48, 258n1
FATF (Financial Action Task Force), 321
Faulk, Lewis, 237–61
federal budget composition, 1940–2015, 72

Federal Election Campaign Act (FECA), 193
Federal Election Commission (FEC), 3–4, 191, 193–95
federal spending:
  aggregate changes, FY 1980 to FY 2015, 90–92;
  caveats for analysis of, 89–90;
  demand effect on nonprofits, 87, 89, 90–94;
  by functional area, FY 1980 and FY 2015, 92–93;
  future outlook, 95;
  in health care, 81, 87;
  indirect versus direct effects on nonprofits, 89;
  nonprofit spending compared to, 86–87;
  percentage change by nonprofit subsector, FY 1980 versus FY 2015, 97, 100n10;
  private giving compared to social welfare spending, 79, 83, 85;
  public assistance spending, 1940–2015, 72;
  social welfare spending growth, 1980–2013, 79, 80–81;
  supply effect on nonprofits, 87, 89, 94–95.
  See also government financing of nonprofits
Federation Employment Guidance Services (FEGS), 57
fee-for-service revenues, 16, 112–16
Filer Commission, 221–22
finances of nonprofits:
  assets, 8, 15–16, 24, 77, 78;
  capital financing, 117–19;
  charity-monitoring organizations and, 16;
  effect of tax deductions on, 138;
  expenses, 14, 15, 95–96;
  fee-for-service income, 16, 112–16;
  governmental fiscal conservatism and, 64–65;
  growth in social welfare spending, 2003–2013, 79, 80–81;
  international nonprofit revenues, 315;
  nonprofit sector in relation to the economy, 77;
  percent of national income, 76, 78;
  performance management resources, 302;
  private giving percentage of revenues, 137;
  private sector models used for, 16;
  program service revenues, by subsector, 87, 88;
  resources concentrated in largest organizations, 14;
  revenues by subsector, 2003 and 2013, 96;
  revenue sources, 2, 14;
  size of monetary contributions, 79–80;
  spending by sector, FY 1980 and FY 2015, 94;
  surpluses by subsector, 2011, 138–39;
  tax incentives benefiting, 13–14;
  tax treatment of capital income, 148–49;
  by type of activity, 14–15;
  trends in, 38.
  See also government financing of nonprofits
Financial Action Task Force (FATF), 321
First Amendment to the Constitution:
  adversarial government-nonprofit relationship and, 60;
  advocacy protected by, 191, 192, 195, 196–97, 207–8
flexible purpose corporations (FPCs), 280–81
Form 1023-EZ, 168–69
Forms 990:
  controversy about, 168, 181n9;
  electronic filing and dissemination of information, 170, 181n10;
  finding information on, 28n1;

multistate registration and the Single Portal project, 173–75;
redesign in 2007, 167–68;
requirements to file, 4
for-profit subsidiaries of nonprofits, 265–66
foundations:
5 percent payout rule, 254;
ability to affect political change limited form, 21;
adversarial role in the 1960s, 59–60;
community, donations to, 245;
congressional attack in the 1950s and 1960s, 62;
corporate, advantages of, 239–40;
Council on Foundations, 62;
diversity of stakeholders and, 256–58;
grants from, 16, 248;
invention of, 52;
performance management by, 295–96, 298–99;
private, heavy regulation of, 239;
private, lobbying not allowed for, 201–2;
private, philanthropy and, 248–49;
private, policy issues and growth in, 254–55;
public policy influence of, 19–20;
public versus private, 245–47;
support grants from, 16;
transparency concerns, 256;
types of, 247–48.
See also philanthropy; private giving
FPCs (flexible purpose corporations), 280–81
Franklin, Benjamin, 54
freedom of speech. See First Amendment to the Constitution
"free riding" problem, 43, 223
Fremont-Smith, Marion, 162–90, 225
fundraising regulation, 165–66, 175, 324
Fyffe, Saunji D., 291–312

Galaskiewicz, J., 250
Gates, Bill, 320
Gazley, B., 53
GEO (Grantmakers for Effective Organizations), 296
giving circles, 240
Giving Pledge, 320
giving pledges, 251–52
Goodwill Industries, 266
Gospel of Wealth, 51
government failure theory, 16, 17, 46
government financing of nonprofits, 103–32;
capital financing, 117–19;
direct grants and contracts, 109–12;
diversification of, 109;
effect on staff costs and professionalism, 122–24;
evolution from accountability to learning, 305, 306–7;
factors affecting, 103–4;
fee-for-service revenue, 112–16;
future outlook, 126–27;
grants, by nonprofit subsector, 88;
growth for education, 108;
growth for health care, 106–8;
history of, 104–6;
international nonprofits, 334nn6–7;
management of, 110, 119–25;
nonprofit governance and, 124–25;
performance management and, 110;
public-private partnerships, 112;
Reagan administration cuts in, 226;
reliance on intermediaries, 111–12;
risk management needed for, 126–27;
scope of, 291;
social impact bonds (SIBs), 110–11;
tax deductions and exemptions, 116–17;
See also federal spending; tax treatment of nonprofits
Government Performance Project (GPP), 295, 297

Government Performance Results Act (GPRA), 294, 297
government representation for nonprofits:
Affordable Care Act and, 228, 229;
Anti-Terrorist Financing Guidelines and, 228;
lack of understanding of nonprofit sector and, 226–27;
late payments and, 227–28;
limited nature of, 217;
nonprofit sector ambivalence about, 221–23;
offices for, 218–20;
options for reform, 230–32;
reasons for lack of, 220–24;
weakness in nonprofit sector and, 223–24;
weakness of government efforts, 225–29
government sector:
agencies collecting data on nonprofits, 219;
constraints on resources, 75–76;
household and workplace economy versus, 74;
hybrid forms involvement by, 271–76;
inevitable inadequacy of meeting social needs, 73–76;
representation of nonprofits in, 217, 218–20;
volunteering, 85, 86.
See also federal spending; government financing of nonprofits
GPP (Government Performance Project), 295, 297
GPRA (Government Performance Results Act), 294, 297
GPRA Modernization Act of 2010, 297
Graddy, Elizabeth A., 246
Grantmakers for Effective Organizations (GEO), 296

grants:
for arts and culture nonprofits, 109;
by DAFs, 252;
donations to grantmakers, 245;
federal, by nonprofit subsector, 88;
from foundations, 16, 248;
performance management for, 110, 296
Great Depression, 52, 54, 56, 104
Great Recession, nonprofits' problems due to, 227
Grønbjerg, Kirsten, 57
gross domestic product of US, nonprofit share of, 8
growth of nonprofits in the US:
civil society and, 313;
number of charitable organizations, 2003–2013, 8;
number of entities, 1998–2013, 8, 9;
private foundations, policy issues and, 254–55;
regional variation in, 11;
small charities, 10;
by type of service, 2003–2013, 5;
types with most rapid growth, 8, 10

Hacker, Jacob, 127
Hall, Peter Dobkin, 49, 51, 52, 53
Hammack, D. C., 237
Hand, Learned, 198, 213n3
Hansmann, Henry, 47
Harvard University, 54, 58
health information-related goods, 268–69
health nonprofits:
ACA and increased funding, 103;
early hospitals, 54;
examples, 5;
growth in, 2003–2013, 5;
growth in funding for, 106–8;
managed-care organizations (MCOs), 111;
shift to outpatient care and, 97.
See also hospitals, nonprofit
Hewlett Foundation, 296
High Priority Performance Goals, 297

history of nonprofits in the US:
  Civil War period, 51, 59;
  colonial period, 51, 53–54;
  early republic period, 51, 54, 58–59, 64;
  federal financing, 104–6;
  late nineteenth and early twentieth centuries, 51–52, 54, 59, 64;
  license required in observations, 51;
  modern times, 52–53, 54–58, 59–63, 64;
  through the adversarial lens, 58–63;
  through the complementary lens, 53–58;
  through the supplementary lens, 51–53
Hodgkinson, Virginia, 71–101
Hoover, Herbert, 56
hospitals, nonprofit:
  conversion to for-profit, 7;
  early hospitals, 54;
  endowment gifts to, 244;
  value added by, 7.
  See also health nonprofits
Hudson Institute, 325
Hull House bankruptcy, 57
human resources for performance management, 302
human services nonprofits, 5
hybrid structures:
  benefit corporations, 279–80;
  B Labs certification, 273, 279;
  Chan Zuckerberg Initiative, 263–64;
  combining business with social missions, 7;
  common alternative structures, 264–69, 271;
  continuum of organizational forms, 264–65, 269;
  customer-beneficiary distinctions and, 283;
  donation of profits to charity, 267;
  factors influencing legislation to create new forms, 274–76;
  financing challenges, 283;
  flexible purpose corporations, 280–81;
  for-profit businesses with social objectives, 267–68;
  for-profit subsidiaries, 265–66;
  future developments, 281–86;
  giving pledges, 251–52;
  government involvement, 271–76;
  government-nonprofit modes combined, 40;
  growth in popularity, 268;
  growth of industries with potentially charitable output, 270;
  in international nonprofits, 26;
  international nonprofits and, 319;
  L3Cs, 277–79;
  mission funding through business operations, 266–67;
  new legal organizational forms, 277–81, 282–83;
  nondistribution constraint and, 264–65, 267, 271;
  operating foundations, 248;
  partnership with for-profit companies, 266, 268;
  problems and pitfalls, 282;
  recent government activity, 285–86;
  regulatory challenges, 284–85;
  social purpose corporations, 281;
  staffing challenges, 284;
  state regulation and, 176;
  states with hybrid legal forms, 272–73

impact investing, 255
independent foundations, 247, 258n1
Independent Sector, 178–79
inequality, private giving and, 83, 85, 100n6
infrastructure for performance management, 302–3
innovation:
  adversarial government-nonprofit relationship and, 46;
  government encouragement of, 276;
  Social Innovation Fund (SIF), 104;

supplementary government-nonprofit relationship and, 42–43
interdisciplinary approaches to studying nonprofits, 18
Internal Revenue Service (IRS):
  501(c)(4) judgments by, 208–9, 213n5;
  Advisory Committee on Tax-Exempt and Government Entities, 171–72;
  Citizens United decision and, 192, 194;
  electronic filing and dissemination of information, 170, 181n10;
  Form 1023-EZ, 168–70;
  Forms 990, 4, 28n1, 167–68, 170, 173–75, 181n9, 181n10;
  forms used for nonprofits, 4, 28n1;
  nonprofits registered with, 2013, 10, 11;
  reasons for limited oversight, 225;
  registration of nonprofits with, 4;
  regulation of nonprofits by, 3, 166–67, 192, 194, 218, 225;
  religion-related nonprofits and, 22–23
international nonprofits, 313–42;
  decrease in trust for, 318;
  demographic changing for, 317–18;
  diversification of the sector, 319;
  diversity of, 25–26;
  examples, 5;
  growth in, 2003–2013, 5;
  hybrid forms, 26;
  measurement issues, 316–17;
  meta-policies, 330–32;
  Millennial generation and, 317–18;
  models of government-nonprofit relationships, 332;
  political and business activity trends, 328–30;
  regulation and oversight of, 4, 26;
  revenues of, 315;
  service functions of, 314–15;
  tax incentive trends, 326–28;
  terrorist organizations' use of, 320–21;
  in transition and developing countries, 316;
  transnationalism in, 320–21;
  transparency and oversight trends, 321, 323–26;
  transparency concerns, 318–19, 334n2;
  US organizations in other countries, 26

Job Training Partnership Act (JTPA), 294
Johns Hopkins Comparative Nonprofit Sector Project (JHCNSP), 314
Johnson, Jasmine McGinnis, 237–61

Kerlin, J. A., 251
Komen, Susan, 266
Kramer, Ralph M., 40

L3Cs, 277–79
Leydier, Béatrice, 1–35
lobbying. *See* advocacy and lobbying
Lobbying Disclosure Act, 197
Lohmann, Roger, 17, 51
Lott, Cindy, 162–90, 225, 230
Low-Income Housing Tax Credit (LIHTC), 105, 118–19
Lutheran Alliance To Create Housing (LATCH), 119

Ma, Jack, 334n3
Malloy, Dan, 220
managed-care organizations (MCOs), 111
market failure theory, 16, 17
McCollum, Betty, 222, 231
McConnell v. FEC, 194
McKeever, Brice, 1–35
Medicaid, 106–8, 114
Medicare, growth in funding for, 106–7
Mellon, Andrew, 55
membership associations, pass-through gifts through, 240–41
meta-policies of international nonprofits, 330–32

Metzenbaum, S., 292
Millennial generation, 317–18
mobile technologies, disruption by, 61–62
Model Act, 279
Model Nonprofit Corporation Act, 177–78
Model Protection of Charitable Assets Act, 177
Moe, Terry, 220–21, 232
Morgan, Donald L., 246
Mosley, J. E., 250
mutual membership and benefit nonprofits, 5

Najam, Adil, 39
National Council of Nonprofits, 179
National Taxonomy of Exempt Entities (NTEE), 5, 28n4, 38
New Community Corporation (NCC), 266–67
Newman, Paul, 267
Newman's Own, 267
Nielsen, Waldemar A., 51, 53, 54
non-charitable nonprofits, 195, 202, 205–6
nondistribution constraint, 47, 264–65, 267, 271
nonprofit failure theory, 16, 17
Nonprofit Sector and Community Solutions Act, 222–23
nonprofits in general:
　ambivalence about government representation, 221–23;
　blurred government-nonprofit boundaries, 40, 65;
　businesses differentiated from, 2;
　common characteristics of, 2;
　constraints on resources, 75–76;
　diversity of, 95–97;
　government differentiated from, 2;
　government spending compared to, 86–87;
　inevitable inadequacy of meeting social needs, 73–76;
　nonprofits, defined, 1–2;
　NTEE categories, 5;
　professionalization of staff, 122–24;
　regional variation among, 11–13;
　scope in the US, 8–11;
　terms associated with organizations, 2;
　types of activities, 6–8;
　weakness in sector policymaking, 223–24
no substantial part test for lobbying, 199
NTEE. *See* National Taxonomy of Exempt Entities (NTEE)

Obama, Barack, 48, 56, 95, 117, 170, 219, 254, 297
Office of Foundation Liaison (OFL), Michigan, 220
Olson, Mancur, 43
Olympic Sculpture Park (OSP), 123
O'Neill, Michael, 51, 60
operating foundations, 248
Owens, Marcus, 225, 229–30

Panera Bread Foundation, 267–68
PART (Program Assessment Rating Tool), 294–95
pass-through giving, 240–41
pay for success (PFS), 110–11
payments in lieu of taxes (PILOTs), 25, 116, 152
Pell, Claiborne, 55
Pennsylvania Hospital, 54
performance management:
　balancing top-down and bottom-up pressures, 305–6;
　culture of learning with, 303–5;
　described, 292;
　environmental influences, 304–5;
　evolution from accountability to learning, 300–301, 306–7;
　by foundations, 294–96, 298–99;
　government funding and, 110;
　Government Performance Project (GPP), 295, 297;
　Government Performance Results Act, 294;

High Priority Performance
    Goals, 297;
nonprofits in the performance
    web, 293;
organization improvement
    through, 292;
performance measurement as part of,
    292, 306;
Program Assessment Rating Tool
    for, 294–95;
resources required for, 301–3;
state initiatives, 295, 297;
strategic philanthropy and, 298
performance measurement:
in the 1970s and 1980s, 294;
in the 1990s, 294–96;
in the 2000s, 296–99;
described, 292;
motivations and drivers of, 293–94;
outputs versus outcomes in, 297–98;
as part of performance management,
    292, 306;
tools and frameworks for, 300–301;
United Way requirement for, 295
Peterson Commission, 221
Pettijohn, Sarah L., 291
PFS (pay for success), 110–11
philanthropy:
corporate giving programs, 239–40;
defined, 237;
donations to community
    foundations, 245;
donations to grantmakers, 245;
donor-advised funds (DAFs), 238,
    242–44, 252–54;
endowment gifts to public charities,
    243–44;
forms in the US, 238–39;
giving circles, 240;
giving pledges, 251–52;
of Giving Pledge signers, 320;
historical forms of, 237;
impact investing, 255;
international, 317;
pass-through giving, 240–41;
performance management and, 298;

private foundations and, 248–49;
public versus private foundations
    and, 245–47;
roles in public policy and
    government relationships, 249–51;
trade-offs between structure and
    control, 238–39;
types of foundations and, 247–48.
See also foundations; private giving
Philips, Susan D., 313–42
Piketty, Thomas, 83
PILOTs (payments in lieu of taxes), 25,
    116, 152
"Pink Ribbon Affinity" program, 266
political activity by nonprofits, 202–7;
501(c)(3) charities, 203–5;
non-charitable nonprofits, 205–6;
political organizations, 202, 206–7
political views of nonprofits:
Citizens United decision and, 61,
    192, 194, 205;
nonprofit roles and, 17–18;
oversimplification in, 37–38;
services and, 37;
social media and new technologies
    and, 61–62.
See also adversarial government-
    nonprofit relationship; advocacy
    and lobbying
"Principles for Good Governance and
    Ethical Practice . . . ," 178–79
private giving:
of appreciated property, 149–50,
    156n9, 213n7;
constancy of, 82–85;
effect of charitable deductions on, 145;
individuals as greatest source of,
    82, 84;
inequality and, 83, 100n5;
moderate amount of, 79–80;
by nonprofit subsector, 84, 88;
as a percentage of nonprofit
    revenue, 137;
social welfare spending compared to,
    79, 83;
taxation preferred over, 80;

tax incentives and, 83, 99–100n5;
tax rates and, 82, 83;
by the top 1 percent of taxpayers, 1979–2013, 72.
See also foundations; philanthropy
Program Assessment Rating Tool (PART), 294–95
program-related investments (PRIs), 255
property tax exemptions:
cost of, 116;
financial effect of, 140, 141;
state and local initiatives to limit, 116, 152–53;
state variations in, 147
public and societal benefit nonprofits, 5
public education by nonprofits, 19, 20
public policy, 19–20, 249–50
public-private partnerships, 112
Putnam, Robert, 18

Randolph, William, 82, 85
Reagan, Ronald, 219, 226
regional variation among nonprofits:
by demographics and motivations, 12–13;
in growth rates, 11;
number and expenses by region, 2013, 13;
number per 10,000 residents, 2013, 11–12;
by type of activity, 12
regulation of hybrid structures, 284–85
regulation of nonprofits:
campaign finance law and advocacy regulation, 193–95;
credibility of regulators and, 324;
DAFs, 244;
DAFs versus private foundations, 253;
by Federal Election Commission, 3–4, 191, 193–95;
Form 1023-EZ for, 168–69;
international nonprofits, 4, 26, 321–26, 334nn6–7;
by the IRS, 3, 166–67, 192, 194, 218, 225;

issues relating to advocacy regulation, 207–12;
lobbying regulation, 197–202;
offices for, 218;
options for reform, 229–30;
reasons for limited oversight, 225;
tax exemption as justification for, 117, 134;
tax law and advocacy regulation, 195–97.
See also Forms 990; state regulation of charities
Reid, E. J., 251
religion-related nonprofits:
Affordable Care Act controversy and, 23;
charitable status automatic for congregations, 4;
controversies over values and, 22–23;
examples, 5;
growth in, 2003–2013, 5;
number of congregations in the US, 29n5;
pass-through gifts through, 240–41;
separation of church and state and, 22
Revenue Act of 1913, 166
revenues of nonprofits:
fee-for-service, 16, 112–16;
international nonprofits, 315;
private giving percentage of, 137;
program service, by subsector, 87, 88;
sources for nonprofits, 2, 14;
by subsector, 2003 and 2013, 96;
tax treatment of capital income, 148–49.
See also government financing of nonprofits; private giving
Revised Model Nonprofit Corporation Act, 177–78
Rockefeller, John D., 52, 222
roles of nonprofits, 16–24;
advocacy, lobbying, and political, 20–21;
civic activities, 19–20;

economic approaches to, 17;
interdisciplinary approaches to, 18;
political approaches to, 17–18;
religious, cultural, and artistic, 22–23;
service, 23–24
Russell Sage Foundation, 52

Sagawa, Shirley, 230–31, 232
Salamon, Lester, 17, 43, 53, 54, 57, 313
Sandfort, J. R., 300
Sarbanes-Oxley legislation, 62–63, 296
Schneiderman, Eric T., 266
schools, pass-through gifts through, 240–41
Schwarzenegger, Arnold, 220
scope of nonprofits in the US:
  gross receipts in 2013, 8;
  impact of tax-exempt status on, 144–45;
  number of charitable organizations, 2003–2013, 8;
  number of entities, 1998–2013, 8, 9;
  number registered with the IRS, 2013, 10, 11;
  percent of gross domestic product, 8;
  percent of labor force employed, 9, 77, 78, 99n2;
  percent of national income, 76, 78;
  small charities, 10;
  total assets, 8, 77, 78
scouting, pass-through gifts through, 240–41
Seattle Art Museum (SAM), 123
Seldon, S. C., 300
service:
  fee-for-service revenues, 16, 112–16;
  functions of international nonprofits, 314–15;
  narrative of government-nonprofit relationship, 37;
  nonprofit growth by type of, 2003–2013, 5;
  to the poor, targeting, 149–50;
  program service revenues, by subsector, 87, 88;
  roles of nonprofits, 23–24

services in lieu of taxes (SILOTs), 25
Single Portal project, 173–75
Small Business Administration (SBA), 230–31, 232
Smetters, Kent, 85
Smith, David Horton, 52
Smith, S. R., 305
Smith, Steven Rathgeb, 55, 103–32
Smithson, James, 55
social capital of nonprofits, 18–19
social impact bonds (SIBs), 110–11
Social Innovation Fund (SIF), 104
socially responsible business certification, 273
social media, disruption by, 61–62
social needs, 72, 73–76
social purpose corporations (SPCs), 281
social welfare organizations. *See* 501(c)(4) (social welfare) organizations
social welfare spending:
  growth in, 1980–2013, 79, 80–81;
  in health care, 81, 87, 106–8;
  private giving compared to, 79, 83, 85
Sowa, J. E., 300
sports groups, pass-through gifts through, 240–41
Standards for Excellence Institute, 179, 183n26
Stanford Social Innovation Review (SSIR), 282
state regulation of charities, 162–90;
  attorneys general roles in, 163–64;
  Charleston Principles for, 166, 175;
  common law and, 164, 180n5;
  electronic filing and dissemination of IRS information, 170, 181n10;
  enforcement trends, 173–76;
  fundraising regulation, 165–66, 175;
  hybrid entities and, 176;
  increased interest in, 2003–2013, 172–73;
  information sharing with the IRS and, 169–70, 181n10;
  IRS ACT on TE and GE, 171–72;
  lack of personnel for, 164, 172, 224;

modernization of nonprofit laws, 164, 176–78, 180n3, 182n22, 183n24;
multistate enforcement, 175–76;
multistate registration and the Single Portal project, 173–75;
nonprofit efforts toward compliance, 178–80;
offices for, 218;
performance management initiatives, 295;
shared jurisdiction within states, 165, 180n6;
shared jurisdiction with the IRS, 166–67;
states with hybrid legal forms, 272–73

Steele, Ellen, 71–101, 253
Steinberg, Richard, 44
Steuerle, C. Eugene, 71–101, 81, 253, 263–89
subsidies. *See* tax subsidies
supplementary-complementary-adversarial model:
adversarial mode, 45–48, 58–63;
blurred government-nonprofit boundaries and, 40, 65;
complementary mode, 43–45, 53–58;
graph illustrating modes, 40;
history viewed through adversarial lens, 58–63;
history viewed through complementary lens, 53–58;
history viewed through supplementary lens, 51–53;
modes described, 39;
other frameworks, 41;
overlap between modes, 39–40, 48–49, 50;
supplementary mode, 41–43, 51–53.
See also specific modes
supplementary government-nonprofit relationship:
basic premise of, 41–42;
complementary lens compared to, 56;
costs of other solutions and, 42;
described, 39;
government action prompted by, 42–43;
graph illustrating, 40;
history viewed through lens of, 51–53, 64;
innovation and, 42–43;
overlap with other modes, 39–40, 48–49, 50;
variations among fields of activity, 42
supply-side tax subsidies, 133
Susan G. Komen Foundation, 266

tax code or tax law:
advocacy regulation and, 195–97;
capital income tax, 148–49;
Citizens United decision and, 194, 205;
DAFs and, 243;
effect of changing tax rates, 148;
expenditure test, 198–201;
neutrality rationale for subsidies, 198, 207, 213n4;
nonprofit lobbying and, 197–202;
no substantial part test, 199;
recent proposals for change, 150–52;
section 527 and advocacy, 194, 195, 196;
targeting service to the poor, 149–50;
using to improve nonprofit governance, 153.
See also tax treatment of nonprofits
tax exemption:
benefits to nonprofits, 134, 153–54;
cap on tax-exempt borrowing, 147;
complex government relationships and, 133;
from corporate income taxes, 138–40;
entity-level, 135;
Form 1023-EZ for, 168–69;
for-profit businesses with social objectives and, 274, 275;
payments in lieu of taxes (PILOTs), 25, 116–17, 152;

premium returns and, 146, 155n5;
from property taxes, 116, 140, 141, 147, 152–53;
regulation justified by, 117, 134;
subsidy view of, 143–44;
tax-exempt bonds, 117–18, 140–41, 155n4;
unrelated business income tax and, 136, 146–47.
See also tax treatment of nonprofits
tax incentives:
benefits to nonprofits, 13–14, 155nn4–5;
costs of, 29n10, 136;
deductions for appreciated property, 149–50, 156n9;
economic value of deductions, 136–38;
higher-income donors and, 145;
indirect value of tax preferences, 141;
international trends, 326–28;
Low-Income Housing Tax Credit, 105, 118–19;
private giving and, 83, 85, 100n6;
subsidy view of deductions, 116, 142–43;
targeting service to the poor, 149;
tax rate changes and deductions, 148;
viewed through the complementary lens, 56–57.
See also tax exemption; tax subsidies; tax treatment of nonprofits
Tax Reform Act of 1969, 60, 249, 254
Tax Reform Act of 2014, 150–52, 254
tax subsidies:
charitable deductions viewed as, 116, 142–43;
neutrality rationale for, 198, 207, 213n4;
supply-side, 133;
tax exemption viewed as, 143–44
tax treatment of nonprofits, 133–161;
capital income, 148–49;
cap on tax-exempt borrowing, 147;
cost of charitable deductions, 136;
estate tax, 148;
future policy directions, 153–55;
potentially taxable income, 139–40;
proposals for tax code change, 150–52;
subsidy view of, 142–44;
supply-side tax subsidies, 133;
tax policy, 135–36;
tax rates, 82, 83, 85, 148–49;
unrelated business income tax, 136, 146–47.
See also tax exemption; tax incentives
technologies:
electronic filing and dissemination of IRS information, 170;
mobile, nonprofits disrupted by, 61–62;
state regulation enforcement and, 173
transaction costs theory, 44–45
transnationalism, 320–21
transparency:
foundations' concerns, 256;
of international nonprofits, 318–19, 334n2;
international trends, 321, 323

Uniform Law Commission, 177
Uniform Prudent Investor Act, 177
Uniform Prudent Management of Institutional Funds Act, 177
Uniform Trust Code, 177
United Way agencies, 246–47
United Way of America, 295
universities, 54, 244
University of Pennsylvania, 54
unrelated business income tax, 136, 146–47
US Freedmen's Bureau, 59

volunteering:
millions volunteer, 25;
ethnicity and, 85;
government sector, 86;
longer-term forces affecting, 100n8;

in the nonprofit sector, 1977–2012, 77;
numbers and value of, 2014, 83, 85;
social benefits of, 18–19;
value of monetary contributions
   compared to, 85–86

Weisbrod, Burton, 41, 42, 46, 47, 48
Williams College, 54
Winkler, Mary K., 291–312

women's movements, 61
Works Progress Administration, 54

Yale University, 54
Young, Dennis R., 37–70, 250
youth groups, pass-through gifts
   through, 240–41

Zuckerberg, Mark, 251, 263–64

About the Contributors

Alan J. Abramson is professor in the Schar School of Policy and Government at George Mason University and founding director of Mason's Center for Nonprofit Management, Philanthropy, and Policy. Previously, he was a program director at the Aspen Institute and on the research staff at the Urban Institute. In 2015–2016, he is serving as president of the Association for Research on Nonprofit Organizations and Voluntary Action (ARNOVA), the nation's leading association of nonprofit researchers.

Mark Blumberg is a charity lawyer based in Toronto with Blumberg Segal LLP and has worked for over twenty years on issues relating to nonprofits, registered charities, and philanthropy, in Canada and abroad. Mark has written and lectured extensively on these topics. He is the editor of two blogs, namely www.CanadianCharityLaw.ca and www.GlobalPhilanthropy.ca™.

Elizabeth T. Boris is the Waldemar A. Nielsen Chair of Philanthropy at the McCourt School of Public Policy at Georgetown University and an Urban Institute fellow. She was the founding director of the Center on Nonprofits and Philanthropy at the Urban Institute, which she led from 1996–2016. She is co-editor with C. Eugene Steuerle of two previous editions of *Nonprofits and Government*, author of many research studies on nonprofits and philanthropy, and an active advisor and board member of many groups.

Erica Broadus is earning her PhD in public policy and public administration at George Washington University. Erica's research focuses on women's participation in social entrepreneurship and policies that help low-income women thrive.

Evelyn Brody is a professor at Chicago-Kent College of Law, Illinois Institute of Technology, and has spent semesters visiting at the University of Pennsylvania, Duke, and New York University law schools. She teaches courses on tax and nonprofit law. She edited the multi-disciplinary volume *Property-Tax Exemption for Charities: Mapping the Battlefield*.

John Casey is associate professor in the School of Public Affairs at Baruch College, City University of New York. Prior to academia, he held executive positions in government and nonprofits in Australia, Spain, and the United States. His latest book is *The Nonprofit World: Civil Society and Rise of the Nonprofit Sector*.

Roger Colinvaux is professor of law at Catholic University of America, where he teaches tax, legislation, and property courses and directs the Law and Public Policy Program. He is the author of numerous articles about regulation of the nonprofit sector through federal tax law, and for seven years served as counsel to the Congressional Joint Committee on Taxation.

Joseph J. Cordes is associate director of the School of Public Policy and Public Administration; professor of economics, public policy and public administration, and international affairs; and co-director of the George Washington University Regulatory Studies Center. He is the co-editor of *The Encyclopedia of Taxation and Tax Policy* and of *Nonprofits and Business*.

Teresa Derrick-Mills is a senior research associate in the Center on Nonprofits and Philanthropy and the Center on Labor, Human Services, and Population at the Urban Institute. She is also an adjunct professor in the Trachtenberg School of Public Policy and Public Administration at George Washington University.

Nathan Dietz is senior research associate in the Urban Institute's Center on Nonprofits and Philanthropy. He has served as associate director of the National Center for Charitable Statistics, and has led Urban's involvement in the Growth in Giving Initiative and the Fourth Sector Mapping Initiative.

Lewis Faulk is assistant professor of public administration and policy in the School of Public Affairs at American University. Dr. Faulk has a PhD in public policy from Georgia State University and the Georgia Institute of Technology. His research focuses on nonprofit management, nonprofit finance, and the intersection of nonprofit organizations and public policy.

About the Contributors

Marion Fremont-Smith is senior research fellow at the Hauser Institute for Civil Society of the Center for Public Leadership at Harvard Kennedy School. She has served as assistant attorney general and director of the Division of Public Charities in Massachusetts. She is the author of *Governing Nonprofit Organizations: Federal and State Law and Regulation*.

Saunji D. Fyffe is a researcher in the Center on Nonprofits and Philanthropy at the Urban Institute. Previously, she worked at several nonprofit trade associations where she oversaw performance management efforts, leadership and management training programs, large-scale organizational change initiatives, and the development and implementation of workforce equity strategies.

Virginia Hodgkinson is a retired research professor of public policy and director at the Center for Voluntary Organizations and Service, Georgetown University Public Policy Institute. Hodgkinson is the author and editor of numerous articles and books on the nonprofit sector, including *The Nonprofit Almanac: Dimensions of the Independent Sector 1996–1998* and *The Civil Society Reader*.

Béatrice Leydier is a dual master's student in management and public policy at HEC Paris (Grande École) and Georgetown University (McCourt School). At Georgetown, she has worked as a research assistant to Elizabeth T. Boris, along with other engagements at the nexus of private, public, and nonprofit sectors.

Cindy M. Lott serves as program director for Nonprofit Management Programs at Columbia University's School of Professional Studies. Prior to her current position, she served as executive director and senior counsel to the National State Attorneys General Program at Columbia Law School and, within that program, was the developer and lead counsel to the Charities Regulation and Oversight Project.

Jasmine McGinnis Johnson is assistant professor in the Trachtenberg School of Public Policy and Public Administration at George Washington University. Her research focuses on the interaction between philanthropic governance and grantmaking decisions, nonprofit grant networks, and the recruitment and retention of Millennial nonprofit employees.

Brice McKeever is a researcher in the Center on Nonprofits and Philanthropy at the Urban Institute, where he performs quantitative research and analysis for the National Center for Charitable Statistics. Previously, he worked as a research analyst at the University of Virginia's Center for Survey Research.

Susan D. Phillips is professor, School of Public Policy and Administration, Carleton University in Ottawa, Canada, and program director of the Master of Philanthropy and Nonprofit Leadership. Susan's research focuses on comparative analysis of public policy governing nonprofits and philanthropy, community foundations and cross-sectoral collaboration. She is co-editor of the *Routledge Companion to Philanthropy* and co-editor-in-chief of *Nonprofit and Voluntary Sector Quarterly*.

Steven Rathgeb Smith is the executive director of the American Political Science Association. He has taught at several universities including the University of Washington, where he was the Nancy Bell Evans Professor of Public Affairs. His most recent book is *Nonprofits and Advocacy* (with Robert Pekkanen and Yutaka Tsujinaka). He is president-elect of the International Society for Third Sector Research.

Ellen Steele is a graduate student at Princeton University and a former researcher at the Urban Institute.

C. Eugene Steuerle is an Institute fellow and the Richard B. Fischer chair at the Urban Institute. He served as deputy assistant secretary of the US Department of the Treasury for Tax Analysis (1987–1989) before co-founding the Urban-Brookings Tax Policy Center, Urban's Center on Nonprofits and Philanthropy, and Act for Alexandria, a community foundation. His other books include *Dead Men Ruling*, *Contemporary U.S. Tax Policy*, and *Nonprofits and Business*.

Mary K. Winkler is senior research associate in the Center on Nonprofits and Philanthropy at the Urban Institute where she oversees Urban's Cross-Center Initiative on Performance Measurement and Management. She is a member of the Leap of Reason Ambassador Community—a private community of nonprofit thought leaders and practitioners—committed to increasing the adoption of high performance in the social sector.

Dennis R. Young is executive in residence in the Maxine Goodman Levin College of Urban Affairs, Cleveland State University, and professor emeritus, Georgia State University. He is editor-in-chief of the journal *Nonprofit Policy Forum*. His recent books as co-editor include *The Social Enterprise Zoo*, *Third Sector and Social Enterprise*, and *Handbook of Research on Nonprofit Economics and Management*.